# I Refuse
# to Raise a
# BRAT

# I Refuse to Raise a
# BRAT

## Straightforward Advice on
## Parenting in an Age of Overindulgence

# Marilu Henner
*and*
# Ruth Velikovsky Sharon, Ph.D.

ReganBooks
*An Imprint of HarperCollinsPublishers*

A hardcover edition of this book was published by ReganBooks, an imprint of Harper-Collins Publishers, in 1999.

First paperback edition published 2000.

*Designed by Laura Lindgren and Celia Fuller*

*Drawings by Ralph Schlegel*

Library of Congress Cataloging-in-Publication Data
Henner, Marilu.
   I refuse to raise a brat : straightforward advice on parenting in an age of overindulgence / Marilu Henner and Ruth Velikovsky Sharon.
      p.   cm.
   Originally published: 1999.
   Includes index.
   ISBN 0-06-098730-8
   1. Child rearing.  2. Discipline of children.  3. Parent and child.  I. Sharon, Ruth Velikovsky.
   HQ769 .H498   2000                                    00-055366
   649'.1—dc21

00 01 02 03 04 ❖/RRD 10 9 8 7 6 5 4 3 2 1

*To Nicky and Joey*
*—Marilu*

*To my grandchildren:*
*Elizabeth, Ashley, Cimarron, Colby, and Dylan*
*—Dr. Sharon*

# CONTENTS

------------------------------------------------

# ACKNOWLEDGMENTS

------------------------------------------------

Without the support, talent, and hard work from the following people, this project would never have been possible.

To Judith Regan, who continues to be my friend and idol . . . her unbeatable team at ReganBooks and HarperCollins, Amye Dyer, Angelica Canales, Rick Pracher, Steven Sorrentino, Paul Olsewski (who stops at nothing to get the news out), Renée Iwaszkiewicz, Claudia Gabel, Cassie Jones, and especially Laura Yorke, who showed me what a truly great editor does to save the day. I hope this is the first of many.

To Mel Berger, Marc Schwartz, Sam Haskell, Rick Bradley, and Jerry Katzman of the William Morris Agency, Dick Guttman and Susan Madore of Guttman & Associates, and Richard Feldstein and Barbara Karrol at Provident Financial Management.

To Stephanie Pierson for her ability to make order out of chaos, and to her husband, Tom Connell, for his tireless support.

To Brent Strickland, who once again brought his magic fingers and great attitude. To Trent Othick for always coming through. To Bryony Atkinson for her organization, speed, and great outfits. To Suzanne Carney and Charlotte Huss for reminding us what it's like to have an infant. To my sister JoAnn Carney for her exquisite photos. To Elizabeth Carney for her full-service troubleshooting. To my sister-in-law Lynnette Lesko Henner, who sorted, filed, and tagged, and inspired. To Caroline Aaron for once again adding her special brand of humor and insight inspired by her children, Ben and Sydney. And to my brother Lorin Henner—I said so much about you in the last book, I've nothing left to say, except that you'll always be my favorite brat.

To Elena Lewis, for her can-do attitude and organizational skills.

To Donna Erickson, who follows the principles in this book without even realizing it.

To my talented husband, Rob, who shares with me the great joy and responsibility of raising our two sons.

And to Nicky and Joey, who are the best reasons for wanting to be a good parent.

—Marilu

■          ■          ■

Thanks to Heather Menozzi for her long hours at the computer and to her son, Corey, for his humor; to Marilyn Frasier for her organizational skills; to Lorna Sharon for her very thoughtful suggestions and recommendations; to Rafael Sharon, whose deep understanding of children makes him a great father; to Naomi Mitchell for her helpful insights and contributions; to Carmel Warner for her brilliant understanding of how children learn; to Dr. Robert Ginsberg for his exemplary approach to children's education; to John O'Donnell, Peter Shukat, Denise Johnson for their help; to Richard Peterson for his help; to Ralph Schlegel, whose drawings capture the human condition; to Stephanie Pierson for her creative expertise and to her husband, Tom Connell, for his help; to Laura Yorke for her editorial skills, and to Judith Regan, whose brilliance, energy, and determination have made this book a reality.

—Dr. Sharon

# Marilu Henner

Being a mom is my favorite, and by far the most important, thing I do in my life. When I look at the beautiful faces of my two little boys, Nicky, age five, and Joey, three and a half, I know I want to be the best mother I can be. But what does being the best mother mean? Does it mean that I'm supposed to do everything for my children, and then one day expect them to be able to do those things for themselves? Should I try to anticipate their needs before they even know and can identify those needs? Does it mean that I'm supposed to shield them from all of life's bumps and hard knocks? And how difficult will it be for them to cope when I'm not there to be their shield? As a parent, you want to do so much for your children, but how much is too much? At what point does giving and protecting too much become what we will refer to throughout this book as overgratification? My parents, who raised six of us, often let us stumble and fall and find our own way. They had to. There wasn't enough time in the day for them to hover over and do too much for six children. We sometimes learned the hard way, and had a few mishaps along the way, but eventually we all had to learn to fend for ourselves.

My children are relatively young right now. As a mom, I know I'm a work in progress. I don't claim to be an expert yet. I am, however, fortunate enough to have had the guidance of Dr. Ruth Velikovsky Sharon. She is a brilliant psychoanalyst who has helped me in my career for many years, and the mother of three adults who have families of their own. The most important lesson she has taught me about child rearing is that the majority of problems we experience throughout our lives can be traced to being overgratified, overprotected, and/or overindulged as children. Giving too much to our children is one of the surest ways to deprive them of the emotional and physical tools they will need to cope with the many challenges and changes of life. Every time I have followed her theories, I can see positive results. And every time I'm having trouble, or anyone around me is having trouble, it usually relates to overgratification in some way. Overfrustration (giving a child too little) is the opposite of overgratification, and can also create problems in one's life. The answer lies in finding a *balance* between frustration and gratification. Finding that balance is what this book is all about.

The world is a frustrating place where every day we must identify what we need and what we want in order to get it. And sometimes it takes a long time to get it, or we *never* get it. That's life. Some people are better equipped to deal with life's frustrations than others, and that's probably because their parents allowed them to work through their frustrations at an early age. But so many parents today do everything they can to avoid teaching their children these important life-coping skills.

From the day my first son, Nicky, was born, I tried to apply Dr. Sharon's advice. I learned to listen to the differences in Nicky's cries. Eventually, I could distinguish his "cry to be fed" from his "cry to be played with" from his "cry to be changed," and so on. If

I hadn't let him cry *first,* I never would have been able to recognize the differences in his cries. Nicky and I soon developed our own "language," and instead of my anticipating his every need (which is an unrealistic way to bring up a child, because the world doesn't work that way), he was able to cry and let me know what he wanted. I was then able to help him.

When Nicky was around fourteen months old, I was explaining to Dr. Sharon that I was having a really hard time putting him to bed. He slept through the night by that time, of course, but getting him to bed was difficult, because early on, despite Dr. Sharon's advice to put him down awake and let him fall asleep on his own, I would rock him to sleep while singing my favorite Beatles songs. It was a time I looked forward to every day, but now the ritual was getting old, and with Joey on the way (I was five months pregnant at the time), it was exhausting. I remember saying to her, "I know, I know, I shouldn't have let this go on so long. He's too old to be rocked to sleep. It's too much, and he now knows he's getting away with something, too. I can tell. There's this bratty quality about it now, and I refuse to raise a brat!"

So, what is a brat? Every kid is a little bratty sometimes, of course. But when we talk about a brat in this book, we're talking about that uncooperative, whining, annoying, demanding, selfish little (or big) person whom no one can control. We've seen them all too often in malls, restaurants, theaters, and playgrounds. Their parents are constantly pleading and bribing and enticing and bargaining. Brats can come in all shapes, sizes, and even ages, because little brats often become big brats. Some grown-ups never stop being brats; they only get better at hiding their brattiness. Throughout this book, we will extensively explore these questions: What makes a child become a brat in the first place? And what can parents do (and more important, *not* do) to keep their child from becoming a brat? What kind of mindset do we need, as parents, to raise our children?

When I became a mother, Dr. Sharon and I started writing this book together. As a new mother, so many questions came up every day of my first child's life. And then, once I had two children and realized that the playing field had changed, I thought, How do I balance the frustration and gratification between the two of them?

We all want to do a great job as parents, but striving to be *perfect* parents is a mistake. The world is not a perfect place, and insisting on perfection can be both paralyzing and crazy-making (for us and our children). It's inevitable that we're going to make mistakes along the way. It's just that it's better to *have* a general mind-set, a sort of blueprint, even if we end up straying from it every once in a while. If we are on the right path, the results will be much better than if we had no structure, no boundaries, and no guidelines. That's why Dr. Sharon and I have written this book: to take you through the different aspects of raising a child. It sounds very simple to say, "Okay, I'm just not going to overgratify my children." But when you've got a crying baby, what do you do? When you can't understand what your five-year-old is upset about, what do you do? Or if you've got a twelve-year-old and some bad habits have crept in, how do you *undo* those habits?

The chapters of this book include a number of elements. I introduce each topic, and Dr. Sharon's ideas, written in her own words, follow. In each of the chapters, there is a series of questions we've appropriately called "Brat-Busters." The questions reflect the issues of the chapter, made real by everyday parents and their concerns. Even if a question doesn't apply to your situation, you may recognize your life somewhere else in the question or answer. In addition to Dr. Sharon's answer, I usually add my insight as a mom, currently and joyously at the frontline of motherhood. There is a brief section in each chapter about the consequences of certain behaviors if children carry them into adulthood. It's aptly titled "When Little Brats Become Big Brats."

I hope you find our book inspiring and helpful in your desire to become a great (but not perfect!) parent.

---------------------------------------------------

# Dr. Ruth V. Sharon

As a psychoanalyst in practice for the past twenty-five years, my perspective on child rearing has given me some fresh views and insights that I believe would be immensely helpful to today's parents. While much of my advice about raising children might seem to go against the common wisdom, I have seen it work time and again, producing successful and long-lasting results and winning over even the most skeptical parents.

All my theories are based on one simple (and surprising) observation: Some of the most difficult patients I've treated have not been those who were poorly treated or neglected as children, but those who were overindulged or who received endless gratification and attention. Patients who, as children, were treated as special and entitled, whose parents did everything to try to keep them happy all the time, had more emotional problems and unresolved issues than children who grew up dealing with adversity and frustration from a very young age. Sadly, these same patients had a harder time in therapy, too—they made less progress and took longer resolving problems. Perhaps most surprising, these over-tended and overgratified children were the most vocal about blaming their parents for a miserable childhood once they themselves became adults, in spite of (or because of) the superhuman efforts their parents made to make their childhoods idyllic. It is most disturbing to observe the emotional damage parents innocently perpetuate on their children, while meaning well. The extent of the damage can be far-reaching. But with some simple understanding of a child's natural development and the right tools, it's fairly simple to be a loving *and* effective parent.

Developmentally, every baby, from day one, needs to feel loved and nurtured and profoundly cared for by responsible parents. But parents need to know that once a newborn comes into the world and starts breathing on his own, he also needs to begin developing a healthy independence from his parents. Too much nurturing, too much bonding, too much togetherness will suppress this natural drive to independence.

The trick is to find a balance between being there for a child and giving him a chance to discover the world (not always an easy place) for himself. Growth from gratification and learning from frustration are equally important, but except in theories and textbooks, there is no possibility of achieving a *perfect* balance. Again at the risk of going against accepted theories, I would suggest that, no matter what the child's temperament is like, it is better in the long run to err on the side of denying him than in overindulging him.

I know that this is a difficult concept for a loving parent to accept, but I've found that overgratifying a child is often the easy way out. And denying a child anything these days is frowned upon. Popular psychology (and a misinterpretation of some excellent psychological theories about self-esteem) have led parents today routinely to confuse love with overgratification and to believe that any amount of frustration is too much. Of course, every child is different. Each child's temperament needs to be considered in finding the right balance of frustration and gratification suited to him. Genetic makeup will also predetermine some of his characteristics that will affect this balance.

Any parenting book that addresses the merits of frustration and denial of immediate gratification runs the risk of seeming harsh and unloving. And at first, some of the advice and suggestions in this book may sound a little harsh or unsympathetic, but it is just this kind of loving and pragmatic advice that will ultimately provide the blueprint for bringing up well-functioning children who, as adults, continue to prosper.

Marilu Henner's dedication to physical and psychological health, her vitality, intelligence, humor, and vibrant personality are evident from her contribution as coauthor of this book, which she titled *I Refuse to Raise a Brat*.

------------------------------------------------------------

# CHAPTER 1

# Twenty-Four-Hour Womb Service

*M*ay 12, 1994. I remember it well. I woke up in the middle of the night and thought, "Today's the day." Even though contractions hadn't started, I knew that was going to be the day I would give birth. I immediately started reorganizing the baby's room, which is what most new mothers do—the whole nesting thing. I became obsessed with wanting everything to be just right for the baby's arrival.

When I brought my son Nicky home, I couldn't believe that only twenty-four hours earlier, he had been growing inside me. And part of me still wanted to feel connected. In retrospect, I think that probably had more to do with my hormones and my needs than it had to do with what was best for him. And just like a new diet, a New

Year's resolution, or the first day of a new school year, I approached this experience wanting everything to be *perfect*.

I'd already found the best crib, picked out the ideal wallpaper, organized all the clothes and toys and bedding that I'd gotten at my baby shower. I was bursting with joy as I picked up every little sock and T-shirt, not really believing that a whole human being could actually fit into those teeny-tiny clothes. Nothing seemed entirely real. During my pregnancy, I felt Nicky growing and kicking, but at that point he seemed to be more part of me than his own person. I think that's why his room became so significant. I realized that this was going to be the place where he would begin his own independent life, wearing those impossibly tiny T-shirts! He was going to be living in this whole new world and I was going to be the one responsible for setting it up. And I wanted it to be just right.

So when I got Nicky home from the hospital, it wasn't enough that I wouldn't let anyone hold him without washing his hands first. I even got squeamish if anyone had too much perfume or garlic breath or the slightest body odor because I didn't want my perfect baby, in his perfect world, to have to smell anything unpleasant! I remember asking everyone to be quiet all the time, especially my husband. I thought his voice was too loud for "my" baby.

Luckily, after a few days, I snapped out of this nonsense. Besides, there were too many people around. Phones were ringing, music was blasting, doors were slamming, odors were permeating, and I just couldn't fight it anymore. I thought, "This is my *real* home. Why am I trying to create an artificial environment for Nicky? This is how I really live. Why am I trying to raise a boy in a plastic bubble?"

I myself came from a very loud, wild, and outspoken family. Our house always had lots of visitors and constant activity. We had a dancing school in our garage, a part-time beauty salon in the kitchen, and art classes going on upstairs. And my bedroom was, by far, the noisiest in the house. It had no door and was actually connected to the kitchen/beauty shop, the busiest and neon-brightest room in the house. My room growing up was the complete opposite of what I was trying to set up for Nicky. Forget about my going to bed early or having a perfectly organized, quiet environment. I had the bright kitchen light shining in my eyes and the family phone ringing in my ears at all hours of the day and night, and while people ate late-night snacks, they could look into my room and see me sleeping in my little bed. I was the original *Truman Show!*

# RE-CREATING THE WOMB

Thanks to a lot of good advice from Dr. Sharon, I've given up the notion of creating a perfect environment. I'm letting my kids see not only who *I* am, the *real* me, but also a little bit of the heritage that they came from . . . a loud and colorful family that was far from perfect. And I feel they will be much better off as human beings because they will be better able to adapt to a variety of situations and people as they move through their lives. Besides, who wants what can never be re-created? Why set up a world for your children that will never exist in the *real* world?

## Dr. Sharon's View

The incredible moment of birth is, from the newborn's point of view, a rude awakening. Birth is his first encounter with frustration. Forced from the perfect environment of the womb where all his needs—nourishment, warmth, comfort, closeness, security—were met, the newborn enters a world where total gratification is no longer guaranteed. He begins to have to figure out how to get these most basic needs met within a reasonable amount of time. And from that moment on, life becomes a progression of steps moving from total dependence to self-sufficiency.

I believe that the parent who hovers over his baby, instantly gratifying every demand and avoiding the slightest frustration, denies the baby the opportunity to begin the wondrous journey of emotional development that will lead to healthy independence and self-sufficiency. Treating a baby as if he were still in the womb does a great disservice to the small but intrepid explorer who is ready and eager to take his first emotional steps in a noisy, imperfect, glorious world.

Overgratification takes many forms and often begins in the first few months of life. And ironically, what seems to a new parent like an enlightened idea or loving gesture can be anything but. One example is the entire category of products intended to simulate the experience of being in the womb. Bassinets that rock and hum, temperature-controlled cribs with vibrating mattresses, stuffed teddy bears that come with a mechanical heartbeat, all send the message that returning to the womb is desirable, thereby delaying the necessary adjustment to life outside the womb.

It isn't just products, it's parenting. The baby who is fed whether he's hungry or not is thwarted from learning to recognize hunger pangs and doesn't have an opportunity to express his needs. The baby who is picked up the minute he makes a sound is deprived of learning to tolerate frustration. Indeed, the most overgratified babies tend to grow into the most demanding, difficult children. The mother who anticipates her baby's needs before he even recognizes them slows down his emotional development. It wouldn't be surprising for this baby to grow into the kind of person who expects the world to read his mind.

There's one other common way that parents overgratify their babies (and almost never know they're doing it). And that's speaking only in soft, hushed tones. Parents who, as children, grew up with lots of

yelling and screaming in their home often make
a conscious decision never to raise their
voices in front of *their* children. But speaking this way paints an unrealistic picture
of the way the world really converses.
It contributes to a child's later inability
to tolerate dissension and conflict. However, as with everything else, there needs
to be a balance. Abusive arguing and
fighting is, in its own way, as detrimen-
tal as speaking in hushed tones.

Friends of mine observed a rather unusual tradition every time a
new child was born into their family. After they would bring each
child home from the hospital, the entire family would not leave
their home or allow visitors for forty days and forty nights. Friends
were told, "Please don't even call the house so that we won't be disturbed while we are bonding with our new baby." They did not want
the new addition exposed to anyone outside their family circle.

On the forty-first day they would throw an enormous party so
that all of their friends could meet the new arrival. Each time I went
to one of these gatherings, I would observe the infant as nervous
and shaky, and the other children as clingy and shy.

Now I know why.

—*Marilu*

What kind of nurturing and positive encouragement contributes
to a baby seeing the world as a challenging and exciting place?
Watch him carefully and observe that he is naturally fascinated with

the visual and auditory stimulation of his environment. Playing alone helps him develop self-sufficiency and tap inner resources. So instead of rushing "to the rescue" to entertain a baby who is playing alone, let him entertain himself. When he finally becomes bored, instead of just amusing him, read to him, sing to him, recite poetry, point to the alphabet and to numbers. Expose him to classical music from day one to help him learn to love music. In short, give him a range of great stimuli in his formative years.

# BRAT-BUSTERS!

## Adjusting to Sounds

We live in a small New York apartment and our baby's crib is off the dining alcove, where we both watch TV and eat. I constantly ask my husband to be quiet and wait until the baby is awake before turning on the television. He thinks the baby should get used to the noise. I think he's being insensitive. What do you think?

*Dr. Sharon:* From the moment of birth, a baby needs to experience the sounds of the world. Silently tiptoeing around creates an artificial environment. Television and garbage trucks are part of life. Furthermore, not to be harsh, but a baby has to discover that the world was not created just to suit him. *He* has to adjust to the world. You cannot insulate him. Turn on the television—he'll probably react much better than you think.

*Marilu:* This reminds me so much of my brother Lorin (the baby of the family), who is now forty years old. He cannot tolerate external noises or discomforts while he is sleeping, such as drafts, the sun rising, birds chirping, or dogs barking. He has a shag carpet draped over his bedroom window and sleeps under a deluxe electric blanket accompanied by a $200 sound machine from Brookstone that simulates Victoria Falls during the rainy season. The only thing missing from this enormous "artificial womb" is some kind of tubular attachment to the refrigerator for overnight feedings. Unfortunately for him, Hammacher-Schlemmer hasn't perfected that yet. I'm not sure, but I suspect that his oversensitivity might have something to do with the fact that when he was a baby, we older kids were forbidden even to whisper while he was sleeping. Our telephone was perpetually buried beneath three or four winter parkas until he was about fourteen. I love my brother dearly now, but back then, we all secretly wanted my mother to put him up for adoption.

## When Barking Is Scary

My family doesn't have any pets because my husband is highly allergic. Consequently, my three-month-old baby is not used to animals. Every time our next-door neighbor's dog barks (a lot!), he startles and starts to cry. No matter how much I reassure him that it's okay, he's inconsolable. My husband insists that we tell the neighbors they have to control their dog. I think our baby will eventually get used to it. Help!

*Dr. Sharon:* Your baby's reaction is normal—the dog's barking *can be* scary. But what seems to be causing his crying is, in part, how you and your husband are reacting. If the two of you would just sit back when the dog barks and continue doing what you were doing, your baby would have (after a few incidents!) the same relaxed attitude you do. The sounds of the world—from barking dogs to loud televisions—are something a baby has to get adjusted to. And he will, with the right cues from you and your husband.

*Marilu:* On the second floor of my family home lived my uncle with ten cats, two dogs, two birds, a skunk, 150 fish, and his friend Charles. You can't imagine the sounds we grew up with.

## Carrying a Fussy Baby

My three-month-old daughter is a fussy baby and cries a lot during the day. At first I thought she was hungry, but feeding her doesn't always work. The only time she really quiets down is when I carry her around with me. How do I break her of this? Or should I just give in and carry her everywhere in a Snugli?

*Dr. Sharon:* It is possible that she is colicky or allergic to formula or breast milk, so check with your pediatrician. But it's more likely that, if she's been overindulged, your three-month-old baby already has expectations and even demands. The best solution would be to hold her several times a day for ten or fifteen minutes, then put her down. If she cries, try to tolerate it. It's much harder to break habits than it is to head them off in the first place!

*Marilu:* It will be much easier to break her of this habit now, since she is only three months old, than it will be at three *years* old. Be grateful that you have the opportunity to correct this so early in her life. Every baby I've seen who was carried all the time seems to become not only dependent, but rather shy and incapable of being separated from his mom. The other day I was at a birthday party, and my girlfriend was there with her seven-month-old, who was never out of my friend's arms. The baby wanted nothing to do with the other children, and she wouldn't let another mother hold her. My friend feels her daughter is already too clingy, but doesn't want to go through the drama of breaking her of her habit. In your case, it may take a few days but in the long run it will be worth it.

## Only Mommy

Our six-month-old son wants to be held only by me. When someone else tries to pick him up he cries. My first instinct is to let him cry, but then I feel guilty, and I reach for him. What should I be doing?

*Dr. Sharon:* Mothers are naturally number one in their babies' lives. If at six months your son wants to be held only by you, go along with his need. Other family members should just refrain from picking him up. That being said, it would have been best if your baby had been held by other people from day one.

*Marilu:* It seems to me that the sooner a mom tries to allow her child to explore other people, the better. I know it can be traumatic to force a child to be held by someone he doesn't want to be with, so of course it's important to use good judgment here. One method that might work well is for the new person to hold the baby so that he always sees you. That way he will know you are around. Gradually, as your son gets comfortable with someone you trust, you can leave the room and have some time alone.

## Falling Asleep on His Own

Is it better to put a four-month-old baby in his crib awake so he can learn to fall asleep on his own, or is it okay to let him fall asleep and then put him down?

*Dr. Sharon:* It's much better to put the baby to bed awake so he can learn to go to sleep by himself. Falling asleep in your arms and then being placed in his crib spares him the slight healthy frustration that will help him adapt to the real world. It's a question of striking the right balance between comfort and too much comfort. However, from the very beginning, *you* will have to learn to tolerate *your* pain and anxiety at hearing your child cry for five or ten minutes as he is put down. Be sure he is dry, warm, well-fed. Then both you and your baby will simultaneously need to deal with this frustration. Once you start the habit of his falling asleep in your arms, it's going to take fifteen minutes of his unhappiness (several nights in a row) to break him of this habit.

*Marilu:* It is often said that you make your mistakes on the first child. Boy, did I make a mistake with Nicky when it came to putting him to bed. He wanted to be rocked to sleep while I sang to him. It was great because I got a chance to sing the hits of Broadway every night, and now Nicky is on his way to becoming the next Andrew Lloyd Webber. But it was too exhausting. With my second son, Joey, I just put him down awake and then let him learn to fall asleep on his own. To this day, he's a great sleeper.

## Bedtime Rituals

I've developed a very successful ritual for putting my five-month-old baby to sleep. I give her a bath, give her a nighttime feeding, place her in her crib with a night-light on, and put on a nursery tape. At the end of the tape, I turn out the light and kiss her good night and close the door. A couple of nights ago as I put her to bed, I put on her tape and the batteries ran out. Without her music, she couldn't get to sleep. I realized that she's way too dependent on this ritual. Should I try to vary this ritual so she becomes more flexible? Or should I keep doing what's she's used to and what usually works just fine?

*Dr. Sharon:* The items (like blankets and stuffed animals) and the rituals that babies become deeply attached to, particularly at bedtime, are the equivalent of emotional medicine to them. The same way you wouldn't forget your baby's medicine, just make sure you have a spare set of batteries in the house! In time, on her own, your baby will outgrow these rituals.

*Marilu:* I remember when Nicky was two months old his favorite thing to look at was a black-and-white bull's-eye card. It would entertain him during diaper changing or calm him down when he got overtired. We carried it with us everywhere and one time left it behind at friends'. I actually had a messenger pick it up and deliver it. (Talk about overindulgence!) Nicky enjoyed the card that evening, but within a week had moved on to trapezoids.

## Relatives Roughhousing

My sister and her husband are my baby's closest family. As much as I love my brother-in-law, he has no instinct for babies. He treats my seven-month-old boy like a football, tossing him in the air and pretending (for fun!) to drop him. When I tell him he's scaring the baby, he laughs it off. Am I being too overprotective?

*Dr. Sharon:* Unless your baby is fearful and crying, you shouldn't automatically assume that your brother-in-law is scaring him. What should scare you is that your baby's neck is not being supported when he's tossed in the air. Make sure he is always held in ways that are safe.

*Marilu:* If you love your brother-in-law, then you should feel comfortable expressing your concerns and he should respect that. Tell him to postpone the football game at least until your boy is in Pull-Ups.

## Working Mom Wants to Stay in Touch

I'm a working mother who travels a lot. Someone suggested I line pictures of myself around the crib when I'm on a business trip. Do you think this makes sense?

*Dr. Sharon:* Oddly enough, lining the crib with your pictures may have a negative effect on your baby, only reminding him that you are gone. He will not be comforted. His birth experience initiated him to the physical and emotional pain of separation. Having survived that, he can contend with your short business trip.

One more caveat: If pictures are unnecessary, recording your voice for the baby to listen to in your absence is equally unhelpful. It serves only to remind the baby that the parent is not physically there with him.

*Marilu:* Lining the crib with photos sounds a bit narcissistic. I have found that the best way to keep my boys happy and content while I'm away is to show them continuous reruns of *Taxi*. (I'm just kidding.)

## Fear of the Pediatrician

My four-month-old daughter is afraid of our pediatrician. This pediatrician has taken care of our six-year-old son since he was born and our son is very fond of him. Should I get a different pediatrician for our daughter? One that would be a better match with her personality?

*Dr. Sharon:* At four months, it's natural for your daughter to be afraid of a doctor. However well-intentioned, it would be wrong for you to change pediatricians on the basis of her age-appropriate fears. Your six-year-old son is attesting to the fact that the pediatrician is okay. Plus, you're there when your daughter is being examined so you could tell if the pediatrician were being too harsh with her. Since that's not the case, stick with the pediatrician and don't let your daughter run the show.

*Marilu:* The most important thing to remember when dealing with a pediatrician (or any doctor, for that matter) is that you must work *with* him to get the best results. It's teamwork. Know as much as you can about your family's history and trust your instincts as a parent. Don't be afraid to ask questions and educate yourself so that you always know what your doctor is talking about.

## Breast-Feeding Isolation

I am a breast-feeding mother of a newborn. I love breast-feeding and I'm committed to feeding on demand. But it makes me terribly self-conscious to breast-feed in front of anyone other than my husband. Consequently, I'm feeling very isolated. I don't have people over and I don't go out much. I don't have enough milk to pump. Do you think I should give up nursing?

*Dr. Sharon:* Being self-conscious about breast-feeding in public is a statement about your modesty, which is an admirable trait. More important, I am a big proponent of feeding on demand (just make sure your baby is only fed when he is really hungry and doesn't get into the habit of using your breast as a pacifier). However, since you say you don't have much milk, teach your baby to get a bottle of formula occasionally. That way you don't have to give up something that means so much to you and your baby. Breast-feed your baby at home, then go out on short excursions where you can see friends and feel more connected, or take a bottle of formula with you so you can spend more quality time with your friends.

*Marilu:* If your milk supply is low, the best way to increase it is to drink more water (and nonalcoholic beer, too!). Eat more protein and mochi (a brown rice product found in health food stores). Breast-feeding and pumping have a demand-and-supply relationship. If you pump after you breast-feed, you will also eventually increase your milk supply. Try to be patient. It may take a while to see the results. Recent studies have shown that if you can breast-feed your baby for a year, the rewards will be great because your child will be so much healthier.

# WHEN LITTLE BRATS BECOME BIG BRATS

We've already learned that finding a balance between frustration and gratification starts from day one, but what happens when the twenty-four-hour womb service continues throughout a child's life?

## Dr. Sharon's View

*At nine months, Jared tries to reach for the toy on top of the table. "Oh, no, Jared," says his mother, pained at his effort, "let me get that." At two years, Jared tries to hang his jacket up all by himself. "That's too hard for you, sweetie," says his loving mother, "let me help." At six years, Jared slowly signs his name with his favorite crayon to a drawing he has just finished, but as he tries to get it straight, his mother prints it neatly for him. "See, Jared, that's how you do it. Isn't that better?" At every stage, Jared's mother only wants to help. But every time she helps, Jared feels certain that he must be helpless, otherwise why would his mother keep interfering? With every passing year, Jared feels closer than ever to—and more dependent on—his mother.*

Having been shielded from frustration, challenges, and painful experiences in childhood, the adult lives not in the real world, but in a kind of cocoon. He is, in essence, an infant in an adult body. Not equipped to overcome problems, he grows up limited both in his personal relationships and in relating to his peers, still hoping that his needs will be anticipated and met. He says "I can't" with great frequency. In fact, the dependency fostered by overindulgence is one of the most important themes of this book, because it is so crucial to determining a child's growth and potential.

Perhaps the greatest tragedy of childhood overgratification is that its damage in adulthood is extremely difficult, if not impossible, to reverse. Laying down the law—"either get a job or get out"—may cause the dependent adult to become further nonfunctioning, slumping into a depression. It's too late to give ultimatums. The problem was not created just by telling the child that he was "special"—*it was created by a lack of demands, expectations, and boundaries.*

And there is one more sad legacy. The adult who was given twenty-four-hour womb service when he was growing up, excessively pampered and indulged, will *not*, quite surprisingly, recall any of this fondly. Indeed, he will honestly recall his childhood as a miserable time and blame his parents for mistreating him, when in fact they did quite the opposite. This is a very important eye-opener for adults who carry lifelong grudges against their parents. There is hope for these adults once they understand this surprising concept of their upbringing, and start to deal with the long-lasting damage that overindulgence created for them.

# CHAPTER 2

# Independence 101

I've always been fascinated by the process of learning. What seems at first to be overwhelming and frustrating (learning to crawl, walk, talk, read, dress, ride a bike, and so on) soon becomes second nature, and we can barely remember those first moments when we felt overchallenged. We tend to associate learning with starting school, but learning begins the day we are born. I was lucky enough to have two older sisters (four and a half and nine years older) who loved to play teacher with me. Along with school-type lessons, like reading and writing, they taught me practical lessons like crawling, using a glass instead of a bottle, brushing my teeth, and tying my shoes. By the time I started kindergarten, they had already exposed me to many of the lessons they had learned, so I felt well-prepared for school from the very beginning. I wanted to provide the same learning environment for my sons when they were born.

One of the most valuable lessons I've learned over the years (sometimes the hard way) is that the best way to teach someone is to let him do it himself. I always keep that in mind when teaching my boys. For example, for Nicky's first lesson on day one, I put him on his stomach so that he would naturally want to push up. This can be frustrating for a baby, especially a one-day-old, but it is a wonderful exercise because it gradually develops his arms, which is necessary for him to begin crawling, which leads to walking, which leads to exploring, which leads to independence. The basic idea is that it is best to let babies and children do as much for themselves as possible. At first, when I put Nicky on his stomach, he really didn't like it. When his arms got stronger, though, he stopped disliking it and was actually proud of himself. Next, I started placing desirable objects, like a set of keys out of reach in front of him, so he would be motivated to reach for it. I let him get it sometimes, but, most of the time, I would place the object farther and farther away, which would frustrate him even more. My friends would say, "You're terrible!" or "How can you frustrate him like that?" But that struggle was just what he needed to learn eventually to crawl. It was a very exciting day when he finally made that breakthrough. His efforts reminded me of what I used to go through as a dancer when I would work through a new dance step that I couldn't get right away. I would practice and practice, and then, all of a sudden, the muscle memory would take over my body and I would nail the step. I thought of this as I watched Nicky reach his moment of accomplishment, first going right, and then moving left, and recognizing that this was getting him closer to the keys. To this day, he approaches learning something new with the same technique, understanding that once he can break through the frustration of repetition, he will accomplish a new goal.

# WHEN YOU PREVENT A CHILD FROM MOVING ON

As I said earlier, the key to teaching your children is to let them do as many things as possible by themselves. Through Dr. Sharon, I've learned that there are two main problems that we as parents run into with this directive. First, many parents hate to see their kids struggle and be frustrated, even for a moment, so they jump in and help after they detect the slightest amount of discomfort. One of the worst things we can do as parents is to hold our children back from the progress that they want to make themselves. The second problem is the time factor. It's often necessary for us to move quickly through our lives, so we expect these little people to work at our pace with the expediency of a grown-up. Because it's so easy just to cruise through our lives with the speed and ease we're used to as adults, we usually take that easier and faster route. But it's important to take the time to let our children dress themselves, feed themselves, struggle on the floor when they're learning to crawl, or walk slowly when they're learning to walk. It's so much easier, and takes so much less time, for us just to pick up the baby and go. I used to pride myself on the fact that I could get both kids dressed and out the door in record time. Now I force myself to let them gather their things, dress themselves, and put on their own shoes. All I can say is . . . thank God for Velcro!

Here's what Dr. Sharon has to say on the subject.

## Dr. Sharon's View

A baby tries to reach for something, he struggles, he has difficulty getting hold of it, he keeps trying, he's still trying his hardest . . . but his mother, watching this, hands it to him. And while she gives the now-smiling baby the object that he wants, what she is taking away from him is much more significant. She is unconsciously taking away her child's emotional and physical muscles, undermining his first brave efforts to become self-resourceful and independent.

The child who fends for himself thinks, "Oh, great! Mommy and Daddy think I can do it. I've got my own arms and legs and brains and my own ability. I *can* do it." And this is the beginning of a highly functioning, independent individual. This is a child who learns and grows with each small challenge he faces. But the parent who cannot tolerate seeing the baby struggle, who believes him to be helpless, will produce a child who *is* helpless, a child who forever wants a parent to help with every task. Interestingly, the parent who has the hardest time watching his child struggling with frustration was probably overgratified himself when he was growing up. His child's struggle will remind him, in painful ways, of his own low frustration tolerance. Occasionally the parent who was neglected will want to give his child a better experience and will err in the same way as the parent who was overindulged.

Not letting a child move forward starts from the very beginning of life. The baby who is given a bottle when he can (and given a choice, *would*) drink from a glass, or the toddler who is carried when he can walk, gets the message that to grow up and fend for himself is not desirable. He suspects that he needs a lot of help. When a parent becomes the child's arms, legs, and brains, that child's independence and self-sufficiency are thwarted. The result? A child who is unequipped to deal with the pitfalls of life. A child who is likely to become bewildered and even resentful of demands made of him.

To what extent the damage of overgratification can be fully undone depends on when parents stop the overindulgence. If the child is two years old when the indulgence stops, the chances of damage being reversed are good. If the child is five and already has trouble in school, it is difficult but not impossible. It takes effort and determination for parents to change their approach and not waver. Once the child has reached his teens the damage is difficult to reverse, but can to some extent be repaired. If a child has been overindulged into the teens, precautions must be taken when making an attempt to put an end to the overgratification. It is unwise to insist that a teenager "shape up" when his "emotional wings" have been clipped by doing too much for him as he grew up. But the lucky child whose parents understand the importance of providing a balance of frustration and gratification will thrive, developing a great capacity for overcoming adversity throughout life.

## Pampering a Sick Child

Even parents who watch their child confront a new task or challenge without interfering or "helping" have a hard time maintaining that admirable independent stance when their child is sick. Of course, it probably goes without saying that it's imperative for parents to make sure their sick child's basic needs are well taken care of; that the child is properly medicated, properly nourished, warm, and resting comfortably. But hovering over a child who's in bed with a head cold or flu, overreacting at the first sneeze, ministering to him with extraordinary attention and sympathy, only gives the child the impression that there are tremendous emotional rewards attached to being sick.

At the risk of making a generalization, children who are showered with attention when they are sick tend to lack resilience in other areas of their lives. They are often the children who take the longest time to recover from emotional wounds, blowing up minor insults and experiencing them as irreparable hurts or treating everyday problems as if they were dire emergencies. This kind of distorted thinking can lead to great unhappiness as well as some serious errors in judgment later on.

When I was in my early twenties, my boyfriend at the time expected me to wait on him hand and foot when he got sick. He would use a mild cold as an excuse to stay home and away from responsibility for a whole week. I would fluff up his pillows, bring him chicken soup, and make sure he had the right amount of magazines and the TV remote control nearby. It was just so ridiculous and seemed so counterproductive to getting well. He told me stories about how his mother overpampered him when he was sick as a child. He simply *loved* being sick.

I grew up in a household where my father would often say, "People should be blamed for their sicknesses, not pitied." So we rarely acted like we were sick. In fact, he would also say, "Why do you want to stay home when you're sick? You should go to school when you're sick and take off on a day that you're healthy." He felt you shouldn't waste a free day being sick.

I remember one rare exception when I was overpampered. I was sick when I was ten years old and had a violent allergic reaction to the penicillin I was given. My recovery took over two weeks. I got extremely attached to my mother during that period, because I was home with her for so long. But it wasn't because she indulged me in the usual way, in fact, quite the contrary. I barely saw her during the day while she did beauty work and taught dancing. But at night, I stayed up with her watching *The Late Show* and *The Late-Late Show* until four o'clock in the morning.

*That* bonded us forever. So it wasn't that she brought me too many cookies and milk in bed, or whatever. It had more to do with living like a grown-up for the two and a half weeks that made me want to get sick more often.

—*Marila*

# BRAT-BUSTERS!

## When to Stop Breast-Feeding

I am still breast-feeding my three-year-old son and being criticized by my family. They say it isn't healthy for a boy who is
already walking and talking and even toilet-trained. Please advise.

*Dr. Sharon:* Since your son has already successfully dealt with the
frustrations of toilet-training and learning to talk, breast-feeding
now is a form of overgratification. There's another reason to stop. If
it is your husband who is critical of this, there is a good chance he
will come to resent your son's relationship with you.

*Marilu:* I am a big advocate of breast-feeding. I breast-fed both of my
sons for a year. In fact, I have an award from the La Leche League for
the work I've done campaigning for breast-feeding. It was one of the
greatest experiences of my life, but when it was time to wean them,
as emotional as it was for me, I felt it was important to let them move
on to the next phase. If your son is capable of talking and using the
toilet by himself, he is certainly capable of using a cup. Put it this
way, any child who can ask for it by name should no longer be
breast-feeding. If he is saying things like, "Okay, let me move to the
right one now," you've probably let him go way too long!

## Eating with His Fingers

Should I spoon-feed my fourteen-month-old or let him eat with
his fingers?

*Dr. Sharon:* Letting him feed himself is a good way to encourage
your fourteen-month-old's independence. And if he's not interested

in eating at one meal, he'll probably get the nourishment he needs in the course of the day at other meals. Check with your pediatrician if you have any concerns.

*Marilu:* Once kids start eating, it's better to let them feed themselves because it's important for them to establish their own rhythms of eating. So many adults are obese because they were overfed as children and not allowed to listen to their own bodies' needs. As messy as it is sometimes, children need to develop their own relationship with food based on their internal signals rather than the timing and volume control assumed by an adult.

## A Child's Lack of Fear Can Be Scary

My fifteen-month-old has no fear of danger and often takes risks. I think he'd go out the window and try to fly if I didn't watch his every move. How can I teach him about danger?

*Dr. Sharon:* Almost every move a baby makes has some risk factor since he is so young and not yet coordinated. So you do have to stay ever-vigilant about keeping him from a potentially dangerous situation. But just as psychologically dangerous would be if you were so worried about your son's safety that you didn't encourage him to explore the world on his own.

*Marilu:* My Joey is a born daredevil. The first time I took him to a kids' gym, at seventeen months, he jumped into the "ball crawl" like he was a salmon spawning. I'm grateful he's more cautious now, but he learned the hard way. He had already been to the emergency room four times for daredevil-type things by the time he was two and a half. Actually, I'm getting a little dramatic here. The worst thing he ever did was crash his tricycle into a tree after rolling down a hill. I'm giving the impression that he's out skydiving and bungee jumping. I won't allow that until he's at least four.

## Skipping Grades

I have a real dilemma on my hands. My daughter has just completed her kindergarten year. Her teacher and the principal of the school are recommending that she skip to second grade. She is already a fluid reader and understands the basic principles of math. The school feels first grade would not be challenging as she is exceptionally bright and hungry to learn. I am reluctant because she is so happy with her classmates, and an enormous part of school for her is friends. The school made it clear that it will support any choice I make on her behalf. Should I keep her where she is or have her begin second grade in the fall?

*Dr. Sharon:* You have two choices—keep her in first grade and provide her with challenging educational materials and books after school, or have her skip to second grade and have friends her age come over after school. There's no reason you can't ask her for her preference. You can simply state that she would learn more if she skips first grade and she would still get to see her friends after school. It depends on the child. Some children can absorb a tremendous amount of information at this age but are too immature to jump a grade. Also, give thought to getting professional help in assessing your child's readiness (her ability to keep up academically as well as her emotional and physical maturity).

*Marilu:* When I was your daughter's age, it was recommended that I skip first grade, too. My mom was a firm believer that it was better to stay with friends my own age than to skip a grade. Her opinion was based more on a "big fish, little pond" theory, but I'll never know whether or not she was right. All I can tell you is that I loved school, graduated first in my grammar school and third in my high school, and challenged myself after and outside school with extracurricular activities.

## Alone in a Public Place

Last Saturday I took my nine-year-old son and four-year-old daughter to see a movie. They were excited and I was thrilled to find one that they'd both like. In the middle of the movie, my daughter had to go to the bathroom, and I told my son he had to come with us and wait outside the ladies' room. He said, "No, Mom, I'll stay right here. I promise I won't go anywhere." I didn't feel comfortable leaving him there by himself but I also felt bad about interrupting his movie. Did I do the right thing?

*Dr. Sharon:* Leaving your nine-year-old son in the theater unattended would have been reckless. Next time, it might be a good idea to bring another adult to the movies or take your children one at a time.

*Marilu:* Because we live in a big city, I know I would have done the same thing. It's a shame we have to worry about things like that nowadays, but we do. Maybe next time you can bring a few of your son's friends along so that there will be more of them.

## Going Alone: New Experiences

My daughter, who is nine, is really interested in art classes. I read her the brochures about all the painting, sculpting, and pottery classes. She seemed really excited, but when I went to enroll her she said she'd only go if a friend went with her. I reassured her that she would make new friends there. None of her current friends is as interested in art as she is. I think she should go by herself and take a chance, but she won't budge. Is it that she isn't open to new experiences? Help!

*Dr. Sharon:* It is not clear what your daughter's problem is, aside from feeling insecure by herself. At any rate, she is coming up with a simple and reasonable solution: namely, get one of her friends to join the art class with her. Such standoffs could have been avoided before your daughter began running the show. Now it's too late.

*Marilu:* Your daughter may also need a friend because she's talented in art and may feel more comfortable showing off in front of someone she knows. I have a friend whose son is an athlete and he often wants a friend along because, being the new guy and alone, it takes him a while to strut his stuff.

## Sleeping Away from Home

My daughter is ten. Almost all her friends are going to sleep-away camp or going to stay with grandparents for a week in another city, and so on. My daughter doesn't want to sleep away from home for even one night. Her summer seems to be lonely but she would rather be alone than away from home. Should we force her?

*Dr. Sharon:* Forced separation is generally not a good idea. There could be any number of reasons your daughter is opposed to staying away from home, among them fear of missing something good during her absence. Or it could be a more anxiety-producing reason: She could feel insecure about being away from you, fearing you might get ill. Fear of separation needs to be respected. Let her decide when she's comfortable being away by herself.

*Marilu:* Your daughter would have loved my mom's rule. We weren't allowed to spend the night away from home until we were twelve. My mother would let anyone stay at our house (the more, the merrier), but when it came to her kids, she wanted us home. Looking back, I'm sure that she didn't want to miss us.

## Creative Freedom

My six-year-old daughter received a paint-by-number game for her birthday. She used to draw pictures and paint her own paintings but now she meticulously fills in little spaces with predetermined colors. What do you think of this activity?

*Dr. Sharon:* Paint-by-number canvases are confining and don't allow for creativity. Coloring books aren't much better. It's best to give a child large sheets of paper, watercolors, brushes, and lots of space to work freely. Don't suggest what he should paint or volunteer your interpretation of his work. Say "good job" and hang up one of his paintings every once in a while.

*Marilu:* Everyone in my family is artistic except me, and I think it's because I got so obsessed with those paint-by-number kits. It was more important for me to fill in the spaces inside the lines perfectly and with the right colors than to look at the big picture and think in terms of creating my own work. I'm great at filling in spaces. No one can touch me when it comes to Tetris. But I'm a terrible artist. And I blame paint-by-number. I would like to gather all the inartistic people in this country and start a class action suit against Hasbro. I'll set up a test on my Web site. Please contact me if you can't draw "Binky."

## Coming Down with "Mommyitis"

I am lucky enough to have wonderful full-time help. My son is in nursery school in the mornings five days a week. Since his first school experience means exposure to more germs, he has come down with the usual kid fevers and infections. When he is home from school with a fever, I feel his "mommyitis" is justified. I want to take off work to be with him. I know by staying with our housekeeper, he is in good, loving hands, but isn't it true that you just want your mommy when you're sick?

*Dr. Sharon:* You sound like a good, sympathetic mother and it's hard not to feel sympathetic when your child wants you. However, what your child wants isn't necessarily in his best interest. Babying your son when he is sick sends the wrong message and creates a destructive bonding between the two of you. Since he is in good, loving hands, stay at work and let him be cared for by your housekeeper.

*Marilu:* Oh boy, this is a tough one. Kids are never more vulnerable than when they're sick, and I know from my own experience that nothing pulls on your heart strings more than a fevered, jammied, little bundle of need who wants to be cozied. But let's think this through. If you indulge him and stay home, your son may enjoy being with you so much that he will learn how to fake or exaggerate sickness in the future just to be with you. Remember your own childhood—we've all tried the old thermometer on the radiator trick at least once.

# WHEN LITTLE BRATS BECOME BIG BRATS

As you can see, our job as parents is all about giving children the tools they need to learn, grow, and cope in the outside world while trying to avoid the temptation of doing too many things for them (even though those things may seem unimportant and harmless). Here's what can happen to children who grow up overpampered and deprived of learning simple skills:

## *Dr. Sharon's View*

*Running on the playground, Cora and Gerry bumped into each other and both fell. Cora's mother scurried over, gasping loudly, "Oh no, are you okay, darling? It's okay!" as she picked up and enveloped her sobbing, inconsolable three-year-old. Gerry's mother, on the other hand, witnessing the same collision take place, stood up and called "Safe!" from a distance as Gerry "slid into home base," then got up, brushed himself off, and announced, "I'm okay." Gerry ran off to play with some other kids, while Cora's mother had to take her home.*

*Cora, of course, didn't mind, since she has a playmate who does not leave her side. Her name is Mommy and she takes up most of the room in the sandbox, to the dismay of the other kids whose faces turn long when she takes off her pumps and sits cross-legged next to her daughter, spooning sand into a bucket. Cora follows her mother everywhere, becoming depressed when she is out of sight. Cora's behavior is easily explained by her mother's behavior. Since Cora was a baby, she had been at Cora's beck and call day and night. Cora is now a helpless child who needs her mother near her at all times.*

The child whose parents anticipated his needs, thereby undervaluing his strengths and skills, will never fully use his talents when he grows up. The child whose parents *overvalued* his abilities by praising him unstintingly will also suffer adult consequences. He will feel a false sense of entitlement, constantly needing compliments for each and every small accomplishment and will have trouble creating and maintaining good relationships.

The child whose worried parents hovered over him when he was sick will, as an adult, seek an overwhelming display of concern and attention from his spouse and his friends. He might live in a state of anxiety. Never feeling really healthy, he will expect sympathy even when he isn't sick at all.

The overtended and overindulged child is not equipped to understand his role in assuming responsibilities for himself as he grows up. The anxiety he lives with is an expression of concern about how to deal with life's daily, as well as long-term, demands. Clearly, then, parents will be helping their children become secure and confident adults by fostering their independence from an early age.

------------------------------------------------

# CHAPTER 3

# "No Screaming, No Biting, No Dairy Products, No Sugar"

Being an actress, I know what contracts are, and I never start work until everything between my new employer and me is agreed upon, and both parties have signed on the dotted line. We all understand what a paper contract is, but do you realize that, as Dr. Sharon explains it, we have a contract with each and every person in our lives? From our most personal relationships to the people with whom we have the briefest, most perfunctory association, there is always an unspoken mutually agreed upon contract as to how each of us is to handle ourselves in that exchange or relationship.

For example, if you are in a restaurant and a waitress does a particularly good job, the contract is that you, the patron, leave a nice tip. You would be in violation of that unspoken contract if you chose instead to hug and kiss her to express your gratitude. When you call Information for a telephone number, it would be a violation of the basic contract that you have with the operator (a total stranger) to discuss anything other than the information she needs to perform her job and supply you with the telephone number or address you requested. In public, it is most generally accepted that we will be properly clothed and will refrain from touching one another. If someone bumps you in a crowd, don't you immediately recoil in defense? When a person on the street solicits you for money and follows you, don't you feel awkward and uncomfortable? In overcrowded situations, physical fights will actually break out because there is an unspoken agreement that we all travel with a certain amount of space around us which is ours, and that contract should not be violated.

These same principles apply to our own families' contracts, albeit with broader boundaries and greater intimacy. In my family, we had an unspoken agreement that no one (especially my parents) would parade around naked or inappropriately dressed (although my mother rarely wore anything other than a leotard or a bathing suit). When I was growing up, there were some funny rules between my mother and us kids, the most important being we couldn't wake her before noon unless we brought her a . . . Pepsi. For instance, whenever I needed a dollar for school, I would cautiously knock (Pepsi in hand) and wait to be called into her darkened room. She would sit up groggily, take a swig, and then tell me to get her purse. But God forbid I should ever open her purse myself. That was another contract. The only person allowed into the inner sanctum of my mother's hallowed purse was my mother.

My father's contract, on the other hand, was simple—"Listen to your mother!" The only other rule was that we all had to help him clean the house on Wednesdays, his day off and our only precious half-day off from school. He would don his sporty Robert Hall gray-and-white speckled shirt, the only thing in his closet that wasn't a suit (my father ran an automobile dealership), and we all knew it was time to get busy. My parents rarely had to spell out the contract. We just knew.

Although I am very different from my parents (times have changed), I have come to realize that my sons also understand most of our contracts without my totally spelling them out. The first time I was aware that I even had a specific contract with my boys was when I overheard Nicky, at two-and-a-half, tell one of his friends who was screaming at the time, "You can't scream. Mommy says, 'No screaming, no biting, no dairy products, no sugar!' "

# THE CONTRACT BETWEEN PARENT AND CHILD

The basic contract that Rob and I have established with our boys is fairly simple: We are the parents, they are the children, they live in our home, they follow our rules. Although this sounds pretty obvious, it is actually a notion that escapes many households for a variety of reasons, such as the idea that kids' feelings should be respected to the point where the child has equal say with his parents. By having our children grasp the basic understanding of our contract, I believe we are experiencing fewer arguments, fewer tantrums, and certainly far fewer lengthy explanations. Dr. Sharon has taught us that by establishing clearly defined contracts with our children, we are trying to give them a greater sense of security, stability, and a more realistic sense of expectation. (We're trying to, anyway!)

Here's what she has to say on the subject.

## Dr. Sharon's View

Corporations, marriages, trade unions—all function because of contracts they've mutually agreed on. On a smaller, but no less important level, *parents and children need to create an unwritten contract* to make the family function. This contract is: "I am the parent, I make the rules. You are the child, you obey them!"

And far from being harsh or absolute, *a parent who consistently respects and adheres to this will help promote healthy, cooperative relationships between every member of the family.* Children who respect this contract will grow up knowing their place in the family and in society. They will know what is expected of them. They will know what they can expect from their parents. They will feel secure.

But the child who controls the household (whether he takes over or the parent abdicates), ordering his parents around and monitoring, criticizing, or nagging his siblings—or the student who "takes over" the class from the teacher or who monopolizes the teacher's time, all break contracts and create confusion. When a parent or teacher permits a child to break the contract, boundaries of safety cease to exist for the child, his sense of security is undermined, and a great deal of emotional confusion can ensue.

Equally troubling is when a child entices the parent into breaking the contract, for on some level the child hopes that the parent will remain steadfast, since this contract is the foundation of the parent-child relationship. When a parent breaks the agreement, the child is likely to experience a great deal of anxiety since he will interpret his parent's action as a weakness. For instance, the child who incessantly nags his parents to let him stay up late and watch TV may wear his parents down. But once they give him permission to stay up, he will become anxious at not having his parents remain in charge and help him maintain a routine. His parents at the same time will gradually become resentful of having given him permission.

It takes a great deal of willpower for a parent to honor the contract, to be steadfast and not budge, especially in the face of a child's constant demands to the contrary. The parent must prevail, though, since it is the parent who sets the example of how other relationships remain intact. Another crucial reason for parents to uphold contracts is that children take their cues from their parents—often unconsciously. If parents break contracts, the child quickly sees that, in his own life, he has a choice to obey or not obey society's rules and laws. For instance, one contract that is frequently disregarded has to do with being punctual and respecting another person's time. A parent who promises to pick up a child at a certain time and is chronically late gives the child the message that it's okay to disregard an agreed-upon time and to make someone wait.

Children naturally imitate the positive qualities of each parent, *providing* they have not been consistently overindulged. But the overindulged child, to the parents' dismay, will imitate the negative qualities of both parents. An example of this might be a parent who is not truthful. The child, picking up on this, will later have a tendency to alter the truth himself. Uncanny as it seems (and of great surprise to Mom and Dad), children pick up their parents' behavior even if the parents keep it "secret."

Doing chores, doing homework, going to bed on time—these are the most basic contracts of childhood. But there are other understood, unspoken "contracts" with the child's environment that children begin to enter into at a very young age. They are dealing with teachers, shopkeepers, bus drivers, neighbors. Simple as they may seem, these relationships in society provide a framework for everyone's life, teaching children how to keep within the boundaries of cooperation and helping them function adeptly. Parents need to help children respect these contracts.

My father, the salesman, with his "get rich quick" schemes, figured out a great way for us to learn the value of money and at the same time honor one of my mother's most important rules of the house. No one was allowed to say "shut up," and if anyone did, they had to pay a quarter to the Family Kitty. This system became so effective my parents introduced another contract as well: If you said something bad about your brother or sister (i.e., "you're a stupid . . .") you had to pay a nickel, and if you said something about yourself ("I'm such an idiot . . .") you had to pay a quarter. This not only taught us about respect and self-esteem but eventually gave us enough money for a family vacation!

—Marila

# BRAT-BUSTERS!

## When Children and Parents Become Peers

My friend confides in her nine-year-old daughter about her personal problems. I think she is burdening her child. What do you think?

*Dr. Sharon:* I agree with you. It's destructive for a child to be burdened with the parent's problems or secrets. In a healthy family, parents and children each have a defined and different role. Contrary to popular belief, parents and children cannot (and should not) be "friends" in this sense.

*Marilu:* I have noticed that this is really common in divorced families. I've seen fathers who treat their teenage boys like buddies, confiding in them about their sex lives or bragging about their conquests. I've also seen divorced moms who wanted their children to know how "wronged" they were by their former husbands. I really feel that parents should be careful not to do this. It is unfair to their children and former spouses, and it definitely breaks the parent-child contract.

## Grandma's Different Rules

My mother baby-sits for our children two evenings a week. I've explained to her our daily routine and method of discipline, but she refuses to follow them. She lets the children watch too much television, stay up an hour past their bedtime, and have more sweets than they are allowed. What effect will Grandma have on the children?

*Dr. Sharon:* Happily, your children are firmly anchored in the disciplined world since you spend much more time with them than their grandmother. You have three options: The children are told that when Grandma comes over, some of the family rules are altered. The second is to make it clear to your mother that she must follow your rules when she baby-sits. The third is not to have her baby-sit at all. If you choose the first option, accept the more liberal rules and don't make an issue of Grandma's "spoiling" the children.

*Marilu:* How lucky you are to have your mother help you once in a while. I always think it is so important for children to know their families. However, if you're really fighting over your opposed methods of routine and discipline, maybe you should let your mom take the kids less often, so that when she *does* take them, she can have her relationship with them. We are never going to be able to control all the people who come in contact with our children.

## Family Trips

We have four children, ages five to twelve. On the weekends, every time we try to decide on an excursion, there is dissension. Should we decide our outings based on democracy and let the majority rule, or should we, as the parents, avoid the arguments and make the choice ourselves?

*Dr. Sharon:* Because your children's ages range so greatly, there's no wonder that they will want to do different things. Make the decision yourselves. If they are accustomed to their parents being in charge, they will cooperate and look forward to the group excursion.

*Marilu:* My parents usually made the decisions about what we would do, but sometimes the kids decided *where* we would do it. For example, every Wednesday, on my father's day off, we made it a point to go "out" for dinner and each kid took turns deciding where we would go. This was a great idea! We would do research to find a good restaurant because we all took pride in our own selection when our turn came up. In fact, we would then rate the restaurants on a one-to five-star system. It was our first lesson in making an informed decision and in taking responsibility for our own choices. Somehow my younger brother Lorin got four-and-a-half stars for choosing Arby's after my choice of the Travelodge coffeehouse only got four stars. And mine was "all you can eat"! Although I must admit that Arby's in the sixties was a more glamorous dining experience.

## Hard Work and Privilege

Our family is affluent and we have worked hard to achieve this. We are generous with our children with respect to money and material possessions. How do we show our children a connection between hard work and privilege? We don't want them to be spoiled.

*Dr. Sharon:* If your children work hard at school, get good grades, go to bed on time, and do their chores when they're asked to, there's no reason for you to be concerned. Responsible children understand the contract that exists between them and their academics—they will make the connection between hard work and privilege, and your generosity will not cause them to be spoiled.

*Marilu:* Out here in Hollywood I've seen parents' generosity either spoil their children or inspire them to work hard and make something of themselves. It all depends on the parents' example and rules. If we have respect for money and material possessions, our children will, too.

## Rewarding Good Grades

My daughter has been falling behind in her grades. I only expect her to do her best, but I believe that a lot of her Bs and Cs are because of her slacking off. Her teacher agrees that she's not working to her full aptitude. Is it a good idea for me to promise her a reward of some kind if she brings up her grades in her next report card? And if she doesn't bring up her grades, should I dock her allowance?

*Dr. Sharon:* There are a couple of issues here. First of all, a good grade ought to be a reward in itself. Promising an additional reward as an incentive is okay, but withholding something like an allowance is not a good idea. In this case, promising a reward is a better option than threatening a punishment. In addition, you might explain to your daughter that excellent grades now could help her get accepted into a good school later, which in turn could strongly determine her success in life.

*Marilu:* I think if a child expects money for good grades, she could also end up only being interested in the classes that are easy. That's not a contract you would want to uphold! School would become a moneymaking opportunity, instead of a learning one.

## "But All the Other Kids Are Going!"

My eleven-year-old son was looking forward to a much anticipated sleepover party. The parents rented an R-rated movie for the children to watch. None of the other parents seemed concerned, but our rule is no R-rated movies. What do we do?

*Dr. Sharon:* It's so important for parents to monitor what their children watch. Since your rule is no R-rated movies, make no exceptions. Tell your son that his friend's parents' decision is unacceptable to you and violates your rules. As hard as it might be, tell him that, because of this, he is not allowed to attend the sleepover.

*Marilu:* When I was a child, the Catholic Church defined what movies we could see by rating them according to the Legion of Decency guidelines—A, A2, A3, B, and C for condemned. This rating system was very similar to the one we have now, but it was reinforced by our school and the church's position. That made it easier for parents to set a standard and have their children respect it. Today, the rules of the house are the rules of the house, and even though occasionally they can be broken, I really do believe that children feel more secure if these rules are defined and upheld.

## What Lateness Means

My thirteen-year-old son is chronically late to every event. My husband and I find this very disruptive and rude. What makes it even more maddening is that I am always early. I'm not sure what these patterns mean or what I can do about them.

*Dr. Sharon:* A person who is frequently late shows contempt (without always realizing it) for the contract that demands punctuality and a regard for other people's time. Chronic lateness is a symptom of breaking the rules, which usually points to having been overgratified by one or both of his parents. Being frequently *early* is a symptom of anxiety. Unfortunately, it takes a great deal of effort to change either of these behaviors. Respect for time and punctuality are part of the foundation of one's upbringing. Encourage punctuality and forgive occasional lapses.

*Marilu:* Oh boy, does this sound like my family. When we were kids, every clock in our house was anywhere from five to forty minutes fast. Each room had its own time zone. If you were running late, you could always move to a room where you were early. To this day, some of the people in our family are always late. My brother Lorin's wedding started an hour and twelve minutes late. I know the precise time because my husband started a $5 pool and that was the winning time. Even some of the parish nuns, who know my family well, entered the pool. In Lorin's wedding video, the entire congregation is visibly concerned about "post time" when the kid (the ring boy) steps on the paper (the official start of the wedding). At that moment everyone looks at my husband for the official time, and then congratulates the winner, completely ignoring the wedding procession.

## When to Stay Out of It

Our sixteen-year-old daughter has received three detentions last month for being late for class. She has served two detentions but forgot to attend the third. Consequently, she has now been given a *full* day—Saturday detention. She feels this is unfair and wants us to call the school to request that it be waived. What should we do?

*Dr. Sharon:* A full day of detention on Saturday seems severe, but for you to intervene gives her the message that she can break the rules. Stay out of it and don't share with her that you agree the punishment is unfair.

*Marilu:* If you get a simple traffic ticket and completely ignore it, the ticket goes to warrant and the fine multiplies from three to ten times the original cost, and in some cases, could even lead to jail time. The consequences of ignoring penalties is a good lesson for a sixteen-year-old to learn before entering the real world. (Can you tell I know someone who teaches traffic school?)

## Son Taking Over the Role of Father

My husband went into a rage and moved out of the house. He lives down the street and refuses to come home. It's been about three months, and as a result, my four children are upset, especially my thirteen-year-old son, who has decided he's now the head of the house and has started bossing everyone around. Aside from the problem with my husband, what do I do about my son taking over the household?

*Dr. Sharon:* When a family functions properly, it is like a mobile with all the pieces hanging in balance. If one piece drops off, all the pieces must be shifted and a new balance achieved. The moment your husband moved out was the time for you to take over complete authority (which was understandably difficult during such a tumultuous time). Your son sounds like he is in a lot of pain and could use a strong parent. Start by explaining to him that you are in charge and that he must defer to you. Then investigate getting your entire family into family counseling—with such a big disruption you could all benefit.

## Chores and Responsibilities

Our nine-year-old has to constantly be reminded to do his chores (setting the table at night, taking out the trash, and feeding the cat). Every day there's a battle. To solve all this fighting, what if we excused him from all chores? It would make for peace and quiet in the house.

*Dr. Sharon:* The child who is not asked to do any chores is overgratified. The examples you give of setting the table, taking out the trash, and feeding the cat seem reasonable chores for a nine-year-old. Maybe it's just a simple problem of forgetfulness, not inattentiveness or defiance. Some children *are* forgetful—they're not bad kids. They'll grow out of it.

*Marilu:* When I was a kid, my sister Christal and I were responsible for doing the dishes (a thirty-minute chore) while my brothers were responsible for taking out the garbage (a thirty-second chore). The dishes were always clean and neatly put away, while the garbage piled up like during a New York strike. Their hands were always too grubby to let them touch the dishes, but they certainly didn't get that way from touching the garbage!

## WHEN LITTLE BRATS
## BECOME BIG BRATS

We all want our government to enforce certain rules and regulations that are meant to protect us. Even though we occasionally want to break or bend those rules (such as income tax, speeding, and so on), we are grateful and feel more secure because those rules exist. Our children, like us, really want to be protected by rules as well. As we can see, children whose parents let them manipulate contracts can grow up with a host of problems.

## Dr. Sharon's View

*Five-year-old Jimmy developed his own anti-parent lock system inside the car. On one side of the window was his frantic father trying to open the door. On the other side, holding down the lock, was Jimmy, with an intent look on his face. "Jimmy, it's getting late and Daddy's getting tired," Jimmy's weary father yelled through the window. Jimmy didn't budge. "You are being really bad," he said, adding, "It's past your bedtime. Stop this nonsense and come inside the house." Jimmy just looked at him. "I'll buy you that video game you wanted if you come out right now!" Jimmy could sense that his father was desperate and that the warnings would have to escalate before anything dire happened to him, so he continued bargaining. "I want the Nintendo and a Happy Meal. Besides, you're not going to bed. It's not fair," Jimmy shouted. It took fifteen minutes to get Jimmy out of the car. Once in the house, Jimmy's father gave him a lecture and Jimmy was so angry he smashed a little glass vase.*

The parent-child contract was disregarded, roles were reversed, and chaos ensued. When this happens perpetually, the child grows up having little regard for the needs of others, ignoring boundaries and

lacking empathy. As an adult, he will demonstrate an inability to adhere to contracts (spoken and unspoken) within his family. He'll have problems as a spouse *and* as a parent. He may pay his bills late (or not at all). He may sleep late when he should be at work. Because he doesn't really know what a contract is, except something to scoff at or disregard, the only contract he is likely to adhere to is seeking pleasure. In extreme cases, he may not even honor the marriage contract or the law. Since there were no consequences to contend with when his parents permitted him to cajole them into breaking the contract, he believes that anything goes.

"I am the parent. I make the rules. You are the child, you obey them" is a contract that seems simple. It is not. It's difficult for the parent to adhere to, particularly because the long-term consequences of not adhering to the contract don't seem too ominous when the child is young. But knowing how devastating the effects of breaking this contract can be in the long run is a good reminder why every parent needs to be consistent and firm.

# CHAPTER 4

# "Wait 'Til Your Father Gets Home"

*I* grew up in the fifties and sixties, when most moms were home with their kids all day long. After a full day of negotiations and pleas, the only threat moms had left in their arsenal was "Wait 'til your father gets home." This, however, never worked for my mom. The problem in our house was that our father got home very late, and he didn't want to waste our precious time together by yelling at us. He was, by nature, a real jokester and entered the house like "Mr. Guest Appearance." It was like—Heeeere's Daddy!

Our mom was always trying to be serious with us and could rarely count on his support as a disciplinarian. Whenever he would scold us, it was only because our mom put him up to it, so it pretty much lost its effect. (Plus, we all knew some cute way to crack him up and lighten up the situation, if necessary.) But this was all part of their contract together as parents. It was a fairly simple contract because he was rarely home, so the two of them hardly ever clashed over how we should be raised. It was always pretty much her call.

Our family dynamic was typical for a sixties American household, but families are different now. Parents are more likely to share the duties of child rearing because it is more common for both parents to be in the workforce. And in some cases, the mother works away at an office, and the father works at home on his computer, so *he* gets to spend more time with the kids. The threat "Wait 'til your father gets home" no longer has the same impact when Dad is working in his home office or exercising down in the basement. It's hard to intimidate your kids with "Wait 'til your father gets off the Internet."

Sharing the duties of child rearing rewards parents because they work as a team to shape these precious lives. However, what if parents have opposing methods for raising their kids? Who should make all the daily decisions? Is it important to choose one parent as the "Main Boss"? Or should each parent develop independent contracts and avoid the temptation of supervising each other?

## THE CONTRACT BETWEEN PARENTS

Rob and I have learned from Dr. Sharon that couples should *not* supervise each others' parenting skills and strategies. We do our best to follow her advice, but at times this can be very difficult. Our biggest problem is that we disagree on strategies for suppressing a tantrum. Rob tends to imitate the tantrum to show them how silly it sounds, and I prefer to ignore it to show how futile it is. I believe that overpowering a tantrum is counterproductive, and he feels that ignoring it doesn't get the point across. We have always quarreled on this issue.

So, what should a couple do when their child-rearing credos clash?

## Dr. Sharon's View

In the best of all worlds, parents would always agree on how to raise and discipline their children. But this is not the way the world really works. The good news is that parents with two different approaches to raising children can work well together and a child can easily adjust to their separate viewpoints. In fact, it's all for the best if a child recognizes early on that no two human beings are alike and that his parents' attitudes aren't necessarily the same. There may be conflicting opinions, but there is a simple rule of thumb that makes allowing for different parenting approaches work remarkably well: When one parent says something to the child first, the other parent then should simply abstain from giving his opinion, as hard as that might be. Privately, they agree not to interfere with each other's opinions. So there is no need to make any decisions behind closed doors. Once they decide ahead of time not to interfere, the rest is predetermined.

However, when one parent tries to supervise the other (whether it's in the presence of the child or behind closed doors), making critical comments like "I think you're too mean to Jimmy" and "Why did you put him in his room? All he said was 'I don't want to do it'" and "What's so terrible about him yelling 'no'?" the child will suffer.

There are certain extreme circumstances in which one parent *should* interfere with the other: when the child is being physically punished, inappropriately touched, or victimized by ongoing relentless derision or verbal outbursts. Under no circumstances should these kinds of violations be tolerated by the other parent.

A parent who engages in controlling or nagging or judging, or trying to will the other parent into conforming to *his* method of parenting, deprives his child of the whole rich gamut of human interactions, of exposure to divergent opinions and different ways of thinking. When the stricter of the two parents gives in and accepts the more lenient approach, the child is denied something else: the necessary discipline he thrives on. Things can be more confusing when a child is aware that one parent is critical of the other. Knowing that the lenient, permissive parent is in his corner silently (or openly) rooting for him will tend to make him uncooperative.

Interestingly, children with emotional problems, such as being overly hostile and aggressive, are rarely the result of parents who have two different approaches to child rearing.

# BRAT-BUSTERS!

## Let Your Husband Do It His Way

My husband teases our three-year-old daughter, imitating her crying when she's cranky and mimicking other sounds she makes. I tell him to cut it out. Should I imitate him when he's cranky to show him how obnoxious it is?

*Dr. Sharon:* Imitating people is hostile, so you should refrain from doing it yourself. But if that is what your husband is doing with your daughter, don't stop him. She is not being harmed and correcting his behavior is a bad idea.

*Marilu:* In the past, my husband tried to curtail our boys' loudness by imitating their volume, but it only made them get louder. I wanted to interfere, but I didn't because Dr. Sharon had explained it was better not to. Eventually, they all got bored with this "yelling game," especially because their audience (me) wasn't interested. The problem hardly exists now.

## Should Children Interrupt Parents?

My husband frequently says "Wait a minute" to our four-year-old son, who interrupts whatever his dad is doing. I don't think it's fair. I believe that when our son interrupts his dad, one of us should pay attention to him, but my husband disagrees.

*Dr. Sharon:* Your husband's request to wait a minute is perfectly fine. Delayed gratification is part of the "wait a minute" request, which will help your son mature. Even if it was wrong, it makes sense for you to stay out of it.

*Marilu:* I think one of the best things a parent can teach a child is how to be patient.

I used to play a game with my boys when they were very little. If they wanted something (and I couldn't get it or it wasn't ready) I would say "patience," and then I would count to twenty, because that's how long it took to get them what they wanted. To this day my boys play the "patience game."

## Mr. Mom

My husband is Mr. Mom, and sometimes when I come home from work, our three-year-old barely greets me, yet cries when her dad is out of sight. Since I am the breadwinner I have no choice but to work, but her reaction to me makes me miserable. What can I do?

*Dr. Sharon:* Could your husband and child visit you at work or meet you for lunch? Maybe on weekends, you and your daughter could spend lots of time together while your husband does the grocery shopping, and so on. As she grows up, your child will love you because of your concern for her and because you have worked to support the family, *not* because of the time you spent with her.

*Marilu:* Could you be acting a little guilty for going to work? Because if your daughter picks up on your dissatisfaction with the situation, she probably doesn't understand why you're not happy at home with her instead of being miserable at work. Be glad that you're such a good role model for your daughter. She'll grow up knowing a woman can be a successful mom and a successful career woman.

## Good Cop/Bad Cop

My husband spends so much time at work that I have no partner in raising the children. I am the "heavy" and the "bad cop" and I resent when my husband spends a few minutes here and there having a good time with the children. Shouldn't he have to be the bad cop once in a while so the kids can see me in the same positive light that they see him?

*Dr. Sharon:* Be glad that your husband spends some fun time with your children. That's good for everyone. And you need to realize that as they grow up, your children will recognize that the day-to-day responsibilities fell on you and that you were there for them through all the difficult times.

*Marilu:* As I've already said, this is very similar to our family, and probably most families of my generation. My father worked six days a week and came home late every night. He was always brief and charming, while my mother, who was with us all day, was often the "heavy" with no sense of humor. Deep down, we all knew that she played the leading role and our father was the very likable supporting comedian. I really respect and admire both of the roles they played in our upbringing, and how committed they were to the same goal of our well-being.

## Delayed Discipline

My husband works long hours. Often when the children do something wrong during the day, he wants me to wait until he's home so that he can discipline them. I feel that delayed discipline is useless. What do you think?

*Dr. Sharon:* It is unusual for a father to volunteer to be the "bad guy." But the threat "wait 'til Dad comes home" is ineffective. Threats have no place in child rearing.

*Marilu:* It's nice that your husband is "willing" to let you palm off some of the responsibility on him so that you're not the only "bad guy." However, I think you're right. The only effective response is an immediate one.

## Dad Says Yes, Mom Says No

I expect my children to keep their rooms tidy. My husband believes that they should be allowed to keep their rooms any way they want to. When I say, "Go clean your room," they respond, "Dad says I don't have to." What do I do?

*Dr. Sharon:* When your children say, "Dad says I don't have to," your response should be that *you* (not your husband) are now in charge and asking them to do something. Don't get into an argument with your husband about it. He might not agree with you on this, but it is possible for you to act independently and for you to get your children to obey you.

*Marilu:* I am an extremely organized person, and yet, when my kids get to be around ten, I will do what my parents did with us. I will let my boys keep their rooms any way they want (with the door closed if necessary). Once every two weeks, however, I will insist that they clean their rooms enough to wipe out any conditions that might be conducive to critter breeding. When we were kids, my brothers' room was so dirty that they created some plant and insect species never before seen.

## How to Be a Stepparent

My wife and her twelve-year-old daughter frequently argue without resolution. As a stepfather, I stay on the sideline, but I dislike the escalating arguments. What can I do to bring some peace to our home?

*Dr. Sharon:* It can be difficult to live with a stepparent, especially one of the opposite sex, so there's even more reason that boundaries be adhered to. It is possible, also, that on some level, the fight might be over you. Consequently, you are right not to interfere in their arguments and to try not to even be around when they are arguing.

*Marilu:* As a parent and a stepparent I have learned that the rules of the road are the same. It's best not to parent your partner's parenting.

## Too Many Phone Calls?

I am a divorced father, and my seven- and eleven-year-old sons stay with me every other weekend. Their mother telephones two or three times a day to speak with them. I find it disruptive. What is reasonable in this situation?

*Dr. Sharon:* It is natural for a mother to want to talk to her children once or twice a day. Providing that she isn't interfering with your parenting, making unreasonable demands of the boys, or upsetting them, don't interfere. It's good for the children to know that both parents are involved in their lives and that their mother is welcome to call when they are at your house.

*Marilu:* Boy, you'd hate to be married to my husband. When he's away from our boys he calls so often that I have to tell him, "Nothing's changed since your last call. Let us live some life before you call again." In your case, two or three times a day doesn't sound unreasonable to me at all, especially with a seven-year-old.

## When to Get Involved in Fights

My five-year-old son reported to us that he is being hit by one of his classmates. My husband taught our son that fighting is wrong and he should walk away. I think he should fight back. Who is right?

*Dr. Sharon:* If there is danger of his being physically harmed, notify his teacher or the school principal. Otherwise, let him work this out himself. Let him know that you understand what he is going through but that you aren't going to interfere unless he is in danger. Your resolve will strengthen his ability to deal with difficulties in life.

*Marilu:* If I sensed that it was just typical school-bully stuff, I would stay out of it. It would be very hard for me to do that, but I know it's probably best for my child to learn on his own how to deal with jerks like that. If he were in danger, that's a completely different story. Then I would intervene. I really hate situations like this. Bullies create so much misery in the world, but bully training really prepared me for a life in show business.

## The Importance of Staying Involved

My husband and I are divorced. When my fourteen-year-old visits his father he hangs out with a teenage boy who had once stolen a walkie-talkie at a street fair and called in a phony burglar report to the police. I have forbidden my son to spend time with this boy but my ex-husband is not concerned. What should I do?

*Dr. Sharon:* It appears your ex-husband is going to continue allowing your son to associate with this teenager, so be pleased that your son is confiding in you. Telling your son not to have anything to do with his friend will pit your son against his father. It's best to let your son continue to see his friend and hopefully, he will continue to keep you involved in his life, so you know what's going on. If you can have open conversations, he will be able to determine for himself that there are better ways to spend his time.

# WHEN LITTLE BRATS BECOME BIG BRATS

Obviously, it is difficult to allow your spouse (or partner) to parent in ways that conflict with your own approach. However, as we have learned in this chapter, it is best to permit each other separate rules for supervision. Think of how often we adults are given conflicting orders from two different authority figures in our lives. No one is always right, just as no one is always wrong. We eventually learn to find our own answers by analyzing which set of rules works best for us. Letting one parent make all the rules deprives the child of understanding that there are usually at least two sides to every issue.

Here are some consequences when one parent supervises the other.

## Dr. Sharon's View

*Four-year-old Kevin wanted to watch a tape and his mother, preoccupied with an urgent matter, said "no." Kevin threw himself on the floor and started crying inconsolably. Kevin's father, on the phone discussing a business deal, overheard what was going on. By the time he hung up the phone and came out to the living room, Kevin had stopped crying and was cheerfully watching his tape. Aghast, the father loudly reprimanded his wife for reversing herself with Kevin. Not one, but three mistakes were made in a matter of minutes. The mother's initial "no" to Kevin was needless, reversing herself was a second mistake, and the father's reprimand (which only compounded the problem) was the third mistake.*

When a lenient parent countermands the other parent's stricter approach to child rearing, their child will grow up with many false expectations. As an adult, he will expect his partner to be excessively tolerant and uncritical. Dealing with the stricter demands of life will be hard for him. Since there were always "open arms" ready to soothe him as he was growing up, nothing less than a totally sympathetic and overprotective partner will do. When the stricter of the two parents interferes with the lenient parent's approach, the consequences are similar: The child gets confused and as an adult will give his partner a "script" and "cue cards" of what loving words to say, or will "run for cover," sequestering himself from the outside world, attempting to avoid that harsh, punitive "ogre" from his early memories.

Whether a child is getting parenting approaches that complement or whose philosophies vary, he will be fine. He learns the validity of different ways of thinking and is able to react accordingly. As an adult he will expect the world to be a complex place, full of different opinions, rules, and regulations, and will know how to cope.

*My* parents had many different kinds of contracts between them, not all having to do with us kids. They had contracts between themselves as well. And while the point of this chapter has been to show the benefit of allowing for differences in parenting, it reminds me of certain differences in my parents that were allowed for within a particular contract. This contract, while never verbally expressed, was considered iron clad nonetheless—the Famous Rhumba Contract.

My parents' behavior at a party was always the same. My father could be found standing in the corner surrounded by any number of people, their heads thrown back in laughter at some outrageously witty and mischievous story he told, while my mom was on the dance floor (she always made sure there was dancing) with one partner after the next. Wives loved their husbands dancing with my mom because the men always picked up the latest dance step while the women got to flirt. Husbands loved their wives talking to my dad because this way they got to dance with my mom. Both of my parents had the unique talent of making every person they came into contact with feel special. This would go on throughout the evening until a prime moment toward the end of the party (like the "eleven o'clock number" in a Broadway show), when my mother, with a knowing smile, would walk over to the stereo, put on a famous Latin song (usually "Cherry Pink and Apple Blossom White") and flirtatiously move over to my father's corner. She would then put out her hand, which he would take with a sexy squeeze, and then would lead him onto the dance floor, which everyone had cleared so that the two of them could do what was known as the famous Joe and Loretta Rhumba. It was the one dance my father knew, and their moment to show everyone who belonged to whom. Remembering my parents showing off their dancing and chemistry as a couple was a beautiful way to share their differences through a binding commitment to one another. To this it is day, it is one of my favorite life-time memories.

—*Marita*

------------------------------------------------

# CHAPTER 5

# "Cut the Drama!"

*I*n my early days of motherhood, I realized that crying is the only means of communication available to an infant trying to get his needs fulfilled. As a child gets older, temper tantrums can often become an extension of that form of communication. And if this radical, dramatic expression of need (the temper tantrum) is not converted into the more socially acceptable form of a verbal request as a child's language skills develop), it can last well into adolescence. In fact, it can become ingrained in an individual's personality for his entire life.

There are two basic components to the "temper tantrum": first, the demand or adamant request (the expression of need), and second, the reaction to the parent's response, should it be unsatisfactory to the child.

When I initially observed this behavior in my first child, I saw it as an entirely exaggerated performance of need . . . a toddler melodrama, as it were. Nicky's tantrums always seemed to be out of pro-portion to what was being requested. Instead of giving in to the tantrum, I would look at him with an expression of disbelief and give the referee signal for "clipping" and announce, "That's ten yards for BAD ACTING." At first he wasn't sure what to make of this other than the fact that I was not buying into his tantrum. Quite the contrary, I was dismissing it. Eventually he couldn't help but realize that he was being busted for his behavior, and he would acknowledge this awareness with his own little smile of recognition. Eventually this routine simplified to my giving him the signal for scissors (as in "rock, paper, scissors") and saying, "Cut the drama." Nicky invariably came to understand not only that I could see through his tantrums, but that there would be no conceding to this behavior. Thankfully, he is growing up to become a child of understanding and resilience. (Most of the time, anyway!)

Occasionally, every child by virtue of his own body chemistry will spin out of control and run amok. Nicky is no exception. When this occurs, my husband or I will send him to his bedroom to let the tantrum run its course. Several times I've seen him moments later, tears quelled, his enthusiastic personality restored, matter-of-factly going back to whatever he was doing, saying, "Boy, I'm glad that mood's over."

# TANTRUMS:
# I WANT WHAT I WANT
# WHEN I WANT IT

Every child (adult, too!) wants to throw a tantrum every once in a while, but how can we as parents keep a tantrum from becoming a daily ritual? And what is the best way to handle them once they've begun? There are many different theories on this topic, but Dr. Sharon's guidelines have been very effective with my children.

## Dr. Sharon's View

Brats throw temper tantrums. Because they want what they want, and they want it right away or else. Or else they will yell, slam doors, hit, scream, kick, bite, throw a toy, cry hysterically. They will sulk, get under the covers, refuse to talk, go limp. Temper tantrums come in a huge variety of shapes and sizes. But they have one thing in common. They are essentially terror tactics intended to intimidate, frighten, and control. Not surprisingly, a child who resorts to tantrums to get what he wants is usually a child who has been overindulged. (A simple test: If the parent's "no" is respected and obeyed, then the child has not been overindulged. If the parent's "no" is ignored and disregarded, the child has been overindulged.)

What all tantrum throwers need, if they have any chance of being effective, is an audience. The way their parental audience understands and handles early tantrums will determine not only what shape that particular incident will take, but whether the family is to be tortured with them for years to come. Parents are often advised that a child's

tantrum is triggered when they are inconsistent about meeting their child's needs, such as parents who agree to play a game with their child one day but don't have time to play the next day. This theory is completely wrong. Parents aren't required to be consistent about playtime. Tantrums are really triggered by parents who are inconsistent about discipline!

The parent's firmness in not giving in to tantrums helps the child's emotional development and stability. Learning that he does not achieve anything except being punished when he throws a tantrum is a lasting lesson. Without this, tantrums become life-long habits. And when they do, the child (and later the adult) no longer has the desire or the ability to control himself. And everyone in the family suffers.

If dealing with tantrums is the parent's job, preventing them is not. Parents should not walk on eggshells worried that they will trigger a tantrum. Their job is cutting off a temper tantrum at its first sign.

## How to Handle a Tantrum

A raging tantrum, like a raging fire, needs to be quickly extinguished. A hug or soothing words will not do. Negotiating, bribing, giving in—none of these is a good option. Discipline is in order. The best way to deal with a child who throws a tantrum—screaming, yelling, and so on—is a firm "No!" If this doesn't work, the next step is to give the child a time-out. In a time-out, the rules are simple and not open to interpretation. The parent tells the child to go to his room for an assigned period of time. His door is shut, the lights are left on, and a monitor is placed there (if the child is young) so his parents can hear (or see) if he is in any danger of getting hurt. If the child is resistant to the idea of the time-out, his parents need to take him by his hand and lead him to his room.

In general, time-outs should be of a predetermined length so that the child knows what to expect consistently. Basically, though, the punishment should fit the crime. Use your judgment. Any further resistance should be handled by simply adding time to the child's time-out. However, threatening him with "If you don't stop crying, I'll make your time-out longer" is counterproductive. The child should not be let out of his room before his assigned time is over, not even if he behaves perfectly once he's in his room. Giving him a reprieve for good behavior is tantamount to once again letting him control the situation.

Sometimes kids innocently do things that are hysterically funny. And even though we grown-ups are dying to laugh, we can't because we know it would hurt their feelings and/or weaken our reprimand. All in all, we do a lot of "inside cheek biting" as parents. One of those times for me was when Nicky, at three years old, threw a huge tantrum after I told him that he couldn't go with Rob and me to the Hollywood Bowl to see "A Tribute to Gene Kelly" (his favorite entertainer at the time). He cried, stomped his feet, and screamed at me. He continued to sob for so long that his cries turned to hiccups. When he realized that he was getting nowhere, he picked up the phone, while still sobbing, and pretended to call the police. "Hello! Is this the police? Hi. My name is Nicky Lieberman. Could you please arrest my mother? Okay! . . . She'll be at the Hollywood Bowl tonight. Her name is Marilu Henner. I think you know her. She's the actress . . . from *Taxi*."

—*Marilu*

# BRAT-BUSTERS!

## Stop Whining!

Our two-year-old whines most of the time, which is unpleasant and annoying. How do I get her to stop?

*Dr. Sharon:* Children who whine often use their voices to evoke sympathy in their parents. Telling a child to "stop whining!" rarely works. Saying, "I will listen if you don't whine" may work for a particular incident, but the child will likely revert to whining. To break a child of whining, the parent must consistently ignore it and not succumb to giving in to what the child is whining about.

*Marilu:* I used to mimic. I used to bargain. Now I completely freeze and don't unfreeze until they stop whining. So far, it's working.

## Distracting a Tantrum

Our baby-sitter tells us she read in a magazine that when our son throws a tantrum we should sit quietly next to him to distract him, play with his toys, and make comments about them. This is supposed to quiet him down. Do you agree?

*Dr. Sharon:* Magazine articles and books may offer child-rearing suggestions that are compelling reading but that make little sense. This is one! Knowing how to cut off a tantrum is confusing, especially for first-time parents. The word "no," followed by a time-out, if necessary, is still the most effective way to stop a tantrum (providing your child has learned that when you say "no" you mean it).

*Marilu:* When you leave a child alone to have his tantrum, and you don't interfere by distracting him, it's amazing how, without an audience, the tantrum just disappears. He *needs* that audience, otherwise the tantrum serves no purpose. My husband claims that he only screams at traffic when I'm with him in the car. There's no point in yelling with the windows rolled up if he's alone.

## Tantrum in the Car

Whenever we try to secure our eighteen-month-old in his car seat, he has a temper tantrum. My husband tries to joke him out of it. This never seems effective. What should we do?

*Dr. Sharon:* Your husband's joking gives your child the message that he doesn't have to cooperate and suggests to him that on some level, your husband enjoys his disobedience. Be clear about your expectations when you put your son in his car seat and hope your husband will follow your example.

*Marilu:* I had to learn something similar to this the hard way. When Joey was very little, we would play a game with him called "Don't You Do That" and he would go ahead and do it, and we would laugh at his doing the opposite of what we said. Later, when he was a little older, we'd ask him not to do something and he'd laugh and do it anyway. After many times of *not* laughing and showing him we meant business, he finally got the message that "Don't do that!" really meant "Don't do that."

## Hugging Doesn't Help

When my eighteen-month-old does not get his way, he bangs his head on a table or other piece of furniture and then proceeds to cry. Even if I pick him up and hug him to comfort him, he still takes forever to calm down. Why doesn't this work?

*Dr. Sharon:* As hard as it is when your child is crying and in pain, resist picking him up and hugging him. This only encourages him to throw more head-banging tantrums. When he purposely bangs his head, say "no" firmly and put him in his crib for ten minutes. As always, for his safety, since he's in his crib, leave his door open and also listen to him on the monitor.

*Marilu:* My friend's two-year-old son would act out by banging his head against a wall. His mother informed me that he ate and drank an excessive amount of sugar and cola. This probably contributed to his tantrums because his nervous system was so impaired from the sugar and caffeine. The tantrums subsided after he cut down on sugar and cola. I believe that diet, especially refined sugar, can play a significant role in hyperactivity.

## Public Tantrums

I get embarrassed when our two-year-old daughter throws a tantrum in public, so to silence her, I give her anything she wants to make her stop. This doesn't seem to work. What can I do to stop the tantrum?

*Dr. Sharon:* When your daughter throws a tantrum in public, simply take her to as private a place as you can find and let her cry it out. Do not reward her because she is making a scene.

*Marilu:* In public, it's usually a different issue because all eyes are on you, you might be disturbing everyone's dinner, and you have to act quickly. When this happens to me, I'll usually take my child away from the situation and let them cry it out or walk around, or I'll try to distract them with something. But again, that's only in public.

## Pretending Not to Hear

My seven-year-old son walks around with his fingers in his ears whenever he doesn't want to hear any instructions. I find it infuriating. What do you think? And what can I do about it?

*Dr. Sharon:* Explain to your son that we were meant to hear everything since we don't have earlids. Next time he does it, put him in his room for a time-out (again, leave his door open and listen to him on the monitor). His behavior is rude.

*Marilu:* Earlids! What a concept! The perfect solution for a whining spouse!

## Threatening to Run Away from Home

My eight-year-old got angry at me and threatened to run away from home. My husband's mother said I should get a suitcase and say, "I'll help you pack your bag." Can you suggest a better way to handle this situation?

*Dr. Sharon:* The best thing would be to ignore his threat. If he heads for the front door, don't try to stop him. If he actually opens the door to walk out, you could say what your mother-in-law suggested, but if you suggest helping him pack, you have to follow through, and are you really prepared to do that? Another possibility is to send him to his room (door open) for a twenty-minute time-out and hope things will cool down.

*Marilu:* Depending on where you live, these days, I would be much too scared to let an eight-year-old walk out the door. I could *only* send him to his room for a time-out. As with any other tantrum, the "I'm running away from here" kind loses its effectiveness if no one reacts. Letting the air out of the balloon means it can't travel.

## Sulking Is a Silent Tantrum

Our seven-year-old sulks when he does not get his way. How should we handle him?

*Dr. Sharon:* Sulking is a silent temper tantrum. Your son is reacting to not getting his way, so don't give in to him. Go on with what you're doing. If the sulking doesn't stop after about fifteen minutes, send him to his room for a time-out.

*Marilu:* I wish I had known about this with my first boyfriend. That guy was a professional sulker, and I spent days trying to figure out what was wrong and to win him over. Do your son's future girl-friends a favor—nip this in the bud.

## The Silent Treatment

When my twelve-year-old is angry he gives us the silent treatment and we can't get him to respond to any questions. He just stares at us or into space and I get incensed. How do we change his behavior?

*Dr. Sharon:* The silent treatment is another form of tantrum. By giving you this treatment, he is symbolically "killing you off" (don't worry—it's only symbolic!), since you lose all power. He is using silence as a kind of weapon. But if he realizes his silence doesn't really bother you, he will give in. He will retreat from his silence the same way he would retreat from any other form of tantrum.

*Marilu:* Try not to take it personally and try to feel compassion for the difficult age he's at. He's getting more out of stripping you of your power when you plead with him than if you simply ignore him. I think people who use tactics like the silent treatment are so ridiculous. It is one of the most vicious weapons people use and it's such a waste of time.

### "I'll Live with Dad!"

Whenever I say "no" to my thirteen-year-old daughter about anything, she gets so angry she threatens to go live with her father (we are divorced). What should I do?

*Dr. Sharon:* Your thirteen-year-old daughter does not have the legal right to decide where she is going to live. Simply tell her that it is not up to her to decide where she lives. At the same time, examine your own behavior and see if maybe you say "no" to her too often.

# WHEN LITTLE BRATS BECOME BIG BRATS

When it comes to getting what we want, we tend to stick with strategies that work. If tantrums work, children, as well as adults, will continue to use them. In short, do not allow your children's tantrums to work from the very beginning, and your child will quickly learn not to intimidate and control everyone with their tantrums. Here are some consequences of tantrums left unchecked.

## Dr. Sharon's View

*Caroline stomped her feet so hard she left heel marks in the carpet. When she didn't get what she wanted, she didn't merely cry. She flopped to the ground and let out a high-pitched shriek. Then she shut up completely, slumping at her mother's feet. She offered no resistance whatsoever, which made it harder for her mother to pick her up. Her mother, tired of this almost nightly occurrence, decided that a display of opposition would stop Caroline's tantrums once and for all. With her husband's help, they picked up the silent, passive child by her arms and legs and carried her to her bedroom, telling her that she was acting like a baby and asking her to explain why she was acting this way. Instead of responding at all to this massive silent tantrum, Caroline's parents should have left her on the floor and walked away. With no attention and no opposition, Caroline would have gotten up (and given up!) by herself. Two nights later, denied a late bedtime, Caroline threw another tantrum.*

Temper tantrums that go unchecked become a habit. An adult who throws loud, out-of-control tantrums has real emotional problems. He will claim he cannot help his tantrums and he is correct. His tantrums are a habit that involves his psyche and his body. Instead of him being professionally treated to eradicate the tantrums, his family cowers. Walking on eggshells around him, no one in the family dares to speak the truth. The result, sadly, is that relationships are never completely genuine. His behavior also creates real problems for his family, virtually forcing them to conform to what he is demanding or risk being further bullied and terrorized by him. It is a form of emotional blackmail.

Silent tantrums, such as sulking, are developed to perfection by the time a tantrum thrower is an adult. Family members tend to go along with this behavior, often without recognizing that they are being controlled. Sadly, the adult who throws either kind of temper tantrum is very often a depressed person. Despite seemingly getting out all his rage with his tantrum, he is unable to alleviate his depression (which is anger turned inward, so ranting and raving won't get rid of it). It's encouraging to know that a few firm "no"'s! and some short time-outs when a tantrum thrower is very young will go a long way to making sure that when he grows up, he will act like a grown-up.

------------------------------------------------------------

# CHAPTER 6

# "I'm Calling Lily!"

When it comes to bringing up children, nothing raises more controversy than the various methods of discipline parents use. Methods range from extreme leniency to mental and physical abuse. Fortunately, today fewer parents hit their children. The wiser we become as a society, the more we realize that hitting is dangerous, degrading, and simply wrong, and it serves no constructive purpose. When I was growing up, hitting and humiliating were not only the norm, they were expected. I don't blame my parents or hold any grudges today because back then, nearly every mom, dad, and nun was doing it. They really didn't know any better. My siblings and I laugh about it today, but at the time, it wasn't very funny. We went to a very strict Midwestern Catholic school, Our Lady of Beat-Me-Senseless-with-the-Rosary-Beads was the name, I believe. Their methods of torture and discipline were handed down through generations of Europe's finest medieval monasteries.

I remember in first grade, after one little boy got caught sticking out his tongue at someone, the teacher forced him to keep his tongue out for the rest of the day. He was not even allowed to swallow. By the time the school bell rang, this poor boy's tongue had moss growing on it. It looked like a petri dish.

My brother Tommy, who suffered most at the hands of the Dominicans, should have been canonized for his martyrdom by the end of the third grade. He once got caught chewing gum by—I think it was—Sister Mary Milosevic. She made him kneel, fold his hands behind his back, and push a wad of gum down the entire length of the hallway—with his nose. He hasn't touched a pack of Juicy Fruit since March of '63.

Another time when he was acting out in school, the nuns taped a sign saying "I am a baby" to his chest, put a bow in his hair and a rattle in his hand, and made him parade around the entire school, classroom to classroom, for public humiliation. Most kids would have been scarred for life. My brother, a true bad-boy hall-of-famer, actually liked the attention.

My parents were not as bad as the nuns, but they weren't entirely innocent either. My mother was a part-time beautician (she ran a beauty salon out of our kitchen) and always had her weapon of choice, a hairbrush, at her side and loaded. My father was not as scary since he was too busy working and rarely home, but when he struck, he had a faster backhand than Pete Sampras.

All these tactics kept us in tow for the most part, but occasionally when serious disciplinary action was necessary, my mother used the one thing that instilled fear deep in our hearts. Our knees would tremble just from hearing the name—LILY!

She was a 300-pound German woman, a kitchen beauty salon

regular, who resided in the apartment complex next door. By day she was a cleaning lady who lived a pretty normal life, but by night, she was my mother's secret weapon against child disobedience. Ready to spring into action at a moment's notice, Lily would come over to "sit" on us. While holding the phone high above our heads, my mother would ask, "You want me to call Lily? You want her to sit on you? Is that what you want? I could have her here in five minutes." I once thought she was bluffing. I paid dearly for that assumption. When Lily arrived, she sat me down on the very hard porcelain edge of our bathtub to prepare me for the "treatment." Next, with the gracefulness of the *Queen Mary*, she turned around and slowly backed in toward the epicenter, me. And then it happened—splashdown! A 9.6 on anyone's Richter scale.

# "NO" IS A COMPLETE SENTENCE

The first thing I vowed when I had kids of my own was this: No spanking, no slapping, no shaking, and definitely—no Lilys! (Besides, with all my friends off dairy, it would be hard to find someone 300 pounds.) I turned to Dr. Sharon for guidance on the subject of discipline.

## *Dr. Sharon's View*

When it comes to raising children, some rules are crystal clear, and this is one of them: Physical punishment is humiliating and dangerous and is never an acceptable way to discipline a child. It is really just a frightening terror tactic used to assert power over a child. It is a paradox that loving parents try to relieve their children's pain when their children are sick or hurt, yet they actually inflict physical pain on these same children as a form of discipline. Whether it's a slap, spanking, or just the threat of being hit, a child will come to think of his parents as cruel and out of control. As an adult, he will recall his parents' threatening gestures—gritting their teeth, lifting their arm, or grabbing a belt or brush—as real physical assaults even though no physical contact was ever made. Getting slapped across the face, a particularly violent form of punishment, can have dire emotional and physical consequences. The eyes, the ears, the nose, the mouth, and in particular, the brain are all assaulted. And those are the lifelines, psychologically and physically, to the person's very existence. Parents who slap a child in the head are intent on harming a child in both ways.

What does work as a form of discipline? An emphatic "no" is one of the most effective words a parent can use. A few years ago, it was believed that "no" would damage a child's self-esteem, and that parents should remove the word "no" from their parenting vocabulary, replacing it with endless warnings, explanations, and negotiations. It has now become increasingly clear that these methods are pointless and ineffective. The message they give the child is that the parent is uncertain of his own rules and is not in charge. A child needs to be aware that children and parents are NOT equals and that the parent is in charge. Rules that are clearly established and boundaries that are clearly defined may make the child momentarily unhappy, but in the long run, they will make him feel safe and secure.

In most cases a child can figure out the reasons for his parent's rules and why the parent is saying "no." But in any case, the child does not need to be told *why* he should or should not do something. "You need to put your toys away" is enough. Adding, "so that tomorrow you will know where they are" is redundant. Spelling it all out and thinking for him undermine his desire to grow up and think for himself.

## The Language of Parents

If parents' rules should be clear, so should their language. Unfortunately, parents often phrase commands to their children in the form of a question, such as, "Do you think you can move a little faster?" or "How about cutting it out?" This gives children the impression that they have the option to disobey. Qualifying words such as "probably," "sometimes," "unless," "hopefully," "perhaps," and "unfortunately" also render the requests ineffective and undermine commands. Take, for example, "You will *probably* be in trouble," "I *hope* you listen," "*Perhaps* you should put your toys away," "*Try* to stop bickering," "*Unfortunately* you must first do your homework." Firm statements such as "Put your toys away," "Do your homework," "Move faster," and "Cut it out" may sound harsh, but are less confusing and much more effective.

A parent should *not* have to resort to statements like "You had better," "Either . . . or," and "Unless you . . . I will . . ." Threats will only compound a child's bad behavior. And idle commands that sound like bribery or blackmail do nothing but lead to a standoff. The parent who is able to remain firm will not have to resort to threats.

There's one other approach to avoid, and that's trying to persuade a child to do something. This is an exhausting and ineffective exercise that the child, far from seeing as enlightened and loving, interprets as a form of weakness on the parent's part. Given an opening, the determined child may continue pestering until the parent gives in. From then on, the child will not take "no" for an answer. Explaining and justifying the "no" are both forms of overindulgence, which inevitably lead to negotiations and arguments. A child should not have the option to negotiate or reject what the parent tells him to do. "Do it!" are two words that say it all.

*Before* I knew Dr. Sharon's position on negotiating with your children, I discovered the perfect two words to get your kids to listen to you and do what you ask—"Hello Santa!"

"Hello Santa" is my shorthand for threatening and bribing your kids daily by pretending to call Santa in order to get them to do whatever you want. It's a tactic that begins right after Halloween and lasts (if you're creative enough) right up until New Year's Day (remember—you can threaten to return the toys, too.)

I know it was wrong, and I know I shouldn't have done it, but it worked *sooo* beautifully. I even had my brother call and pretend he was Santa, although he sounded more like Ed McMahon. Now they're scared of Santa and Publishers Clearinghouse.

—*Marilu*

# BRAT-BUSTERS!
## Punishing and Protecting

The one and only time I left my five-year-old in the care of my parents my father slapped her across her face because she said something fresh to him. This is not unusual for him. He hit me throughout my life. I disapprove of slapping or any form of physical discipline, and I cannot forgive my father for slapping my little girl. What should I do?

*Dr. Sharon:* As a child you were unprotected, but now you have the power to control your father's behavior toward your child. You simply must not leave her in your parents' care again. If your mother never stopped your father's abuse of you, she probably still has no control over him. Tell your five-year-old that you disapprove of Grandpa's behavior and you will not leave her there again.

*Marilu:* Your father is probably from a generation in which it was acceptable to slap children. Public awareness has changed a great deal on this subject, and by now your father should have changed, too. Anyone who could slap a five-year-old out of anger, especially in the face, should not be given the opportunity to do it again. I would forgive your father and move on (at least for your sake), but don't leave your child alone in his care again.

## Confronting a Stranger

If you see a stranger spanking his child, is it okay to say something in order to protect the child from the humiliation?

*Dr. Sharon:* If you tell a stranger not to spank his child, the spanking may go underground where the child will be put in more jeopardy. If you fear the child is in psychological or physical danger, report it to the authorities.

*Marilu:* I understand Dr. Sharon's position on this, but it would be very difficult for me to keep my mouth shut if I saw a stranger spanking his child. Maybe someone reading this will be afraid to hit his child if he knew that I or someone else would say something to stop him.

## Trashing His Room

I put a lock on my seven-year-old son's bedroom door because he kept leaving the room during a time-out. I do have a monitor

in his room. Now he gets so angry he trashes his room. He emp-
ties his drawers, throws his clothes on the floor, takes the bed
sheets off, and throws toys and books all over the room. It takes
him a week to clean it up. What should I do?

*Dr. Sharon:* When you open the door to your son's room and see
that he has trashed it (you may have been forewarned by the
sounds), make sure he doesn't leave his room until everything is put
back in place. Allowing him a week to clean up the mess negates the
effectiveness of the original time-out.

*Marilu:* This kid has the makings of a rock star. His room is only a
stepping-stone for future hotel suites. Seriously though, at age seven,
this couldn't be a new pattern. Behavior like this is established gradually. You'll have to hang tough to get him to respect you again.

## Biting Baby Back?

Our eighteen-month-old son is going through the biting stage.
When he bites it really hurts. I heard that biting the baby
back—not too hard—gets the baby to realize it is painful and
he then will stop biting. It sounds barbaric to me. What do you
recommend?

*Dr. Sharon:* You don't teach a child not to bite by biting him, just as
you don't hit a child for hitting his brother. Inflicting physical pain
in order to teach about pain is perverse and accomplishes nothing. A
firm "no" should accomplish the desired results. If it does not, put
the baby in his crib for fifteen minutes (while observing him on the
monitor).

*Marilu:* This question is right up my alley. I was a major biter as a child. I didn't do it in a mean way. I was no baby Mike Tyson or anything like that. It was just my way of expressing uncontrollable love. I bit my brothers mercilessly. My mother did everything short of driving a stake through my heart to get me to stop. I wore a garlic necklace until I was twelve! Thank goodness neither of my children is a biter.

## Ending a Time-Out

When I give my four-year-old daughter a time-out, should I greet her with open arms when she comes out? I want to include some positive reinforcement in a negative situation. Also, should I shorten her time-out once she calms down?

*Dr. Sharon:* Greeting your daughter with open arms when she comes out only softens the message she received when she was sent to her room. It's best just to go about your business, yet be pleasant. The length of the time-out should not depend on her calming down. Once it is established, stick to it.

*Marilu:* Giving more attention and coddling after a tantrum teaches the lesson, "Tantrums bring affection, therefore I should throw more tantrums." Put another way, "The squeaky wheel gets the oil." Stop giving your kids the "oil," and they'll stop squeaking.

## Saying "No" Too Much

It seems that lately I'm always saying "no" to my two-year-old. If I say "no" too often, will it become less effective and will he tune me out?

*Dr. Sharon:* The word "no" will remain effective as long as you are not wishy-washy about it, in which case it will become an exercise in futility.

*Marilu:* You'll never say "no" more often than while your child is two. Don't worry. It gets easier as your child gets older and learns what he can and cannot do. But if you don't say "no" often, and back it up with an action that is consistent with the word, he'll never learn.

## Parent and Child Aren't Equal

Our five-year-old daughter has started saying "no" to everything we ask of her. She complains that it's unfair that we say "no" to her and that she can't say "no" to us. What do we do?

*Dr. Sharon:* Your daughter needs to learn that parents and children are not equals. According to her reasoning, if you command her to go to bed, she should be allowed to tell you to go to bed as well. When she says "no," tell her it's unacceptable. If she repeats it, put her in her room for a time-out. In the long run, she will feel safer knowing that you are in charge and that you are the one saying "no."

*Marilu:* Throughout her life, your daughter will be in the same situation without her authority figures. If you set a good example, her future teachers and bosses will thank you. And your daughter will thank you for teaching her respect for, and cooperation with, people in charge.

## Anticipating Bad Behavior

Whenever our six-year-old is about to do something wrong his facial expression betrays it and I warn him not to go ahead and do it. My husband thinks I should let him do it and then say "no."

*Dr. Sharon:* Whenever your son looks suspicious, disregard it. The word "no" should not be used when anticipating a problem (unless it's a potentially dangerous situation, like a toddler about to touch a hot stove).

*Marilu:* If all mothers warned their kids every time they made a facial expression, the world would have no more Jim Carreys.

## Words That Help Discipline

Our pediatrician says we shouldn't use the words "good" and "bad" when we describe our four-year-old's behavior. Instead, we should use "acceptable" and "unacceptable" when disciplining him. What do you think?

*Dr. Sharon:* In the final analysis, consistency of discipline is what counts, not the words.

*Marilu:* Tell your pediatrician that this is "bad" advice and that his bill is "unacceptable."

## Do Threats Work?

Threatening my four-year-old with "If you don't put your shoes on quickly then you can't go with Mommy" almost never works. I end up taking her with me because I'm a single mom and there's no one else at home. I don't know how to get her to cooperate. Please help.

*Dr. Sharon:* It's best not to use threats at all. But if you do threaten your daughter and she doesn't obey, you must follow through with your threat or you weaken your position from then on. Whenever you threaten your child with a consequence, make sure it is one you can carry out. One or two such threats that are followed through with consequences are probably all it will take to get her to know you're serious.

*Marilu:* I once told Nicky that if he didn't get ready on time, I was going to leave him at home. He didn't comply, but I was able to follow through because I could leave him at home with my husband. It broke my heart, but Nicky was able to learn the definition of consequences. (Not that staying home with my husband is facing dire consequences.)

## Ignoring a "No!"

My twenty-month-old has started throwing food and utensils on the floor. He thinks it's fun to watch Mommy pick it all up. When I say "no!" he gets angry and tries to stand up in his high chair. What do I do? I am concerned he is not getting enough nourishment.

*Dr. Sharon:* Most likely your son ignores your "no" because he knows you don't really mean it. He may, by now, feel like it's a game. Your strategy should be to place his food in front of him and a big towel under his high chair. Make sure he's safely and securely fastened in his high chair, so he can't stand up. Let him eat and don't worry about his getting enough nourishment (unless the pediatrician disagrees). If everything in front of him lands on the floor, don't give him more food to replace it. He'll quickly learn not to throw it next time.

*Marilu:* When my kids started throwing their food, I took the food away so they couldn't play with it anymore. Usually children will eat when they're hungry at the beginning of the meal. When they're no longer hungry, they will start entertaining themselves by playing with their food. Try taking your son's food away when he starts playing with it. However, if he starts to shape his mashed potatoes like Devil's Tower, it might mean something. Keep your eyes out for UFOs.

## Disciplining a Hitter

I read in a book that one way to help a child stop hitting other children is to tell him to take his own hand and talk to it, and say, "Hand, you should not hit people!" Do you recommend this?

*Dr. Sharon:* Having conversations with different parts of one's body is very odd and accomplishes nothing. The impulse to have a child talk about hitting is legitimate, but not to his hand.

*Marilu:* I have a friend who once went through this bizarre therapy that involved placing an article he was wearing (a belt, a shoe, a tie, and so on) on the chair next to him so that he could talk to it. I guess the object represented "him," and this was a way to physically talk to himself. The therapy worked fine until he started dating one of his shirts. . . . No, I'm sure it didn't help much. He looks back now and says, "What was I thinking?"

# WHEN LITTLE BRATS BECOME BIG BRATS

Discipline can be a complicated and emotionally charged issue. Consequently, I would like to summarize three important points in this chapter: 1) Physical and verbally abusive discipline is humiliating, debilitating, immoral, and illegal; 2) Truly effective discipline comes from the appropriate, firm, and consistent use of the word "no," complemented, when necessary, with a time-out; and 3) Weak negotiations and explanations are simply ineffective. Here are some final examples to illustrate what happens when these points are not followed.

## Dr. Sharon's View

*"Nathan," said his mother in a no-nonsense voice, "if I let you stay up and watch one more television show you will not get a good night's sleep and you'll be tired at school tomorrow and your grades will suffer and your health will deteriorate from the stress and you'll get kicked off the softball team and then you won't get into Harvard and you won't go to*

*medical school and nobody will want to marry you and then you won't have a big house with a swimming pool and a three-car garage. Would you like that to happen?" Nathan's mother is saying "no" to his request to watch more television, but at the end of her narration Nathan's mind reeled from the predictions of a doomed life. Nevertheless, Nathan once again insisted on staying up another half hour to watch his favorite show. Back to square one, for his mother's words had had absolutely no effect on Nathan. "Explaining" must take the form of telling the child it is his bedtime. Period! And a response to his insistence is "no," which is to the point and much more effective than predictions of consequences.*

When parents are reluctant to say a firm "no" to their children, their children will be reluctant to obey them. Their halfhearted commands, long-winded explanations, weak threats, and mixed messages will all be ignored or disregarded by the child. The result is a confused and inconsistently disciplined child who often will grow up to be a shy, insecure adult in public and an ornery, irreverent, and difficult person at home. The child who is inappropriately and harshly disciplined, frequently spanked or slapped (particularly because the parent is in a bad mood), will later in life allow other people, even his spouse, to treat him poorly. His self-esteem will be shaky and based on other people's approval. In contrast, the consistently disciplined child is given every opportunity to grow up stable and cooperative, both at home and in the world.

# CHAPTER 7

# He's in the Middle of His Own Movie

Comedian Judy Toll said it best: "After years of therapy, I realized I'm the biggest piece of crap . . . that the world revolves around."

We all know them. We've all dated them. Some of us have even married them . . . twice. They're those princes or princesses who think they walk above ground (or on water) and the rest of us are merely their subjects. They believe they are starring in their own movies, and we're just the wanna-be extras hoping to get a line. I know so many people like this (especially in show business). They walk around as if they're entitled to anything. They tend to be histrionic, too. Everything that happens around them often has this sense of high drama. Nothing is ever right, and every problem is always somebody else's fault.

A guy I went out with was exactly like this. I wondered how he became such a "prince," and then I met the queen. My boyfriend's mother completely doted on her precious baby (my boyfriend), and nothing was good enough for her sonny boy. I was lucky she liked me, but it was only because she hated his last girlfriend. This guy approached every encounter as if he were doing you a favor by being there, and he put very little energy into his personal relationships. His attitude was "I'll show them," but it really evolved into "I'll show me." I saw him as a real challenge and fell madly in love with him, until I got older and wiser and moved on to healthier people.

# THE CURSE OF "SPECIAL"

When I had children I swore that I wouldn't let them turn out like this. I'm always asking Dr. Sharon how to prevent this from happening. What can parents do to keep their child from becoming a person who is full of himself, yet dissatisfied and completely unaware of other people?

## Dr. Sharon's View

Some children are told by their parents that they were born special and that they should always have the best. Their parents spare no energy or expense to do this, at the same time protecting them from a world that might not recognize their innate gifts. These parents, only wanting to do the right thing, have read or heard that telling a child he is special will help him develop the self-esteem and confidence he needs to grow and prosper. They believe that a child who is told this often enough will know he is loved. It's not just parents who buy into this myth—in later years, the child's teachers will probably use the same hyperbolic phrases in the mistaken belief that this will convince the child that his talents are appreciated.

And it is a myth. Praising a child excessively and indiscriminately by using superlatives like "special," "amazing," "brilliant," "extraordinary," and "gifted" will *not* create the well-loved, well-balanced child, so secure he feels he can achieve anything he sets his mind to. On the contrary, it will produce an overindulged child who feels *insecure* physically and emotionally, who will never have an accurate perspective about who he is and what his place is in the family and in society. The curse of "special" is that it gives him the most unrealistic expectations, sentencing him to a lifetime of disillusionment. A gap will always exist between his insistence that he is a genius and his less-than-superlative functioning. Yet he can't figure out why everyone around him doesn't behave as if he's special.

Furthermore, most children *know* that everything they do isn't brilliant or incredible, so they may end up confused *and* dubious about what people tell them because they can't buy into their parents' constant exaggerations.

The child who has his needs tended to and receives consistent discipline will have a far better chance of becoming successful than the coddled child who hears nothing but admiring words.

## The Problem with "Happy"

Another way of indulging a "special" child is to tell him, "All I want for you is to be happy in life." This sentiment may seem harmless and loving, but it does a real disservice to a child, assigning him an impossible, unobtainable task. For happiness, as a life goal, is elusive, intermittent, often random, and unpredictable. As an adult, he will pursue one career after another, one relationship after another, never settling down and always in search of what will make him happy.

Parents who don't make happiness a goal but who concentrate on the basics—making sure their child works hard in school and takes his chores and responsibilities seriously—will produce a child whose talents and values will bring him success.

*A* few months ago, I had the privilege of sitting next to a wonderful woman in her sixties at a dinner party. As usual, the conversation got around to every mother's favorite topic (her children), and she told me all about her two grown daughters, who are as close in age as my two boys. When I talked about writing this book, she told me that she found the theory in this chapter particularly interesting. Her older child had been the "Golden Child" growing up, with everyone telling her through her whole life how special she was. The woman had expected her older daughter to grow up and be very successful, but, as yet, she doesn't know what she wants to do with her life and is having a hard time finding herself. Her younger daughter, however, who wasn't constantly being told she was "special" while she was growing up because her older sister was getting all the attention, is now one of the most successful women in America. Her mom told me how hard this daughter had had to work to get to where she is today. She explained that nothing came easily, but her daughter learned early in life that it takes hard work and discipline to get anywhere. The younger daughter didn't grow with the curse of "special."

—*Marilu*

# BRAT-BUSTERS!

## Exaggerated Praise

I heard it is good to praise a child throughout the day for all his little accomplishments. ("You buttoned your shirt—that is *wonderful!*" or "You brushed your teeth. I am so proud of you!") and that these compliments are the building blocks for self-esteem. What do you think?

*Dr. Sharon:* Praising a child's ordinary, everyday accomplishments burdens him with a sense of entitlement. And exaggerated praise like "You are the best," "the greatest," "a genius," "one of a kind," gives a child false expectations of what he will achieve in life.

*Marilu:* If a child gets the same praise for doing the dishes as he did for getting A's on his report card, it gives him less incentive to work hard for the A's next semester. When a child receives praise, he should feel truly proud that he strove for something and succeeded.

## Winning

My son and I are just starting to play games together. Should I let him win most of the time in order to build his self-esteem?

*Dr. Sharon:* Winning all the time will not build your son's self-esteem. He will not learn to tolerate setbacks in life, and he will recognize that you are bending the truth, which sets a bad example. In life, we sometimes win and sometimes lose. Also, in the real world, other people won't let him win all the time.

*Marilu:* I took my kids to their friend's birthday party recently and the mother throwing the party actually said to me, "Because it's his birthday, I hope you don't mind if I let my son win all the games today." Can you imagine this? What will happen to this boy when he faces the real world and starts losing once in a while?

## Too Young to Share?

My friend brought her three-and-a-half-year-old son to my home to play with my son, who is the same age. My son is an only child and he's not used to other people playing with his toys. When his friend wanted to play with his toy he started to fuss. I forced him to share because I don't want him to grow up to be selfish. Did I do the right thing, or is he too young to share?

*Dr. Sharon:* He is not too young to know how to share. I don't know what you mean by *forcing* him to share. Simply say "no" when he takes away a toy from his friend and return it to the friend. And make sure you set a good example since his learning to share will be reinforced by your good examples. Sharing is so important because we don't live in a vacuum. We all benefit when we share our talents, ideas, and abilities.

*Marilu:* One of the best children's videotapes is called "Learning to Share," from *Sesame Street.* It stars Elmo, Zoey, Big Bird, and Katie Couric. It's all about sharing and compromising. My kids learned so much from this tape that every time there's a question about sharing with each other or with friends, some phrase from this tape comes up. You might want to get this for your children. (I hear they're coming out with one called "Learning to Obey" for husbands. I can't wait!)

## Too Much Birthday

In my family the "birthday child" has always been special. It was a family tradition to spend an entire week celebrating each child's birthday with a different treat each night. I'd like to continue this tradition with my children. Do you think that would be okay?

*Dr. Sharon:* It is overgratifying to celebrate a child's birthday for an entire week. One birthday party is enough—but not one at school, one at home, *plus* a whole week of family celebrations. A child accustomed to ongoing celebrations will later in life become depressed if his spouse and friends won't fuss over his birthday. Besides, it is narcissistic to fuss that much over anyone's birth.

*Marilu:* I would like to know how you do it all week. Is it fiesta night on Monday, Chinese food on Tuesday? How do you keep the spirit fresh without making everybody sick? What is the expense?

What if you have a really big family? Practically every other day would be a birthday.

## On the Phone

Every time my sister and I are on the phone, her six-year-old daughter interrupts our conversation. I find this frustrating and intrusive, but my sister claims that a child's needs should always come first. Is she right?

*Dr. Sharon:* Your sister should have told her daughter to wait until she was off the phone instead of permitting her to interrupt. There's very little that can't wait. It is a bad lesson to teach a child that her needs always come first. She is going to grow up into a demanding adult.

*Marilu:* I do a lot of business on the telephone. I have made it clear to my kids that most of my time on the phone is work, and I shouldn't be interrupted unless it's important. If they didn't understand this, I would never get any work done. My children's needs are the most important thing in the world to me, and one of the things I believe they need most is a sense of other people. Deferring to them first will deprive them ultimately of sharing themselves with the great big wide world out there.

## Difficult or Creative?

I heard that there is a connection between a child being difficult and being creative. Our four-year-old is a very difficult child and I find it worrisome. My husband thinks I'm overreacting, and he believes that our son's combativeness will help develop his creativity and intelligence. What do you think?

*Dr. Sharon:* I don't subscribe to the notion that there is a connection between a child being difficult and being creative. A self-effacing parent who has not achieved his own goals may encourage his child to be difficult, thinking that will help his child achieve what the parent has not. Your husband is actually limiting your son's creativity by encouraging him to be difficult, unleashing emotional problems.

*Marilu:* Oh boy! This sounds like so many guys I went to acting school with in the seventies. (Don't worry, I am not going to mention any names.) So many actors use this as an excuse for not giving up drugs or alcohol or not getting into therapy. They believe their being "difficult" is what makes them creative. Unfortunately, their emotional or substance abuse problems waste so much of their time and energy, it keeps them unemployed as actors. The key element that makes a person talented and creative is, believe it or not, talent and creativity, and perhaps even more important, discipline. Being disciplined is the opposite of being difficult.

## Really Gifted

I am the mother of four and although I know that many mothers believe their children are special and gifted, my family and friends agree that my five-year-old son is a genius. I don't want my other children to be hurt by how much attention their brother gets for being so advanced, but on the other hand, I don't want to deliberately deny my special son praise just to protect his siblings. How should I handle this?

*Dr. Sharon:* Your children are aware that their five-year-old sibling is advanced, but constant praise will cause them to resent him and he will grow up feeling above the masses, which will land him on the psychoanalytic couch. Provide him with educational stimuli—books, classical music, and music lessons, as well as special educational programs. Leave the excessive praise out.

*Marilu:* My mom, the mother of six, made us all feel special and advanced, each in our own way. Your son's talent may be in the academic world, but make sure your other children's talents are not being overlooked.

## Menial Jobs

Our sixteen-year-old son has been offered a job busing tables in a neighborhood restaurant. We don't want him to do it. We would rather he not work than do a menial job that will not make use of his sharp mind. Do you agree?

*Dr. Sharon:* What does your son want to do? Let him decide. Collecting garbage and waiting tables are demanding jobs that require hard work and responsibility, and someone has to do them. Not all lessons are academic. If, on the other hand, he thinks he is too good or too smart for menial work, his self-perception will interfere with his creativity.

*Marilu:* One of the best jobs I ever had was being a waitress at a summer resort. It taught me discipline, decision-making, timing, and coordination, and it sharpened my memory. It laid the groundwork for almost every job I ever had. Menial? What's menial?

## Happiness

In talking to my son the other day I happened to say, "I just want you to be happy." My husband said, "What about me? I'm not happy. I'd love to quit my job, go back to school, and study the Greeks." I'm not sure he was kidding. Should he pursue his "bliss"?

*Dr. Sharon:* The same way it doesn't benefit a child to pursue happiness, an adult who pursues his "bliss" will have a hard time and so will his family. None of us can pursue our bliss, except for moments here and there, unless we want to become parasitic (namely, having others taking care of our responsibilties). Pursuing "bliss" is the unrealistic ambition of an adult who was told as a child that he deserved to be happy in life.

*Marilu:* I read somewhere that only two percent of all people love their jobs, five percent like their jobs, and the other ninety-three percent hate their jobs! My friends in Italy seem to live a certain way so that they "work to live, not live to work." They don't necessarily like their jobs, but they all seem to have jobs, and they adjust their lifestyles to their jobs. In America, we've come to believe that we should have to work only at what we love. Real happiness in life comes from taking responsibility for yourself and your loved ones in adulthood.

## The Key to Life

As I was growing up, my father repeatedly told me, "The key to life is to discover what it is you truly love to do, then find some fool to pay you for it." My question is: Where do I find someone to pay me to watch ESPN with Chee-tos and a six-pack?

*Dr. Sharon:* Your question is humorous, but the concept is destructive. Your father would have done a better job had he advised you to go to school and obtain a degree that would qualify you for a profession, unless you did not follow his advice and you really are a successful comedian.

*Marilu:* Some people are lucky enough to know at an early age what it is they truly love doing. This gives them an enormous advantage in their field. The earlier they start, the greater the potential for long-term career growth and success. Most people, however, don't discover this until they are much older, and quite a few spend their entire lives searching for the one career they think will make them happy. I basically believe your father's advice is good but he should add this: It's great to discover what it is you truly love doing . . . and the best way to discover it is to dive passionately into your education. The trick is to strive for excellence in all your subjects, not just the ones you think are interesting or have the greatest potential for being useful later in life. This way, many more avenues are explored and you'll have a better chance of finding your passion. There is no better way to explore the range of career and life possibilities at a young age than by making a commitment to your education.

## Success . . . or Else

My husband is basically a loving and supportive man, but he becomes inconsolable and depressed when a colleague succeeds. He can't read of promotions or participate in celebrations honoring others in his field. What is this about?

*Dr. Sharon:* It sounds like when your husband was growing up he was told that *he* was the special one, and as a result, nothing short of enormous success will satisfy him. Unable to achieve success and jealous of his colleagues who are successful, he is vindictive and wants to undermine them. Since he can't do that, he turns his anger inward and becomes depressed. At home, be prepared to live with a man who is disillusioned.

*Marilu:* I would recommend to your husband that he get into an exercise program to help relieve *stress.* My business (show business) is a very competitive one in which the "best man" does not always win. My husband, who is a talented director, has eased the stress of show business by running every day. Maybe your husband would benefit from this as well.

# WHEN LITTLE BRATS BECOME BIG BRATS

Bestowing *too* much adulation on our children is a detriment because it gives them an unrealistic perception of themselves and their abilities. Later on, they may become confused by the mixed reactions they'll receive from the rest of the world. They will also have a more difficult time improving the social, intellectual, and practical skills that are necessary to become a contributing member of society. The following is an example of what may happen when a child grows up thinking all she has to do is be "special."

## Dr. Sharon's View

*Mary has been told she was "special" from the day she was born. "A jewel . . . a treasure . . . our precious angel," her parents often told her. Now, at thirteen, Mary knows she is special with all her heart, although she could not begin to tell you what is special about her. All she knows is that she deserves to be treated like a princess. So, soon after the school bell rings, Mary pulls out her cell phone and admonishes her mother for being five minutes late in picking her up. Mary is mad at her music teacher, too. She didn't get the lead in the school play in spite of the fact that her father has always sworn to her that she was the best singer—head and shoulders above the others. She can't believe the housekeeper is sick today and her room is a mess (Mary never learned to pick up after herself) and she is used to everything being perfect. As if that wasn't enough, she is upset because her teachers gave her more homework than ever. Why, Mary thinks, should I have to do homework? Mary is a princess, but she has no kingdom, and the only people who treat her like royalty are her parents. When she grows up, she will still be living in an ivory tower, only, chances are, there will be no prince, no subjects, and no happiness.*

Narcissism (self-love that disguises self-hate) flourishes in an adult who was treated as though he was the greatest creature, someone his lucky parents were blessed with. This child grows up very jealous of his peers, and as an adult will covet what others have. The very jealous person will hide his jealousy and reveal it in lots of different ways—by trying to make others jealous of him, by having an attractive partner, fancy clothes, and a sharp car, and so on. If all that doesn't make his friends jealous, as a last resort he undermines his friends by becoming vindictive, thereby eliminating the necessity or reason for him to be jealous of them. Lack of resilience rears its head in the jealous person— for within the family structure, living with a non-resilient person means being subjected to his end-

less pouting, which is oppressive to everyone near him. To make matters worse, if he turns his anger inward, onto himself, having no other outlet, he will become depressed.

Having been told how special he was, he will not tolerate a life of obscurity, pining to have his name in lights (and rarely seeing them). Sadly, his grandiosity will torture his family, but it will torture him more.

One way emotional health is measured is by a person's ability to be resilient. Ironically, *not* being told he is the greatest and the best is probably the best way to help a child become a sensible, grounded adult who knows that the only way to get praise is to do something praiseworthy and that the only way to be on top is to work from the bottom up. Such a child will tolerate disappointment much more easily as an adult—which is a great part of coping with whatever comes his way in life.

# CHAPTER 8

-------------------------------------------------------------

# "But I'm Not Tired!"

As I mentioned in the Preface, right from birth, I unknowingly helped Nicky develop some bad going-to-bed habits. Since the time he started to talk, he found ways to prolong the process. "But I'm not tired" became the nightly chant when he was told it was time for bed. I would remain steadfast, countering with suggestions like "Just close your eyes and count sheep." To which he'd reply, "How many?" After a great deal of protracted negotiations he would eventually tire of the process, but this ritual took a long time to reverse. By the time Joey arrived, I had found the error of my ways and allowed him to go to sleep on his own. He developed the habit of *wanting* to be left alone to go to sleep. He would actually volunteer that he was tired and that he wanted to go to bed. But once Nicky and Joey began to room together, sharing a bunk bed, Nicky's residual habits took precedence, and a new nightly ritual was born. About thirty to forty-five minutes before I want them to go to sleep I have to get them into their pajamas, have a glass of "milk" (Rice Dream, of course), brush their teeth, and snuggle down for a story, either one I read from a book or one we make up.

When we are finished playing our story game or reading a book, they usually want a little water, then "final potty," at which time Rob and I tuck them in with a kiss, turn off the light, and close their door. We then jointly pray that that will be it. Often it is. I think I indulge this ritual as much for my own need as I do for its help in getting them down. Being as busy as I am, I look forward to our quiet time together.

"The Story Game" is a game I invented to get my kids more involved than just listening to a story; it stimulates their imaginations and (I hope) tires them with a satisfying challenge. (We share a few laughs to boot!) I ask them to give me six words that will then be used in the story. For example, I'll say, "Joey, give me a color. Nicky, give me a superhero. Joey, give me a city." We go on and on until we have six different elements. (It can be anything—a food, a toy, a song, and so on.) We then proceed to make up a story, working those words into the plot. One child starts the story, then when that child is out of ideas, the story gets passed to the next person. This continues until all the words have been included and the story has come to a natural conclusion. It is a joy to witness how inventive your children can be and I feel it is a wonderful way to stimulate their imaginations as they ready themselves to enter the sleep state.

—*Marilu*

Nevertheless, I do have a bedtime contract, just like any other contract with my children: "When it's time to go to bed, it's time to go to bed, one tuck-in and one tuck-in *only*." This policy was established after putting up with five to ten tuck-ins per child, per night. Rob and I were determined we wouldn't give into "one more and that's it" no matter what. One night I had put the boys to bed in the usual manner and went upstairs. I no sooner got into bed when Rob and I heard the patter of two little feet down the hallway. The footsteps stopped just outside our bedroom door. There was a short pause (I'm sure it was to gather his courage), and then a faint knock. (The boys know they are not allowed to enter our room without knocking.) We tried to ignore it but the knock just got louder until finally we had to acknowledge it. "Who is it?" I asked. The tiny voice answered, "It's Joey." He opened the door and crossed the darkened room to stand next to our bed. "What do you want, Joey?" I asked matter-of-factly without turning on the light. "I need you to tuck me in," he sweetly implored. "I already tucked you in," I countered. And in the cutest voice imaginable, he replied, "I need you to tuck me in again." "But Joey, you know I'm only going to tuck you in once from now on. Now go back to bed." He stood there for a few moments assessing his options. Then finally he turned and walked down the hallway, softly whispering to himself as he went. I think it was the most difficult thing I've ever had to do as a mother. He broke my heart, and every maternal instinct in me wanted to go and pick him up, give him a hug, and tuck him in again. But I knew that would be the wrong message. By hanging tough and sticking to the contract, I allowed my three-year-old to feel his strength and independence while sending the message that my word could be trusted, and in that trust, I believe my children find security. He hasn't come up for an extra tuck-in since.

# SLEEP DRAMAS

Here's what Dr. Sharon has to say about helping our children develop good sleep habits.

## *Dr. Sharon's View*

No matter how they are being raised, all babies and all toddlers require a great deal of sleep. This shouldn't be surprising considering how much they have to learn about the world and how exhausting that job is. The newborn must learn who is who, what everything is, how to reach, how to stretch, how to ask for something, and so on. Everything involves the mind, which had been a clean slate, and the body, which had been fed by the umbilical cord. The mother has done all the thinking and all the nurturing, and now the amount of work for the baby is overwhelming. Toddlers, too, are discovering the world by leaps and bounds, mentally and physically, so it is no wonder they need a good night's sleep *and* an afternoon nap.

We spend close to a third of our lives asleep. And while sleep may be a physical activity, it has many emotional components and ramifications. The overindulged child (less motivated and ambitious) will generally require more sleep than the child who is subjected to a balance of frustration and gratification. The child whose parents erred on the side of overfrustration will generally require the least amount of sleep, growing up determined to rise with the sun and become a success.

Sleep habits are formed early. The child who obeys his bedtime will also be likely to get up on time and be ready for school. However, parents who give in to tampering with the parent-child contract and let bedtime become loose and unstructured will end up with irritable children who, in addition to being overtired, are unsure of their parents' true limits. Parents who are casual about a child not staying in his bed make a mistake, too. If the child appears in the doorway of the parents' bedroom in the middle of the night, it's important that the parent send or lead the child back to his room and then promptly return to his own bed. That is the clear contract; parents have their bed and must retain their privacy. To accomplish that, the child has to know his place in the family and in the house.

# BRAT-BUSTERS!

## Waking Up

My six-month-old daughter wakes up several times each night to feed. I am exhausted, so I bring her into bed to nurse her. My husband complains that he is disturbed. Should he move to another room until my daughter sleeps through the night?

*Dr. Sharon:* Your husband shouldn't move out of the bedroom. If he does he will start to resent your daughter even more. First she disturbs his sleep, then she takes over his place next to you in bed! What might help is changing your way of nursing. Try nursing her sitting up in a chair (safer than nursing her in bed), then put her back in her crib. There is no reason she should demand to be fed so frequently, so begin to reduce the number of feedings (just make sure she isn't still hungry if she falls asleep while she's nursing). If it's difficult for you to get up so many times a night, pump your milk during the day and your husband can give her the bottle at night. That would also strengthen his relationship with her.

*Marilu:* A possible explanation for your daughter's waking up to feed several times in the night could be *your* diet. Breast-feeding moms don't realize how much their own diet affects their babies.

The breast milk you give her is the result of the food you ate about eight hours earlier. Therefore, spicy foods and meals that are heavy in protein eaten eight hours before nursing her at night can affect your baby's sleep pattern and keep her awake when you most want her to sleep.

## "I'm Thirsty!"

Lately my two-year-old wakes me up in the middle of the night crying for a glass of milk. I thought this would end after a night or two, but it seems to have become a ritual. How do I break him of this habit?

*Dr. Sharon:* Since your two-year-old drinks from a glass and no longer from a bottle, it shows he can cope with frustration. The best solution is to let him cry until he falls asleep. As heartbreaking as it may be for you and him, don't get him a glass of milk.

*Marilu:* The same thing happened with Joey around the same age. We were living in a New York apartment at the time, and I was really puzzled why all of the sudden he started to wake up asking for "milk" (Rice Dream), especially since he's ordinarily such a good sleeper. He seemed genuinely thirsty, drinking an entire glass two nights in a row. On the third night he woke up, I realized that the reason it was so easy for me to wake up with him was that I, too, had gotten up three nights in a row craving something to drink. What I finally figured out was that the weather had changed and the building we were living in had started heating the apartment. It was so dry, we were dying for something to drink. The next day I bought humidifiers for each of the bedrooms and Joey and I stopped waking up thirsty. Could this be the problem at your house?

## Night-Light

My two-and-a-half-year-old son, who has been sleeping in the dark, suddenly has begun to wake up crying and demanding that we put on a bright light in his room. I don't know what the cause of this might be. Should we just keep a bright light in his room all night?

*Dr. Sharon:* It is not clear why your son suddenly insists a light be kept on all night. However, the request isn't unreasonable; many children between the ages of two and six like to sleep with a light on. Your son may have had a bad dream and can't distinguish between dreaming and reality when he wakes up. Cooperate with his request. Put a night-light in his room. If that doesn't satisfy him, leave a brighter light on. He will eventually outgrow this need.

*Marilu:* This also must be something that happens around two and a half, because at that age Joey made the same request. Up until then he had chosen to sleep in a room so dark, his nickname was Batty Bat. Anyway, after he requested a light, I put him to bed with one on, although week by week the light became less and less bright per his request.

## Working Parents

My wife and I both work long hours and don't arrive home until about eight at night. We miss our five-year-old daughter and wish to spend some "quality time" with her, so we let her stay up until nine-thirty or ten on school nights. Our families think this is wrong and that she should be in bed by eight or eight-thirty P.M., and that we should wait until the weekend to spend time with her. What do you think?

*Dr. Sharon:* If your five-year-old can nap after school and is able to get up for school feeling fresh and rested, going to bed at nine o'clock is unlikely to harm her. Take your cues from her. In addition, your work ethics are impressive and set a good example for your daughter.

*Marilu:* My father worked every night until ten. If my siblings and I didn't stay up late, we would never have seen him. This schedule didn't adversely affect our grades or our health. If anything, it made us feel better to spend time with our dad. I grew up discovering that there is nothing wrong with children changing their schedule a little in order to spend time with their parents.

## Negotiating Bedtime

My husband and I have to negotiate with our two-year-old son to go to bed. It has become an exhausting ritual. We watch his favorite tape, then tell him a bedtime story, he then insists on a bowl of cereal followed by a glass of juice. On the nights we don't have the energy to go through these rituals, he refuses to go to sleep. What should we do?

*Dr. Sharon:* A child must recognize that bedtime is not negotiable. Brace yourselves for his outrage once you remove one ritual each week. As hard as it is, he has to learn to live in the real world of limits and frustrations. Give him a little time to adjust to your new firmer bedtime rules and he will.

*Marilu:* If it were up to Nicky, he'd watch *Conan O'Brian* every night. Sometimes I say to him, "You tuck *me* in." When I say this, however, within five minutes, he's begging to be tucked in. Try it. I hope it works (and if you have any other good suggestions, send them to www.marilu.com).

## Family Bed

I'm pregnant with my first child and nervous that I won't have the baby's room ready in time. My sister, the mother of a three-year-old, tells me there is no rush because the baby should sleep with us and he won't be needing his own room for a long time. In fact, her son still sleeps with her and her husband. She calls this the family bed. Although it sounds sweet in theory, I'm not sure. What do you think?

*Dr. Sharon:* A newborn kept in a bassinet next to his parents' bed for the first two or three months of his life is both customary and harmless. It makes sense to have the newborn close to his parents. But after that, it is best to put his crib or bassinet in another room with a monitor on so that he learns to sleep by himself—and try to comfort himself when he wakes during the night. This will foster his independence.

With the exception of newborns, children should not sleep in the same room with their parents and not in a family bed. It is a form of togetherness and symbiosis that is too emotionally loaded on many levels. A heavy answer, perhaps, but one that's important to ponder.

*Marilu:* The family bed is such a controversial subject for people that I devoted an entire hour to it when I had my own talk show. At the end of the show, the credits were rolling and people were still arguing. I heard stories that hour that haunt me today. There was one family of nine with seven boys ranging from four months to seventeen years that slept in the same large bed (several beds pushed together). They still did this despite the fact that one night the father awoke to discover his elbow in the throat of the four-month-old, cutting off the baby's windpipe. The father quickly got out of bed with the passed-out infant. He revived him in the bathroom before the mother woke up. If that story isn't enough to scare you away from a family bed setup, I don't know what is.

## Sleeping Late

When I was a teenager I was not allowed to sleep late on weekends. My father pounded on my door yelling "Up and at 'em!" at seven-thirty on Saturday mornings. As a result of my early experience I let my son sleep until eleven A.M. on Saturdays. When my dad comes over to visit on weekends, he is appalled to find his grandson still sleeping. Am I hurting his progress in life—and am I making him lazy?

*Dr. Sharon:* There is a connection between a teenager's sleeping late and being lazy. Habitually sleeping late and staying up late are often signs of a teenager or adult who was overindulged as a child. It can demonstrate a disregard for others, because while he sleeps late, he hopes other people will carry on his daytime tasks and responsibilities for him.

*Marilu:* The body easily develops habitual sleep patterns. If you regularly sleep ten hours a day, the body will think it needs ten hours a day. It can also become accustomed to six hours. If you allow kids to sleep as much as they want, they could develop lazy sleep patterns. It is probably better to take charge and force them into good sleep habits. On the other hand, I believe some people are naturally nocturnal. They stay up very late and sleep very late.

## Wake-Up Call

Our eighteen-month-old wakes up at five every morning and then he wants to play. I'm exhausted. What do I do?

*Dr. Sharon:* Don't blame your baby. What time does he go to sleep? If he gets nine or ten hours' sleep, he has every right to wake up at five A.M. What *you* can do is prepare a few safe toys in his crib so he can occupy himself until you get up yourself an hour or so later. Just because he wants to play at five A.M. doesn't mean you have to be included. Children who are constantly entertained will expect the parent to play with them any time of the day or night.

*Marilu:* If he's eighteen months old, he may be on the cusp of needing only one nap a day. I know as a mom it's hard to give up those few precious morning and afternoon hours that you are used to having for yourself, but pick your battles. If your baby is waking up before the rooster crows, it may be because he's getting too much sleep during the day. When I cut my boys to one nap a day, they started to wake up at a more humane hour.

## Only Mommy

When our two-and-a-half-year-old son wakes up in the middle of the night, he only wants his mother. If I go in his room to make sure he is all right, he demands his mother come stay with him. My wife is tired of getting up. I really want to help her with the demands of our son. I can see how sleep-deprived she is and I know it's not fair for me to be the only one in the family who needs a good night's sleep, but I am at a loss as to what to do.

*Dr. Sharon:* It seems your wife has become the most important person in your son's life. A mother who wants to feel needed sometimes makes the mistake of training her baby to want *only* her, then eventually she starts to resent it. Here's how you can help: When your toddler wakes up in the middle of the night, neither you nor your wife should linger in his room, and as difficult as it may be for you to break him of the habit, let him cry. You can go in and check to see that your son is all right, then go back to your bed. Your wife should try to control her desire to go into the baby's room. It's better for him and means more sleep for her. Be sure to have a monitor in his room.

*Marilu:* The middle of the night is one of the most difficult times for parents and children. You're all tired, you're all vulnerable, and sometimes (though not often), something is really wrong. You're lucky that there are two of you to share the work of raising your son. Single parents don't have that option, so the solution has to come from getting your son to sleep through the night without needing a parent. Crying it out is really the only way to go, and after a few days, he'll know that everything is okay and he should go back to sleep by himself.

# WHEN LITTLE BRATS BECOME BIG BRATS

How we sleep is one of the most important aspects of our lives because our sleep habits tend both to affect and mirror our emotional state. The long-term sleep patterns that we develop are established in infancy. When a parent doesn't help to establish good sleeping habits in a child it is a form of breaking a contract. The consequences—other than fatigue—can carry over into adulthood.

## Dr. Sharon's View

*Leslie's mother, on her way out to a dinner party, was speaking to her daughter in the most heartfelt mother-daughter way. She was telling Leslie what she expected of her that evening. "So if you wash up, brush your teeth, have your pajamas on by eight, and go to bed on time, then tomorrow we'll stop at Carvel's after school for a hot fudge sundae. But if your teeth aren't brushed and you're not ready for bed, then no dessert for you. Not even an ice cream sandwich at home. Do you understand?" Leslie nodded as she mulled it over. The contract Leslie's mother was proposing involved bribery. The parent-child contract cannot be part of a bargain, nor can it be conditional. "I'm going out. Your bedtime is nine o'clock," was what her mother should have said. Since children are faced with bedtime every night, negotiating implies that the child has a choice, which she doesn't (or shouldn't). Just suggesting that bedtime is negotiable filters into other areas, leading the child into thinking that maybe everything is open for discussion.*

Always going to sleep late and getting up late are the most notable bad habits of the adult who was overindulged. But there are other reasons for unhealthy sleep patterns. The adult who is prone to silent temper tantrums or who is depressed may get under the covers and actually pull the covers over his head to escape responsibility or sleep fourteen hours in a row. To make it worse, if he suffers from anxiety he may be unable to fall asleep for hours. If it's a temper tantrum, he'll resist getting up and starting his day. Sleep becomes, for him, not a way of resting, but a safe haven. When the person had been overindulged, he will become angry and punitive toward whoever dares to try to get him out of bed when the sun rises. And like so many other issues of childhood (tantrums and sharing come to mind) that can be dealt with when they first come up, sleep issues don't *have* to turn into problems that persist into adulthood. When parents demonstrate a balance of fairness and firmness, possess the right knowledge, and set up the right boundaries, everyone is likely to get a good night's sleep.

# CHAPTER 9

# "And What Are We Going to Do About This?"

*A*friend of mine told me a funny story that happened when she was four years old and her new baby brother had recently come home from the hospital. One night, while their parents were downstairs watching television, my friend snuck her brother out of his crib, carried him to the top of the stairs, dangerously dangled him upside down by the ankle over the stairwell, and shouted to her parents, "And *what* are we going to do about *this*?" Of course, her parents didn't want her to drop him, so, to avoid scaring her by overreacting, they very cautiously walked up the stairs and negotiated with her to gently put him down. It was your typical sibling rivalry baby-hostage situation.

The baby brother is in his forties today, so I know he's okay. But he still won't go near any staircases with his sister. It's my favorite, although very scary, sibling rivalry story.

I love being part of a big family. I've always been proud of the fact that my five siblings and I continue to have a great appreciation and respect for one another. People ask me, "Why is it that you all get along so well?"

I believe it's because my mother never pushed or forced us to love one another. We just organically found our way into each other's hearts. We're all different and yet, between any two of us, there's a unique bond which only that pairing shares. I guess what I'm saying is that any one of us can end up sitting next to any one of the others and still feel like he's sitting next to one of his best friends. Believe me, we all gladly show up for every family event.

# SIBLING RIVALRY

Growing up, we had our sibling rivalries, but I always felt that it was healthy. I loved hanging around with my older sisters. I loved hanging around with my younger siblings, too, although I was never above a good old-fashioned game of "Ditch 'Em." For those of you who don't know, Ditch 'Em is a game in which an accomplice (usually my brother Tommy) and I would cruelly and spontaneously decide to yell, "DITCH 'EM!" We would then run as fast as we could to get away from our victim(s)—usually our little sister Christal and/or our brother Lorin, the baby of the family. (You know, come to think of it, we haven't seen or heard from Lorin since 1962.) I realize now that Christal and Lorin were probably grateful to get away from us two meanies.

*My* parents had some great solutions for sibling rivalries, especially when we traveled in the family car and fought over who would sit next to the window. We took most of our family trips in the sixties when seat belts were just an overlooked accessory. My parents always sat in the front seat with my two younger brothers wedged between them, and my three sisters and I sat in the backseat. My parents decided the big sisters would sit by the windows on odd days, and on even days, it would be us little sisters. Because there were more odd days throughout the year, the older sisters had the advantage. This way they felt they had seniority, and we little sisters felt we were lucky even to be considered. This solution was carried out through our entire family life. When my boys started fighting over who got to do what (for example, press an elevator button or choose a book for a bedtime story), I remembered the Henner odd/even-days solution and I use it to this day.

— *Marilu*

A lot of people don't realize how many positive things come from having a big family. I find that kids from large families are better equipped to deal with the real world outside their family life. They have already learned how to deal with compromise, sharing, competition, teasing, jealousy, and, perhaps most important, "pride in teamwork." Put it this way: Who was healthier, the Brady Bunch or Dennis the Menace? (All right, I'll admit, Jan was a little screwed up, but otherwise . . . )

Here's what Dr. Sharon has to say on the subject.

## Dr. Sharon's View

Parents who treat all their children the same do them a disservice because every child is different. So it follows that parents must try to tailor a balance of frustration and gratification to that particular child's needs and temperament. The parent-child contract that exists between that child and his parents is also unique (although it still comes under the heading of "I am the parent. I make the rules. You are the child. You obey them"). But if each contract is honored by the parents and the child, that in itself will go a long way toward fostering cooperative relationships between siblings.

Sibling rivalry is a volatile area where issues have to be handled with care. One of the worst mistakes parents can make is doing anything to exacerbate it, thereby creating lifetime friction and acrimony among their children. There are many opinions about what parents should do. Some authorities suggest curbing sibling rivalry by trying to acknowledge children's feelings. For example, a parent might say, "You feel your brother is doing that to irritate you, don't you?" or "You wish your sister would stop annoying you." But telling a child what he is feeling, as well-intentioned as it is, is presumptuous, intrusive, and very often off the mark.

Also intrusive and unhelpful is interfering with children who are having a disagreement or are verbally sparring. When two siblings fight, both take part in the entanglement, regardless of which one appears to be the victim. Parents who play judge and jury, attempting

to establish guilt, will get nowhere asking what happened and hearing details like "Daddy! Jordan hit me!" followed by "Why did you hit your brother?" and "Jackie broke my dinosaur game!" and "Jordan called me stupid!"

It helps to remember that most sibling fights have to do with trying to get their parents on their side. Which is why parents must try not to interfere. Simply by appearing on the scene, they unintentionally prolong the fighting. And there are no good answers to parents who ask, "Why are you being difficult?" or "Why are you upsetting your brother?" If siblings' arguments become intolerable, the best idea is to give both children a time-out.

## The Firstborn

The firstborn often experiences the birth of a sibling as both an intrusion and disruption of life as he knew it. His feelings about suddenly having a new brother or sister have been likened to those of a wife whose husband one day, out of the blue, brings home another wife. The ways parents handle the new arrival greatly determines how the older child adjusts to the change. The first child, upon the birth of a sibling, is often seen by his parents as a "huge child," by comparison to the new baby. But if he remains important when a sibling is born, still getting time and attention from his parents, he will be able to tolerate the newcomer. Parents who suddenly become short or harsh with the older child or who err in the other direction by communicating their guilt at having disrupted his perfect world will cause the child's natural jealousy to become exacerbated and will make it much harder for him to accept his new brother or sister.

The way parents handled their first arrival will also affect the siblings. If the parents fawned over the older child and praised him excessively for every little thing, exclaiming, "Look what we've created! The greatest baby in the world!" it will follow that he'll have a hard time tolerating the frustration of losing his parents' undivided attention and affection. The second child, on the other hand, is born into a household where, from day one, there's someone else he has to share his parents' time and love with.

# BRAT-BUSTERS!

## Regressing to a Bottle

We have recently weaned our eighteen-month-old daughter off the bottle. When she sees us give our newborn son a bottle she cries for one, too. Sometimes she grabs his bottle and puts it in her mouth. What do we do?

*Dr. Sharon:* Your daughter is expressing her jealousy. It would be best to get her a sippy cup or a large plastic cup with colorful straws and tell her it belongs to her. Then put juice or milk in it for her.

*Marilu:* Nicky was eighteen months old when Joey was born and regressed in little ways, too. He wanted a bottle, wanted to be held more often, and so on. After a few days, he recognized that he wasn't the "baby" and, of course, preferred being the "big boy" and went back to his "big boy" ways.

## Who Started It?

When our two children (ages six and ten) have a fight, each accuses the other of starting it. How do I find out who really started the fight?

*Dr. Sharon:* It doesn't really make a difference *who* started it and it's not your job to find out. You are not an attorney establishing guilt. Just remove yourself from the scene and let your children sort it out. Of course, in the case of physical fights, send them both for a time-out.

*Marilu:* I am grateful that my parents rarely got involved with our arguments when we were kids. We learned to verbally fight our own battles. But if you see blood or dismemberment, act quickly (think of the carpet)!

## The "Gift" of Sharing

Should I force my children to share their toys, clothes, and so on, or should I leave it up to the children if they want to share?

*Dr. Sharon:* Urge your children to share. As to "forcing"—if you mean putting verbal pressure on them, the answer is yes. If you *don't* urge them, you are silently condoning their not sharing. One of the greatest gifts parents can give their children is the skill they need to get along and share with siblings throughout life.

*Marilu:* Growing up in a house with eight people, four bedrooms, and one bathroom, we were forced to share. To this day I wish we all still lived together. I really like sharing. I've always liked it. I think it teaches you how to negotiate, how to compromise, and how to respect another person's property and personal space. Some of my favorite childhood memories involve sharing. That's why my boys share a room.

## To Hug or Not to Hug

Our five-year-old daughter refuses to kiss or hug her new baby brother. She insists she hates him. What do we do to encourage her to like him?

*Dr. Sharon:* Unfortunately, the more you encourage your five-year-old to hug and kiss the baby, the more she will experience you as partial to him. But if you don't pay too much attention to her when she announces she hates her baby brother, in time she will learn that he is here to stay and that she will have to get along with him. Her feelings are understandable. Just because he has intruded into her life (a painful reality for her to accept), she probably reasons, why should she also have to love him?

*Marilu:* I remember my mother always saying, "You don't have to love her because she's your sister," or "You don't have to like him because he's your brother," that kind of thing. I think that our mother gave us a lot if space not to like each other, and that's probably why we like each other so much today. Also, I think the advantage of coming from a large family is that if you are fighting with someone, there's always someone else to play with. Still, I was never forced to hug or kiss my siblings.

## Equal Treatment

Whenever I buy something for my four-year-old child, the older child (age six) expects the same, even if it is just a pair of socks. Should I buy the older child socks as well, even though he doesn't need them?

*Dr. Sharon:* The younger child was born into a family where a sibling already existed, so from the start he was accustomed to unequal distribution of "goodies" in the family. The older child has it harder, for he has to learn to cope with his feelings of jealousy. If you, as the parent, don't act or feel guilty about not equalizing all gifts and purchases, your older child will learn to cope with his jealous feelings, and that will be a valuable lesson.

*Marilu:* In my family, shopping for practical things is on an as-needed basis for each child. However, if I'm away for a few days and bring home gifts, it's always for both of them.

## A Gift for the Big Brother

We have requested our relatives and friends to bring a gift for our three-year-old son when they bring a gift for our new baby, for we don't want the three-year-old to feel left out. Is this overindulgence?

*Dr. Sharon:* Trying to eliminate jealousy from your three-year-old's repertoire of feelings will only make him vulnerable when he has to deal with jealous feelings later in life. Coping with his frustration of having people fuss over the new baby in the household will strengthen his resolve to cope with whatever difficulties life has in store. Parents who equalize gifts among their children and their friends, making certain, for example, that if the neighbor's child gets a new bicycle, their child gets one as well, prevent their child from experiencing jealousy and limit his ability to cope later in life when confronting jealous feelings—not to mention life's difficulties.

*Marilu:* Can you imagine in my childhood if every sibling got a present because one of us got a present? It would be six gifts—I mean, where does it end? I guess you could start by saying, "No wonder nobody has big families anymore—everyone would be using up their time buying presents."

## Allowances

We give our ten-year-old more allowance than our seven-year-old. The younger says this is not fair and wants the same allowance that the older child receives. What do you recommend?

*Dr. Sharon:* This one is clear-cut: The older child has seniority and *should* get more. The younger child has to adjust to that fact.

*Marilu:* It's kind of like seniority in the workplace. The older child has been with the "company" longer, so he deserves a bigger "salary" as his "expense account" increases. Usually older kids get more privileges compared to the younger ones, but the younger kids usually get to do things earlier because the older ones have paved the way. I remember in my family, you had to be ten years old before you could wear nylons. It was a big deal for me to turn ten and wear them. When I was eleven and my younger sister Christal was nine, our older sister got married and wanted us to be junior bridesmaids. For the ceremony, we had to wear nylons . . . one whole year before Christal was turning ten! Believe me, after that ceremony was over, I tried to force her to switch to anklets for the reception.

## Sibling and Friends

When our ten-year-old daughter has a friend over, her eight-year-old sister follows them around, which results in the older one calling her sister a "pest." Should I force the older one to include her younger sister at least once in a while, especially when the younger one's friends are not available?

*Dr. Sharon:* When older children shut out and act in a mean way to their younger siblings, they in a sense retaliate for the younger sibling's original intrusion of being born into their lives. So don't try to force inclusion. In life, some people are includers and some are excluders. If you look at families, you'll see that, understandably, younger siblings most often are *includers*, and the firstborns *excluders*.

*Marilu:* I really think behavior like this starts with the parents. My mom and dad were both includers; our house was always filled with a lot of people. Consequently, for the most part, my older siblings included me and I included my younger siblings. I would bet that if *you* included the eight-year-old when the ten-year-old wanted to play only with her friend, eventually they would all be playing together.

## Praising Only One

Whenever I praise my ten-year-old son in the presence of his eight-year-old sister she gets uneasy, as if I'm comparing them. Should I praise him only when his sister is not around?

*Dr. Sharon:* The real problem may be how *much* you're praising your son. Praise can be overdone. A child whose parent praises him ad nauseam will often grow up to be an adult who will expect and insist on endless praise from the people he is close to. In this case, whenever you praise your son, your daughter feels criticized simply by being left out of the praise.

*Marilu:* With six children, if my mother had praised us only when the others weren't around, we never would have heard any praise from her.

## Making Comparisons

**We have different feelings for each of our children. How does that affect the children? I've heard that it is not a good idea to compare one child to another, for example, "Johnny gets his homework done on time, why can't you?" What is your opinion?**

*Dr. Sharon:* It's never a good idea to compare siblings, calling attention to where one excels. Children already notice the difference between themselves and their brothers and sisters. Parents who reaffirm those differences are destructive. Each child is conceived at a different time in the parents' lives—the pregnancy is different, the father's treatment of the mother is different, and so on. The reality is, parents develop different feelings for each child and each child affects them differently.

*Marilu:* I believe that comparisons with siblings can rarely be done in a positive way. But oh boy, is it tempting. It's the hardest thing not to do and probably the best thing for parents to avoid. With two boys close to the same age, it would be so much fun for me to pit them against each other, especially when getting dressed or at bedtime.

# WHEN LITTLE BRATS BECOME BIG BRATS

For a number of reasons, it is best not to interfere too much with our children's relationships with one another. What can happen when parents do this? Here are some possibilities.

## Dr. Sharon's View

*Three-year-old Jeremy, who was much too old for a pacifier (but insisted on it anyway), suddenly spit it out and bit into the biceps of his little brother. He then calmly picked up his pacifier and put it back in his mouth, as his brother screamed in pain. Jeremy's mother stood nearby, mortified by what she had just observed. What Jeremy had witnessed just moments earlier was the sight of his mother furtively kissing his eight-month-old brother, then turning to her friend and asking, "Did Jeremy see me kiss the baby?" By trying to prevent Jeremy from feeling jealous of his brother, she was creating problems for both children. Jealousy between siblings is normal. And Jeremy will remain unequipped to deal with his feelings, resorting to hurting his brother, getting a perverse pleasure from his mother's reaction, and always resenting his brother and his mother.*

Sadly for everyone, the older child—if overindulged—will grow up to see the younger not as a friend or ally but as a threat. On a more sophisticated level in adulthood, these feelings remain much the same. Long-established sibling rivalries continue to flourish and very often come to a head when the parents die. That's when the *real* fights begin, not over who had gotten more affection, but over the parents' wills—who is being treated better, who feels slighted with his inheritance. Overindulged from birth, he can never get adjusted to the competition of a sibling. The saga of siblings as they grow up is too often one of ongoing jealousy. It is a compliment to parents whose children get along with each other throughout life.

# CHAPTER 10

# Liar, Liar, Pants on Fire

Rob tells a story about taking my then five-year-old nephew Adam out for a banana split at the world-famous Rumpelmayer's in New York City. As he tells it, the two of them were sitting on stools at the soda fountain when Rob, in an effort to make conversation, and knowing that Adam had recently returned from visiting his grandparents in Florida, started out, "How was your trip to Florida?" The adorable and extremely bright little fella, deep into his ice cream treat, was not forthcoming with his answer. "Fine," he replied. Trying harder to find a common base for conversation, Rob went on. "You know, my grandparents used to live in Florida and I would visit them when I was your age." Without hesitation, while shoveling another spoonful into his mouth, Adam asked, "Where do they live now?" Rob was then faced with a dilemma. Not knowing what my sister Melody had already told her son about death, he was hesitant to open the issue. Instead he decided to circumvent it by creating a small deception. "They moved away," Rob answered sheepishly, hoping it would suffice. For the first time since the waitress had set the banana split down in front of him, the five-year-old stopped cold in his eating frenzy and stared directly up at Rob incredulously. "They'd be dead by now, wouldn't they?" he exclaimed. Rob, shocked that a five-year-old could be so perceptive, had no choice but to admit to Adam, "Yes, you're quite right. They are both dead."

# TELLING THE TRUTH

This story is one of the best examples I can think of to demonstrate how children are never too young to distinguish truth from dishonesty. Dr. Sharon often says that the unconscious mind knows everything, and that is never more apparent than in small children. Even when a parent believes that he has done an expert job of fibbing or covering up the truth, his behavior will betray him. Children, even babies, are far more perceptive than they are given credit for. How honest should we be with our children? And how safe can we make it for them to tell the truth?

## Dr. Sharon's View

Parents who are consistently truthful will raise children who tell the truth. Children who are lied to grow up sooner or later tampering with the truth. Lying to a child in an effort to spare him the frustration of dealing with the pitfalls and difficulties of life is just another form of overprotection and overgratification. For example, parents who reassure their child that they are not going out to dinner, and then sneak out once he is asleep, are doing him a disservice. Once a child is lied to, he will never fully trust that person to tell the truth.

Withholding information, such as not telling a child that his mother is expecting a baby in an attempt to protect him from the frustration of waiting months for the birth, is another form of over-protection. When told the truth belatedly, the child will be puzzled and will feel unsettled. Another form of withholding information, in an effort to protect him, is sparing him the pain of learning about death (when he asks and wants to know). Not knowing the truth, he will conjure up fantasies from which he will be rudely awakened, and his resilience will be replaced by anxiety.

Similarly, giving a child a dishonest explanation of a situation, particularly if it affects him deeply, is both deceptive and unwise. For instance: A two-year-old boy thought his stepmother was his biological mother. When he turned nine, his stepmother divorced his father, and the older siblings, who had known the truth all along, informed and consoled him. "She wasn't your real mother anyhow, so why are you so upset?" This long deception played havoc with the boy's ability to trust. And indeed, the longer the delay in truthfully answering a child's question, the greater the fall once he discovers the truth.

Clearly, not telling the truth is harmful. So is misrepresenting the truth when a child asks questions. And while giving the child honest explanations is important, this is best done when the child *asks* for the information. Most of the time, giving the child information he did not request, or giving too many details, is a mistake. In a different vein, a child who is instructed by his parents to misrepresent something—such as a family secret—is put in a painful and conflicted position. Children should not be told to misrepresent anything.

Some well-known parenting authorities believe that children lack an understanding of the difference between lying and being truthful and that their boundary between reality and fantasy is very shaky. However, it is quite the contrary. A child can absolutely distinguish between honesty, lying, reality, and fantasy. Parents need to give him credit for this and set a good example for him to follow as he grows up.

*When Nicky was in preschool in New York, two of his teachers were pregnant. Nicky knew about it, but none of the other kids seemed to know because the teachers didn't want to tell them. These teachers even asked the parents not to tell their kids. But, Nicky had already figured out from their growing tummies. When one of the teachers went into premature labor and had to leave the school early in her seventh month, the school had a real dilemma on their hands. They decided it was best to tell the kids that she was sick. I found this particularly offensive. So I said to them, "Well, have we learned our lesson? Are we now going to tell them the truth about the second teacher being pregnant?" They said, "Oh no! It is way too much to tell them all at once." I completely disagree with this way of withholding information. Adults often wait until the last possible second to impart this kind of news because they're afraid that telling kids early will be too overwhelming or frustrating for them. So what? I say we should use the pregnancy experience as a way of teaching our children about patience and anticipation.*

*—Marilu*

Setting a good example includes making it possible for a child to feel he can tell the truth. If a parent simply listens to whatever the child says and comments, "Thank you for telling me," he makes it safe for the child to express something he might otherwise be uncomfortable sharing. The message that the parent is giving the honest child is that he will listen without being judgmental or critical. He is not reprimanding the child in any way, but neither is he expressing his approval. He is, however, keeping the lines of communication open and giving his child permission to tell the truth.

# BRAT-BUSTERS!

## Confronting a Lie

Our four-year-old daughter has been lying lately. Do we confront her or ignore it?

*Dr. Sharon:* Confront her. Lying can become a habit. Sometimes a child lies when he picks up that one of his parents is untruthful. Be vigilant about consistently being truthful yourselves and tell your child not to lie. Once a child finds a refuge in lying, it is difficult to reverse.

*Marilu:* I always think lying should be nipped in the bud. Kids will try to test you with lies because they don't even understand what lying is, and they're so afraid of getting in trouble. I think it's best to make it safe for a child to tell the truth by not overreacting or overly punishing them when they tell the truth.

## White Lies

How do I explain to my children the difference between "white lies" (lying to protect someone's feelings) and serious dishonesty, like cheating on a test?

*Dr. Sharon:* What is the purpose of explaining the difference between one type of lie and another? Why are "white lies" okay . . . because they protect another's feelings? All lies are intended to protect someone, mostly oneself. Explaining the difference between types of lies imparts unconscious condoning of lying.

*Marilu:* To protect someone's feelings, you don't have to tell someone a white lie, you can simply not tell them *all* of the truth. There can always be truth in what you say to them, but it doesn't have to be hurtful. You can always answer, "How do you like my new haircut?" with "That is going to grow out so nicely."

## Honesty Pact

A friend had each member of her family sign an "honesty pact" evaluating his honesty during that week. Does that help children learn about honesty?

*Dr. Sharon:* Being honest should be taken for granted. An "honesty pact" implies that people may not be honest. Furthermore, evaluating family members' honesty may deal with the myriad ways a person can be dishonest, which makes dishonesty sound both creative and entertaining—a destructive consequence of an "honesty pact."

*Marilu:* There is something Orwellian-Big-Brother about this. My guess is that one family member started this in order to control the other members of the family. It's kind of strange. I know one family that keeps this enormous chart in their kitchen which they use to mark down every little dishonest and bad feeling they have, so they can later "clean up." One day during lunch, the six-year-old daughter got up and marked something on the chart. I said, "What did you do?" She said, "I just had a bad thought about my sister" (who was only four). It was so bizarre. I felt like I was eating with the cast of *Children of the Corn*. People must be allowed to have their own feelings. If I had to tell my husband every time I wanted to kill him, he would never sleep with his eyes closed again.

## Don't Tell Mommy

Whenever I drop off my seven-year-old son at his mother's (we are separated) after a weekend with me, I always instruct him not to tell Mommy that "my friend" spent the weekend with us. I do this to help him spare his mother's feelings during this difficult time. Am I doing the right thing?

*Dr. Sharon:* It's best not to instruct your child to withhold information from his mother. It puts your child in a tough position. Your wife's feelings may be spared, but your son's relationship both with you and his mother will be compromised. Do you care more about your wife's feelings than your son's?

*Marilu:* This exact situation happened to a friend of mine, and when she realized that her son was withholding information, it made it very difficult for all parties involved. She found herself grilling the boy after every excursion with Dad because she knew what he was capable of doing. Once again, honesty is the best policy.

## Scared to Tell the Truth

I heard the sound of my nine-year-old son falling down the stairs. I frantically rushed over as he ran to the refrigerator to put ice on his lip and his eye. After he removed the ice I could tell that he had been in a fistfight and faked the fall to explain the bruises on his face. He denied being in a fight so I don't know how to find out the truth. I'm upset not only because he is fighting in school but also because he doesn't feel he can be honest with me. How should I handle this?

*Dr. Sharon:* Do you make it safe for your son to tell you what is happening in his life? Could you be too hard on him? And how honest are you and your husband? Deception is learned behavior. At this point, don't try to establish the truth. Asking him questions now will feel like prying to him and won't help your relationship with him. Just be supportive.

*Marilu:* Your son sounds like a real character. He actually forced himself to fall down the stairs? What does he want to be when he grows up, a stunt man? His resourcefulness is interesting. I hope he can put it to better use.

## Lying and Stealing

Our ten-year-old steals money from his mother's purse, and we don't know how to handle it. He also lies and denies lying. We are both honest, hardworking people, and we try to reason with him. Is dishonesty an emotional illness?

*Dr. Sharon:* Since both of you are honest, an emotional problem may be brewing. The time for reasoning with him is gone. You need to establish consequences for his behavior. If it continues over time, seek some professional help.

*Marilu:* When kids steal, it can be serious or just that innocent phase that all kids go through during adolescence. Sometimes adolescent theft, however, should not be taken lightly. All big-time thieves had to start somewhere. Most of them will tell you that they started with what was most accessible, namely stealing from their family and friends. If you determine that it's serious, treat it seriously.

## Truthful About Death

At what age should a child attend funerals and wakes? Isn't it unhealthy for a child to see people grieving over the loss of a loved one?

*Dr. Sharon:* Protecting children from taking part in the grieving process is not recommended. Taking a child to a funeral at any age is okay, although it is preferable to wait until a child is eight or nine years old. As for wakes, once you've told him about the open casket, leave it up to him whether or not he attends.

*Marilu:* I went to dozens of open casket wakes by the time I was nine. Because I saw so many at such a young age, it was never really frightening for me. I never had nightmares. I think the bigger "deal" that is made about this creates a greater potential for scaring a child.

## No Big Deal

I took my thirteen-year-old son and his friend to the movies the other day. His mom always gets him into the movies at the child's price. When I said, "Three adults," the friend said, "No, I only pay the child's price." My son didn't think it was any big deal and thinks that rigidity about telling the truth is ridiculous. He said Cineplex Odeon is richer than his friend's parents. Am I a stick in the mud?

*Dr. Sharon:* You are not a stick in the mud. You are a person of integrity. You should have insisted on paying for three adults or you would have been drawn into a dishonest situation. By paying for three adults, your son would have had the benefit of your good example.

*Marilu:* I have always believed that it's better to be honest about money, even when it's to my disadvantage. One time a salesgirl gave me too much change, but I didn't realize it until I had left the store. I went back to return the money, but the line was so long, by the time I had corrected the mistake, I got back to my car to face . . . a parking ticket.

# WHEN LITTLE BRATS
# BECOME BIG BRATS

Lying creates more lying, and that lying creates even more. The cycle continues until you have a huge junk pile of lies. Unfortunately, our children often inherit these piles and create piles of their own. Here are some consequences in families that condone lying.

## Dr. Sharon's View

*Because Joshua's father was going to be on a business trip, Joshua's mother arranged to celebrate his fifth birthday two days late. Then, in order not to upset him, she told Joshua that his real birthday was, in fact, two days later. On the morning of his real birthday, the house-*

*keeper inadvertently greeted Joshua with "Happy Birthday." As a result, his teachers at school (who had been told to "pretend" his birthday was two days later) were alerted to the fact that Joshua knew the truth. The web of deception in the service of not upsetting Joshua only made him anxious and upset. He began to eye his parents and teachers with suspicion. His birthday was a miserable experience for everyone. Joshua's mother should have told him that his birthday was going to be celebrated two days late, thereby avoiding a whole string of lies and deceptions. To spare a situation she thought would frustrate her son, Joshua's mother resorted to behavior that was dishonest and far more damaging.*

A child who lies because he lives in a family where honesty isn't sacred is likely to have little regard for the truth all his life. Adults who don't tell the truth tend to cheat and act deceptively. They are frequently charming people who have developed their lying skills to perfection, always hiding behind their innocent demeanor. These people often have other related problems. In adulthood, one of the most serious consequences of years of lying is promiscuity. Straying from the truth so freely and easily can pave the road for straying in marriage and not honoring contracts. Cheating in business is another adult consequence of years of lying.

Consequently, as painful as the truth may be, it helps the child to hear it from loving and forthright parents. Being truthful is one of the best ways to make a child feel secure.

# CHAPTER 11

# It's a Hard-Knock Life

One morning in New York when Nicky was three and a half, he was so excited because his dad was going to pick him up from preschool and take him to lunch. This was all Nicky talked about during breakfast. To him, it had the makings of a big event.

Well, about fifteen minutes before Nicky was supposed to be picked up, Rob called me at home and said that he couldn't get out of an important business meeting, and there was no way he could pick up Nicky or take him to lunch. Our poor little guy sobbed uncontrollably in the cab all the way home when I told him that his special day with Daddy was not going to happen.

Every fiber of my being wanted to protect Nicky from feeling the way he did at that moment. As a parent, you always want to protect your children from that kind of a letdown. I wanted to treat him to everything that Rob had planned, and more. I felt like taking him not only to lunch but also to an afternoon movie and a shopping spree at FAO Schwarz. Instead, I knew that it was better in the long run for him to endure the disappointment. He will have to face moments like that for the rest of his life, and I knew that facing this frustration offered a much better lesson than if I had done my best to protect his feelings. So I said, "Nicky, I know you're upset, but you know what you can tell Daddy later, when he gets home? You can say that you've now been to three schools—you've been to Oakdale [his preschool in Los Angeles], to the 92nd Street Y [his preschool in New York], and now to the School of Hard Knocks." He understood the humor, and it eased the pain a little bit. The experience was still a tough pill for him to swallow, but I could see that it was helpful for him to experience all of his feelings about it. It's the sort of lesson that fortifies his character, so that later on he won't be shattered by every disappointment.

We went home, hung out, and basically continued as we would on any other day. Now, whenever Nicky is let down about something, he'll say, "Oh boy. I guess I'm at that School of Hard Knocks again." It has become our little phrase that represents our having to adjust to "Plan B." I have talked about Plan B in every one of my books because it's such an important concept to me. I truly believe that the key to your life is how well you deal with Plan B. Plan A is what we hope for and plan for, but Plan B is what actually happens. It's our reaction to Plan B, to what *really* happens, that makes up our lives. Life is full of disappointments. It's our resilience to disappointment and how creatively we adjust to disappointment that determines how we ultimately live our lives.

*R*ecently, my boys and I set out to have a great day at the beach. As we got closer to our destination, I realized that this was a terrible idea. It was the hottest day of the year and everyone else had the exact same plan. I turned off the freeway and said, "You know what, guys? Going to the beach was Plan A, but we're now going to have a Plan B Day." We decided to explore the area where we exited and be open to any serendipitous experiences that this random neighborhood offered. Thank goodness it turned out to be a fun and safe one. We ended up having a blast. We discovered a bookstore, a craft store, a kids' gym, even a magic shop. To this day, my boys say, "Can we have another Plan B Day?" You can make all the plans that you want, but it's your adjustment to what really happens that counts most. The more resilient you are, the easier it will be to accept Plan B.

*—Marila*

# LEARNING TO ACCEPT DISAPPOINTMENT AND UNPLEASANT FEELINGS

Dr. Sharon taught me the following truism: If our parents shield us from painful feelings by replacing them with a pleasurable distraction, we never learn to develop the capacity to deal with emotional pain. Here are her thoughts about accepting our feelings.

## *Dr. Sharon's View*

Parents who attempt to eliminate an unpleasant or unhappy feeling from their child's repertoire of feelings give him a very shaky foundation. Having a feeling, as unpleasant or painful as it may be, is not the problem. *Trying to get rid of the feeling is a problem.*

If a child, early in life, is deprived of experiencing such feelings as fear, jealousy, anger, frustration, and sadness, he will grow up to become anxious when he is forced to confront those feelings for the first time. A well-adjusted child needs to be in touch with all his feelings—developing new feelings while keeping old ones—so he doesn't grow up trying to escape from the realities of life.

Parents who tell their child how he is feeling, like "You feel I'm being a bad mother, don't you?" or "You wish your dad would spend more time with you," are presumptuous and intrusive, for no one knows how another person feels. Consequently, a parent who tells his child what to think and how to feel will bring up a child who will have difficulty relying on his own resources, a problem difficult to repair.

Just as a child whose parents deny him his own feelings will suffer, so will the child who is deprived of the *parent's* full range of feelings. Not having the benefit of this range of emotions, he will be inexperienced in dealing with all feelings and attitudes. It's better to witness anger and sadness, for instance, to understand that these are a part of life and aren't "bad," or feelings to be afraid of. This reasoning applies to positive emotions as well. A child who has not experienced loving feelings from his parents will not respond positively to loving communications from others. It is important for a child to be told that his parents love him and equally dangerous to tell him that they do not.

# BRAT-BUSTERS!

## Pacifying Feelings

Our ten-month-old frequently uses a pacifier. Are we giving him the message not to make any sounds by stuffing it in his mouth? Is thumb sucking preferable?

*Dr. Sharon:* Although a pacifier in a baby's mouth is visually unattractive it satisfies the baby's sucking instinct. When the baby sucks his thumb he solves his own problem. Whether thumb sucking is preferable would depend on your dentist's opinion.

I would suggest weaning a child from a pacifier after he is a year old. Otherwise he will be dependent on oral satisfaction to quell his frustrations instead of learning to tolerate them.

*Marilu:* By its very name, a pacifier is designed to keep a child from being frustrated, bored, or loud. When I lived in New York, I was amazed at how many kids three and four years old were sucking on pacifiers. This is probably because their living space is so close to their neighbors, and parents want their kids to be quiet. Before my children were born, I had read several studies suggesting that pacifiers and thumb sucking lead to dental problems and a dependency on cigarette smoking later in life. Because of this, I made sure that my kids rarely used pacifiers, and that was only during their first three months. I would give them one for a short moment right after breast-feeding so that I wouldn't become a "human pacifier" after they had eaten. By four months old, they were completely off the pacifier. The longer a child stays with one, the harder it is to break him of the habit. When I look at smokers I think of them as adults with pacifiers. Learning to live with uncomfortable feelings is part of life.

## Anticipating Needs

My friend says that it's best to hand a baby what he wants, and that by anticipating her six-month-old baby's needs she prevents him from becoming bored, while making him feel secure. She also quickly replaces one toy with another before he gets bored or frustrated. Is this good to do?

*Dr. Sharon:* This approach will have the opposite effect, making the baby insecure. When the baby struggles to reach for a toy and the mother intercedes and hands it to him, the baby is deprived of the satisfaction of accomplishment. With such repeated experiences, he will expect people to anticipate his needs and hand him whatever he wants.

*Marilu:* I worked very hard not to be a hovering mother. I didn't want my children to think I was the *only* thing in their lives, or that everything around them had to be filtered through me. Consequently, I would put several toys and books in their crib so when they woke up they would find something to amuse themselves and to this day my kids are very good at playing by themselves, getting books on their own and playing with blocks. You can be sure someone like Robin Williams didn't have a hovering mother. He developed his talent by performing elaborate shows as a child just for himself.

## Punching Bag for Feelings

I read in a magazine that a punching bag helps a child get his anger out. Do you agree?

*Dr. Sharon:* A punching bag is good for exercise, but not to get out anger. It symbolically represents hitting another person. Running up and down a flight of stairs or taking a brisk walk is a better release of anger. Confronting a family member and telling him "I am angry at you" will constructively release anger using language.

*Marilu:* Exercise works for children as well as adults. If you make exercise part of their routine while they're young, it can make all the difference in the world in how they handle stress throughout their lives.

## Jealousy

My two-and-a-half-year-old daughter is very jealous when I pay attention to other children. Recently I was holding my sister's baby and my daughter insisted I put the baby down. I did so just because I didn't want to hurt her feelings. Is this jealousy normal at this age? What do I do about it?

*Dr. Sharon:* Jealousy is normal at an early age. When your daughter complains about your holding the baby, don't give in by putting the baby down. You don't want to prevent your child from dealing with a feeling that she will have to confront as she grows up. Her jealousy, if properly channeled (by not pacifying her), can be a constructive feeling propelling her to excel later in life.

Allowing jealousy to exist in a healthy manner curbs it from becoming too intense. This is important because emotional health is measured by a person's resilience, degree of jealousy, and intensity of vindictiveness. The resilient person will recover from an emotional injury in a brief time—in minutes or a few hours—while the nonresilient person will bemoan his emotional injury and remain unforgiving for days, years, or even a lifetime. A child who has a healthy amount of jealousy will not become overly vindictive and will develop into a resilient adult.

*Marilu:* My mother hated jealousy so much; she couldn't even say the word. She called it JEA instead. To her, it was the worst feeling a person could have because it was so counterproductive. She always encouraged us to take our jealous feelings and turn them into energy to improve ourselves. She always said, "You only compete with yourself."

## Crying Is a Feeling

When I am about to take my two-year-old outside, I carefully put sunscreen on his arms and face. He cries and I try to calm him down by repeating, "Mommy is almost done—it's okay just one more minute," but he keeps on crying. What do I do?

*Dr. Sharon:* Little children will frequently complain when suntan lotion and other medications are administered. Just put sunscreen on as carefully but as quickly as you can. Don't be obsessive about it.

*Marilu:* This is Joey all the way. I am Polish and Greek and my husband is Jewish. Somehow Joey ended up with bright red hair and pink, almost translucent skin. He looks like a Jewish leprechaun. If I didn't put gallons of sun block on him, his skin would bubble up like a slice of pizza with extra cheese. He hates it, but too bad! I apply it fast and abundantly no matter how much he cries. When it comes to important health practices (brushing their teeth, wearing weather-appropriate clothing and sunblock, and so on), it's better not to give in to the drama.

## Getting Upset and Avoiding Bad Feelings

When our six-year-old daughter breaks or loses something, my wife, to prevent our daughter from getting upset, immediately offers to replace it. Is this a good idea?

*Dr. Sharon:* A six-year-old should deal with the consequences of losing something. If her mother stops replacing the items, the girl will learn to recover on her own and she will learn to be resilient, not despondent over the loss. The sooner a child is permitted to feel a loss, the better she will be equipped to deal with the hard knocks of life.

*Marilu:* With six kids my parents would have gone broke replacing everything we broke or lost in the house. Things were always put back together with glue, tape, or safety pins. Maybe one of the best gifts you could get your daughter is a repair kit.

## Masking Feelings

When our four-year-old daughter gets upset I say something funny, turning the problem into a joke so she forgets about it. It works. My mother says I do this too much and that it is not healthy to turn everything into a joke. What is your opinion?

*Dr. Sharon:* Occasional joking is okay. But always joking to distract your daughter from being upset will prevent her from dealing head-on with frustrating situations. In the long run she will profit by experiencing all feelings, including feeling upset, so your mother is correct.

*Marilu:* I often use humor to lighten situations with my sons. For example, one time Joey fell and hit his head on the ground and wouldn't let me apply a bag of ice to it until I pretended to place the bag on the ground first to take the swelling out of *it*. That cracked him up and he then let me put the ice bag on his head.

## What Does a Feeling Look Like?

I've heard that a healthy way of handling an angry child is to let him draw pictures of what his "anger" looks like. Do you recommend this?

*Dr. Sharon:* Getting out his anger in language is good, providing it's not repetitive. But asking a child to draw a picture of what his anger looks like is not constructive or helpful. Who is to say what anger looks like? It will likely conjure up destructive images—which the child would otherwise not have thought of. I don't recommend this approach.

*Marilu:* I am glad I wasn't asked to do this as a child. I was a horrible artist. It is hard to express anger using bad stick figures.

## Appropriate Emotions

I don't know how to help my nine-year-old daughter when she is sad and wallows in self-pity. Growing up I was not allowed to show my emotions. I don't want to do this to my daughter, but on the other hand I don't want to encourage her to wallow in self-pity. How should I deal with her?

*Dr. Sharon:* You may not have been permitted to show emotions, but you have empathy for your child, so, luckily, your parents' attitude did not make you an unfeeling adult. It is okay for your child to feel sad. If she wants to talk to you about it, listen to what she volunteers. Just listening will be therapeutic for her, and at the end of her story tell her she did a good job of telling you why she was upset. If she continues to wallow in self-pity, try to ignore it. If no attention is paid to her, she will soon give up wallowing in self-pity, which essentially is a silent temper tantrum.

*Marilu:* I think it is really important to let children feel all their emotions. I saw teachers at my sons' old preschool suppressing the kids' feelings. They would say things like, "All right now, let's take that bad feeling and put it in that drawer over there. Okay, we've said good-bye to that feeling now. It is in the drawer." That is so unnatural! And it has to be confusing and crazy-making for the kids. Not only that, but I think one day that drawer is going to get so steeped in bad feelings, it is going to lash out at the teachers like the final scene in *Raiders of the Lost Ark*.

## How Parents Feel

Our seven-year-old neighbor gets picked on at home by his mother and at school by his peers. He is really not a bad kid. Why is this happening?

*Dr. Sharon:* A child often induces in others the predominant feeling one of his parents had for him. A child who is disliked by a parent may trigger the same feeling in his teachers, caregivers, and play-mates. It's difficult to dislodge from the way the world reacts to this child. They may have to seek family counseling.

*Marilu:* This is a great explanation for why some people just "rub people the wrong way" and do so their entire lives. Now I under-stand why, when meeting someone with whom I have no prior his-tory, I can have a feeling about him that something is just not right. I remember showing someone my first-grade class picture and they picked out a little boy they thought was cute. I couldn't believe it. It was a kid nobody liked. Upon closer examination I realized he *was* very cute but just gave off a vibe that was very unlikable.

## Feeling Excluded

My eight-year-old son complains that his friends exclude him. I don't want him hurt. How do I handle this?

*Dr. Sharon:* If you protect your child from getting hurt, later in life he will crumble if you are not there to "hold his hand." Try not to involve yourself. It probably hurts you more than it hurts him. Listen to his complaint and tell him, "I understand." Let him figure out a way out of his own dilemma. Struggling and resolving a problem will make him stronger.

*Marilu:* I remember feeling hurt as a child when two of my girlfriends would pair up and exclude me, but somehow there was always some new friend to come in and take their place. Has your son explored all the possibilities in the neighborhood or he is counting on these particular friends? Maybe there is some other little boy like him who needs a friend.

# WHEN LITTLE BRATS BECOME BIG BRATS

Just as inoculations and booster shots prepare us in small doses to later fight a serious disease, frustrations and disappointments throughout childhood prepare us for more traumatic experiences as adults. What can happen when children are frequently protected from unpleasant feelings and experiences?

## Dr. Sharon's View

*Fearing that Johnny would be upset, his mother decided not to tell him that his dog, Scottie, was put to sleep. Instead she told him that Scottie collapsed and died naturally. Johnny was unconsciously aware of what had actually happened to his beloved dog. And at some point, Johnny would realize that he had been deceived. It would have been far better for Johnny to have been told that Scottie was very ill and that the vet recommended that the dog be put to sleep with a painless injection. And that was what had been done. Had Johnny been told, he would have dealt with his feelings at the time it happened and his questions could have been answered truthfully.*

A child who was prevented from dealing with all of his emotions, having been shielded by the well-meaning, overprotective parent will, in adulthood, become extremely distressed in the face of painful feelings. This child will grow up trying to escape any unpleasant situation, shutting himself off from the real world when possible. This will be the adult who turns to some kind of sedation. Often he can't socialize without alcohol or he frequently tries to conquer his "bad" feelings by overeating or smoking.

Feelings are wonderful and important to experience; pity the child who was taught to run from them.

# CHAPTER 12

# Spooky, Spunky, and Sleepy

My brother Tommy has always said that the ideal mom is a balanced combination of Spooky, Spunky, and Sleepy. Spooky represents our cautious side. It's the parent who warns kids about potential dangers. A little bit of Spooky is good because it instills some protective fears in children. Too much Spooky creates unnecessary paranoia. Spunky represents the rah-rah side of parents. It's important to be Spunky to encourage kids to do their best and to be proud when they succeed. But too much Spunky makes children feel as if they're being hovered over or pushed too hard (think Mama Rose). And Sleepy is the parent who allows his kids a lot of freedom, the laissez-faire parent. The right amount of Sleepy helps develop healthy independent kids; too much Sleepy creates feelings of neglect. A good parent has a natural blend of all three.

My mother had a balanced, yet eccentric, combination of Spooky, Spunky, and Sleepy. Her Spooky side came from her bizarre rules and fears such as: You couldn't be a cheerleader because it might ruin your female organs. You couldn't live away from home your first year of college because you might commit suicide. And my personal favorite: You couldn't wear a bra until you were at least a B-cup because it might stunt your growth. (True or not, *that* seemed to work.)

Even though my mother had these odd fears, her overall temperament leaned more toward Sleepy. She didn't care whom we dated as long as he had sisters. She didn't care how close we sat to the TV as long as we didn't have the volume on while she was sleeping. (In fact, I was a grown-up before I found out that Mighty Mouse was an opera.) She didn't even care whether or not we ate breakfast (talk about Sleepy!). She had silly rules about bras, but she couldn't have cared less about breakfast. Her Spunky side was a contradiction, too. She didn't really encourage, or discourage, our getting involved in scholastic or science projects. But when it came to acting, singing, or dancing, she was the first mom to get involved. She was a real *showbiz* mom. Staying up late on school nights to watch a classic movie musical or Lana Turner film on *The Late Show* was actually encouraged. She always knew the latest dances and hippest songs. She often threw record parties where everyone had to bring a newly released 45 to attend. It was a great way for us to restock the record supply for our dancing school.

My mother may not have had the conventional balance of Spooky, Spunky, Sleepy, but it worked for me. Not all children feel that way, however. How can we as parents give our children a good balance without putting too much on them in any one category?

## Dr. Sharon's View

As Marilu writes, her parents' attitudes toward child rearing, both laissez-faire and vigilant, worked well for her. Her good relationships with all her siblings, in particular, attest to her parents' intelligent approach to the family structure.

Indeed, there is great value to a parenting style that combines a healthy dose of all three approaches. A parent who acts cautiously on a child's behalf, gives him encouragement, and offers him the freedom to act independently, once boundaries are established, gives him healthy messages. In the home where a sense of humor prevails, where just being alive is a privilege, where parents' rules are respected—that is the home in which children will grow up secure and successful.

# FINAL THOUGHTS FROM MARILU

I guess the best way to recognize what it is we're doing to our children is to know and understand who *we* are and why we do the things we do. Are we passing on (without even thinking about it) the behaviors and fears our parents gave us? Or are we automatically doing the opposite just to be different? Either way, we need to parent consciously in order to find the right balance.

The theories in this book are meant to help us become more aware of the things we parents do (although well intentioned) that could be holding our children back in some way and/or creating behaviors in them that are undesirable. It is information that I am finding helpful as I experience the joys and trials of motherhood. I hope that you have found Dr. Sharon's advice throughout the book to be provocative information that inspires you to look at your parenting skills from a different angle.

Just remember: As much as no one wants to raise a brat, no one wants to *be* a brat.

------------------------------------------------------------

# More Commonly Asked Questions

## DEVELOPMENTAL ISSUES

### Babies in a Place of Worship

My one-year-old was whimpering during the service at our place of worship. Afterward, one of the parishoners accused our family of being insensitive to the other worshipers. Should parents take their babies to service?

*Dr. Sharon:* Alienating parents who bring their babies to a house of worship is hypocritical. Places of worship should encourage the entire family to attend, babies and children included.

*Marilu:* There are always crying babies at a service. Mass wouldn't be Mass without a crying baby. The church I go to in Los Angeles has an actual crying room with a glass window right on the altar. I had kids just to get a box seat at church.

## Toilet Training

My son is three-and-a-half and very bright but is still not potty trained. What can I do to get him to use the toilet?

*Dr. Sharon:* It's a huge transition from diaper to the potty. Be patient with him. If no one shames him he will eventually, on his own, decide to use the potty. A standoff between parent and child during toilet training will only fortify the child's stubbornness.

*Marilu:* Is he wearing Pull-Ups or diapers? My guess would be Pull-Ups because I think we have a generation of children who are training late because of disposable pants. When a child first starts training he's given a Pull-Up and told, "They're big boy pants and not a babyish diaper." Then when we want him to move on and be totally trained, the Pull-Up is considered babyish. It's confusing. I think if children wore only diapers or real underwear they would train earlier. In your son's case, he probably wouldn't want to wear a diaper at three and a half.

## Baby-Sitting Barney

My three-year-old daughter is obsessed with Barney and Disney tapes. I find myself using them throughout the day as a baby-sitter. Is it bad to allow tapes to become a major part of her life? I don't want her to become a dull couch potato.

*Dr. Sharon:* Exposing children to tapes such as Barney is a mostly harmless distraction. However, don't let the tapes become the major part of her life. Expose her to art and to classical music and let her express her creativity through drawing and watercolors.

*Marilu:* I've never been a Barney basher because he teaches children good manners. And I love *Sesame Street* because, besides being educational, it has such a great sense of humor. If you're worried about her becoming a couch potato, try supplementing Barney with Elmo-cize. However, I don't think it's a good idea for anyone to get obsessed with tapes.

## Playing a Part

My four-year-old son likes to play make-believe with his thirty-year-old aunt whom he assigns the role of the pretty damsel in distress, and his uncle is the bad guy. My son is the hero who destroys the villain (his uncle). Are games like this confusing or innocent fun for a four-year-old?

*Dr. Sharon:* If this is the product of your four-year-old's imagination and he made up the whole scenario, that's fine. If it was inspired or thought of by his aunt or uncle, I would encourage him to be his own scriptwriter.

*Marilu:* This happens all the time in my family because we are all so theatrical. Our ethnic background is Polish and Greek and as kids, we used to play "Greek Gods and Heroes." I was Aphrodite, Tommy was Apollo, and my thirty-five-year-old eccentric uncle was Zeus. Because our younger brother Lorin felt bad for our Polish side, he started a rival make-believe troupe, "Polish Gods and Heroes." He was Lubaleski the Polish god and warrior, and Christal was Portky, the Polish slave girl.

## Childhood Fears

Our four-year-old son is terrified when we start letting the water
out of the bathtub before he gets out (as if he is afraid of going
down the drain). Is this normal?

*Dr. Sharon:* It is not uncommon for a child to be fearful of going
down the drain when the bathwater is let out. It is not an emotional
problem. Take him out of the tub, then open the drain. He will outgrow these fears in time. Forcing a child to confront one of his fears
is counterproductive. It will only exacerbate the fear and cause the
child to mistrust his parent.

*Marilu:* When my children were afraid of the drain, I would take
them out of the tub and let them pull the stopper. My sister JoAnn
was afraid to take a bath because she was afraid that Superman
might break through the wall and see her. But the funniest childhood fear was my sister Christal's. She was afraid of the painting
"Whistler's Mother." (Although I think it had more to do with the
poster for *Psycho* than the painting.)

## No Dresses, Only Sweatsuits

My daughter, age five, refuses to wear dresses and wants to wear
only sweatsuits. I let her wear whatever she wants. My husband
says I'm spoiling her by not setting limits on her choices. What do
you think?

*Dr. Sharon:* It isn't clear why your five-year-old refuses to wear
dresses. I would not make an issue unless she is in kindergarten and

there is a dress code, in which case, insist she conform. At other times, let her wear whatever she wants—you are not spoiling her. She will outgrow that phase.

*Marilu:* Friends of mine had a daughter who would only dress as a Disney character. Believe me, it's just a phase kids go through. You don't usually see a twenty-year-old Princess Jasmine unless she's auditioning for a remake of *I Dream of Jeannie.*

# RESISTING OVERGRATIFICATION AND RESPECTING THE PARENT-CHILD CONTRACT

## Self-Discipline

**My wife feels that our children should discipline themselves. As a result, our home is chaos. What do you think?**

*Dr. Sharon:* Children are not capable of disciplining themselves. If during the first few years of their lives children are disciplined by their parents and caretakers, they will eventually become self-disciplined, a natural outgrowth of living within parental imposed limits.

*Marilu:* Oh boy, does this remind me of a household I visited recently. The children were completely out of control, and their nanny took me aside begging me for a job because she had absolutely no authority over the children. The mother, who is a friend of mine, explained to me that her children are allowed to do what they want because they're little and when they are adults she will pick her battles. I would suggest you sit your wife down and make her read this book. Come to think of it I'd better send my friend this book as well.

## Mom as Playmate

My eight-month-old son crawls after me and wants me to play with him all the time. At the end of each day I am exhausted. I have childproofed my home so he will be safe. How can I get him to play by himself?

*Dr. Sharon:* Your eight-month-old has become dependent on your constant company. Place him in a safe confined space where you can observe him and play with him for only a few minutes at a time. Be prepared for a day or two of misery for both of you as he objects, but don't give in or you will teach him one more bad lesson: namely, that if he fusses and cries, he wins.

*Marilu:* I can really relate to an eight-month-old boy crawling everywhere. Nicky was like the road runner at this age and could even crawl out of his Exer-saucer. I put a safety gate at the door of his baby-proofed bedroom and let him play on the floor while I worked right outside his room where I could always see him. That way he was safe, had a lot of room to explore and toys to play with, and I could get my work done and still be readily available.

## No Time as a Couple

Our three-year-old daughter stays up too late and as a result my wife and I don't have time together in the evenings. I want to have an intimate relationship with my wife, but by the time she gets into bed she is too exhausted. What do I do?

*Dr. Sharon:* Don't try to persuade your daughter to go to bed. Endless persuasion, discussion, or negotiation won't work. Bedtime is bedtime. Once this part of the parent child contract is reinforced and honored, everyone will be happier.

*Marilu:* If your daughter stays up late, I'm assuming she wakes up late. What about being intimate in the morning? Or during the day when she's in preschool? Who knows? Out-of-the-ordinary times often make for some out-of-the-ordinary encounters.

## Bribing to Stop Crying

My wife bribes our four-year-old to get her to stop crying. What do you think?

*Dr. Sharon:* Bribing, "If you stop crying I will give you . . ." will momentarily spare the child from having to deal with the predicament he is crying about, but from then on it will weaken the child's resolve to deal with similar frustrating situations without being bribed.

*Marilu:* Sometimes it's so hard not to bribe. Every time I do, though, I'm always sorry because the next time they cry, a bribe is expected and I'm back to square one.

## When It's Good to Be "Mean"

My five-year-old's aunts, uncles, and nanny all overgratify her. I don't want to be the only "meany" in her life. What do I do?

*Dr. Sharon:* You may be the only "meany" in your daughter's life, nevertheless you will keep your daughter anchored in the real world. When she grows up she will recall that you were the most sensible and caring person in her early years. It's the overgratifying parent that is frequently remembered as a "meany." Grandparents, aunts, and nannies don't have the power that you, the parent, have. You cannot prevent your daughter from being overgratified by others (although you do have a say over the nannies who work for you).

*Marilu:* I am proud to be this kind of "meany." I feel like I must be doing a good job if my kids see me this way. When I watch my children at first get frustrated or angry about something, then overcome those problems using their own ingenuity and willpower, I know I am doing the right thing. It is okay if they get mad at me or think I am the bad guy. They never stay mad long and, even though they are too young to understand this, deep down I know they appreciate my honesty and disciplinary consistency.

## Clean Plate

My husband believes very strongly that our children—ages five and eight—should finish all the food on their plates at every meal. I disagree and believe it is too rigid. What do you think?

*Dr. Sharon:* It is not necessary for a child to finish everything on his plate at every meal. Avoid putting a whole lot of food on his plate. If the child piles food on his own plate and then does not eat it, he is overindulged. Instruct him to take a taste before putting more on his plate.

*Marilu:* I think the clean plate edict is a mistake. I believe such a rule can create a compulsion to always clean your plate, which could then lead to overeating and obesity. I have a very strong opinion about the way kids should eat. I believe that they should be allowed to listen to their own natural "gauges." My kids rarely finish everything on their plate and that is fine. I do, of course, determine what they eat at home by keeping only healthy foods in the house. Simply put: I am in charge of the quality and they are in charge of the quantity.

## A Break from School

> About two or three times a year our six-year-old daughter likes to take a day off from school even though she is not sick. She says she "just needs a break." I let her stay home because I know that every once in a while I, too, need to take a "mental health" day from my job. My husband says this will make her irresponsible later in life. I think it is teaching her that it is okay to take care of herself. What do you think?

*Dr. Sharon:* I agree with your husband. Why does your daughter need a break from school? She has to learn that work can be pleasurable and does not have to be something that one needs a break from. If she is sick she stays home; otherwise she should attend school regularly. Overgratified children grow up to be adults who need frequent breaks throughout the year and look forward to the calendar of pre-holidays, holidays, and post-holidays, leaving little time for work.

*Marilu:* "Just needs a break"? This sounds like something kids would say because they've heard their parents say it. It's good to teach your daughter that it's okay to take care of herself, but staying home from school when she's not sick doesn't seem like a responsible way to do it.

## Putting Away Toys

When I ask my six-year-old son to put away his toys, he is often resistant. I usually end up putting them away myself. It takes less time than struggling to get him to cooperate. Punishing him with time-out doesn't necessarily get his room cleaned up any faster so it is just more practical for me to do it myself. What do you think?

*Dr. Sharon:* A six-year-old complaining that he is too tired to pick up his toys hints at being overgratified, or that one of his parents complains about being too tired to do something around the house. It sounds like imitated behavior. If he refuses to pick up his toys, give him a time-out.

*Marilu:* Joey would not pick up his toys one time and it became a battle of wills. By the time I finally got him to pick up his toys I felt like Annie Sullivan. He finally picked up his toys. . . . The next thing is folding his napkin.

## Piano Lessons

Our ten-year-old son is musical, but he refuses to practice the piano and wants to quit his lessons. I regret not having been "forced" to practice the piano. What do you think? It's become a battle of wills between him and me. Would you push it?

*Dr. Sharon:* Your son is unaware that when he grows up he will regret having given up music lessons. Find a teacher who will work with him in a way that will not discourage him. Permitting a musically gifted child to give up music lessons is a form of overgratification.

*Marilu:* If your son is that talented there has to be some way to tap into his being interested enough to practice. Maybe he finds the lessons dull because his music choices are limited to classical music. Take him to a music store and let him pick out music he's really interested in, and maybe the challenge of being able to play it will light that spark.

## Starting Smoking

> I suspect that my eleven-year-old son is smoking cigarettes. I battled this dreadful habit for twenty-five years until I quit five years ago. I don't want him to follow in my footsteps. Do I confront him?

*Dr. Sharon:* Your son saw you smoke the first six years of his life, and that message was imprinted in his mind. Ask your pediatrician to explain to him the dangers of smoking and show him the printed warning on each pack of cigarettes.

*Marilu:* Almost every smoker I know had at least one parent who smoked. Their parents' secondhand smoke has become such a part of their respiratory system that many of them are addicted to nicotine. A lot of people I know who had two parents that smoked find it almost impossible to quit. Your son is still so young that I think you should hang tough on this one. You'll probably be saving his life.

## Teens on the Phone

Our teenage daughter talks to her friends on the phone when she should be doing her homework. If she is not on the phone she has the radio on. Whenever I remind her that it is homework time, she says, "We *are* talking about homework." Unless I stand by her door and listen I have no way of knowing if she is being truthful. How should we handle this?

*Dr. Sharon:* Don't stand by her door and listen. If your daughter's grades have not dropped since she began phone conversations with her friends or listening to the radio, don't interfere. If her grades have deteriorated, set limits about use of both the phone and radio.

*Marilu:* I talked a lot on the phone as a teenager, but because I was able to keep my grades up my parents never had to remind me to do my homework. Is this about homework or spending money on phone calls, or is it about something else? Maybe you could get her her own phone and she could contribute to the monthly bill if it goes over a certain amount. That might teach her responsibility and curtail her phone use at the same time.

# ISSUES OF PRIVACY, SELF-ESTEEM, AND SEXUALITY

## Dinnertime Nudity

My three-year-old niece took off all her clothes at the dinner table on more than one occasion. Her mother just laughs and says, "Here she goes again." I was uncomfortable. What do you think?

*Dr. Sharon:* The three-year-old is out of control and her mother is too lenient, which is clear from her reaction. The little girl should be told to go into her room and get dressed and return to the table. It is not cute for a three-year-old to behave in an inappropriate manner. Does one of her parents tend to be exhibitionistic? Children's behavior often betrays the parents' problems, even if the child is not consciously aware of them.

*Marilu:* It sounds like it has been communicated to this child that taking your clothes off is entertaining and even appealing. This mother should be really careful to communicate the right things to a little girl in terms of respecting her body.

## Privacy at School

On a visit to my daughter's preschool I saw a little girl using the toilet and a little boy was urinating in a toilet next to her within her view. There were no partitions between the toilets and there was a large mirror facing them. What do you think about that?

*Dr. Sharon:* The fact that the school has this setup sends a bad message to the children, in a sense encouraging exhibitionism and voyeurism. It is unsettling when teachers and other professionals, who might not be trained in psychological matters, make such important psychological decisions in children's lives. Children's privacy needs to be guarded.

*Marilu:* This is so prevalent in the L.A. school system that I had to get myself on the cover of *Parents* in order to protest. When I saw this very situation while evaluating preschools for the first time, I ended up calling twenty-one before I found a preschool that has a potty with privacy.

## Touching

When I change my two-year-old's diaper he reaches down and pulls on his penis. What is the best way of dealing with that?

*Dr. Sharon:* It's not uncommon for little babies to reach for their genitals when being diapered. Make certain you are not obsessive about wiping him or putting creams on him. Taking a long time to wipe and powder his genitals is sexually stimulating. Babies have sexual feelings and are reluctant to give up the "pleasure" of being diapered and becoming toilet trained. When your two-year-old pulls on his penis, refrain from saying "No" or removing his hand. Simply diaper him quickly.

*Marilu:* My son started pulling on his penis when he was around four months old. When I told my pediatrician, he said, "Don't worry about this. It is very normal. He'll outgrow that in about six or seven . . . decades!"

## Daddy/Daughter

My husband refuses to give our one-month-old daughter a bath because he says it "feels weird." Should he force himself to bathe her so he can bond with her?

*Dr. Sharon:* Since your husband claims he "feels weird" when he bathes your daughter, don't insist. He may feel awkward or embarrassed because he is of the opposite sex. His feelings are not unusual and he may outgrow them.

*Marilu:* Your husband may also feel "weird" because he lacks the confidence that is required to give an infant a bath. Try letting him assist you. If he doesn't want to, I'm sure that your husband and daughter can bond in other ways.

## Dressing Up and Dressing Older

My teenage daughter is very flat-chested. The other day when we were going to a wedding she came down all dressed up in a very tight-fitting tank dress with an obviously stuffed Wonderbra. I wanted her to take that ridiculous thing off but she was so happy and confident that I didn't want to hurt her feelings. Anyway, the staredowns and flirting from the cousins at the wedding were so obnoxious I almost got sick—unfortunately, she didn't. She's been living in her Wonderbra ever since. What should I do?

*Dr. Sharon:* Is your daughter thirteen or eighteen? It makes a difference. If she is under eighteen, I would tell her not to wear the Wonderbra. You still have a say about her dress code. Explain to her that beauty comes from within and a genuine person is much more appealing in the long run than a fake.

*Marilu:* This is a tough question because there's so much going on here: self-image, self-esteem, role playing, even cousin attraction (flirty, but safe). Your daughter is the one who thought of doing this in the first place, so it's something she feels she has control over. I would bet anything this is a phase she'll go through for a short period of time. Eventually, she'll get tired of stuffing and get into styles that look better on girls with less bosom.

## Olympic Hopeful

My seven-year-old Olympic hopeful daughter just loves acrobatics and wants to enroll in the advanced tumbling program in school. Her coach leveled with me, saying she really just isn't built right for the movements involved in this sport and consequently will have difficulty in advancement as well as a higher risk of injuries. I'm so proud of her achievements and enthusiasm that even though I know the facts, I feel like signing her up. What should I do?

*Dr. Sharon:* Your daughter is only seven. If, however, she truly wants to proceed into an advanced tumbling class, since the coach has warned you of possible injury, discuss it with her pediatrician first.

*Marilu:* If I listened to every person in my life who told me I wasn't "this or that enough" to succeed, I would never have become a dancer, an actress, or an author. Make sure your daughter is safe, but applaud her enthusiasm. Besides, she's only seven and her body can change. She may also develop different passions as she grows.

# TEACHING VALUES
# AND LISTENING TO FEELINGS

## No Compromise

I try to teach my six-year-old son the value of compromise. Whenever we disagree about something such as bedtime, unhealthy snacks, or television we always negotiate until we reach an agreement. Is that okay?

*Dr. Sharon:* Negotiating with a child until you reach an agreement gives the child the impression that he is an equal. A six-year-old must understand that the parent is in charge and that what the parent says goes, and as unfair as it may sound, compromises should not be a part of the parent/child relationship. A child will feel secure, and in fact you are doing him a favor, when his role is clearly defined. Although the word "compromise" generally conjures up the image of conciliatory agreement between the parent and child, it is counterproductive. The parent, at all times, must remain in charge.

*Marilu:* Even as a car salesman's daughter I know that negotiating with a child can be a never-ending process. A child should not learn the value of compromise by negotiating like it's a Middle Eastern bazaar, unless they want to go into the flea-market business.

## Competition: Good or Bad?

The world is a competitive place. Does this mean we should encourage competition among our children in order to get them prepared for life?

*Dr. Sharon:* There is natural competition and a struggle for survival from day one of a baby's life. Encouraging competition is an additional burden.

*Marilu:* I don't think you need to encourage competition. It's there anyway. I feel it's most important not to shield or protect your child from competition with his peers—it's natural.

## Honesty

We have begun to share with our children situations that required our honesty and courage and how we handled them. Is that a good idea?

*Dr. Sharon:* It is a good idea to share with your children personal anecdotes of how you practiced honesty and courage. Your children will profit from both the moral of the anecdote and your willingness to share these experiences with them.

*Marilu:* Children are such "tape recorders," and it's always amazing to hear your own language come back to you from the mouth of such a little person. They pick up everything that you do, and if you are an honest and courageous person, more than likely, they are going to be the same way. If you feel that there is some experience that they are going through that is similar to what you've been through, I think it's always good to use that as an example.

## Forgiveness

*How do we teach our children forgiveness, and at what age can children understand it?*

*Dr. Sharon:* Forgiveness is not taught, it is a natural outgrowth of observing how parents behave toward each other, toward others, and toward their children. It is virtually imitated.

*Marilu:* My parents were very forgiving, and I think my siblings and I learned forgiveness by their example. I don't remember ever actually having explained to me the value of forgiveness.

## "If Only I Had . . ."

*My sixteen-year-old keeps saying "I wish I hadn't done this, I wish I hadn't done that, I should have bought this, I should have gotten the homework from someone," and so on. He constantly regrets things. How should I handle it?*

*Dr. Sharon:* Tell your son that regret is a waste of time because it "kills" the present and it doesn't use the brain cells to be creative in present time. Tell him that the only regret he should have is that he regrets.

*Marilu:* After an experience, it's best to assess the situation, figure out what you can do better next time, then move on. There's nothing worse than living in regret.

## Family Pets

My four-year-old wants a cat. He's too young to take care of it, and I'm concerned he may be too rough with it. Should I wait until he is older?

*Dr. Sharon:* Aside from asking whether it would be fair to the cat, is it fair to your son? If the cat is injured and it's his fault, it will be a destructive experience. Wait a couple of years until he understands how to take care of a pet.

*Marilu:* Four years old seems awfully young for a cat. Maybe you should buy him a hamster or an animal that's easier to take care of because it's in its own cage. If your son demonstrates that he can be responsible for a pet, maybe you can buy him a cat when he's five or six.

## "Your Mom Is Pregnant!"

What is the best way to prepare a two-year-old and a six-year-old for a new baby brother or sister? My wife just found out she is pregnant.

*Dr. Sharon:* Tell the children the truth the moment you find out you are expecting. The two-year-old should be included in the information you impart. Parents who are truthful and share such information from the beginning make the family a closer unit. Share information right along, except for the feelings you have for the growing baby, or what feelings you expect the children to have for the baby when it is born. Let your children have their own reactions.

*Marilu:* I have the cutest picture of my son, Nicky, at age one, when I was three months pregnant with Joey. He's got a big smile on his face and he's pointing at my stomach. So, I've always been a big believer in telling kids the truth about what's going on, because their unconscious mind knows it anyway and could conjure up all kinds of strange things trying to understand it. By the time Joey was born, Nicky, then eighteen months old, felt like he was in on the whole thing because Joey was not some major shock or dirty secret.

---------------------------------------------------------------

**Marilu Henner** is an acclaimed actress who has made numerous appearances in film and television and is best known for her co-starring roles on the hit television series *Taxi* and *Evening Shade*. She recently completed successful runs in productions of the award-winning Broadway musical *Chicago*, in both New York and Las Vegas, in the lead role of Roxie Hart. A promoter of mental, physical, and emotional health, Marilu is also the bestselling author of *Marilu Henner's Total Health Makeover* and *The 30-Day Total Health Makeover*. Marilu is married to producer/director Robert Lieberman. They have two children, Nicky and Joey.

**Dr. Ruth Velikovsky Sharon** holds B.A. and M.A. degrees from N.Y.U. and a Ph.D. from the Union Institute. She is a certified psychoanalyst and training analyst for general psychoanalytic institutes. Dr. Sharon and her son, Rafael, co-host a weekly radio talk show, *The Couch*, in New Jersey. Dr. Sharon was influenced by her father, Dr. Immanuel Velikovsky, a psychiatrist and colleague of Freud.

# INTRODUCTION to RESEARCH
### Understanding and Applying Multiple Strategies

# INTRODUCTION to RESEARCH

## Understanding and Applying Multiple Strategies

### 2nd edition

**Elizabeth DePoy,** PhD, MSW, OTR

Professor
School of Social Work
Coordinator of Research and Evaluation
Center for Community Inclusion
University of Maine
Orono, Maine

**Laura N. Gitlin,** PhD

Professor
Department of Occupational Therapy
Director
Community and Homecare Research Division
College of Health Professions
Thomas Jefferson University
Philadelphia, Pennsylvania

*A Harcourt Health Sciences Company*

St. Louis   London   Philadelphia   Sydney   Toronto

Mosby

*A Harcourt Health Sciences Company*

Publisher:  **John Schrefer**
Executive Editor:  **Martha Sasser**
Developmental Editor:  **Amy Christopher**
Associate Developmental Editor:  **Christie Hart**
Project Manager:  **Gayle Morris**
Manufacturing Manager:  **Betty Mueller**
Cover Designer:  **David Zielinski**

Printed in the United States of America

ISBN 0-8016-6284-2

00  01  02  /  9  8  7  6  5  4  3  2

To Don, Sam, and Lynn
Edward, Eric, and Keith
and our students

# Foreword

The second edition of this book remains focused on the theoretical and practical conduct of human inquiry. It is about people doing work with other people; it is about making sense of human experiences, thoughts, and actions.

In this new edition, Elizabeth DePoy and Laura Gitlin provide an integrating framework, not only for the conduct of naturalistic and experimental inquiry but also for the relationship of theory and practice. These experienced health professionals and researchers describe *ways of knowing* about health and illness and about people who are embedded in contexts of delivering health and human services. Unlike other textbooks, their work is integrative. It recognizes that each way of knowing is incomplete, fragmentary, partial. Consequently, because of this, any single methodology is at the same time both trustworthy and untrustworthy in what it helps people to illuminate and understand. It recognizes that each way of knowing is not independent of the other—not *alternative to* but *complementary with* other ways of knowing. The ideas of complementariness and connectedness are celebrated rather than bemoaned, legitimatized rather than delegitimatized, as is too often the case. These scholars recognize that an important task of "post-empiricist" epistemology is to reconfigure the consensus regarding the canons of rationality. Because DePoy and Gitlin allow these values to influence their writing explicitly, they avoid presenting material and argu-ments in smorgasbord fashion. And more importantly, in an intellectual sense, they are able to write about and illustrate methodology at multiple levels—political, philosophical, technical, cognitive, and linguistic. Herein lies a unique and important strength of their treatment. DePoy and Gitlin recognize that the act of doing research, as well as the product of that act, is a complex blend of political, ethical, technological, social, and linguistic engagements between human beings. Both the structure and content of their text reflect this idea.

DePoy and Gitlin have benefited from the methodological debates characteristic of the 1970s through the mid-1990s. In this new edition they bring to their work, at both theoretical and practical levels, an interpretation of methodological pluralism, which avoids the philosophical confusion that pluralism condones or legitimatizes alternative standards of rationality. Rather, they adopt a process perspective that suggests different research traditions attend to a similar set of challenges. In doing so, their project integrates the fragmentation or discontinuities often generated by the actors in debates of meaning and method in the social sciences. Their text reflects an interest for integrated approaches to inquiry. And just what is integrated? And at what levels does this integration take place? Ideas of what constitutes sound inquiry in one tradition (e.g., ethnography) are related to those of another tradition (e.g., quasi-experimental). In turn, how one goes about this integrated work and how one writes up such integrated work are both described. Thus the language, cognitive processes, and value systems of those engaged in integrative designs at different levels are carefully articulated throughout the text.

Those who do research in health care settings will find a great deal of practical knowledge grounded in a sophisticated philosophical and sociological context. This should be refreshing. Those who are about to embark on doing research will not only learn how to do good work, but, and perhaps most importantly, they will understand why they do what they do. Consistent with the viewpoint taken by DePoy and Gitlin, their text ends by empowering those who do the work. "Stories from the Field," the final chapter, is a powerful and constructive narrative way to know about the conduct of research.

John D. Engel, PhD
Vice President for Academic Affairs and
    Executive Associate Dean
Professor of Behavioral Sciences
Northeastern Ohio Universities College of
    Medicine
Rootstown, Ohio

# Preface

Our main purpose in writing this second edition is similar to our original intent. We are committed to sharing with the student, health and human professional, and beginning researcher our great enthusiasm and passion for conducting research in health and human services using multiple research strategies. We hope this edition with its conceptual refinements, updated and expanded information, and use of current research demystifies the research process and provides a foundation from which to critique, understand, and apply multiple research strategies to health and human service concerns. With this second edition, we have refined our conceptual framework from which to examine and integrate different research traditions. In so doing, our goal remains to challenge traditional teaching approaches to research processes and to contribute to narrowing the gap between quantitative and qualitative paradigms.

Why do health and human service professionals still need another research text and this second edition? As in the first writing of this book, health and human service professions continue to stand at the crossroads of significant megatrends in the delivery and financing of services to clients, families, and communities. These trends continue at a rapid pace and include the movement from an acute, medical framework to community-based models of care; a focus on health promotion and disease prevention; the development of new paradigms for examining the interplay of behavioral, environmental and biological interactions; and an increased emphasis on innovative services for underserved, culturally diverse populations and individuals with disabling conditions.

These new directions in health and human services require the need to consider new approaches to research. The traditional research paradigm taught to students of the social sciences and health professions, referred to as quantitative, empiricist, positivist, or rationalist, represents only one approach to scientific inquiry. Historically, the quantitative or experimental-type approach to research has been upheld as the most scientific, valid, and precise methodology. Unfortunately, this belief still lingers in the health and human service worlds and has significantly limited the effective use of other research strategies, which, in turn, has restricted knowledge building. In light of this, another research tradition, referred to as discovery-oriented, interpretive, qualitative, or naturalistic, is rapidly gaining importance and recognition as a form of inquiry with its own rules and systematic approach to understanding human behavior.

The viewpoint we continue to present in this second edition reflects a new school of thought that recognizes and values multiple research strategies. This contemporary perspective proposes that naturalistic and experimental-type research strategies have equal value and contribute in complementary and distinct ways to the science of practice. Knowledge of these different research traditions presents new opportunities for addressing the complex health and human service research questions that are emerging as a consequence of today's health care environment. Students, professionals, and researchers need a research text that prepares them for using the full range of research traditions to meet the scientific challenges posed by a changing service systems. For example, to develop effective health promotion programs for communities composed of individuals from diverse cultural backgrounds requires understanding specific health beliefs and self-care practices of different groups. Traditional survey techniques have not been successful in identifying different self-care practices, and existing standardized health belief questionnaires do not represent the varied values of culturally diverse groups. Different methodologies and approaches that uncover and accurately represent personal beliefs and practices are required for knowledge building in this area.

Since our first edition was published, there has been a plethora of new articles, books, and texts that discuss and evaluate new methodologies, particularly those from the tradition of naturalistic inquiry. However, our approach in this second edition continues to differ significantly from other research texts. Most texts for health and human service professionals still identify quantitative research as the only valid approach to scientific inquiry. Some of these research texts include a brief discussion of other research traditions more or less as an afterthought. Still other texts explain naturalistic inquiry by using the framework or lens of the experimental researcher. In doing so, the authors assume that naturalistic and experimental approaches differ only with respect to specific procedures. They are unable to present the essential thinking processes that underlie the activity of qualitative research. Thus the research student cannot come to understand and accurately implement different design strategies from this tradition. There are a number of new books that focus only on qualitative research, many of which we cite in this second edition. Although these books are greatly welcomed and broaden our understanding of the scope of human inquiry, they in turn provide insight into only one type of research tradition. The student does not obtain an understanding of the truly vast array of research possibilities nor learn strategies by which to select a particular research approach or integrate different methodologies and theoretical frameworks.

In contrast, this text provides a comprehensive understanding of how researchers think and act in both naturalistic and experimental-type social and behavioral research. It provides a basic introduction to the essential components of both approaches. The reader learns how to critically evaluate, respect, and implement each research strategy from its own philosophical perspective, thinking process, language, and specific actions that engage the researcher. In this text we concur with the new wave of qualitative books and suggest that it is possible to explain the thought and action processes of naturalistic inquiry and advance the standards by which such research is understood, evaluated, and conducted.

Writing the second edition of *Introduction to Research: Understanding and Applying Mul-*

*tiple Strategies* has given us an important opportunity to reflect on and advance our initial concept of the research traditions and their potential integration. Providing a balanced discussion of the different research traditions and their specific design strategies continues to pose a great challenge to scholars and teachers of research. In our first edition we developed a schema by which to compare and contrast research design strategies from the traditions of experimental-type and naturalistic inquiry. The continua of designs, as we called it, ordered designs according to their degree of structure, control, and investigator involvement. This structural approach served as a heuristic device that enabled the research student to examine and respect differences in approaches in research. It also, however, imposed a language and way of thinking about naturalistic research that was not as clear as we would have liked. In this second edition we have refined our thinking and present an understanding of the two research traditions from a process perspective. We have replaced the continua with the concept that each research tradition must address 10 essential thinking and action processes. These highly integrated processes are thought about and solved differently, depending on the particular research tradition being pursued. A process approach, we believe, improves our ability to describe and capture the essence of both naturalistic and experimental-type research. Readers of our first edition will experience the second edition as an improvement and just a small change in emphasis and chapter restructuring. Our underlying assumptions about the purpose and conduct of research and much of the discussions remain intact. We believe all readers will benefit from the clarity that a process approach brings to

understanding the fundamentals of doing research in all research traditions.

The second edition is organized similarly to the first in that there are four major sections. Each section moves the reader from an understanding of the meaning and importance of research (Part I) to examining the specific thinking processes (Part II), design strategies (Part III), and action processes (Part IV) of distinct research traditions. Each chapter focuses on one of the 10 essentials of the research process, all of which are discussed using the language of both the experimental-type and naturalistic researchers. In this second edition we have significantly expanded our discussions on specific design strategies used in quantitative and naturalistic research. Our emphasis continues to be on the application of these strategies to the practice setting. Many research examples are provided from diverse bodies of literature that are relevant to all service providers. As in the first edition we end with field stories, real-life snapshots of what it is like to participate in different types of research processes. These brief accounts, in the tradition of ethnography, reveal the hidden side of the research process, how a study unfolds, what it is like to be an investigator, and what really happens after entering the field. Research, after all, is a human endeavor. Too few researchers dare to discuss the personal ups and downs and common blunders that inform knowledge construction.

We do not intend to solve the qualitative-quantitative controversy in this text. Nonetheless, we urge health and human service professionals to transcend the debate and go beyond attempts of the health care community to polarize research practices. Health and human service professionals must learn the purposes, values, and uses of each research tradition. We propose that knowing the strengths and weaknesses of each tradition provides the basis from which to combine and use multiple strategies to answer research questions. Ultimately this text is designed to facilitate the integration of traditions with the belief that integration is the most comprehensive and productive approach to health and human service research. We hope this text advances the movement toward a new paradigm of integration that can guide research practices.

Who should use this text? This second edition can be used by undergraduate and advanced students in the health and human service professions. It can also be used by practitioners and beginning researchers who want to broaden their understanding of research traditions to which they have not been previously exposed. Health and human service professionals will continue to experience increasing pressure to initiate research, participate as members of research teams, and use research findings to justify their practice and service programs. This text provides a solid foundation from which to pursue these activities effectively.

Elizabeth DePoy
Laura N. Gitlin

# Table of contents

# Table of contents

## PART III Design approaches

# PART IV Action processes

# Table of contents

# INTRODUCTION to RESEARCH
## Understanding and Applying
## Multiple Strategies

*Research…*

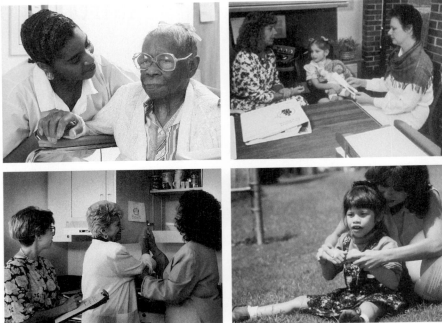

...is a group of multiple, systematic strategies that generate knowledge about human behavior, human experience, and human environments in which the thought and action processes of the researcher are clearly specified so they are logical, understandable, confirmable, and useful. This collection of photographs illustrates the multidisciplinary role that research plays in today's health and human service professions. Research is a human endeavor. It is also a challenging, creative, and intellectually satisfying professional activity that develops and advances knowledge to enhance the lives of clients, their families, and their communities.

# PART I Introduction

Welcome to the world of research!

Conducting research is one of the most challenging, creative, and intellectually satisfying professional activities. Research is an important professional responsibility that develops and advances knowledge from which to base practice. This knowledge is essential if we, as health and human service professionals, are to provide quality services that enhance the lives of our clients, their families, and their communities.

Part I begins with our definition of *research*. We identify and discuss the 10 elements of the *research process* that are essential to the traditions of both experimental-type and naturalistic inquiry.

At this point you may be thinking, "What is research?" "Why is it necessary?" "How does research differ from other ways of learning about things?" "How does one engage in research?" "What is the process?"

These are all important questions that are examined in the chapters of Part I.

# Chapter 1

# Research as an important way of knowing

**Key terms**
Abductive reasoning
Action processes
Confirmable
Deductive reasoning
Experimental-type

Inductive reasoning
Logical process
Naturalistic inquiry
Thinking processes

Why is research necessary?
What is research?
    Research as multiple systematic strategies
    Research as thought and action processes
    Research as four basic characteristics
Summary

*A 74-year-old single African-American woman with a fractured hip will be discharged shortly from rehabilitation to her home. She appears unwilling to use the self-care techniques you taught her. You wonder if rehabilitation has been effective and what her future functional capabilities will be once she returns home.* ■

*You have learned how to use a new tool to assess functional status in children with developmental delays. You wonder if this instrument is more accurate and useful than previous ones you have tried.* ■

*A research article describes an interesting discharge planning procedure for cognitively impaired adults. You wonder if you should implement these planning procedures in your own department and if they will be effective.* ■

*You need to initiate a new program to prevent low-back injury in Hispanic migrant farm workers. Existing prevention strategies have not been effective in reducing the incidence of low-back injury in this population. You wonder why traditional approaches have failed and how to develop an appropriate knowledge base from which to develop an effective program.* ■

*You notice in your home care practice that some patients need more visits than others to achieve the same level of functional gain. You wonder what factors determine service need.* ■

## Why is research necessary?

Health and human service professionals routinely have questions about their daily practice. Many of these questions, like the ones above, are answered best through systematic investigation—or the research process. It is unfortunate that many practitioners are hesitant to engage in research. This hesitancy is due, in part, to an unfamiliarity with and a misconception of the research process. Research is challenging, exhilarating, and very stimulating. Like other professional activities, it can be time-consuming, tedious, and frustrating. The challenges and frustrations of conducting research occur because it is not a simple activity. This is especially true for health and human service research because of the complexity of conducting research in service environments and understanding human behavior. Implementing a research study in the home, community, outpatient clinic, or medical facility can be more challenging than research

conducted in a laboratory or setting controlled by the investigator. Throughout this book, we discuss the specific dilemmas and design implications that are posed by research implemented in different settings.

There are five important reasons why you should understand the research process and participate in research activities (Box 1-1).

First, research is a systematic process to obtain scientific knowledge about specific problems encountered in daily practice.[1] Thus it is an important way of finding answers to clinical irritations. The fundamental goal of research for health and human services is to develop and advance a body of knowledge to guide professional activity. Research contributes to the development of a scientific body of knowledge in several ways. It generates relevant theory and knowledge about human experience and behavior; it develops and tests theories that form the basis of specific practices and treatment approaches; and it validates or determines the effectiveness of different practices.[2]

The second important reason to understand and participate in research is its impact on

---

**Box 1-1** | **Five reasons to learn about the research process**

- To systematically build knowledge and test treatment efficacy
- To impact health policy and service delivery
- To participate in research activities
- To become a critical consumer of research literature
- To enhance understanding of daily practice

health care policy and service delivery. The knowledge obtained through research is often used to inform legislators and regulatory bodies about the best health and human service policies and service delivery models. Federal regulatory agencies and other fiscal intermediaries base many of their decisions and practice guidelines on empirical evidence or knowledge generated through the research process. In managed care facilities, measures are used to assess the outcomes of different treatments for patients. Outcomes data are then used to develop clinical pathways, evaluate cost effectiveness, and refine service delivery. Additionally, facilities are requested to "benchmark" their services to other facilities. This means that facilities must compare their clinical outcomes for different patient populations with other facilities to determine their level of efficiency and effectiveness. For example, let us assume that the average length of stay at your facility for stroke patients is 21 days, and within that time 85% of the patients return home requiring minimal assistance to perform daily activities of living. You may consider this an effective outcome. However, comparing your outcomes with other similar institutions, you learn differently. Other institutions with the same case mix report an average length of stay of 10 days with patients achieving the same level of function as your patients. This information enables you to examine the specific clinical practices of your institution critically in comparison with others. By comparing outcomes data, each institution can evaluate and refine its best practices.

The third reason to learn about research is to enable you to participate in research activities in your own practice setting. Many health and human service settings require practitioners to establish or maintain a database of clinical information and derive statistical reports on patient outcomes. In some settings, you or other members of your agency will be expected to participate in research to advance the research goals of the institution. This will be particularly the case if employed in an academic health science center or teaching hospital. There are many diverse roles you may play as a member of a research project. You may initially want to participate in the process as a data collector, chart extractor, interviewer, provider of an experimental intervention, or recruiter of clients into a study. These are all excellent, time-limited roles to learn firsthand—the art and science of the research process. When you feel more comfortable and gain some experience with the process, you may want to serve as a project coordinator and become responsible for the coordination of the detailed tasks and daily activities of a research endeavor; or you may choose the role of the co-investigator and assist in the conceptual development, design, implementation, and analytical components of a study. If you really become hooked on research, you may want to be a principal investigator and assume responsibility for initiating and overseeing the scientific integrity of the entire research effort.

The fourth reason to learn about and participate in research is to become a critical consumer of the growing body of research literature that is published in professional journals. Understanding research will provide the necessary skills to determine the adequacy of research outcomes and their implications for daily practice.[3] Most importantly, the knowledge you gain about research findings has the potential to improve your clinical practice and, as a result, the quality of life of the people you serve—your patients and their families and communities.

There is one more important reason to learn about the research process. The procedures and methodologies used in research can help improve your daily practice. This text offers a range of methodologies and techniques, such as case study, audiotape or videotape analysis, single-case design, observation, or in-depth interviewing. As a clinician or health care professional, you can use each to gain better insight into a particularly difficult case or to advance your practice. For example, if you are experiencing difficulty effectively interacting with and thus treating a child who has a developmental disability, videotaping a session and systematically analyzing verbal and nonverbal interactions frame by frame may provide important insights to better approach this particular case. In another example, let us assume you have been asked to assess the functional ability of a nursing home resident and improve his or her self-care abilities. You may want to set up a single-subject design to monitor your treatment program and its effectiveness. The outcome of the case will be important to share with staff and administrators. First, take several baseline assessments of the resident's functioning over several days using a standardized functional measure. Second, introduce your strategies to improve self-care. Then, reassess the resident over several days using the same functional assessment. This is a simple and easy approach that allows you to obtain systematic information about your treatment and its outcome. The point is that many aspects of the research process can be borrowed and in-corporated into your daily practice to improve your knowledge about a clinical irritation or to systematize your approach in providing health or human services.

One final note about the importance of participating in research. As health and human service professionals engage in the research process, they contribute to the development of knowledge and theory and help validate practice. Through this research activity, health professionals are participating in the advancement and refinement of the research process itself and its applications to professional issues and service settings. Health and human service professionals who are involved in research today will make significant contributions to the evolution of research methodologies.[4-7]

## What is research?

*Research* is not owned by any one profession or discipline. It is a systematic way of thinking and knowing and has a distinct vocabulary that can be learned and used by anyone.

There are many different definitions of research that can be found in texts. These definitions range from a very broad to a very restrictive understanding of the research endeavor. A very broad definition suggests that research includes any type of investigation that uncovers knowledge. On the other hand, a formal and more restrictive definition of research implies that only one type of strategy, that of a quantitative-orientation, is valid. The standard definition used by many researchers is the restricted definition offered by Kerlinger. He defines scientific research as "systematic, controlled, empirical, and critical investigation of natural phenomena guided by theory and hypotheses about the presumed relations among such phenomena."[8] Whereas a broad definition includes any type of activity as research, a restricted definition, such as Kerlinger's viewpoint, implies that the only legitimate approach to scientific inquiry is hypothesis testing.

In contrast, we define research as multiple, systematic strategies to generate knowledge about human behavior, human experience, and human environments in which the thought and *action processes* of the researcher are clearly specified so that they are logical, understandable, *confirmable*, and useful.

Our definition has three important components (Box 1-2).

First, we state that research is more than one type of investigative strategy; that is, research is not just hypothesis testing, as suggested by Kerlinger, but it reflects a broad range of strategies that is systematically implemented. In contrast to the definition offered by the restrictive view, we recognize the legitimacy and

value of many distinct types of investigative strategies. Second, research is composed of *thinking processes* and specific actions that must be clearly delineated. Third, we characterize thinking and action processes as logical, understandable, confirmable, and useful to meet the criteria of research; that is, in contrast to the broad inclusive definition of research, our approach clearly delineates the boundary between research and other forms of knowing by establishing these important criteria. Let us examine the three major components of our definition in greater detail.

### Research as multiple systematic strategies

The first component of our research definition emphasizes the value of varied systematic strategies to understand the depth and range of research questions asked by health and human service professionals. These multiple research strategies can be categorized as representing either *naturalistic inquiry* or *experimental-type* research. These two broad categories of research strategies are based in distinct philosophical traditions, follow different forms of human reasoning, and define and obtain knowledge differently. Naturalistic inquiry refers to a wide range of research approaches that is characterized by its focus on understanding and interpreting human experience within which the natural context occurs. Experimental-type research refers to a range of designs that is characterized by its focus on prediction and hypothesis testing. In Chapter 3, we examine the differences between these research traditions and their philosophical roots and their

 **What is research?**

*Multiple systematic strategies*
- Experimental-type
- Naturalistic inquiry

*Thought and action processes*
- Inductive
- Abductive
- Deductive

*Four criteria*
- Logical
- Understandable
- Confirmable
- Useful

implications for health and human service research.

Our viewpoint, however, reflects a new school of thought that has been expressed in numerous professional and academic disciplines. This school of thought proposes that both naturalistic inquiry and experimental-type research strategies are equal in importance to establishing a scientific base of health and human service practice and adequately examining the diversity of human experiences and behaviors. This viewpoint also firmly asserts that it is not reasonable to critique naturalistic research using experimental language because each approach represents a distinct epistemology or way of knowing and obtaining knowledge.[9,10,11] As Gareth Morgan eloquently claims:

It is not possible to judge the validity or contribution of different research perspectives in terms of the ground assumptions of any one set of perspectives, since the process is self-justifying. Hence the attempts in much social science debate to judge the utility of different research strategies in terms of universal criteria based on the importance of generalizability, predictability and control, explanation of variance, meaningful understanding, or whatever are *inevitably flawed: These criteria inevitably favor research strategies consistent with the assumptions that generate such criteria as meaningful guidelines for the evaluation of research....*Different research perspectives make different kinds of knowledge claims, and the criteria as to what counts as significant knowledge vary from one to another.[10]

## Research as thought and action processes

The second important component of our definition of research refers to thought and action processes. Thought and action processes represent the different ways of reasoning and the specific series of actions that distinguish naturalistic and experimental-type investigators in the conduct of their research. Experimental-type research uses primarily a deductive form of human reasoning. Naturalistic inquiry primarily uses inductive and abductive forms of reasoning. Each leads to a different type of research action and generates different information or knowledge. The major characteristics of these approaches to reasoning are summarized in Table 1-1.

*Deductive reasoning and actions.* Experimental-type researchers use primarily *deductive reasoning.* This type of reasoning involves moving from a general principle to understanding a specific case. Based on a theory and its propositions, hypotheses are derived and then formally tested. Health and human service professionals use this type of reasoning everyday in practice. For example, let us assume a physician refers a particular case to you. You receive the patient's chart, and it contains basic information. The patient, who has a diagnosis of possible dementia, is 75 years of age and is a widowed woman who lives alone. From this general information and your knowledge about dementia, you begin to conjecture about this patient's future needs and whether she can return home alone. You may hypothesize that the patient will need assistance in performing daily activities of living, and you may hypothesize that she will be unsafe alone at home. When you meet the patient, you apply this

| Table 1-1 | Major characteristics inductive/abductive and deductive thinking | |
|---|---|---|
| *Inductive/abductive* | *Deductive* |
| • No *a priori* acceptance of truth exists | • *A priori* acceptance of truth exists |
| • Alternative conclusions can be drawn from data | • One set of conclusions is accepted as true |
| • Theory is developed | • Theory is tested |
| • Relationships are examined among unrelated pieces of data | • Relationships are tested among discrete phenomena |
| • Concepts are developed based on repetition of patterns | • Concepts are tested based on application to discrete phenomena |
| • Perspective is holistic | • Perspective is atomistic |
| • Multiple realities exist | • Single separate reality exists |

general knowledge to understand this specific case. You begin to test your hypothesis that the person is unable to return home alone. You may use a functional assessment tool to determine the level of personal assistance that is required by the patient. You may evaluate her ability to make judgments as a basis from which to determine home safety risks.

A similar process occurs in research. Using a deductive type of reasoning, the researcher begins with the acceptance of a general principle or belief based on a particular theoretical framework. This principle is then applied or used to explain a specific case or phenomenon. This approach involves "drawing out" or verifying what already is accepted as true.[12] For example, a researcher is interested in testing an intervention to improve the health of caregivers of dementia patients. In this case the researcher may begin from a framework of stress theory that assumes that the characteristics or behaviors of the care recipient are objective stressors that negatively impact the health of caregivers. Accepting this principle as truth, the deductive researcher will be interested in testing the effec-

tiveness of interventions that are designed to reduce objective burden, through providing education or teaching behavioral skills management.

***Inductive reasoning and actions.*** Researchers who work within a naturalistic framework use primarily *inductive reasoning*. This type of reasoning involves moving from a specific case to a broader generalization about the phenomenon under study. In some forms of naturalistic inquiry, inductive reasoning involves fitting data, such as a set of observations or propositions of an existing theory. Health and human service professionals also use this form of reasoning in everyday practice. For example, let us assume you need to determine the discharge plans for the dementia patient as in the previous example. You have concerns about the ability of the person to live alone, based on your knowledge of dementia as a progressively deteriorating condition. However, you do not know anything about the circumstances of this particular patient, her personal goals and those of her family, or her specific living arrangements. Through observation of the patient in the clinic, as well as in-depth interviewing of the patient and family members, you discover that an adequate plan for monitoring and caring for the patient has been put into place. Thus you make a discharge decision based on the specifics of this case and the information you uncovered inductively.

A similar reasoning process occurs in research. Using inductive reasoning, the researcher searches for general rules or patterns by linking specific observations. There is no "truth" or general principle that is accepted *a priori* or before the study begins. Consider the example of caregiving previously given. To derive an understanding of the nature and scope of stress, one type of inductive research approach will involve examining the daily life experiences of caregivers and their own perceptions of their activities. Using a variety of data collection techniques, such as observation and in-depth interviewing, the researcher will reason inductively by searching for patterns across observations of different caregivers. From this approach the researcher will develop an understanding of the specific situations that cause stress, as well as the types of intervention that will be most useful in promoting caregiver health. The researcher, proceeding inductively, will seek to reveal or uncover a truth based on the perceptions of caregivers. Intervention principles, then, will be developed based on the researcher's interpretations of the perceptions of caregivers.

***Abductive reasoning and actions.*** As we illustrate here, the two research traditions are typically characterized as using deductive and inductive reasoning processes; experimental-type research

uses the former and naturalistic inquiry uses the latter. However, as Agar, an ethnographer, points out in *The Professional Stranger* (1996), this representation is not completely accurate. Some approaches in naturalistic inquiry are best characterized as "abductive."[13] Abduction is a term first introduced by Charles Peirce,[14] and is currently used by Agar and other ethnographers to refer to the iterative process of naturalistic inquiry. This process involves the development of new theoretical propositions that account for a set of observations, which cannot be accounted for or explained by an old proposition or theoretical framework. The new theoretical proposition becomes validated and modified as part of the research process. In this way, ethnography and some other forms of naturalistic inquiry, such as grounded theory, are considered to be theory generating. In deductive reasoning, the data are controlled by the hypotheses. In inductive reasoning, an attempt is made to fit the data to a theoretical framework or to a set of identified and well-defined concepts. In *abductive reasoning*, the data are analyzed for their own patterns and concepts, which in some cases may relate to available theories and in other cases may not.

***Differences in knowledge.*** Each type of reasoning will result in the generation or production of a different form of knowledge. An inductive or abductive reasoning approach in research is used to "uncover" or "reveal" theory, rules, and processes. A deductive reasoning approach is used to test or predict the application of theory and rules to a specific phenomenon. Both approaches can be used to describe, explain, and predict phenomena, although traditionally only deductive reasoning has been valued as contributing to explanation and cause-and-effect relationships.

Let us examine the kind of knowledge that is generated by each reasoning approach. The researcher working deductively will assume a truth before engaging in the research process and will apply that truth to the investigation. In the caregiver example, the researcher will assume that all caregivers will experience a form of stress and therefore will benefit from a stress-reduction intervention. The stress-reduction intervention may take the form of group psycho-educational counseling sessions and will be based on existing stress theory. Actual research that has tested this intervention approach has found it to be only mildly effective in reducing caregiver stress and only for some caregiver study participants.[15,16] Thus the question remains as to why all caregivers do not benefit at the level at which researchers expect.

In a study proceeding inductively or abductively, an intervention approach will emerge from that which is learned from those who will receive the intervention. Caregiver research that uses an inductive process will find that caregivers express different levels of stress and identify issues and difficulties about their experience that cannot be explained by stress theory or addressed by stress-oriented interventions alone.[17] Interventions that may be developed as a consequence of these insights may include a much broader array of services based on the specific needs and care issues identified by the study participants.[16]

The deductive approach will show that a stress-reduction intervention may benefit some caregivers. The inductive approach will show that stress theory is too limited to understand the multiple needs of this group and that other types of interventions are required.

As you can see, each type of reasoning and research approach produces important information from which to advance services to caregivers. It is also possible to use both types of reasoning to answer a research problem. For example, you can use an inductive or abductive approach to identify specific areas of caregiver needs and then use a deductive strategy to systematically test an intervention that addresses the identified needs. This inductive-abductive-deductive approach is currently being used to develop and test community-based health programs for underserved and culturally diverse populations. First, investigators use qualitative strategies to uncover the health beliefs and needs of the target group. Based on the findings and theoretical frameworks that are refined, health care strategies are developed, implemented, and evaluated.

Certainly, the integration of different forms of reasoning makes intuitive sense. In our daily lives, we naturally engage in all forms of reasoning. Likewise, health and human service professionals combine knowledge gained from both deductive and inductive reasoning to derive appropriate treatment plans.

## Research as four basic characteristics

The third important component of our research definition refers to the criteria we use to characterize the research activity and differentiate it from other ways of knowing about a phenomenon. We have stated that scientific knowledge may be generated by multiple research strategies using inductive or abductive and deductive reasoning. Any research strategy, whether it is based on inductive or abductive or deductive reasoning, must conform to the four criteria of being logical, understandable, confirmable, and useful. Let us examine the meaning and significance of each criterion.

**Logical.** In research there is a unique way of thinking and acting that distinguishes it from other ways in which we come to know, understand, and make sense of our experiences. Charles Peirce,[14] one of the founders of the scientific research process, identified other ways of "knowing" as the following: (1) authority—being told by a respected or trusted source; (2) hearsay—secondhand information that is not verified; (3) trial and error—knowledge gained through incremental doing, evaluating, and modifying actions to achieve a desired outcome; (4) history—knowing indirectly through collective past experiences; (5) belief—knowing without verification; (6) spiritual understanding—knowing through divine belief; and (7) intuition—explanations of human experience based on previous unique and personal organization of one's own experience.

In these forms, knowledge is gained haphazardly, and it is not necessary to clarify the logical thinking and action processes by which the information is obtained. Think about how an individual gains knowledge about parenting or providing care to a person with a disability. Caregivers tend to learn how to provide care through trial and error. Information as to what works and what does not work is gained incrementally, over time, by trying different techniques and informally evaluating their effectiveness. Caregivers

also use intuition and hearsay or information from other caregivers, family, and friends who may make suggestions based on their own history and experience. Research, however, must be based on systematic thought processes and methodical investigative activities that include documentation, analysis, and drawing conclusions.

By *logical*, we mean that the thought and action processes of a research study are clear, rational, and conform to accepted norms of deductive or inductive reasoning. Logic is a science that involves defined ways of thinking and methodically relates ideas to develop an understanding of phenomena and their relationships. The systematic nature of research requires that the investigator proceed logically and articulate each thought and action throughout the research process.

**Understandable.** It is not sufficient for a researcher to articulate a *logical process*. This process, the study outcomes, and its conclusions need to be explicit, make sense, be precise, be intelligible, and be credible to the reader or research consumer. If you cannot *understand* the research process, then it cannot be used, confirmed, or replicated.

Historically, researchers using naturalistic inquiry did not typically identify the specific steps involved in their investigative process. Today, however, there is a growing body of literature that describes and makes explicit the thinking and action processes of different forms of naturalistic inquiry.[18,19,20,21,22] Investigators who work out of the naturalistic tradition are advancing the standards of quality by which to judge such research. How are we to distinguish, for example, a casual observation of emergency room behavior from a scholarly interpretation of underlying patterns in that setting? Currently, researchers are actively addressing this critical issue.[9,10,11,23,24]

***Confirmable.*** By *confirmable,* we mean that the researcher clearly and logically identifies the strategies used in the study so that others can reasonably follow the path of analysis and arrive at similar outcomes and conclusions. The claims made by the researcher should be supported by the research strategy and be accurate and credible within the stated boundaries of the study.

***Useful.*** Research generates, verifies, or tests theory and knowledge for use. In other words, the knowledge derived from a study should inform and potentially improve professional practice and client outcome. Each researcher, consumer, or professional judges the utility of a study based on his or her own needs and purposes. *Useful*ness is a subjective criterion in that it is based on the researcher's judgment about the value of the knowledge produced by a study. However, the value of a study and the usefulness of knowledge become more widely accepted as the new knowledge increasingly stimulates further research and promotes the testing or verification of new or existing theory and practice.

### Summary

In this chapter, we introduced the basic elements of our definition of research that guides our subsequent discussions. Our definition of research represents our conceptual framework. It is based on a philosophical position that the multiple realities that shape health and human services require an approach to research that is informed by multiple research traditions and design strategies. Our approach to research is practical; that is, the purpose and question of an investigator guides the selection of appropriate methodologies, and, in turn, the questions asked and the knowledge gained must be useful to the clinical, professional, and consumer communities.

Research is important to health and human service professionals. It informs knowledge development and daily practice, and there are many different ways in which professionals can participate in this activity.

### Exercises

1. Select a research article in your professional journal. Identify the source from which the investigator obtained the research question. Determine whether the study fits the four characteristics of research as being logical, confirmable, understandable, and useful.

2. Write down three issues that represent a concern to your profession or that have emerged from your daily practice. Determine whether each issue reflects a topic that can be researched. How do you currently address these issues?

## References

1. Yerxa E: Seeing a relevant, ethical and realistic way to knowing for occupational therapy, *Am J Occup Ther* 45:199, 1991.
2. Payton OD: *Research: the validation of clinical practice,* ed 2, Philadelphia, 1988, FA Davis.
3. Ottenbacher KJ: *Evaluating clinical change: strategies for occupational and physical therapists,* Baltimore, 1986, Williams & Wilkins.
4. Burns N, Grove S: *The practice of nursing research: conduct, critique and utilization,* Philadelphia, 1987, WB Saunders.
5. Whyte WF: *Participatory action research,* Newbury Park, Calif, 1991, Sage.
6. Parse RR, Coyne AB, Smith MJ: Nursing research traditions: quantitative and qualitative approaches. In *Nursing research: qualitative methods,* Bowie, MD, 1985, Brady Communications.
7. Morse J: *Qualitative nursing research,* Rockville, MD, 1989, Aspen.
8. Kerlinger FN: *Foundations of behavioral research,* ed 2, New York, 1973, Holt, Rinehart, & Winston.
9. Guba EG: Criteria for assessing the trustworthiness of naturalistic inquiries, *Educ Commun Technol J* 29:75-91, 1981.
10. Patton M: *Qualitative evaluation and research methods,* ed 2, Newbury Park, Calif, 1990, Sage.
11. Salomon G: Transcending the qualitative-quantitative debate: the analytic and systematic approaches to educational research, *Educ Researcher* 20:10-18, 1991.
12. Hoover KR: *The elements of social scientific thinking,* ed 2, New York, 1980, St Martin's Press.
13. Agar MH: *The professional stranger,* ed 2, San Diego, 1996, Academic Press.
14. Peirce CS: *Essays in the philosophy of science,* Indianapolis, 1957, Bobbs-Merrill.
15. Zarit SH: Do we need another caregiver study? *The Gerontologist* 29:47, 1989.
16. Corcoran MA, Gitlin LN: Environmental influences on behavior of the elderly with dementia: principles for home intervention, *Occup Ther Geriatr* 4:5-22, 1991.
17. Hasselkus B: Meaning in family caregiving: perspectives on caregiver/professional relationships, *The Gerontologist* 28:686, 1988.
18. Spradley JP: *Participant observation,* New York, 1980, Holt, Rinehart, & Winston.
19. Geertz C: *The interpretation of cultures,* New York, 1973, Basic Books.
20. Glaser BG, Strauss AL: *The discovery of grounded theory: strategies for qualitative research,* New York, 1967, Aldine.
21. Lincoln YS, Guba EG: But is it rigorous? Trustworthiness and authenticity in naturalistic evaluation. In Williams DD, editor: *Naturalistic evaluation,* San Francisco, 1986, Jossey-Bass.
22. Denzin NK, Lincoln YS, (editors): *Handbook of qualitative research,* Thousand Oaks, Calif, 1994, Sage.
23. Smith JK: Quantitative vs. qualitative research: an attempt to clarify the issue, *Educ Researcher* 112:6-13, 1983.
24. Miles MB, Huberman AM: *Qualitative data analysis,* ed 2, Newbury Park, Calif, 1994, Sage.

# Essentials of research

**Key terms**   Ethics
Ten essentials

Researchers who pursue either naturalistic or experimental-type inquiry confront similar challenges and requirements when conducting research. However, these challenges and requirements are interpreted and acted on differently, depending on the type of inquiry pursued. We categorize the challenges and requirements of any type of research endeavor into what we call the *10 essentials* of the research process (Box 2-1). The focus of each subsequent chapter in this book describes one particular research essential and examines its components from the perspectives of both naturalistic inquiry and experimental-type research. Consider this chapter as a brief summary of the entire text. You may want to read this chapter quickly and then refer to it as you make your way through the text as a way of summarizing the meaning of each essential. You can refer to Table 2-1 as a quick guide as well.

## Ten essentials of research

The 10 research essentials and their order of presentation in this book should not be construed as representing a step-by-step, procedural, or type of recipe approach to the research process. Each essential is highly interrelated and may not necessarily occur in the order in which it is presented in Box 2-1 and in this text.

Experimental-type research is hierarchical in its sequence and approach. It tends to follow the 10 essentials in an ordered and highly structured manner in which each essential purposely builds on the other in a linear, step-wise fashion. Figure 2-1 depicts this linear approach.

However, even in this type of research, the 10 essentials are not mutually exclusive. Naturalistic inquiry, on the other hand, embodies the 10 essentials using an iterative process, whereby each essential is related to the other and revisited at different points throughout the research process. This spiral approach (Figure 2-2) links the 10 essentials in different orders, depending on the specific philosophical foundation in

**Figure 2-1** Linear approach.

| Box 2-1 | Ten essentials of research |
| --- | --- |

- Identify philosophical foundation
- Frame a research problem
- Determine supporting knowledge
- Identify theory base
- Develop specific question or query
- Select a design strategy
- Set study boundaries
- Obtain information
- Analyze information and draw conclusions
- Report and disseminate conclusions

Ethical considerations

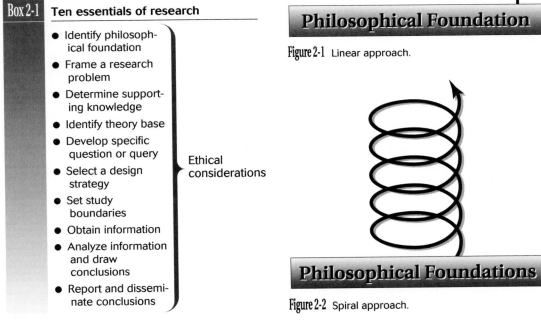

**Figure 2-2** Spiral approach.

which the research is based. The sequences of the 10 essentials within each research tradition in naturalistic inquiry will become clear as you make your way through this book. Let us briefly examine the meaning of each essential.

## Identify a philosophical foundation

Identifying a philosophical foundation is an important essential that must occur first or in the early stages of the research process. By philosophical foundation, we mean an individual's particular orientation to how one learns about human behavior, health and personal abilities and experiences, or other phenomena of importance in health and human service. In Chapter 3 you learn that there are essentially two different ways of viewing the building of knowledge. The researcher's particular orientation toward learning about phenomena determines the specific research tradition that is selected—experimental-type, naturalistic inquiry, or an integration of the two.

In naturalistic inquiry, articulating a philosophical tradition is very important because of the many distinct philosophical tradi-

**Table 2-1** Ten essentials of research

| Essential | Explanation | Process |
|---|---|---|
| Identify philosophical foundation | Reveal underlying assumptions of ontology and epistemology | Thinking |
| Frame a research problem | Identify broad topic or problem area | Thinking |
| Determine supporting knowledge | Review and synthesize existing literature to examine knowledge development in identified problem area | Thinking |
| Identify a theory base | Use existing theory to frame research problem and interpret result; or construct theory as part of research process | Thinking |
| Develop a specific question or query | Identify specific focus for research, based on knowledge development, theoretical perspective and research purpose | Thinking |
| Select a design strategy | Develop standard procedures or broad strategic approach to answer research question or query | Thinking |
| Set study boundaries | Establish scope of study and methods for accessing research participants | Action |
| Obtain information | Determine strategies for collecting information that is numeric, visual, auditory, or narrative | Action |
| Analyze information and draw conclusions | Employ systematic processes to examine different types of data and derive interpretative scheme | Action |
| Report and disseminate conclusions | Write and disseminate research conclusions | Action |

tions that inform this research approach (see Chapter 3). For example, researchers who identify their philosophical perspective as symbolic interaction tend to use highly interpretative forms of naturalistic inquiry that focus on the meanings and behaviors of individuals in social interaction. These researchers tend to pursue ethnographic research methodology. On the other hand, researchers who identify with the philosophical foundation of phenomenology will focus on particular personal experiences of individuals (i.e., what it is like to have acquired immunodeficiency syndrome [AIDS], service experiences of ethnic minorities) or on how each gender perceives sense of self. These researchers tend to pursue methodologies that elicit the telling of a person's personal story. In writing a proposal to conduct a research study or in writing a report of the completed study, the researcher using naturalistic inquiry usually discusses his or her philosophical perspective.

In contrast, experimental-type research is based on one unifying philosophical foundation—logical positivism. Positivism is a broad term that refers to the belief that there is one truth that is independent of the investigator and that this truth can be discovered by following strict procedures. Positivism is described in greater detail in Chapter 3. It is not necessary for an experimental-type researcher to identify the philosophical root of his or her research when submitting a research proposal or a published report, because all experimental-type inquiry is based on a single philosophical base. For example, a researcher trained in survey techniques will quite naturally assume a positivist or empiricist approach to describe a particular phenomenon. It is not necessary for this researcher

to state formally the epistemological assumption embedded in his or her study.

A philosophical foundation provides the backdrop from which specific methodologic decisions in research are made. This does not mean that you have to first become a philosopher to participate in research. It does mean, however, that you need to know that research methodologies reflect different assumptions about human behavior and knowledge and about how we learn about phenomena. By selecting a particular research strategy you will automatically adopt a particular world view and philosophical foundation. We believe that, at the very least, you should be aware that you are adopting a specific set of assumptions about human behavior and how people come to understand it. Understanding this philosophical foundation is particularly critical since assumptions about knowledge and their use have major implications for how health and human service professionals serve different ethnic, gender, ability groups. Consider the example of a social worker who is hired to design and examine a pregnancy prevention program for Asian-American teenagers. Using a logical positive approach, existing and validated programs will be implemented and tested to ascertain the efficacy in pregnancy prevention. However, a naturalistic researcher may want to begin by finding out about the cultural norms before selecting or developing an intervention. Each approach has its advantages and limitations.

You probably have a particular philosophical foundation or preferred way of knowing without fully labeling or recognizing it as such. Sometimes personality, or how one naturally approaches the world, influences the particular research direction that is adopted. If you are not very flexible or feel uncomfortable examining your own biases and personal values or just "hanging out" in someone else's world, then you may have difficulty with naturalistic inquiry. There are a number of interesting articles written about the personality types of individuals who pursue ethnography versus those who pursue experimental-type research. However, there is nothing definitive about this literature. Certainly, all types of personalities are capable of learning the practices of multiple research paradigms.

### Frame a research problem

To engage in the research process the investigator must identify, up front, a particular problem area or broad issue that necessitates systematic investigation. Research is a focused endeavor that answers a social issue, practice question, or personal concern. One of the first thinking processes in which you engage is to identify the problem area and the specific purpose for your research. Research topics should come from personal, professional, theoretical, political, or societal concerns. To engage in research, it is important that you identify an area that holds personal interest to you. The research process is challenging and requires time and commitment. You will quickly lose momentum and interest if you do not pursue a topic of personal intrigue. Some researchers study areas that have been problematic in their own lives. For example, some researchers who pursue disability studies have had a personal encounter with disability, such as growing up with a disabled sibling or parent. Research in an area that has personal sig-

nificance provides a scholarly forum from which to examine and then personally understand the issues. Obviously, this is not to say that you have to be an individual with a disability to want to study disability or need to have experienced child abuse to study that phenomenon. However, something about a topic should "grab" you. It has to have personal meaning or some level of importance to your life—intellectually, emotionally, or professionally—for the research endeavor to be personally worthwhile.

Once you have identified a topic (e.g., coping strategies of African-American caregivers of dementia patients; impact of maternal alcohol abuse on early childhood development), you can begin to think about your particular purpose in exploring the topic. What do you want to know about the topic? What will be the purpose of your particular research? To determine the direction and purpose of a study, the researcher must read what is already known about the topic.

### Determine supporting knowledge

Another research essential involves a critical review of existing research studies that concern your topic or area of inquiry. Let us assume, based on your practice with hospitalized African-American patients with spinal cord injuries, that you want to know more about their self-care practices once they return home. This information will help determine the types of skills training to introduce in the hospital and how best to prepare your patients for the challenges they will confront at home. You believe this area of concern is important to investigate. Your first task will be to determine what is known in the published literature. If there is little or no knowledge about the topic, you will need to design a study that describes self-care practices. If there is some descriptive knowledge of daily practices but little information about whether these practices differ for men and women, you may want to conduct a study that investigates this aspect of the topic. If there is a body of well-constructed knowledge about gender and ethnic differences, you may want to examine the impact of self-care practices on the general well-being of the patients and on the coping mechanisms of diverse groups. Existing literature should be used to help guide the next directions that need to occur in research to build knowledge in your area of interest. A critical review of the literature initially helps the investigator frame a specific research direction so that the study will systematically contribute to the building of knowledge in the topic or area of concern.

A critical review of the literature is also used for other purposes throughout the research process. In some forms of naturalistic inquiry, for example, literature review is used as an additional set of data. Literature review can also be used to help the investigator further explore his or her emerging interpretations of observations. All researchers must draw on previously existing studies when recording their own findings. Your findings will be interpreted within the context of existing studies.

## Identify a theory base

Theory is formally defined as a set of interrelated propositions that provide a framework for understanding or explaining phenomena. (Theory and its relationship with research are described in greater detail in Chapter 6.) The purpose of research is to either construct theory or test theory. Research that does not contribute to the building of theory or is not based on theory produces findings that are basically useless. Findings from a study that are not based in or related to a theoretical context cannot be adequately interpreted or understood. Atheoretical research does not contribute to the systematic building of knowledge. Experimental-type researchers tend to test different aspects of a theory; that is, the research begins with a theoretical framework from which specific hypotheses (hunches about what should occur) are generated and tested using different design strategies. Even in a descriptive or correlational study that is not designed to test a specific theory, theory is essential in guiding the research process and interpreting study results.

Naturalistic inquiry either generates new theories, expands existing theories, or relates research findings to existing theoretical frameworks. In actual research practice, theory is used by both research traditions for multiple purposes and in many different ways. Thus the use of theory is interjected at different points of the research process, especially in naturalistic inquiry.

## Develop a specific question or query

Once a problem area has been identified, the researcher must specify a particular research direction. This direction will take the form of a highly specified question in experimental-type research that details the exact factors and the characteristics or phenomena that will be examined. For example, the experimental-type researcher may pose the question, "What is the relationship between self-care practice and the psychologic well-being in African-American men with spinal cord injury?" With this question, the researcher identifies two concepts that will be studied: self-care practices and psychological well-being. The researcher will then carefully define each term and determine how each will be measured. A study design is selected that will enable an analysis of the relationship between these two concepts.

In naturalistic inquiry, the research direction will be broadly represented and becomes highly specified only through the process of conducting the study itself. In this type of research, the investigator will develop a broad working question, or what we call a "query," that will initially identify the who, what, and where of the boundaries of the study, but nothing further. For example, the naturalistic-type researcher may pose the question, "What are the experiences of African-American men with spinal cord injuries in performing basic self-care activities upon return home?" With this question, the researcher has identified *who* will be studied (African-American men with spinal cord injuries), *where* the study will occur (at home), and *what* the focus of the query will be (how self-care is accomplished). Other concerns may emerge in the course of the study that may lead the researcher to redefine the initial query or consider more specific questions, such as the relationship between specific self-care practices and personal well-being. However, the decision to examine such a relationship occurs in the field based on an initial analysis of the situation that leads the researcher to the conclusion that it is important to examine these aspects. Thus in

naturalistic inquiry, you should frame the research question broadly so that you can develop research approaches to questions that arise in the course of learning about a group. The questions that emerge in the field cannot be anticipated before entering the research setting.

In any type of research approach, however, a broad topic or area of concern must be framed or specified in such a way as to facilitate its exploration. For example, within the broad topic of aging with a disability, there are many subtopics and specific research questions or queries that can be formulated. The level of knowledge development and theoretical understanding of the topic will direct the researcher to the specific research question or query that represents the next logical step to build knowledge in the area.

## Select a design strategy

Design is perhaps the most fundamental aspect of the research process. Based on one's philosophical position, research purpose, theory, and specific research question or query, the researcher will select a method by which to explore or answer the query. In naturalistic inquiry, research design is fluid and evolves as the investigator gains access to a natural setting and explores the phenomenon of interest. Further, terms that refer to designs can represent both the process and the end product. For example, ethnography is a term that refers to the process of performing field work to understand the cultural patterns of a specified group. Ethnography also refers to the end product—the published report or book about the particular cultural group. Design in naturalistic inquiry means a set of strategies that are employed by the investigator to gain access to a natural setting (e.g., the homes of African-American men with spinal cord injuries), and to collect and analyze information using a combination of procedures that unfold in the course of conducting the study (e.g., videotape, participant observation, interviewing).

In experimental-type research, design is highly structured with a specified set of procedures that are implemented uniformly and systematically by the investigator. In this tradition a design is similar to a "blueprint" that details each procedure or action. Methodologic decisions and all procedures are detailed before beginning the study or entering the field. For example, let us assume an investigator plans to conduct a survey of high school students to determine their level of knowledge about safe sexual practices. Before conducting the study, the investigator will develop a sampling plan (how subjects will be recruited and selected), will frame a set of questions with a fixed response set, and will identify specific statistical analyses that will be conducted. All of this will be decided before the study begins.

It is impossible to discuss the vast array of research design strategies in each of the research traditions in one text. We present the most fundamental and useful approaches for health and human service professionals.

## Set study boundaries

A researcher must establish boundaries or the scope of a study. Boundaries are set for a number of reasons, the most important of which is to limit the scope of the study so it is doable. Ways of setting boundaries include determining the length of study, who will be in the study, the conceptual dimensions that will be examined, or the type and number of questions that will be asked. Setting boundary strategies is different for experimental-type and naturalistic inquiry studies. In experimental-type designs, the boundaries of the study are clearly and precisely defined before entering the field. The researcher establishes a concise plan for identifying and enrolling subjects into the study, determines which questionnaires or data collection strategies to use, and identifies up front the specific conceptual dimensions that will be included. In naturalistic-type studies, the setting of boundaries is an evolving process that occurs once the investigator enters the research setting. After gaining access to the research setting, the investigator continually makes decisions as to who is interviewed, how and what data are collected, and what conceptual issues are explored.

## Obtain information

A researcher can choose from a wide variety of techniques for obtaining information or data. Later in this text, we examine these techniques along a continuum, from unstructured looking and listening techniques to structured, fixed choice observation and ways of asking questions.

## Analyze information and draw conclusions

Analyzing information, the ninth essential of the research process, involves a series of planned activities that differ depending on the specific research tradition in which one works. One of the initial analytical tasks of experimental-type researchers is to reduce numerical data into meaningful and manageable indicators, such as means, mode, and median. Other statistical techniques are then employed depending on the characteristics of the measures, the size of the sample, and the specific research question. In naturalistic inquiry, other approaches are employed that are appropriate for the analysis of narrative and other nonnumeric types of datum. The purpose of analysis is to systematically apply techniques that can lead to an interpretation of the information that has been obtained.

### Report and disseminate conclusions

Reporting and using research are necessary tasks that complete the research process. Reporting conclusions involves writing a report and disseminating the knowledge gained from the research. Each research tradition approaches this research essential somewhat differently. However, researchers usually describe the purpose of their study, how it contributes to a particular field or topic, the specific procedures that were followed by the researcher including analytical strategies, and the findings and interpretations of the information that was obtained.

### Ethical considerations

We have identified 10 essentials or characteristics of any type of research study. Researchers must address each essential at different points in the research process. The application of these essentials in health and human service settings raises special issues and ethical dilemmas. Ethical concerns focus on the rights of the human subject to full knowledge of the purpose of the study and the nature of his or her involvement, the specific behaviors or conduct of the investigator, and the ethics of the question and design procedures. These issues are explored throughout this book.

### Summary

As we have discussed, all research, regardless of the topic, approach, and use, consists of 10 essentials. In experimental-type research, these essentials are ordered, linear, and performed in a stepwise fashion. In naturalistic inquiry, the essentials are carried out in different sequences, depending on the particular research tradition and the design that is being used. Figure 2-3 is used throughout this text to signify the tradition and essential that we are discussing. As you proceed through the world of research with us, you will note that the graphic is also meant to

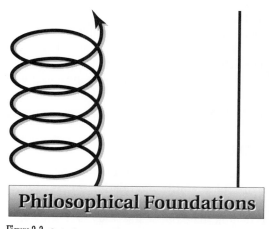

Figure 2-3 Spiral approach and linear approach.

suggest that experimental-type and naturalistic research can be used in tandem or integrated. Research integrating experimental-type and naturalistic traditions can occur in any of the thinking or action processes that comprise the 10 essentials as discussed throughout the book.

## Exercises

1. Select two research articles, and identify the ten essentials in each.

2. Using both articles, compare and contrast how the essentials are sequenced and described by the investigators.

# PART II *Thinking processes*

In Part I of this text, we introduce the definition, purposes, and essentials of research.

We now delve into Part II, the thinking processes in which all researchers engage to make sound decisions about how to frame, conduct, and use research. These efforts include understanding the philosophical foundations that underpin diverse research traditions, framing the research problem, critically reviewing the literature, linking theory and research, developing a research question or query, and using the appropriate research language to understand and explicate the research process, findings, and interpretations.

# Chapter 3

# Philosophical foundations

**Key terms**  Epistemology
Holistic
Integrated design
Interactionists
Logical positivism
Multimethod
Ontology
Phenomenologists
Pluralism

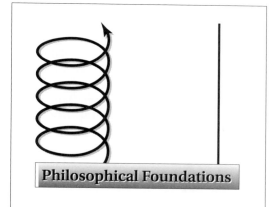

Philosophical Foundations

Although you do not have to be a philosopher to engage in the research process, it is important to understand the philosophical foundations and assumptions about human experience and knowledge on which experimental-type and naturalistic research traditions are based.  By being aware of these assumptions, you will be more skillful in directing the research process and in selecting specific methods to use and combine. Also, an understanding of these philosophical foundations will help you recognize that "knowledge" is determined by the way you frame a research problem and the strategies that are used to obtain, analyze, and interpret information.

The questions, "What is reality?" *(ontology)* and "How do we come to know it?" *(epistemology)* have been posed by philosophers and scholars from many academic and professional disciplines throughout history. As we have suggested, in western cultures there are two primary but often competing views of reality and how to obtain knowledge. These two perspectives reflect the basic differences between naturalistic inquiry and experimental-type research. *Logical positivism* is the foundation for deductive, predicting designs we refer to as experimental-type research. On the other hand, a number of holistic and humanistic philosophical perspectives use inductive reasoning and are referred to as naturalistic inquiry. Let us examine these philosophical traditions.

## Philosophical foundation of experimental-type research

Experimental-type researchers share a common frame of reference or epistemology that has been called rationalistic, positivist, or logical positivism. Although there are theoretical differences between these terms, we use the term logical positivism to name the overall perspective on which deductive research design is based.

David Hume, an 18th century philosopher,[1] was most influential in developing this traditional theory of science. This viewpoint posits that there is a separation between individual thoughts and what is real in the universe outside ourselves; that is, traditional theorists of science define knowledge as part of a reality that is separate and independent from individuals and that is verifiable through the scientific method. These theorists believe the world is objectively knowable and can be discovered through observation and measurement that is considered unbiased. This epistemologic view is based on the fundamental assumption that it is possible to know and understand phenomena that reside outside ourselves, separate from the realm of our subjective ideas. Only through observation and sense data, defined as information obtained through our senses, can we come to know truth and reality.

Philosophers in subsequent centuries further developed, modified, and clarified Hume's basic notion of empiricism to yield what today is known as logical positivism. Essentially, logical positivists believe that there is a single reality that can be discovered by reducing it into its parts, a concept known as reductionism. The relationship among these parts and the logical, structural principles that guide them can also be discovered and known through the systematic collection and analysis of sense data, finally leading to the ability to predict phenomena from that which is already known. Bertrand Russell, a 20th century mathematician and philosopher, was instrumental in promoting the synthesis of mathematical logic with sense data.[2] Statisticians, such as Fischer and Pearson, developed theories to logically and objectively reveal "fact" through mathematical analysis. The logical positive school of thought therefore provided the foundation for what most laypersons have come to know as experimental research. In this approach a theory or set of principles is held as true. Specific areas of inquiry are isolated within that theoretical perspective and clearly defined hypotheses (expected outcomes of an inquiry that investigate only those phenomena) are posed and tested under carefully controlled conditions. Sense data are then collected and mathematically analyzed to support or refute hypotheses. Through incremental deductive reasoning, which involves theory verification and testing, "reality" can become predictable.

Another major tenet of logical positivism is that objective inquiry and analysis are possible; that is, the investigator, through the use of accepted and standard research techniques, can eliminate bias and achieve results through objective, quantitative measurement.[3,4,5,6]

## Philosophical foundation of naturalistic inquiry

Another school of theorists has argued the opposite position—individuals create their own subjective realities and thus the knower and knowledge are interrelated and interdependent.[7,8,9] This group of theorists believes ideas are the lenses through which each individual knows the universe, and they believe that it is through these ideas that we come to understand and define the world. This epistemologic viewpoint is based on the fundamental assumption that it is not possible to separate the outside world from an individual's ideas and perceptions of that world. Knowledge is based on how the individual perceives experiences and how he or she understands his or her world. A number

of research strategies share this basic holistic, epistemologic view, although each is rooted in a different philosophical tradition.

Although research based on *holistic* perspectives is relatively new, these perspectives are not. Ancient Greek philosophers struggled with the separation of idea and object, and philosophers throughout history continue this debate.[10] The essential characteristics of what we refer to as holistic philosophies are as follows:

1. Human experience is complex and cannot be understood by reductionism, that is, only by identifying and examining its parts.
2. Meaning in human experience is derived from an understanding of individuals in their social environments.
3. Multiple realities exist, and our view of reality is determined by events viewed through individual lenses or biases.
4. Those who have the experiences are the most knowledgeable about them.

In addition to these common characteristics, holistic philosophies encompass a number of principles that guide the selection of particular designs in this category. For example, *phenomenologists* believe that human meaning can be understood only through experience.[8] Thus a phenomenological understanding is limited to knowing experience without interpreting that experience. On the other hand, interpretive and social semiotic *interactionists* [8,11,12] assume that human meaning evolves from the context of social interaction. Human phenomena can therefore be understood through interpreting the meanings in social discourse, exchange, and symbols. The holistic philosophies therefore suggest a pluralistic view of knowledge or that there are multiple realities that can be identified and understood only within the natural context in which human experience and behavior occur. Coming to know these realities requires research design that investigates phenomena in their natural contexts and seeks to discover complexity and meaning. Furthermore, those who experience are the knowers, and they transmit their knowledge through doing and telling.[11]

## Implications of philosophical differences for design

How you implicitly define and generate knowledge and how you define the relationship between the knower (researcher) and the known (research outcomes or phenomena of the study) will direct your entire research effort—from framing your research question or query to reporting your findings. Let us consider some examples of these important philosophical concepts and their implications for research design.

Let us suppose three researchers want to know what happens to participants in group therapy who have joined the group to improve their self-confidence. The researcher who suggests that knowing can be objective may choose a strategy in which he or she defines self-confidence as a score on a preexisting, standardized scale and will then measure participants' scores at specified time intervals to ascertain changes. Changes in the scores suggest what changes the group has experienced.

A second investigator, who believes that the world can be known only subjectively, may choose a research strategy in which the group is observed and the members are interviewed to obtain their perspective on their own progress within the group.

A third researcher, who believes in the value of many ways of knowing, may integrate both strategies. This researcher tries to understand change from the perspective of the participants and from the perspective of existing theory as measured by a standardized self-confidence scale.

## Research traditions

We have indicated that there are two primary philosophical traditions in research, which we categorize as either experimental-type or naturalistic inquiry. Within each of these categories we have said that there are many systematic research strategies. We suggest, however, that research strategies fall within two primary research traditions. The first tradition shares the philosophical foundation of experimental-type research. In this tradition a prescribed sequence of linear processes (as discussed in detail in subsequent chapters) is designed and implemented.[4,6] Throughout this text we refer to this tradition as experimental-type research.

On the other hand, strategies that share the principles of a holistic perspective or naturalistic inquiry follow a nonlinear, iterative, and flexible[13] sequence of processes. Throughout this text, we include these strategies in the tradition of naturalistic inquiry. Each design tradition has its own language, its own thought-and-action processes, and specific design issues and concerns. We use the concept of the two traditions throughout this text as a basis from which to discuss and compare design essentials and research processes within the same philosophical perspective and across philosophical traditions.

## Experimental-type

Let us begin with the philosophical foundation of the experimental-type tradition. First, remember that logical positivists believe one can come to know a single reality through a deductive process. This process involves the following: theorizing to explain the part of reality about which the investigator is concerned; reducing theory to observable parts; examining the parts through measurement; and determining the degree to which the analysis verifies or falsifies part or all of the theory. Second, a central principle of logical positivism is that it is possible and desirable to understand the world through systematic objectivity and by eliminating bias in our observations. Given these two critical elements of logical positivism, let us examine how each research essential as it occurs in a linear sequence supports the tenets of logical positivist inquiry.

After identifying a philosophical foundation, the researcher begins by articulating a topic of inquiry. We name this step "framing the problem," which identifies and delimits the part of the "real world" that an investigator will examine. Once a research problem is identified, supporting knowledge is obtained by conducting a literature review. This research essential discerns how the problem has been theoretically approached and explained. It examines the extent to which the theory has been objectively investigated. The literature review therefore provides the researcher with knowledge for developing a theoretical foundation for the inquiry. With this information, the investigator is now ready to propose a specific research question. This question will build on previous inquiry, isolate the theoretical material to be scrutinized, and incrementally advance knowledge about the subject under study. The ultimate goal is to predict a part of reality from knowing about other parts. To objectively answer the research question, the investigator selects a research design that answers the research question and control factors that introduce bias into a study. The design clearly and succinctly specifies all action processes for collecting and analyzing information so that the study may be replicated by other investigators. To ensure that the goals of objectivity and the elimination of bias are met, these actions must be followed exactly as designed. Through data analysis the investigator examines the extent to which the findings have objectively confirmed or raised doubts about the truth value of the theoretical tenets and their capacity to explain and ultimately predict the slice of reality under investigation.

Many designs are anchored in the philosophical foundation of logical positivism. Box 3-1 displays the four major categories of designs that form this tradition, each of which is discussed in detail in Part III.

| Box 3-1 | Major designs in experimental-type research |
|---|---|

- Nonexperimental
- Pre-experimental
- Quasi-experimental
- True experimental

## Naturalistic inquiry

There is great diversity in the strategies that are categorized as naturalistic inquiry. As indicated in this chapter, designs that fit with this tradition are rooted in different philosophical and theoretical perspectives. The language and thought processes used by naturalistic researchers vary within the tradition and are significantly different from the language and thought processes found in the experimental-type tradition. However, all naturalistic approaches have characteristics in common and use qualitative methodologies, although often for different purposes and often to answer very distinct types of inquiries.

These designs vary according to the extent to which inquiry involves the personal "essence," experiences, and insights of the investigator, the extent to which individual "experience" versus patterns of human experience is sought, the extent to which the investigator imposes structure in the data collection and analytical processes, and the sequence of the research process.

Neither the point of entry into the spiral of inquiry nor the sequence of the thinking and action processes is prescribed. Thus an investigator may begin with any of the essential thinking and action processes, change the design or specific action strategies in response to findings throughout the research process, and revisit steps that have already been conducted. The term, iterative, has been used by many methodologists to describe the repetitive, flexible, and progressively building process of naturalistic inquiry.[13]

Although there are many design variations, the major categories of design that make up this tradition are listed (Box 3-2) and discussed in detail in Part III.

**Box 3-2** | **Major categories of design**

- Endogenous
- Participatory action research
- Critical theory
- Phenomenology
- Heuristic design
- Life history
- Ethnography (classical and new)
- Grounded theory

## Integrating two research traditions

As briefly discussed, there has been significant and heated debate over which research tradition is most efficacious in advancing our understanding of human experience. Because experimental-type researchers believe that reality can only become known incrementally through implementing objective thinking and action processes, they may not value the naturalistic foundations of *pluralism* and subjectivity. Conversely, many naturalistic researchers question the extent to which human experience can be reduced to a single, observable, and predictive reality. Moreover, because of the philosophical differences between the traditions, many scholars and researchers suggest that the two cannot be integrated because of philosophical incompatibility. Most recently, however, there is a growing movement in both traditions to recognize the strengths and values of the other. Experimental-type methodologists are beginning to recognize that naturalistic inquiry represents a legitimate and logical alternative research strategy, and naturalistic researchers are giving greater attention to the standardization of analysis and procedures and to the complementary role of experimental-type designs. Consistent with a growing number of methodologists, we believe that the following five points of tension in the health and human service research world have led many investigators to eschew the traditional opposition of qualitative-quantitative research in favor of strategies that overcome or transcend the limitations of each research tradition. (1) The focus on the experimental-type tradition as the only viable research option has been brought into question by findings that repeatedly indicate little or no measurable effects of experimental treatments in health and human service research. (2) There is growing recognition that many of the persistent and unanswered issues that are critical to health and human service cannot be answered by the experimental paradigm alone. (3) There is an increasing realization that quantitative information, in and of itself, does not necessarily provide insight to the various processes that underlie the "hard facts" of a numerical report. (4) There are often great discrepancies in knowledge generated from qualitative and quantitative studies. (5) The increasing emphasis placed on the empirical demonstration of the need for outcomes of health and human services has led naturalistic researchers to consider using replicable strategies.

Both traditions have strengths and limitations, both have value in investigating the depth and breadth of research topics that informs us about human experience, and both can be integrated in a single study or throughout all or some of the parts of a research project involving multiple studies. We suggest that an integrated approach can strengthen health and human service inquiry. An integrated approach involves selecting and combining designs and methods from both traditions so that one complements the other to benefit or contribute to an understanding of the whole. However, as discussed throughout this text, effective integration is contingent on an investigator's firm understanding of the strengths and limitations of the thinking and action processes, the design strategies, and the particular methodologic approaches of each tradition. Based on this understanding, the investigator can mix and combine strategies to strengthen the research effort and to strive for comprehensive understanding of the phenomenon under consideration. Brewer and Hunter use the term *multimethod* research and explain the premise of this approach to inquiry in this way:

> Our individual methods may be flawed, but fortunately the flaws in each are not identical. A diversity of imperfection allows us to combine methods not only to gain their individual strengths but also to compensate for their particular faults and limitations.... Its [multimethod research] fundamental strategy is to attack a research problem with an arsenal of methods that have nonoverlapping weaknesses in addition to their complementary strengths.[14]

The integration of the research traditions as a way to strengthen and advance scientific inquiry has a 30-year history in sociology, anthropology, and education. However, only more recently has the integration of the traditions become a focus in health and human service research. Many researchers implicitly use one or more forms of integration that we discuss throughout the text. For example, there is a long history of the use of simple descriptive statistics, such as frequencies and means, in ethnographic research; and quantitative studies frequently use an exploratory, open-ended series of questions before establishing closed-ended and numerically based interview questions. What is new today is the purposeful and logical development of an integrated perspective that combines elements of the thinking and action processes from both the naturalistic and experimental-type traditions at each step of a research project. These integrated studies transcend the paradigm debate and enhance scientific inquiry.

In Table 3-1, we summarize the essential characteristics of experimental-type, naturalistic, and integrated inquiries. Examining the differences will help you understand the foundations of each tradition and its integration with the other.

We suggest five distinct ways in which the research traditions can be integrated. Figure 3-1, A shows a study design that initially involves a form of naturalistic inquiry that is followed by an experimental-type approach. Usually, in this strategy the purpose of the naturalistic inquiry is to gain an understanding of the boundary or dimensions of a particular construct or to generate a theory or set of propositions. If the pur-

pose is to define a particular construct or concept, the investigator uses the naturalistic process to inform the development of an instrument or set of measures for use in a quantitative study. If the purpose is to generate or modify a theory using the naturalistic process, this study phase is followed by an experimental-type design, which formally tests an aspect of the theory that has been developed. Consider the study on women's health by DePoy and Butler. The first phase of the study involved a naturalistic approach in order to derive definitions of health and well-being by rural elderly women. The second study phase involved a nonexperimental, survey design with a larger cohort of rural elderly women to examine the distribution of the constructs that were generated in the first study phase.[15]

Figure 3-1, B presents a strategy for integrating the research traditions, which involves the opposite sequence. In this integration scheme the investigator begins with an experimental-type approach and then introduces naturalistic techniques. Usually, in this approach the quantitative findings suggest the need for more in-depth and complex exploration of a particular phenomenon. For example, assume you are conducting an experimental-type study to test the outcome of an acquired im-

| Table 3-1 | Four distinguishing characteristics of the research traditions |

| | Experimental-type | Naturalistic | Integrated |
|---|---|---|---|
| Epistemology | Logical positivism | Humanistic or holistic | Multiple |
| Approach to reasoning | Deductive | Inductive and abductive | All |
| Theoretical aim | To reduce complexity; test theory | To reveal complexity; develop theory | All |
| Context | Arranged by researcher | Natural context | Multiple |

munodeficiency syndrome (AIDS) prevention program for urban teenagers. Your findings reveal that knowledge about human immunodeficiency viral (HIV) transmission increased. However, actual sexual behaviors did not change. Your initial inquiry is followed with a naturalistic examination of the intervention process to discover why the program did not have an impact on actual behaviors.

In Figure 3-1, *C*, integration occurs at several points throughout the research process. As a naturalistic study unfolds, elements of emerging theory are tested with experimental-type strategies. For example, in the study conducted by DePoy and Butler previously discussed, it appeared as if the use of health services was associated with the women's definitions of health. To examine this connection systematically, specific experimental-type strategies were introduced.

Similarly, Figure 3-1, *D* depicts an *integrated design* in which experimental-type in-

quiry reveals the need to develop insights using naturalistic techniques. For example, let us assume you are testing a preventive AIDS program and you observe that cultural normative values among teenagers appear to influence sexual behaviors. To explore this phenomenon more closely, you may integrate open-ended interviewing techniques or conduct a series of focus groups as one component of your experimental-type testing. This exploration will enable you to gain insights that will help you restructure the prevention program to yield a more desirable behavior change.

In an experimental-type design that examined the frequency of assistive-device use among older adults discharged from rehabilitation, Gitlin et al. found that older adults expressed a range of meanings and personal attributions to devices, which were not systematically addressed in the closed-ended questionnaires. They added a naturalistic approach by which the statements

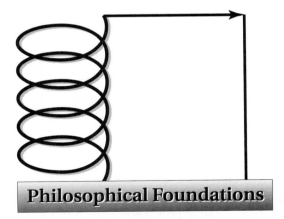

Figure 3-1, *A* Design strategy that involves naturalistic inquiry followed by an experimental-type approach.

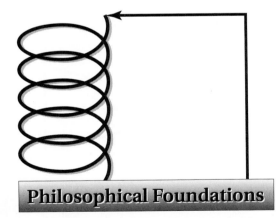

Figure 3-1, *B* Design strategy that begins with an experimental-type approach and then introduces naturalistic techniques.

of research participants were recorded, transcribed, and then analyzed using a content and thematic analytical strategy.[16]

Finally, Figure 3-1, *E* depicts the most fully integrated design. In this scheme the investigator integrates a study from the beginning and throughout all thinking and action processes. Consider the example of a study of the service and support needs of adolescents with special health care needs. In this study the investigators integrated participatory action research that used focus group methodology with the administration of a closed-ended, structured survey of service needs. Both approaches were conducted simultaneously and reported as a single study.[17]

## Selecting a research tradition and design strategy

How does one decide which tradition to work from and which particular design strategy to

choose? The selection of a design strategy is based on three considerations: (1) what you want to do or your purpose in conducting the research, (2) the way in which you think or reason about phenomena, and (3) the level of knowledge development in the area to be investigated.

### Purpose of research

Research is a purposeful activity; that is, research is conducted for a specific reason—to answer a specific question or to solve a particular controversy or issue. We have not yet met anyone who wakes up one morning and says, "I just want to do a research project." Purpose drives the decision to engage in research. For example, you may need to conduct a research project to validate a health care intervention to obtain necessary resources and continued support for a social service program; or perhaps you want to conduct a research study to help you sys-

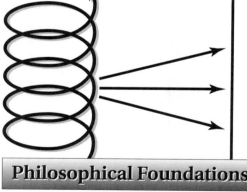

**Figure 3-1,** *C* Design strategy in which integration occurs at several points in a naturalistic study.

**Figure 3-1,** *D* Design strategy in which integration occurs at several points in an experimental-type study.

tematically determine the elements of a new therapeutic approach in a previously untested area. Let us consider another example of how purpose drives the selection of a design.

Consider a case in which an administrator of a rehabilitation unit in a large teaching and research hospital has just been informed that her social work unit may be closed if she cannot demonstrate the value of the department's programs. The administrator decides that she will implement a research project to demonstrate the value of the service to the patients who are being discharged. She selects three criteria for measurement to define valuable intervention: (1) patient satisfaction, (2) social work staff time spent with each patient's family in preparation for discharge, and (3) level of daily living skill performance in the occupational therapy clinic before discharge. She selects and measures these three criteria deductively, because she knows that these strengths can be clearly de-

monstrated by her unit staff. Her purpose in conducting the research is to improve the chances of survival of her unit. She selects a deductive strategy based on her previous knowledge of the strengths of her programs and the types of positive outcomes she hopes to achieve.

In another hospital, the rehabilitation administrator has been asked to develop new programming for Asian immigrants with AIDS and their families. In the absence of a well-developed body of knowledge in this area, the administrator selects an inductive strategy to find out what type of rehabilitation programming will be most valuable. She conducts in-depth, unstructured interviews with immigrants who have AIDS, their families, and service providers to reveal needs and the culturally relevant methods by which those needs can be addressed within her institution.

As you can see, purpose is a powerful force that drives the selection of a research strategy. In the first example, the administrator selected a strategy that she, as the researcher, could control and one that was based on the *a priori* assumptions she was willing to make. In the second example, the administrator selected a strategy that would uncover information that had not been previously determined. Because patient needs as perceived by patients and families were shaping institutional programming, an inductive, naturalistic design strategy was selected.

It is not uncommon to have more than one purpose for your study. Perhaps you already know that your intervention is successful, but you want to improve a service or obtain an understanding as to why the intervention is effective. This dual purpose may lead to a study that integrates a design from the experimental-type

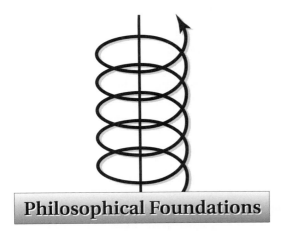

**Philosophical Foundations**

Figure 3-1, $E$  Design strategy in which integration occurs throughout all thinking and action processes.

tradition with a design from the naturalistic inquiry tradition. The purpose of such an integrated study is to verify what is valuable, as well as to reveal new avenues for programmatic improvement and explanation of effectiveness.

## Preference for knowing

Your preferred way of knowing is a second important consideration when selecting a particular category of research design. Selecting a design strategy is based, in part, on your implicit view of "reality" (ontology), your view of how we know what we know (epistemology), and your comfort level with epistemologic assumptions. Often our preferred way of knowing is not something on which we consciously reflect. It is usually demonstrated in which research approach makes the most sense to us and feels the most comfortable. Also, investigator personalities often influence the inclination to participate in one of the two traditions or in integrated inquiry.

## Level of knowledge development

The third consideration involves the level of knowledge that has been developed in the particular topic area of interest. When little or nothing is understood about a phenomenon, a more descriptive and naturalistic approach to inquiry is more appropriate. When a well-developed body of knowledge has been advanced, predicting designs may be more appropriate and suit the purposes of the investigator. However, this is not to suggest that naturalistic inquiry is chosen only when little knowledge has been developed. Again, choice is based on a combination of the level of knowledge and the investigator's purpose. We explore the relationship of knowledge to design selection in more detail in subsequent chapters. Table 3-2 summarizes the criteria for selecting designs across the research traditions.

## Summary

We have made five major points in this chapter:

1. Experimental-type research is based in a single epistemologic framework of logical positivism and involves a primarily deductive process of human reasoning.

2. Naturalistic inquiry is based in multiple philosophical traditions that can be categorized as holistic in their perspectives and involves inductive and abductive processes of human reasoning.

**Table 3-2** Criteria for selecting designs by research tradition

|  | Experimental-type | Naturalistic | Integrated |
|---|---|---|---|
| Practical purpose | Need to control and delimit scope of inquiry | Reveal new understandings | Multiple |
| Preferred way of knowing | Singular reality; objectively viewed | Multiple, interpreted realities | Multiple |
| Level of knowledge development | Well-developed theory | Limited knowledge; challenge to current theory | Both |

**3.** Integrated research draws on strategies from both experimental-type and naturalistic traditions and may involve multiple and varied thought and action processes.

**4.** Research strategies involve two primary traditions: experimental-type or naturalistic inquiry. Each has a distinct language and flow of thinking and action procedures. Moreover, the two traditions can be used in tandem with one another. These types of inquires have been named integrated or multimethod research.

**5.** The selection of a strategy is based on your preferred way of knowing, your research purpose, and the level of knowledge development in the topic area of interest.

## Exercises

1. Select a topic of interest, and determine how you may approach it using experimental-type reasoning and the sequence of the ten essentials.

2. Using the same topic in exercise 1, suggest how you may approach the topic using naturalistic inquiry.

3. Compare and contrast both approaches, and think of how you will approach your topic area using integrated strategies.

### References

1. Hume D: *A treatise on human nature: being an attempt to introduce the experimental method of reasoning into moral*, London, 1974, Longrans, Green, & Co.

2. Russell B: *Introduction to mathematical philosophy*, New York, 1919, Macmillan.

3. Hoover KR: *The elements of social scientific thinking*, ed 2, New York, 1980, St Martin's Press.

4. Cook TD, Campbell DT: *Quasi-experimentation: design and analysis issues for field settings*, Boston, 1979, Houghton Mifflin.

5. Babbie E: *The practice of social research*, Belmont, Calif, 1992, Wadsworth.

6. Campbell DT, Stanley JC: *Experimental and quasi-experimental designs for research*, Boston, 1963, Houghton Mifflin.

7. Denzin N: *Interpretive interactionism*, Newbury Park, Calif, 1988, Sage.

8. Husserl E, Boyce WR, translator: *Ideas: general introduction to pure phenomenology*, New York, 1931, Macmillan.

9. Guba EC: Carrying on the dialogue. In Guba EC, editor: *The paradigm dialogue*, Newbury Park, Calif, 1990, Sage.

10. Randall JH, Buchler J: *Philosophy: an introduction*, New York, 1962, Barnes & Noble.

11. Orcutt BA: *Science and inquiry in social work practice*, New York, 1990, Columbia University Press.

12. Reason P, Rowan J: *Human inquiry*, New York, 1981, John Wiley & Sons.

13. Anastas JW, McDonald ML, Anastas JW: *Research design for social work and the human services*, New York, 1994, Lexington Books

14. Brewer J, Hunter A: *Multimethod research: a synthesis of styles*, Newbury Park, Calif, 1989, Sage.

15. DePoy E, Butler S: Health: elderly rural women's conceptions, *AFFILIA* 11(2):207-220, 1996.

16. Gitlin LN, Luborsky M, Schemm R: Emerging concerns of older stroke patients about assistive device use, *The Gerontologist* 38(2)169-180, 1998.

17. DePoy E, Gilmer D: *Healthy and ready to work: adolescents with special needs in transition*, (paper presented at the Pacific Rim Conference), Honolulu, 1997.

# Chapter 4

# Framing the problem

**Key terms**  Problem statement
Purpose statement
Research topic

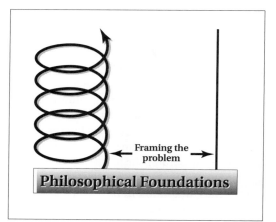

Framing the problem

**Philosophical Foundations**

Where do you begin, now that you are ready to participate in the research process? The first challenge of research is the selection of a problem that is meaningful, appropriate for scientific inquiry, and purposeful. By meaningful we suggest that the problem generates knowledge that is useful to the individual or to his or her profession. By appropriate we mean that the selection of a problem can be submitted to a systematic research process and that the research will yield knowledge to help solve the problem. By purposeful we suggest that health and human research be designed with purposes that serve investigators, consumers, professionals, funders, policy makers, and others concerned with the delivery of health and human services.

Most beginning researchers are able to identify a topic of interest to them. However, many find the identification of a specific research problem a difficult task. This difficulty is caused in part by an unfamiliarity with problem formulation and its relationship to the research process. How you frame a research problem influences and shapes the development of each subsequent thinking and action process. Considerations are summarized in Box 4-1.

As depicted in Figure 4-1, the way the research problem is framed will lead to the development of a specific research question in the experimental-type tradition of research or to a line of query in the naturalistic tradition or to a question and query that integrate both research traditions. This chapter examines the thought process involved in identifying a topic, framing a research problem, and linking design selection to purpose.

| Box 4-1 | Considerations in framing research problems |
|---|---|

- Personal interest
- Relevance
- Need
- Epistemology
- Purpose
- Resources

## Identifying a topic

The first consideration in beginning a research project is identifying a topic from which to pursue an investigation. A *research topic* is a broad issue or area that is important to a health and human service professional. One topic may yield many different problems and strategies for investigation. Examples of topics include post-hospital experience, health promotion in diverse ethnic communities, pain control, community independence, adaptation to disability, drug abuse, hospital management practices, gender differences related to retirement, psychosocial aspects of illness, and impact of interventions on specific outcomes. It is usually easy for someone to identify a topic of interest or one that is relevant to and important for professional practice.

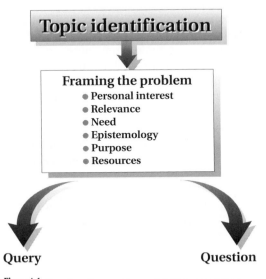

Figure 4-1 Framing the problem: thinking sequence.

Where do topics and specific problem areas come from? There are five basic sources that help professionals select a topic and researchable problem (Box 4-2).

## Professional experience

The professional arena is perhaps the most immediate and important source from which research problems come. The daily ideas and confusions that emerge from cognitive dissonance, or "professional challenges,"[1] (similar to those posed at the beginning of Chapter 1) often yield significant areas of inquiry. Many of the themes or persistent issues that emerge in case review, supervision, or staff conferences may provide investigators with researchable topics and ideas. Themes that cut across individual cases, such as family involvement and consumer perceptions of their experiences in health and human services, provide topics that may stimulate the framing of a specific research problem. For example, a rehabilitation professional in an inpatient rehabilitation hospital posed to us an observation that she and her staff found intriguing. They observed that many of the adaptive devices for self-care that were routinely issued and used with inpatient training were often left behind by patients at discharge. Although she believed patients needed adapted devices to function independently in their homes, she wondered why patients did not feel similarly. When the devices were taken home, she also wondered whether they were used, and, if so, did they enhance the individuals' functioning in their environments? Discussions with practitioners in other hospital sites revealed similar observations and concerns. We identified a research problem and a series of questions to examine these issues systematically in collaboration with rehabilitation practitioners.[2]

## Societal trends

Social concerns and trends reflected in the policies, legislation, and funding priorities of federal, state, and local agencies, foundations, and corporations provide a second and critical area of potential inquiry for health and human service investigation. For example, the report, *Healthy People 2000,*[3] a Public Health Service document, establishes the health-related objectives and priorities for the nation. This document provides a rich foundation for the development of research problems.

Another social arena from which research problems emerge is the set of specific requests for research generated by federal, state, and local governments. Government agencies have established funding streams that provide monetary support to researchers who identify meaningful and appropriate research problems within topic areas relevant to the delivery of health and human services. For example, in the arena of health promotion and disease prevention, the Centers for Disease Control and Prevention issued a call for research that focuses on

**Box 4-2 Five sources for topic identification**

- Professional experience
- Societal trends
- Professional trends
- Published research
- Existing theory

the identification of risk factors related to secondary disability and the prevention of such. The Department of Health and Human Services has issued requests for research proposals to study the effects of welfare reform on the health of children living in poverty. To publicize research priorities set by the federal government, the *Federal Register,* a daily publication of the U.S. government (appearing both in hard copy and on-line), lists funding opportunities and policy developments of each branch of the federal government. Most libraries receive the hard copy publication, and the on-line version can be accessed through the world wide web. The *Federal Register* is an invaluable resource to help identify problem areas and funding sources. Numerous other sources list grant opportunities, including the *National Institutes of Health (NIH) Guide for Grants and Contracts,* the *Federal Grants and Contracts Weekly,* and the *Chronicle of Higher Education*—just to name a few.

## Professional trends

Other resources for identifying important research topics are the weekly newsletters and publications of each health and human service profession. Investigators frequently read these resources to determine the broad topic areas and problems of current interest to a given profession. Also, professional associations establish specific short- and long-term research goals and priorities for their profession. For example, the American Occupational Therapy Foundation identified the need to develop more research in the area of client assessment and intervention outcomes; as a result, the Foundation

has sponsored funding competitions that support research addressing these priorities. Examining the goals and policy statements of professional associations provides a good source from which to establish a research direction.

## Research studies

The research world itself also provides a significant avenue from which to identify research topics and problem areas. Health and human service professionals encounter research ideas by interacting with peers, attending professional meetings that report research findings, participating in a research project, and reviewing published research reports. Reading research in professional journals provides an overview of the important studies that are conducted in a topic area of interest. Most published research studies identify additional research problems and unresolved issues generated by the research findings. Journals, such as the *Journal of Dental Hygiene,* the *Journal of the American Medical Association, Research in Social Work Practice, Occupational Therapy Journal of Research, Nursing Research, Medical Care, Physical Therapy, Qualitative Research in Health Care, The Social Service Review, American Journal of Public Health,* and *Social Work Research,* publish current research findings that are useful and relevant to the helping professions. Routinely reading journals also provides an idea of what issues professional peers believe are important to investigate, as well as the studies that need to be replicated or repeated to confirm the findings. There are many other journals published by the helping professions and related disciplines that may assist in identifying a topic. Substantive topic journals that cross disciplines, such as *Archives of Physical and Rehabilitation Medicine, Psychiatric Services, Journal of Gerontology, Childhood and Adolescence, Topics in Geriatric Rehabilitation, The Gerontologist,* and *Journal of Rehabilitation,* provide specific ideas for research studies that need to be conducted in topics relevant to health and human service professionals.

## Existing theory

Theories also provide an important source for generating topics and identifying research problems. As we discuss in Chapter 6, a theory posits a number of propositions and relationships between concepts. To be considered a theory, each specified relationship within the theory must be submitted to systematic investigation for verification or falsification.[4] Inquiry related to theory development is intended to substantiate the theory and advance or modify its development by refuting some or all of its principles. Consider, for example, the well-known theory of cognitive development put forth by Piaget in the mid-1920s.[5] Piaget developed his theory of the structural development of cognition by observing his two children. Over 60 years, Piaget, his peers, and other scholars interested in human cognition, subjected Piaget's theoretical notions to extensive scientific scrutiny. Hundreds of studies, if not more, have been conducted to corroborate, modify, or refute Piaget's principles. Further study related to Piaget's theory has been initiated to determine the application of the theory to education and health-related intervention, as well as many other arenas.

## Framing a research problem

An endless number of problems or issues can emerge from any one topic. The challenge to the researcher is to identify one particular area of concern or specific research problem in a broad topic area. A specific research problem identifies the phenomenon to be explored, the reason it needs to be examined, and the reason it is a problem or issue. You may believe that it is simple to select a topic for research since there are many problems to be explored. However, how you frame and state the problem is critical to the entire research endeavor and influences all subsequent thought and action processes; that is, the way a problem is framed determines the way it will be answered. Therefore this first research step should be thought through carefully.

The questions in Box 4-3 can help guide your thinking as you move from the selection of a broad topic area to the framing of a concrete research problem. Answering these reflective questions will begin to narrow your focus and help you hone in on a researchable problem.

---

**Box 4-3** **Guiding questions**

- What about this topic is of interest to me?
- What about this topic is relevant to my practice?
- What about this topic is unresolved in the literature?
- What is my preferred way of coming to know about phenomena?
- What societal or professional purpose does knowing about this topic serve?
- What resources do I have to investigate this topic?

## Interest, relevance, and need

It is important to be certain that whatever topic you develop is interesting to you. Research, regardless of the framework and type of methodology used, takes time and is thought consuming. Additionally, you should be convinced of the relevance and need for the inquiry. If the problem is not challenging, exciting, relevant, and needed, the process will quickly become tedious and lack meaning for the investigator.

## Research purpose

As discussed in Chapter 3, all research is purposeful. We suggest that there are three levels of purpose that each research project addresses. The first purpose is professional. Much of the research in health and human services is initiated to determine empirically the need for an intervention program, to inform professional practice, or to examine the extent to which an intervention is efficacious in achieving its outcome. Second, researchers have personal purposes for conducting research. For example, a significant part of the research literature is generated by faculty who are committed or required to contribute to the knowledge base in their respective fields. Practitioners, administrators, and others in the health and human service professions may conduct research for numerous personal reasons, such as adding new challenges to their jobs, career advancement, commitment to funding new projects, and desire for academic collaboration. Third, there are methodologic purposes that both emerge from the literature (as discussed in detail in Chapter 5) and frame the nature of knowledge to be generated by a research effort. Methodologic purpose is based on the formula-

tion of a problem and identifies the specific goals of a research project. In the experimental-type tradition, the researcher is interested in describing, explaining, or predicting phenomena, as demonstrated in the following examples of a *purpose statement:*

*Descriptive.* "Little is known about the nutrition knowledge and beliefs of adults with mental retardation. The present study is a preliminary investigation of nutrition knowledge of persons with mental retardation."[6]

*Explanatory.* "While the use of informal support has been the focus of extensive study…little or no attention has been paid to the role of informal support on the employment activity of women who are AFDC [Aid to Families with Dependent Children] recipients. This study is an attempt to fill that knowledge gap. Specifically, this study examines the relationship between informal network support and the labor force activity for women who are on AFDC compared to women not on AFDC."[7]

*Explanatory.* "This study, with a relatively large national sample, examines specific coping strategies that caregivers have used to manage their day-to-day responsibilities and how the strategies are related to outcomes of caregiver well-being."[8]

*Predictive.* "This study was undertaken to examine changes in family functioning from pre-injury to 3 years after pediatric TBI (traumatic brain injury) and to determine those factors that best predict a 3-year family outcome."[9]

In naturalistic designs the purpose is to understand the meanings, experiences, and phenomena as they evolve in the natural setting. The following are examples of purpose statements by investigators using different naturalistic designs:

*Ethnography.* "The purpose of the study was to 'gain an understanding of the families' demographics, status as immigrants, beliefs about deafness, attitudes toward school and health care professionals, expectations for their children and communication with the deaf child.'" [10]

*Ethnography.* "The purpose of the study was to gain understanding of the meaning of the family caregiving experience with the hope that greater understanding would assist health professionals in working together with caregivers." [11]

*Phenomenology.* "The purpose of the study presented here was to evolve a structural definition of health as it is experienced in everyday life." [12]

*Grounded theory.* "This article discusses the multidimensional relationship that developed between researcher and participants during an exploratory study of enrichment processes in family caregiving to frail elders." [13]

*Grounded theory.* "The purpose of the present study was to identify processes used by family members to manage the unpredictability elicited by the need for and receipt of a heart transplant." [14]

Integrated designs can have multiple purposes that reflect both traditions or only one. Consider the following example in which the purpose combined both traditions: "The purpose of this integrated study was to reveal the ways in which elder rural women defined health and wellness and then test the accuracy of these definitions in a large cohort of the population." [15]

## Epistemology-preferred way of knowing

In addition to problem formulation and study purpose, your preferred way of knowing, or epistemology, will also influence either the development of discrete questions that objectify concepts (experimental-type tradition) or a query to explore multiple and interacting factors in the context in which they emerge (naturalistic tradition) or the development of a query that integrates both approaches. The age-old epistemologic dilemma of what is knowledge and how do we know (discussed in Chapter 3) is an active and forceful determinant of how a researcher frames a problem. The researcher's preferred way of knowing is either clearly articulated or implied in each *problem statement.* Reexamine the previous purpose statements to determine the investigator's preferred way of knowing.

## Resources

Resources represent the concrete limitations of the research world. The accessibility of place, group, or individuals and the extent to which time, money, and other resources are necessary and available to the researcher to implement the inquiry are examples of some of the natural constraints of conducting research. These real-life constraints actively shape the development of the research problem an investigator pursues and the scope of the project that can be implemented.

## Summary

In this chapter we discuss many considerations in framing an inquiry. We begin by looking at the diverse sources and methods through which investigators identify topics for inquiry. Six questions that guide the refinement of the topic into a research problem are offered. These questions organize thinking processes along personal, professional, social, ontologic, and practical lines. For example, considering your interest in a research topic is a personal thinking process, whereas assessing existing resources available for conducting a project is a practical thinking process. We move to an expansion of the purposive aspects of conducting research, suggesting that investigators organize their research to meet personal, professional, and methodologic goals. Finally, the role of your preferred way of knowing, or epistemology, in framing an inquiry is illuminated. How a researcher frames a problem has significant design implications for the selection of design from the experimental-type tradition, the naturalistic tradition, or an integration of the two, as seen in subsequent chapters. Equipped with an understanding of why and how investigators frame research problems, you are ready to begin the thinking process of examining and critically using literature as a basis for knowledge development.

## Exercises

1. Select an experimental-type and a naturalistic article, and compare and contrast the way in which the problems in each are framed.

2. Identify the purpose statement in each article selected for exercise 1.

3. In each article, identify the source of the topic.

### References

1. Schon D: *The reflective practitioner*, New York, 1983, Basic Books.
2. Gitlin LN, Levine R, Geiger C: Adaptive device use in the home by older adults with mixed disabilities, *Arch Phys Med Rehabil* 74:149-152, 1993.
3. U.S. Department of Health and Human Services: *Healthy people 2000*, Washington DC, 1990, US Government Printing Co.
4. Wilson J: *Thinking with concepts*, Cambridge, Mass, 1966, Cambridge University Press.
5. Piaget J, Warden M, translator: *Judgment and reasoning in the child*, New York, 1926, Harcourt Brace.
6. Golden E, Hatcher J: Nutrition knowledge and obesity of adults in community residences, *Mental Retardation* 35(3):177-184, 1997.
7. Lundgren-Gaveras L: Employment and informal network support among AFDC and non-AFDC single mothers, *Journal of Children and Purvey* 2(2):41, 1996.
8. Palmore EB: Predictors of outcome in nursing homes, *J Appl Gerontol* 9:1172-1184, 1990.
9. Rivara JB and others: Predictors of family functioning and change 3 years after traumatic brain injury in children, *Archives of Phys Med* 77:754-64, 1996.
10. Steinberg AG, et al: A little sign and a lot of love: attitudes, perceptions and beliefs of Hispanic families with deaf children, *Qualitative Health Research* 7(2):202-222, 1997.
11. Hasselkus BR: The meaning of activity: day care for persons with Alzheimer disease, *Am J Occup Ther* 46:199-206, 1992.
12. Parse RR, Coyne AB, Smith MJ: Nursing research traditions: qualitative and quantitative approaches. In *Nursing research, qualitative methods*, Bowie, MD, 1985, Brady Communications.
13. Cartwright J, Limandri B: The challenge of multiple roles in the qualitative clinician researcher-participant client relationship, *Qualitative Health Research* 7(2):223-235, 1997.
14. Mishel M, Murdaugh C: Family adjustment to heart transplantation: redesigning the dream, *Nurs Res* 36:332-338, 1987.
15. DePoy E, Butler S: Health: elderly rural women's conceptions, *AFFILIA* 11(2):207-220, 1996.

# Developing a knowledge base through review of the literature

**Key terms**   Concept/construct matrix
Database
Literature review chart

**Why review the literature?**

Determine what research has been conducted on the topic of inquiry

Determine level of theory and knowledge development relevant to your project

Determine relevance of the current knowledge base to your problem area

Provide a rationale for selection of the research strategy

**How to conduct a literature search**

Step 1: Determine when to conduct a search

Step 2: Delimit what is searched

Step 3: Access databases for periodicals, books, and documents

Step 4: Organize information

Step 5: Critically evaluate the literature

Step 6: Write the literature review

**Summary**

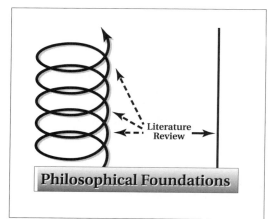

Literature
Review

**Philosophical Foundations**

Once you have decided on a research problem, the literature will help refine your thinking and the way in which to develop a specific query or question. Reviewing the literature is an important and significant aspect of the research process.

Most of us have recollections of long hours at the library poring through literature to discover what others have written about a topic in which we are interested. However, it is often a misunderstood and undervalued activity. However, a literature review in the world of research serves a slightly different purpose than a review you may conduct for other types of activities or classes. It is a process in which the researcher critically reviews literature that is directly or indirectly related to both the topic and proposed strategy of conducting the research. The information obtained from a critical review directs you to a particular research focus and strategy. Discovering what others know and how they come to know it will help determine how your research fits within the body of existing knowledge, and it will help identify the unique contributions of your research to the scientific enterprise.

In this chapter we begin with a discussion of the different reasons for conducting a literature review. We then present specific steps in conducting a literature review. Because there is often so much literature directly related to a topic and many other related bodies of research, the review process may feel overwhelming. However, there are "tricks of the trade," so to speak, to facilitate a systematic and comprehensive review process that is manageable and even enjoyable.

## Why review the literature?

Literature needs to be reviewed for four major reasons (Box 5-1). Let us examine each of these reasons in depth.

| Box 5-1 | Reasons to review the literature |
|---|---|

*To determine:*
- Previous research on topic
- Level of theory and knowledge development
- Relevance of current knowledge base to problem area
- Rationale for selection of research strategy

## Determine what research has been conducted on the topic of inquiry

Why conduct a study if it has already been done and done to your satisfaction? The key words are "to your satisfaction." To determine if the current literature is sufficient to help you solve a professional problem, you must critically evaluate how others have struggled with and resolved the same question. An initial review of the literature provides a sense of what has been done in your area of interest. The review helps identify the current trends and ways of thinking about your topic, the contemporary debates in your field, the gaps in the knowledge base, the ways in which the current knowledge on your topic has been developed, and the conceptual frameworks used to inform and examine your problem.

Sometimes an initial review of the literature will steer you in a research direction different from that which you originally planned. For example, let us say you want to examine the extent to which mild aerobic exercise promotes cardiovascular fitness in the elderly population. You find several studies that already document a positive outcome. However, many of these authors suggest that further inquiry is necessary to determine the particular exercises that promote cardiovascular fitness, as well as those that maintain joint mobility. Although this area may not be what you originally had in mind, the literature review refines your thinking and directs you to specific problem areas that need greater research attention than the one originally intended. You will need to decide if replication of the reported studies is important to verify study findings or whether your focus should be modified according to the recommendations in the literature.

Let us consider another example of the way in which literature influences the investigator's research direction. Gitlow was interested in examining the attitudes of occupational therapy faculty toward students with disabilities in higher education. She performed an extensive literature review to ascertain what studies had been conducted and what instrumentation would be available for her study. Because she was unable to locate much literature on her topic and because no instrumentation was available, she shifted her initial study to revising and validating an instrument to measure the attitudes of higher education faculty toward inclusion of students with disabilities.[1] It was necessary for Gitlow to shift the research focus to conduct her study.

## Determine level of theory and knowledge development relevant to your project

As you review the literature, not only do you need to describe what exists, but, more importantly, you need to analyze critically three important related factors in each work (Box 5-2).

**Box 5-2  Three factors to review critically**
- Level of knowledge
- How knowledge is generated
- Boundaries of a study

*Level of knowledge.* When you read a study, first evaluate the level of knowledge that emerges from the study. As addressed in detail in Chapter 7, studies produce varying levels of knowledge from the descriptive to the theoretical. The level of theory development and knowledge in your topic area is a major determinant of the type of research strategy you select. As you read related studies in the literature, consider the level of theoretical development that exists. Is the body of knowledge descriptive, explanatory, or at the level of prediction?

*How knowledge is generated.* Once you have determined the level of knowledge, evaluate how that knowledge has been generated; in other words, identify the research strategy or design that is used in each study. As you identify the design, critically examine whether it is appropriate for the level of knowledge the authors indicate exists in the literature and whether the conclusions of the study are consistent with the design strategy.

We all know that there is a tendency to read the introduction to a study and then jump to the conclusions to see what it can do for you. However, it is important to read each aspect of a research report, especially the section on methodology. As a matter of fact, you will be surprised to find that, unfortunately, the literature is full of research that demonstrates an inappropriate match among research question, strategy, and conclusions.

As you read a study, ask yourself three interrelated questions (Box 5-3).

| Box 5-3 | **Questions to ask as you read a study** |
|---|---|

- Are the research methods congruent with the level of knowledge reviewed by the investigators in their report?
- Do the research procedures adequately address the proposed research question?
- Is there compatibility or fit among literature, procedures, findings, and conclusions?

The answers to these questions will lead you to understand and determine critically the appropriateness of the level of knowledge generated in your topic area.

***Boundaries of a study.*** It is also important to determine the boundaries of the studies and their relevance to your study problem. By boundaries, we mean the "who, what, when, and where" of a study. For example, suppose you are interested in testing the effectiveness of a hypertension reduction program in a rural setting. Let us assume previously published studies report positive outcomes for a range of interventions. However, on closer examination, you discover that these studies have been conducted in urban areas and include primarily white and male participants with backgrounds very different from the population you plan to include in your study. Therefore it will be important to examine studies that test health promotion interventions in rural settings and include participants with characteristics similar to the intended targets of your study. By extending the literature review in this way, you will obtain a better understanding of the issues and design considerations that are important for the specific boundaries of your study. Also, you may discover that the level of theory and knowledge development in hypertensive risk reduction programs is advanced for one particular population (e.g., white urban men) but undeveloped in respect to another population (e.g., rural African-American women).

If you do not find any literature in your topic area, you may choose to identify a body of literature that is somehow analogous to your study as a way of directing how to develop your strategy. For example, in a study of clinical mastery in occupational therapy, DePoy found relatively little or no research; yet, studies of excellence and achievement had been conducted in fields such as business and music. DePoy reviewed these bodies of literature to shape her methods.[2] Determining the boundaries of the literature helps you to evaluate the level of knowledge that exists for the particular population and setting you are interested in studying.

## Determine relevance of the current knowledge base to your problem area

Once you have evaluated the level of knowledge advanced in the literature, you will need to determine its relevance to your idea.

Let us assume you are considering conducting an experimental-type study. In your literature review, you must find research that points to a theoretical framework relevant to your topic and research that identifies specific variables and measures for inclusion in your study. Your literature review must also yield a body of sufficiently developed knowledge so that hypotheses can be derived for your study.

For example, in a study that examined the factors that predict whether a family will decide to plan for or place an adult member with mental retardation in residential placement, Essex et al. presented an extensive literature review to support the explanatory level of their inquiry.[3] Not only did their literature review posit and define single predictors, such as satisfaction with current living arrangements and the fit between family needs and available formal services, but it presented well-developed, relevant models of family change as a function of stress and coping from which to extract predictor variables. This comprehensive review was more than adequate to support the substance and structure of the study.

If your literature review reveals a clear gap in existing knowledge or a poor fit between a phenomenon and current theory, you probably should consider a strategy in the naturalistic tradition. Let us examine a the work of McCauley, Travis, and Safewright as an instructive example. These researchers were interested in understanding the process by which families choose to institutionalize elder family members in nursing homes.[4] In their review of the literature, they presented existing research that laid the foundation for the study, specifically focusing on the understanding created by sound inquiry that challenges "the myth that the majority of families abandon or ignore the needs of their older dependent members…."[4] However, they note current research using survey methodology has revealed only a linear process of decision making. They identified a clear gap in the literature, implying that existing knowledge cannot support an examination of their topic within the experimental-type tradition; thus they used a naturalistic design to fill the conceptual chasm they found in their review of the literature.

## Provide a rationale for selection of the research strategy

Once you have determined the content and structure of existing theory and knowledge related to your problem area, the next task is to determine a rationale for the selection of your research. A literature review for a research grant proposal or research report is written to directly support your research and choice of design. You must synthesize your critical review of existing studies in such a way that the reader sees your study as a logical extension of current knowledge in the literature.

First, let us discuss how to conduct a literature search; then we will offer guidelines for developing a written rationale.

## How to conduct a literature search

Conducting a literature search and writing a literature review are exciting and creative processes. However, there may be so much literature in the area of interest to you that the review process can initially seem overwhelming. In this section, we identify six steps to guide you in searching the literature, organizing the sources, and taking notes on the references that you plan to use in a written rationale (Box 5-4).

| Box 5-4 | **Six steps to literature review** |
|---|---|

Step 1: Determine when to conduct a search.

Step 2: Delimit what is searched.

Step 3: Access databases for periodicals, books, and documents.

Step 4: Organize the information.

Step 5: Critically evaluate the literature.

Step 6: Write the literature review.

## Step 1: Determine when to conduct a search

The first step in a literature review is to determine when a review should be done. In studies in the experimental-type tradition, a literature review always precedes both the final formulation of a research question and the implementation of the study. As we have discussed, in the experimental-type tradition, variable definitions and the level of theoretical complexity underpinning a study must be presented for a study to be scientifically sound and rigorous. (We discuss rigor in greater detail in subsequent chapters.)

In the tradition of naturalistic inquiry, the literature may be reviewed at different points in time throughout the project. Although the literature is not critical for defining variables and instrumentation, it serves other purposes. Sometimes, for example, the literature is used as an additional source of data and is included as part of the information gathering process that is subsequently analyzed and interpreted. Another purpose of the literature review in naturalistic

inquiry is to inform the direction of data collection once the investigator is in the field. As discoveries occur in data collection, the investigator may turn to the literature to obtain some guidance about how to interpret emergent themes and what other questions should be asked in the field.

To the extreme are forms of research in which no literature is reviewed before or during fieldwork. In a study of prison violence using an endogenous research design (discussed in Chapter 10), the researcher and the research team of prison inmates did not believe that a review was necessary or relevant to the purpose of their study.[5]

For the most part, however, researchers working in the naturalistic-type tradition review the literature before conducting research to confirm the need for a naturalistic approach. For example, in the study by McCauley et al. previously discussed, the literature provides a sound rationale for their approach. Although an extensive review of the literature refines the research approach and design, keep in mind that investigators are continually updating their literature review throughout their study.

## Step 2: Delimit what is searched

Once you have made a decision about when to conduct a literature review, your next step involves setting parameters as to what is relevant to search; after all, it is not feasible or reasonable to review every topic that is somewhat related to your problem. Delimiting, or setting boundaries, to the search is an important yet difficult step. The boundaries you set must ensure a comprehensive review but one that is practical and not overwhelming.

One useful strategy used by investigators in all research traditions is to base a search on the concepts and constructs that are contained in the initial inquiry. For example, suppose you want to determine whether participation in an exercise program for elderly nursing home residents improves perceived health status. The concepts and constructs contained in this initial formulation include exercise, nursing home residents, and perceived health status. You would begin a search using these variables to identify literature and determine how these have been studied.

## Step 3: Access databases for periodicals, books, and documents

Now that you have determined when the literature search will take place and have established some limits on what will be searched, you are ready to go to the library. Over the past 15 years, library searches have become technologically sophisticated and are a big advantage over conventional searching mechanisms. However, the most valuable resource for finding references in the library is still the reference librarian. Working with an experienced librarian is the best way to learn how to navigate the library and the numerous databases that open the world of literature to you.

Once in the library, you have choices about how to begin your search. You can access literature through an on-line (computerized) *database* or through other indexes and abstracts. Some libraries still have card catalogs, which can be most useful in locating resources offered by the library in which you are searching. However, many libraries have discarded these resources, placing the card catalog on the "endangered species" list or in the antique store. In health and human service research you will more likely want to search three categories of materials: books, journal articles, and government documents. You may also find newspapers and newsletters useful, especially those from professional associations. In addition, you can construct a literature search based on the references of research studies you have obtained. However, do not exclusively depend on what these authors identify as important. References from other articles may not represent the broad range of studies you probably will review, nor will they represent the most current literature. There is sometimes a delay of 1 year or more between the submission of a manuscript and its publication date; therefore the citations that precede each article may be seriously outdated.

***Searching periodicals and journals.*** Usually most researchers begin their search by examining periodicals and journals. To begin your search, it is helpful and time efficient to work on the on-line databases. Searching databases can be fun, but you must know how to use the systems. You can search databases by examining subjects, authors, or titles of articles.

Let us first consider a search based on subject. Begin by identifying the major constructs and concepts of your initial inquiry, and then translate these into what is referred to as key words. In addition to the title, author, and abstract, most journals in on-line databases require authors to specify and list key words that reflect the content of their study. Each database groups these studies according to these key words. For example, Box 5-5 presents part of the title page of a study of gender identity in individuals with head injury conducted by Guttman and Napier-Klemic.[6]

Without these key words, this study containing assessment of activity configuration could not be identified in a search on gender role and activity constellations. This example illustrates how valuable key words are in adding dimension to a study, ensuring that its future use in research can be maximized.

You can obtain help from the librarian in formulating key words, or the computer will help direct you to synonymous terms, if the words you initially select are not used as classifiers. Most on-line systems are user-friendly and interactive, in other words, the computer provides step-by-step directions on what to do.

If you search any of the key words listed in the Guttman and Napier-Klemic article, you will come across a citation of the article.

Let us return to the example of the exercise study to show the importance of key words. We will begin our search with the key words, "exercise" and "elderly." The combination of terms is critical in delimiting and focusing your search. For example, when we searched "Carl's Uncover," a database of journal and newspaper

articles available in many university libraries, we first entered the key word, "exercise." The computer counted the citations that were relevant to the subject of exercise and indicated that there were 4495 different sources in the past 5 years. A review of all of these sources will be too cumbersome, to say the least. We then entered our second key word, "elderly," at a prompt that requested further delimiting. The computer then searched for works containing both topics and indicated a total of 46 articles.

After the computer indicates how many citations are found, the next step is to display the sources. Often you have a choice of examining only the citation or the abstract. If your on-line system is connected to a printer, you can select a print command and print the citation and abstract.

You may also search the system by entering authors' names or words you believe may appear in the titles of sources. This entry expands your search to relevant articles that may not have included the combination of key words initially used. The computer will search the references and compile a list of sources from which to choose.

In some cases it is more efficient to ask the librarian to conduct a search for you. Sometimes, large databases, such as ERIC (Educational Information Resources Information Center) and Medline, are accessed in this manner. Asking the librarian to conduct an evening search will be less expensive than a daytime search, because the telephone lines that are used to connect the library's computer to the central database charge less in off-peak hours.

It is also possible to conduct a more limited search by accessing databases that index or

---

**Box 5-5** | **Experience of head injury on impairment of gender identity and gender role**

Sharon A. Guttman, Jean Napier-Klemic

*Key words:*

● Activity configuration analysis
● Personality development

abstract studies in only a specific field or subject. For example, many libraries have a database titled "PsychLIT," which contains sources from the field of psychology and related areas. "Mini-Medline" is another limited database frequently available in universities with health and medical departments. Each of the databases gives user-friendly directions for access and use.

You also may want to do a manual search in the important indexes and abstracts to ensure that you have fully covered the literature relevant to your study. In health research, useful indexes and abstracts include those listed in Box 5-6.

You can search these indexes and abstracts by author, subject, or title, just as you have done with the on-line database. Of course, there are many abstracting and indexing services; it is impossible to list all of the relevant ones here. However, "Ulriche's International Periodical Directory" is a useful reference because it lists all periodicals and databases in which these periodicals are indexed.

---

**Box 5-6    Useful indexes and abstracts**

- Social Science Citation Index
- General Science Index
- Reader's Guide to Periodical Literature
- Index to Government Periodicals
- New York Times Index
- Psychological Abstracts
- Medical Psychological Abstracts
- Cumulative Index to Nursing and Allied Health
- Social Work Abstracts

---

One major directory of abstracts that is not frequently used but is extremely helpful in locating sources is "Dissertation Abstracts International." Because a literature review in a dissertation is usually exhaustive, obtaining a dissertation in your topic area may provide the most comprehensive literature review and bibliography available.

***Searching books and other documents.*** Most libraries, particularly those in colleges and universities, have already computerized the listing of their collections of books and documents. As in searching periodicals, on-line book searching is equally efficient and fun. In these searches, you obtain information about the title, author, and source, as well as the subject, listed by key words and concepts. Also a description of the location of the book and its availability are included in the full citation. If you are unfamiliar with conducting a search, ask the librarian how to use the library system.

Most beginning investigators are concerned with the number of sources to review. Although there is no magical number, most researchers search the literature for articles written within the previous 5 years. A search is extended beyond 5 years to evaluate the historical development of an issue or to review a breakthrough article that was published earlier. The depth of a review is dependent on the purpose and scope of your study. Most investigators try to become familiar with the most important authors, studies, and papers in their topic area. You will have a sense that your review is comprehensive when you begin to see citations of authors you have already read. Also, do not hesitate to call a researcher who has published in your topic area and ask for his or her recent work or articles that he or she recommends you review.

## Step 4:  Organize information

With your list of sources identified by your searches, you are ready to retrieve and organize them.  We usually begin by reading abstracts of journal articles to determine their value to the study.  Based on the abstract, we determine if the study fits one of four categories, as suggested by Findley.[7]  If a study is highly relevant, it goes into what Findley calls the A pile—those studies that absolutely must be read.  If the study appears somewhat relevant, it goes into a B pile—those studies that probably will be read, depending on the direction taken.  If the study might be relevant, it goes into a C pile—those studies that may be read, depending on the direction taken.  Finally, if a study is not relevant at all, it goes into an X pile—those studies that will not be read but will be kept, just in case.  With books, do the same type of categorizing based on the table of contents and the preface.

Next, begin with the A pile, and classify the articles according to the major subjects or concepts.  It is helpful to pick a reading order to outline a preliminary conceptual framework for your literature review.

Because it is not possible to remember all the important information presented in reading, note taking is critical.  There are many different schemes for note taking. Some find that taking notes on index cards is effective because index cards can be shuffled and reordered to fit into an outline.  Others take notes on a database or word processing system.  In general, your notes should include a synopsis of the content, the conceptual framework for the work, the method, and a brief review of the findings.  Whatever method you use, always be sure to cite the full reference.  All researchers have had the miserable experience of losing the volume or page number of a source and then having to spend hours finding it later.

Although each investigator organizes and writes in his or her unique way, we offer two strategies you may want to try or modify to fit your own purpose and style.  We suggest using a chart and concept/construct matrix to organize your reading.  These two organizational aids will also assist in the writing stage of your review.

***Charting the literature.***  In this approach, select pertinent information from each article you review and record it on a chart.  You need to determine the categories of information you will record or place on the chart.  The categories you choose should reflect the nature of your research project and how you plan to develop a rationale for your study.  For example, if you are planning an experimental exercise study for elderly patients with diabetes, your review may highlight the limited number of adequately designed exercise studies with this particular population.  The categories of your chart may therefore include the designs of previous studies and health status of the samples.  An excerpt of a chart is shown in Table 5-1 to illustrate this method of organization.  This chart was developed for a review of literature on exercise intervention studies for healthy older adults.  Charting research articles in this way will allow you to reflect on the literature as a whole and critically evaluate and identify research gaps.

*Concept/construct matrix.* The *concept/construct matrix* organizes information that you have reviewed and evaluated by key concept/construct (the X axis) and source (the Y axis). Table 5-2 displays an excerpt from a concept matrix used in a study by Butler.[5] In this naturalistic study of homeless, middle-aged women, Butler began her literature review by searching three major constructs: homelessness, gender, and middle age. Two other constructs, pathology and poverty, were also identified in the literature on homeless persons. Butler integrated these constructs into her theoretical discussion of existing knowledge, and they were added to the concept matrix. As you begin to write the literature review, the concept/construct matrix facilitates quick identification of the articles that address the specific concepts/constructs you need to discuss.

## Step 5: Critically evaluate the literature

There are several guiding questions you can use to help critically evaluate the literature. Use the questions in Table 5-3 to guide your reading of research literature and the questions in Table 5-4 to prompt your evaluation of nonresearch literature. Your responses to these evaluative questions will inform your research direction.

An evaluation of nonresearch sources involves examining the level of and support for the knowledge presented. Nonresearch sources may include position papers, theoretical works, editorials, and debates. Another important resource is work that presents a critical review of research in a particular area. These published literature reviews provide syntheses of research as ways of summarizing the states of knowledge in particular fields and identifying new directions for research.

### Table 5-1 Literature review chart

| Author (date) | Sample boundaries | Design | Dependent constructs | Claims |
|---|---|---|---|---|
| Blumenthal et al.[8] (1982) | 24 elderly adults from retirement homes (mean age 69 yr) | No control group | Mood (profile of mood) | No change |
| | | | Temperament (Thurstone scale) | No change |
| | | | Self-report of improvement | 40% improved |
| | | | Personality type | No change |

### Table 5-2 Butler's concept/construct matrix[5]

| | Concept 1 | Concept 2 | Concept 3 | Concept 4 | Concept 5 |
|---|---|---|---|---|---|
| Concept | Homelessness | Gender | Middle age | Pathology | Poverty |
| Source | Hosp and Com 1100-1100 | Miller | Hunter and Sundrel | DSMIII-R | Axinn and Levin |

| Table 5-3 | **Evaluating research articles** | |
|---|---|---|
| | *Experimental-type* | *Naturalistic Inquiry* |

| *Experimental-type* | *Naturalistic Inquiry* |
|---|---|
| _____ Was the study clear, unambiguous, and internally consistent? | _____ Was the study clear, unambiguous, and internally consistent? |
| _____ What is (are) the research question(s)? Are they clearly and adequately stated? | _____ What is (are) the research query(ies)? Are they clearly and adequately stated? |
| _____ What is the purpose of the study? | _____ What is the purpose of the study? |
| _____ How does the purpose influence the design and the conclusions? | _____ How does the purpose influence the design and the conclusions? |
| _____ Describe the theory that guides the study and the conceptual framework for the project. Are they clearly presented and relevant to the study? | _____ Describe the theory that guides the study and the conceptual framework for the project. Are they clearly presented and relevant to the study? |
| _____ What are the key constructs identified in the literature review? | _____ What are the key constructs identified in the literature review? |
| _____ What level of theory is suggested in the literature review? Is it consistent with the selected research strategy? | _____ What level of theory is suggested in the literature review? Is it consistent with the selected research strategy? |
| _____ What is the rationale for the design found in the literature review? Is it sound? | _____ What is the rationale for the design found in the literature review? Is it sound? |
| _____ Does the design of the project fit the level of theory? Is relevant knowledge presented in the literature review? | _____ Does the design of the project fit the level of theory? Is relevant knowledge presented in the literature review? |
| _____ Diagram the design. | _____ Describe the design. |
| _____ Does the design answer the research question(s)? Why or why not? | _____ Does the design answer the research query(ies)? Why or why not? |
| _____ What are the boundaries of the study? How are the boundaries selected? | _____ What are the boundaries of the study? How are the boundaries selected? |
| _____ What efforts did the investigator make to ensure validity and reliability? | _____ What efforts did the investigator make to ensure trustworthiness? |

*Continued*

| Table 5-3 | **Evaluating research articles—cont'd** |
|---|---|

| *Experimental-type* | *Naturalistic Inquiry* |
|---|---|
| _____ What data collection techniques were used? Is the rationale for these techniques specified in the literature review and/or in the methods section? | _____ What data collection techniques were used? Is the rationale for these techniques specified in the literature review and/or in the methods section? |
| _____ How does data collection fit with the study purpose and study question? | _____ How does data collection fit with the study purpose and study query? |
| _____ How are the data analyzed? Does the analysis plan make sense for the study? How does the analysis plan fit with the study purpose and study question? | _____ How are the data analyzed? Does the analysis plan make sense for the study? How does the analysis plan fit with the study purpose and study query? |
| _____ Are the conclusions supported by the study? | _____ Are the conclusions supported by the study? |
| _____ What are the strengths of the study? | _____ What are the strengths of the study? |
| _____ What level of knowledge is generated? | _____ What level of knowledge is generated? |
| _____ What use does this knowledge have for health and service practice? | _____ What use does this knowledge have for health and service practice? |
| _____ Are there ethical dilemmas presented in this article? What are they? Did the author(s) resolve the dilemmas in a reasonable and ethical manner? | _____ Are there ethical dilemmas presented in this article? What are they? Did the author(s) resolve the dilemmas in a reasonable and ethical manner? |

## Step 6: Write the literature review

You have now searched, obtained, read, and organized your literature. Finally it is time to write a review. The review is written for a proposal to justify doing the research or for a manuscript that describes the completed research project. A good literature review not only presents an overview of the relevant work on your topic, but it also includes a critical evaluation of the works. There is no recipe for writing a narrative literature review. Most investigators, regardless of which approach to design they use, include the categories of information in their narratives (Box 5-7).

**Table 5-4** **Guiding questions for evaluating nonresearch sources**

1. What way of knowing and level of knowledge are presented?
2. Was the work presented clearly, unambiguously, and consistently?
3. What is the purpose of the work? Is the purpose implicit? It is stated? How does the purpose influence the knowledge discussed in the work?
4. What is the scope and/or application of the paper?
5. What support exists for the claims being made in the source?
6. What debates, new ideas, and trends are presented in the work?
7. What are the strengths and weaknesses of the work?
8. What research queries, or questions, emerge from the work?

**Box 5-7** **Elements of writing a literature review**

- Introduction
- Discussion of each related concept, construct, principle, theory,and model in current literature
- Brief review of related study designs and their results
- Critical appraisal of current related research and knowledge
- Integration of various works reviewed
- Fit of investigator's study with the collective knowledge related to topic under investigation
- Overview and justification for study and design

A suggested outline for writing the narrative is presented in Box 5-8.

**Box 5-8** **Suggested outline for writing narrative**

- Introduction (overview of what the review covers)
- Review of specific concepts
- Description of how each concept has been studied
- Overview of studies
- Design
- Results
- Critical evaluation
- Critical summary of current knowledge and gaps in literature
- Integration of concepts; relationships proposed in studies
- Identification of research needs
- Rationale for study and design
- Overview and niche for proposed study

## Summary

In this chapter four major purposes of a literature review and six steps for conducting a search are discussed. Guidelines for writing a sound review are also provided.

The literature review is a critical evaluation of existing literature that is relevant to your study. Because it is a critical evaluation, reviewing the literature is a thinking process that involves piecing together and integrating diverse bodies of literature. The review provides an understanding of the level of theory and knowledge development that exists about your topic. This understanding is essential so that you can determine how your study fits into the construction of knowledge in the topic area.

The literature review is also an action process whereby concepts are organized and sources are logically presented in a written review. The *literature review chart* and concept/construct matrix are two organizational tools that will help you conceptualize the literature and write an effective review. An effective written review is one that convinces the reader that your study is necessary, and it represents the next step in knowledge building. Remember, the primary purposes of writing a literature review and including it in the written report of your research are to establish the conceptual foundation for your research, establish the specific content of your study, and, most important, provide a rationale for your research design.

## Exercises

1. You are interested in studying the effectiveness of a joint mobilization program to increase the range of motion of the lower extremities of children with spinal cord injuries. Define the key words you will use to conduct a search for relevant literature.

2. Select a research article and develop a concept/construct matrix from the literature presented. What level of knowledge and theory development is presented? Was the design selected appropriate for the level of knowledge in the literature?

### References

1. Gitlow L: *Attitudes of occupational therapy educators toward inclusion*, Minneapolis, Minn, 1997. Paper presented at the Society for Disability Studies.
2. DePoy E: Mastery in clinical occupational therapy, *Am J Occup Ther* 44:55-59, 1991.
3. Essex E, Seltzer MM, Krauss MW: Residential transitions of adults with mental retardation: predictors of waiting list use and placement, *AJMR* 101(6):613-629, 1997.
4. McCauley W, Travis SS, Safewright MP: Personal accounts of the nursing home search and selection process, *Qualitative Health Research* 7(2):236-254, 1997.
5. Butler SS: *Middle-aged, female and homeless: the stories of a forgotten group*, New York, 1994, Garland.
6. Guttman SA, Napier-Klemic J: The experience of head injury on the impairment of gender identity and gender role, *Am J Occup Ther* 50(7):535-544, 1996.
7. Findley TM: The conceptual review of the literature or how to read more articles than you ever wanted to see in your entire LIFE, *Am J Phys Med Rehabil* 68:97-102, 1989.
8. Blumenthal JA, Schocker DD, Needels TL, et al: Psychological and physiological effects of physical conditioning on the elderly, *J Psychosom Res* 26:505-510, 1982.

# Chapter 6

# Theory in research

**Key terms**    Concept
Construct
Hypothesis
Levels of abstraction
Operationalize
Proposition
Theory
Theory generating
Theory testing

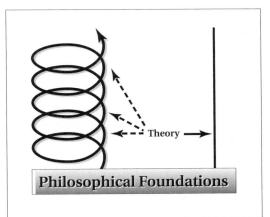

Philosophical Foundations

As we have discussed in previous chapters, the level of knowledge and theory development in a particular field or in your area of interest determines, in large part, the type of design you choose and the specific methods and analyses of a study. In this chapter we discuss the relationship between theory and research and explain the ways in which theory is used by both the experimental-type and naturalistic researchers.

## Why is theory important?

When people hear the word *theory,* they often feel overwhelmed and assume that the term is not relevant to their daily lives or is too abstract and complicated to understand. Think, however, how difficult life would be without theory. Theory informs us each day in many aspects of our lives, from knowing how to prepare for the weather to guiding our professional practice. For example, predicting the weather is based on existing theory. The meteorologist looks at present weather conditions and past weather patterns and makes a prediction in the form of a forecast. In health and human service delivery, you make a decision about which intervention to use based on theory. You use a theory to guide your decisions, even though you may not be fully cognizant that you are actually doing so.

Let us assume you are a social worker in a psychiatric hospital. A new member comes to your group therapy session with a diagnosis of a major depressive disorder. Theoretically you know that this diagnosis is associated with a set of symptoms and behaviors, particularly self-degradation, faulty thinking, and melancholia. Based on this cognitive–behavioral theoretical understanding of the symptoms[1] and the prediction of the individual's behavioral outcomes, you approach this client with support and engage him or her in a cognitive behavioral program in which self-degrading ideation is incrementally decreased. Without the theory, you would not know how to work skillfully with this client.

As discussed in Chapter 1, a primary purpose of research is to test theory using deduction and experimental-type designs or generate theory using induction or abduction and naturalistic-based designs. In this chapter we add the idea that the researcher must have a theoretical framework to conduct adequate research. Let us examine the reasons why. As discussed throughout this text, thinking and action processes are equally important parts of research. The thinking processes that are critical to research are the set of human ideas that can be organized to understand human experience and phenomena. As described later in this chapter, these ideas are theories or parts of theories. Even though we may not realize it, theory frames how we ask, look at, and answer questions. Theory provides conceptual clarity and the capacity to connect new knowledge that is obtained through data collection actions to the vast body of knowledge to which it is relevant. Without theory, we cannot have conceptual direction. Data that are derived without being conceptually embedded in theoretical contexts do not advance our understanding of human experience. As simply stated by Neuman, "…theory helps a researcher see the forest instead of just a single tree."[2]

Let us consider the debate about "race" and "ethnic" data collection in the census to illustrate this important point. Every 10 years, the United States government conducts a national census in which characteristics of individuals, families, and neighborhoods ascertained by collecting information. Over the last 3 decades, there has been a significant debate about the need and ethical rationale for recording race and ethnicity.[3] Proponents rationalize the inclusion of these questions in the census by suggesting that no useful data on ethnicity are available. However, opponents highlight the conceptual vagueness of the concepts of race and ethnicity as a result of atheoretical data collection and analysis. Both are problematic and suggest that any attempt to use the data for understanding, service planning, and policy formulation is futile at best and discriminatory at worst. No one knows what race and ethnicity mean. As stated by Ahmad and Sheldon, "Our first concern is that the 'ethnic' question in the census is both rigid and externally imposed. It uses a culturalist, geographic, and 'nationalist' notion of race dressed up as ethnicity."[3] The authors urge that the inclusion of ethnic data collection be preceded by careful consideration of the definition and use of ethnicity as a theoretical construct to avoid the harm that can be done to significant numbers of people by ungrounded and vague use of the critically important terms of race and ethnicity.

Now that we know the importance of theory, let us examine its definition and components.

## What is theory?

Numerous definitions of theory can be found in research texts and books on theory construction. We believe Kerlinger's definition of theory is the most comprehensive and useful. Kerlinger defines theory as "...a set of interrelated constructs, definitions, and propositions that present a systematic view of phenomena by specifying relations among variables, with the purpose of explaining or predicting phenomena."[4] In this definition, theory is a set of related ideas that has the potential to explain or predict human expe-

rience in an orderly fashion and is based on data. The theorist develops a structural map of what is observed and experienced in an effort to promote understanding and to facilitate the ability to predict outcomes under specific conditions. Through deductive research approaches or empirical investigations, theories are either supported and verified or refuted and falsified. Through inductive approaches, theories are incrementally developed to explain and give order to observations of human experience.

As implied in Kerlinger's definition, there are four interrelated structural components subsumed under theory, which range in degree or level of abstraction. Whereas there are many taxonomies for the parts of a theory,[5] we suggest that the four basic structures are concepts, constructs, relationships, and propositions or principles. Let us examine the meaning of abstraction and then discuss each level.

## Levels of abstraction

Abstraction often conjures up a vision of the ethereal, the "not real." In this book, however, we use the term abstraction as it relates to theory development, to depict symbolic representation of shared experience. For example, if we all see a form that has fur, a tail, four legs, and barks, we name that observation a dog. We have shared in the visual experience and have created a symbol (the word dog) to name our sensory experience. All words are merely symbols to describe shared experience. Words are only one form of abstraction, and different words represent different *levels of abstraction*.

Figure 6-1 displays four levels of abstraction within theory and the relationship of each

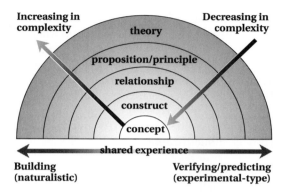

**Figure 6-1** Levels of abstraction

to the other. Shared experience is the foundation on which abstraction is built. It is important to recognize that we do not use the term reality as the foundation. Reality implies that there is only one viewpoint from which to build the basic elements of a theory. In contrast, this text is based on the premise that human beings experience multiple realities and multiple perspectives about the nature of reality. As such, levels of abstraction must be built on shared experience, defined as the consensus of what we obtain through our senses. For experimental-type researchers working deductively, shared experience is usually thought of as sense data, or that which can be reduced to observation and measurement. For researchers working inductively and abductively within the naturalistic tradition, shared experience may include meanings and interpretations of human experience. Let us use the example of the furry being with four legs and a tail that barks to illustrate the multiple meanings that can be attributed to shared experience. Shared experience tells each of us that this is a dog, but the meaning of

that experience may be fear for some and love for others. Each type of experience is equally as important to acknowledge.

As depicted in Figure 6-1, a *concept* is the first level of abstraction and is defined as a symbolic representation of an observable or experienced referent. Concepts help us communicate our experiences and ideas to one another. Without them we would not have language.[6] In the case of the furry being, the word dog is a concept. It describes an observation shared by many. The words furry, tail, four legs, and bark are also concepts because they are directly sensed. In experimental-type research, concepts are selected before a study is started and are defined in such a way as to permit direct measurement or observation. In naturalistic research, concepts are derived from direct observations throughout engagement in the field.

A *construct*, the next level of abstraction, does not have an observable or a directly experienced referent in shared experience. Continuing with the example of dog—for those who do not experience fear, fear is a construct. The fearless observer of the dog may infer that others are fearful. In this case, fear is a construct because it is not directly observed or experienced by the fearless. What may be observed are the behaviors associated with fear, that is, someone who sweats, shakes, turns pale, and moves away from the dog. These observations are synthesized into the construct of fear. Thus fear itself is not directly observed but is surmised, based on a constellation of behavioral concepts. Categories are also examples of constructs. The category of mammal or canine is an example of a construct. Each category is not directly observable; however, it is composed of a set of concepts that can be observed. Other examples of constructs relevant to health and human service inquiry include health, wellness, life roles, rehabilitation, poverty, illness, disability, functional status, and psychological well-being. Each is not directly observable but is made up of parts or components that can be observed or submitted to measurement.

So far, we have been discussing single-word symbols or units of abstraction. At the next level of abstraction, single units are connected and form a relationship. A relationship is defined as an association of two or more constructs or concepts. For example, we may suggest that the size of a dog is related to the level of fear that one experiences. This relationship has two constructs, size and fear, and one concept, dog.

A *proposition* is the next level of abstraction. A proposition or principle is a statement that governs a set of relationships and gives them a structure. For example, a proposition suggests that fear of large dogs is caused by negative childhood experiences with large dogs. This proposition describes the structure of two sets of relationships, the relationship between the size of a dog and fear and the relationship between childhood experiences and the size of dogs. It also suggests the direction of the relationship and the influence of each construct on the other.

Let us consider a theory to illustrate these different levels of abstraction and their relationship. A theory related to the furry being may look like this: Fear of large dogs derives from childhood experiences. It therefore can be cured by psychoanalysis that aims to reverse the negative effects of childhood experiences.

This theory explains the phenomenon, fear of dogs; it is verifiable and can lead to prediction. If, through research, we can support a positive relationship between childhood experiences and the fear of dogs and the effectiveness of psychoanalysis in reducing that fear, we can predict this relationship in the future and control its outcome.

## Levels of abstraction and design selection

We conclude our discussion of levels of abstraction with principles that relate these levels to design selection. We view abstraction as symbolic naming or the representation of shared experience. The further a symbol is removed from shared experience, the higher the level of abstraction. Each level of abstraction, as depicted in Figure 6-1, moves farther away from shared experience. The higher the level of abstraction, the more complex your design becomes. This principle is based on common sense. If the scope of your study is to examine a construct, a complex investigation (such as that required for the development or testing of a full-fledged theory) is not necessary. Consider the following example. Assume you are interested in determining the level of cognitive recovery in a group of persons with head injuries. This type of investigation is an inquiry into the construct of cognitive recovery and requires that one construct be defined and measured in your population. However, suppose you want to move into the realm of propositions and determine the extent to which age at the time of injury affects recovery rate. In this type of investigation, you need to define the construct, "recovery," and state the nature of the relationship between it and the concept of age. As you add more constructs, such as the level of severity of injury and the status before injury, your design increases in complexity.

Let us consider another example that requires a different type of inquiry. Assume you are interested in understanding the behaviors that place rural teenagers at risk for contracting the human immunodeficiency virus (HIV). Because the body of knowledge on the risk of HIV in the teenage population focuses on urban teenagers, you have no theory or set of constructs to investigate; consequently, you simply collect data through asking questions and observing behaviors of the referent group. However, as your observations proceed you find that many factors emerge that impact rural teenage behavior and risk. The complexity of your research approach increases as you focus on discovering specific patterns or relationships among constructs that you observe.

Although concepts, constructs, relationships, and propositions or principles provide the basic language and building blocks of any research project, each research tradition handles the levels of abstraction differently. Let us examine the role of theory in design selection.

## Role of theory in design selection

When theory is well-developed and fits the phenomenon under investigation, deductive studies are likely to be implemented. When theory is poorly developed or does not fit the phenomenon under study, inductive and abductive studies that generate theory may be more appropriate. The degree of knowledge development and relevance of a theory for the particular phenomenon under investigation determines in part the nature and type of research that you will

conduct. Let us consider an example that reflects the differences in knowledge development and use of research to test and build theory.

Lawrence Kohlberg is a well-known scholar who developed a theory of moral reasoning. He suggested three basic levels of moral reasoning that develop and unfold throughout the life span: preconventional, conventional, and postconventional.[7] Briefly, in the preconventional reasoning stage, individuals develop notions of right and wrong, based on reward or punishment; in conventional reasoning, individuals use accepted norms of right and wrong to guide their moral decisions; and in postconventional reasoning, humans use their own intrinsic notions of morality to formulate decisions and actions. Many investigators have accepted this theory as truth and have attempted to characterize and predict the moral reasoning of different populations. Scales to measure moral reasoning have been developed based on Kohlberg's theory and have been used with different groups of people representing diverse socioeconomic, age, and gender groups. Based on these studies, populations and individuals have been categorized contingent on the level of moral reasoning they exhibit. This information has been extremely valuable in promoting our understanding of morality in human beings. The characterization of moral reasoning based on Kohlberg's theory is an example of a deductive relationship between theory and research; that is to say, the theory has been accepted as true, and subsequent studies have intended to verify and advance the application of the theory in varied populations.

However, in the majority of studies in adults, women have been found to reason at a lower level than men. Researchers have concluded that women are not as morally advanced as men. Carol Gilligan, who uses a feminist framework, did not accept Kohlberg's theory as true for women because it was intuitively contrary to what she experienced and believed. Although knowledge had been well-developed in this area, the theory did not seem to fit or to be relevant to the experiences of women. She used inductive research strategies to discover and understand the nature of moral reasoning in women. Through extensive in-depth interviews with women, Gilligan found that women were not less moral than men but used different criteria on which to base their moral decision making. These criteria were substantially different from those identified by Kohlberg's theory and those operationalized in the scales that had been developed to reflect his theory. Although there was extensive theory development, Gilligan's research suggested that Kohlberg's notions did not explain moral reasoning in women. Inductive strategies were essential to reveal the processes by which women reasoned and to develop theory that reflected their thought processes. Not surprisingly, Kohlberg had developed his theory of moral reasoning by studying men. Therefore the deductive strategy was most valuable in expanding knowledge of the moral reasoning in men but not necessarily in women. Gilligan's research strategy illustrates the relationship between theory and naturalistic inquiry; in other words, naturalistic inquiry is extremely valuable as a theory-generating tool, but it also can be used to verify or refute a theory.

Now, let us discuss in detail the relationship between theory and research in each of the research traditions.

## Theory in experimental-type inquiry

Experimental-type researchers begin with a theory and seek to simplify and reduce abstraction by making the abstract observable, measurable, and predictable (see Figure 6-1). Usually this process involves first specifying a theory and then developing hypotheses. A *hypothesis* is linked to a theory and is a statement about the expected relationships between two or more concepts that can be tested. A hypothesis indicates what is expected to be observed and represents the researchers "best hunch" as to what may exist or be found, based on the principles of the theory.

As an example, control theory has been used extensively in medical sociology to explain deviant behavior of adolescents. Developed by Hirschi, this theory posits that people with strong attachments, or bonds, to society are less likely to participate in deviant behavior (including cigarette smoking and alcohol abuse) than those with weaker ties.[9] As you can see, this theory identifies two basic constructs,

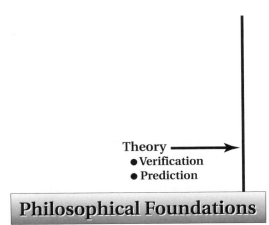

Theory ⟶
- Verification
- Prediction

**Philosophical Foundations**

bonds and deviant behavior, and suggests a relationship between these constructs. Based on this theory, a major hypothesis has been formulated and tested suggesting there is a negative association between attachment to parents and adolescent smoking, regardless of the smoking behavior or the attitudes of the parents. The hypothesis suggests that the greater the attachment or bond, the less likely an adolescent will smoke. This hypothesis also suggests that such a relationship will hold regardless of the smoking behavior of the parent.

Hypotheses can be written in one of two forms, nondirectional or directional. Consider, for example, the following nondirectional hypothesis derived from stress theory:

For persons who care for individuals with Alzheimer's disease, there is a relationship between caregiver stress and the level of function of the care recipient.

A hypothesis can also indicate the direction or nature of a relationship between two concepts or constructs, as illustrated in this example of a directional hypothesis:

Caregivers of persons with Alzheimer's disease experience increasing stress as the care recipient with Alzheimer's experiences deterioration in function.

Thus, as shown in Figure 6-2, a hypothesis is the initial reduction of theory to a more concrete and observable form. Based on the hypothesis the researcher develops an operational definition of a concept so that it can be measured by a scale or other instrumentation. The operational defi-

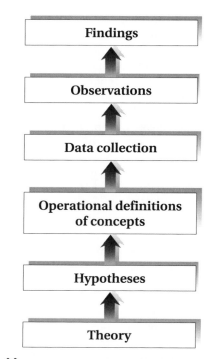

**Figure 6-2** Using theory in experimental-type research.

nition of the concept further reduces the abstract to a concrete observable form. An operational definition of a concept specifies the exact procedures for measuring or observing the phenomenon. In the previous example, the investigator will need to *operationalize* stress and functional level. The process of operationalizing a concept is not easy or straightforward. Each researcher may develop his or her own way of operationalizing. (This process is discussed in greater detail in Chapter 17, where we examine measurement issues.) Using an operational definition, the researcher makes observations that result in data that are then analyzed. Analysis determines if the findings verify, refute, or modify the theory. This scientific process of reducing abstraction is used primarily to test relationships among concepts of a theory and ultimately to determine the adequacy of a theory to make predictions and thus control the phenomenon under study.

The six basic characteristics of the way in which experimental-type researchers use theory are depicted in Box 6-1.

The process, referred to as logical deduction, begins with an abstraction and then focuses on discrete parts of phenomena or observations. Constructs are defined and simplified and, in turn, operationalized into concepts that can be observed to allow measurement. As you can see, this process moves from a more abstract level to a less abstract or more concrete, observable level.

### Theory in naturalistic inquiry

Whereas *theory testing* is the primary goal of the experimental-type researcher, researchers working within the naturalistic tradition are more frequently concerned, although not always, with developing theory from observations. Thus in naturalistic research, the researcher begins with shared experience and then represents that experience at increasing levels of abstraction. In this approach, definitions of concepts and constructs are not set before a study is begun; rather, definitions emerge from the data collection and analytical processes themselves. In many of the orientations of naturalistic research, the aim is to ground or link concepts and constructs to each observation or datum. This theory-method link,[10] or ground-

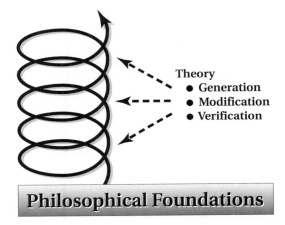

**Box 6-1** **Six characteristics of theory use in experimental-type design**

- Logical deductive process
- Primarily theory testing
- Movement from theory to lesser levels of abstraction
- Assumption of unitary reality that can be measured
- Assumption of knowledge through existing conceptions
- Focus on measurable parts of phenomena

Theory
- Generation
- Modification
- Verification

**Philosophical Foundations**

ed theory approach, is described by Glaser and Strauss in this way:

Generating a theory from data means that most hypotheses and concepts not only come from the data, but are systematically worked out in relation to the data during the course of the research. Generating a theory involves a process of research.[11]

As discussed later in this text, each strategy classified as naturalistic inquiry is based on a different set of assumptions about how we come to know human experience. However, all researchers in this tradition tend to use qualitative methodologies to ground theory in observations. That is, definitions of concepts and then constructs emerge from the investigative process and analysis of the documentation (the data) of shared experience.[10] Based on emergent concepts and their relationships, the investigator develops theory to understand, explain, and give meaning to social and behavioral patterns.

Although each design structure describes this process somewhat differently, the illustration on page 64 (Figure 6-1) gives you the basic idea of the inductive process.

In some naturalistic inquiries, theory is used in a similar manner to experimental-type research. Once the investigator is immersed in observations, he or she frequently draws on well-established theories to explain these observations and make sense of what is being observed. Consider how social exchange theory, for example, may provide the ethnographer with an understanding of observed gift giving. In the process of observing gift exchange, the ethnographer may be reminded of a theory that he or she has previously read that seems to fit with the data set. Thus the theory is applied to the data set as an explanatory mechanism. However, the use of theory in this way occurs after the data have already been collected. Even in this way, theory does not guide data collection nor is it imposed on the data; rather, the data suggest which theory may be relevant.

This is not to say that naturalistic inquiry is atheoretical. Theory use, however, has a different function than in experimental-type research. All research begins from a particular theoretical framework based on assumptions of human experience and reality. This theoretical framework is not substantive or content-specific, but it is structural and frames the research approach. In naturalistic inquiry, the researcher may also begin within a substantive theoretical framework to explore its particular meaning for a specific group of people or in specified situations (e.g., the Kohlberg and Gilligan examples regarding moral reasoning). However, the function of the substantive theory in the naturalistic tradition is to place boundaries on the inquiry. The purpose is not to fit the data into the theoretical framework by reducing concepts to predefined measures. For example, in a study of an adult day care center, Hasselkus[12] explored the application of a theoretical framework of the therapeutic use of activities by staff who work with clients with dementia to promote development, maintain health, and restore function. The purpose of her study was to explore the meaning of activity in that setting. Although she questioned the assumptions of the therapeutic use of activities, this framework guided the types of observation she made. Her findings suggested that the use of a framework, such as the therapeutic use of activities by staff caring for individuals with dementia, may be inappropriate and lead to staff frustration.

The basic characteristics of the use of theory in naturalistic inquiry can be summarized as presented in Box 6-2.

The use of theory occurs primarily within inductive and abductive processes that move from shared experience to higher levels of abstraction. The focus is understanding complexity and *theory generating* that provides meaning to multiple subjective understandings. In this process, knowledge emerges from informants or study participants. Table 6-1 presents an overview of the use of theory in both experimental-type and naturalistic research traditions, as well as how theory can be used in integrated research.

| Box 6-2 | Use of theory in naturalistic inquiry |
|---------|----------------------------------------|

- Primarily uses inductive and abductive processes
- Primarily generates theory
- Moves from shared experience to higher levels of abstraction
- Assumes discovery of meaning through multiple subjective understandings
- Focuses on depicting complexity

## Summary

In this chapter we have discussed five major points:

**1.** Theory is fundamental to the research process.

**2.** Theory consists of four basic components that reflect different levels of abstraction. These levels are concepts, constructs, relationships, and propositions.

**3.** The level at which a theory is developed and its appropriateness determine, in part, the nature and structure of research design.

**4.** Experimental-type research moves from greater levels of abstraction to lesser levels of abstraction by reducing theory to specific hypotheses and operationalizing concepts to observe and measure as a way of testing the theory.

**5.** Naturalistic inquiry moves from less abstraction to more abstraction by grounding or linking theory to each datum that is observed or recorded in the process of conducting research.

| Table 6-1 | Use of theory among research traditions | | |
|-----------|---------------------------------|--------------|------------|
| *Experimental-type* | | *Naturalistic* | *Integrated* |
| Deductive | | Inductive and abductive | All |
| Theory testing | | Theory generating<br>Theory validating | Both |
| Decrease level of abstraction | | Increase level of abstraction | Both |

## Exercises

1. Select an experimental-type article, and determine the level of abstraction presented in the literature review.

2. In the article, search for the important constructs and determine how the authors have operationalized them.

3. Select a naturalistic article, and examine the use of theory in the study. What level of abstraction is developed in the article?

### References

1. Beck A: Cognitive therapy: past, present & future, *J Consult Clin Psychol* 61(2):194-198, 1993.
2. Neuman WL: *Social research methods: qualitative and quantitative approaches,* ed 3, Boston, 1997, Allyn Bacon.
3. Ahmad W, Sheldon T: Race and statistics. In Hammersley M, editor: *Social research: philosophy, politics and practice*, Newbury Park, Calif, 1992, Sage.
4. Kerlinger FN: *Foundations of behavioral research,* ed 2, New York, 1973, Holt, Rinehart & Winston.
5. Mosey AC: *Applied scientific inquiry in the health professions: an epistemological orientation,* Rockville, MD, 1992, AOTA.
6. Wilson J: *Thinking with concepts,* Cambridge, Mass, 1966, Cambridge University Press.
7. Kohlberg L: *The psychology of moral development,* New York, 1984, Harper & Row.
8. Gilligan C: *In a different voice: psychological theory and women's development,* Cambridge, Mass, 1982, Harvard University Press.
9. Hirschi T: *Causes of delinquency,* Berkeley, Calif, 1969, University of California Press.
10. Patton MQ: *Qualitative evaluation and research methods,* ed 2, Newbury Park, Calif, 1990, Sage.
11. Glaser B, Strauss A: *The discovery of grounded theory: strategies for qualitative research,* New York, 1967, Aldine.
12. Hasselkus B: The meaning of activity: day care for persons with Alzheimer's disease, *Am J Occup Ther* 46:199-206, 1992.

# Chapter 7

# Formulating research questions and queries

**Key terms**    Breakdowns
Descriptive questions
Directional hypothesis
Hypotheses
Nondirectional hypothesis
Predictive questions
Query
Relational questions

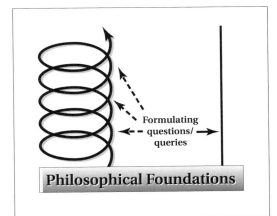

Formulating
questions/
queries

**Philosophical Foundations**

In Chapter 4 we discuss the thinking processes of identifying and framing research problems. In Chapter 5 we examine literature review and the role theory and previous work play in refining the structure and content of an inquiry. In this chapter we move beyond those two starting points to examine the development of questions in the experimental-type tradition and queries in the naturalistic tradition. You may note that we have used two terms, question and *query*, to describe the initial formal point of entry that precedes and bounds the collection of information in each of the two research traditions. The reason for this distinction will become clear as you read this chapter and learn how problems evolve into a question in experimental-type design and into a query in naturalistic research.

## Research questions in experimental-type design

In experimental-type design the researcher identifies a broad topic and then articulates the question that guides the investigation. The question is concise and narrow and establishes the boundaries or limits as to what concepts, individuals, or phenomena will be examined. The

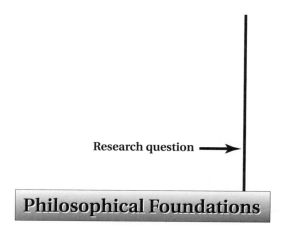

question is posed *a priori* to engaging in the research process and forms the basis from which all subsequent research action processes emerge. The purpose of the research question in the experimental-type tradition is to articulate not only the concepts but also the structure and scope of the concepts that will be studied. The research question leads the investigator to specific design and data collection action processes that involve a form of observation or measurement to answer the question. Questions are developed deductively from the theoretical principles that exist and that are presented in the literature. Questions seek to (1) describe a phenomenon, (2) explore relationships among phenomena, or (3) test existing theory or models. Each type of question reflects a different level of knowledge and theory development concerning the topic of interest: a Level 1 question is asked when little to nothing is empirically known about the topic; a Level 2 question is asked when descriptive knowledge is known, but relationships are not yet understood; a Level 3 question is asked when a substantial body of knowledge is known, and well-defined theory is developed. Let us examine each type of question in greater detail.

## Questions that seek to describe phenomena

Questions that aim to describe phenomena are referred to as Level 1 questions.[1] Level 1 *descriptive questions* are designed to elicit descriptions of a single topic or a single population about which there is theoretical or conceptual material in the literature but little or nothing is

**Research question** ⟶

**Philosophical Foundations**

empirically known. Level 1 questions lead to exploratory action processes where the intent is to describe. For example, let us assume that a body of knowledge exists regarding the attitudes of kindergarten to grade twelve teachers toward including children with disabilities in regular education classrooms; however, little is known about the attitudes of occupational therapy educators toward including students with disabilities in professional occupational therapy education. Therefore research based on a Level 1 question will be meaningful and appropriate to describe the attitudes of occupational therapy faculty toward accepting and teaching students with diverse disabilities in occupational therapy classes. Level 1 questions focus on a description of one concept or variable in a population. To describe a variable, which can be defined as a characteristic or phenomenon that has more than one value, you must first derive a lexical definition of the concept from the literature and operationalize or define it in such a way as to permit its measurement. Thus Level 1 questions focus on measuring the nature of a particular phenomenon in the population of interest.

Another example of this type of question concerns the study of the use of adaptive devices by older patients. A literature review shows only a limited body of knowledge regarding adaptive equipment use by older rehabilitation clients and little theoretical development to explain patterns of use. Thus Gitlin et al. designed a Level 1 descriptive study to describe the use of adaptive equipment in the home by rehabilitation clients and to develop an understanding of the reasons for use and nonuse by older clients

with a range of disabilities.[2] Specific research questions included: What is the frequency of use of adaptive devices by older adults discharged to their home from rehabilitation? What are the reasons for use and non-use of devices in the home?

In these research questions, the main concept or variable that was measured was the use of adaptive equipment. The population of interest was older adults with mixed disabilities who were discharged from rehabilitation to home. The focus of the Level 1 questions was on "the what," as seen in the wording of the questions. Some examples of other Level 1 questions are depicted in Box 7-1.

Each of these questions uses the stem of "what are" or "what is" and refers to one popu-

---

**Box 7-1**    **Level 1: Descriptive research questions**

- What are the attitudes of occupational therapy faculty toward including students with disabilities in professional occupational therapy education?[3]
- What are student enrollments, numbers and types of faculty, and student-faculty ratios in accredited Masters of Social Work (MSW) programs of the past 18 years?[4]
- What is the prevalence of fear of falling among community-dwelling older persons with impaired mobility?[5]

lation. In these examples one population is identified, such as occupational therapy faculty, social work students and faculty, and older, community-dwelling adults. Also, single concepts are examined in each study—attitudes toward inclusion, enrollment and student faculty ratios, and fear of falling, respectively. Each of these concepts can be measured or empirically examined. In essence, Level 1 questions describe the parts of the whole. Remember, the underlying thought process for experimental-type research is to learn about a topic by examining its parts and their relationships. Level 1 questioning is the foundation for clarifying the parts and their nature. In the scheme of levels of abstraction, Level 1 questions address the lowest levels of abstraction—those of concepts and constructs.

As discussed in later chapters, Level 1 questions lead to the development of descriptive designs, such as surveys, exploratory or descriptive studies, trend designs, feasibility studies, need assessments, and case studies.

## Questions that explore relationships among phenomena

The Level 2 *relational questions* build on and refine the results of Level 1 studies. Once a "part" of a phenomenon has been described and there is existing knowledge about it in the context of a particular population, the experimental-type researcher may pose questions that are relational. The key purpose of this level of questioning is to explore relationships among phenomena that have already been studied at the descriptive level. Here the stem question asks,

"What is the relationship?"or a variation thereof, and the topic contains two or more concepts or variables. For example, a researcher may be interested in asking, "What is the relationship between exercise capacity and cardiovascular health in middle-aged men?" In this case the two identified variables that are measured are exercise capacity and cardiovascular health. The specific population is middle-aged men. As you can surmise, Level 1 research must have been accomplished for the two variables to be defined and operationalized.

Return to the example of the last three questions. Suppose we have conducted studies to address the three Level 1 questions in Box 7-1. If we continue our research agenda in each of these areas of inquiry, we will be ready for the Level 2 questions (Box 7-2).

Referring to the levels of abstraction previously discussed, Level 2 questions address the level of relationship. Studies with this level of

---

Box 7-2 **Level 2:  Relational-type questions**

- What is the relationship between the attitudes of occupational therapy faculty and the number of students with disabilities admitted into occupational therapy education programs?
- What is the relationship between student learning and student-faculty ratio in MSW programs?
- What is the relationship between fear of falling and falling incidence in African-American elders who live alone in community-based settings?

questioning represent the next level of complexity above studies that rely on Level 1 questions. These questions continue to build on knowledge in the experimental-type framework by examining their parts, their relationships, and the nature and direction of these relationships. Level 2 questions primarily lead to research that uses passive observation design, as discussed in detail later in the text.

## Questions that test knowledge

Level 3 questions build knowledge that is generated from research conducted at Levels 1 and 2. A Level 3 question asks about a cause-and-effect relationship among two or more variables to test the knowledge or theory behind the knowledge. At Level 2 we asked the question, "What is the relationship among the attitudes of occupational therapy faculty and the number of students with disabilities admitted into occupational therapy education programs?" Assume the study revealed that there was a larger representation of students with disabilities in programs where occupational therapy educators had positive attitudes toward their inclusion, when compared with programs where the faculty had negative attitudes toward inclusion. Building on this knowledge, you are able to ask the Level 3 question, "To what extent do faculty attitudes influence the number of students with disabilities who are accepted into occupational therapy programs?" The resultant study will test the theory behind the reasons positive attitudes promote opportunity for students with disabilities, and the study will be able to predict the opportunity for disabled students to be accepted

into occupational therapy programs on the basis of faculty attitudes. At this level of questioning, the purpose is to predict what will happen and provide a theory to explain the reason(s). Based on a Level 3 question, specific predictive hypotheses, statements predicting the outcome of one variable on the basis of knowing another, are formulated. Action based on this knowledge can be taken to promote educational opportunity if you know where, why, and how to intervene.

In a Level 3 question, it is assumed that two concepts are related, based on previous research findings (from Level 2 research). The point of study at Level 3 is to test these concepts in action by manipulating one to affect the other. Level 3 is the most complex of experimental-type questioning. Once the foundation questions formulated at Levels 1 and 2 are answered, Level 3 questions can be posed and answered to develop knowledge, not only of parts and their relationships, but of how these parts interact and why they interact to cause a particular outcome. Level 3 questions examine higher levels of abstraction, including principles, theories, and models.

To answer a Level 3 question, the research action processes must be capable of revealing causal relationships among variables. A true experimental design or variation of it can be implemented to support the effectiveness of including client and caregiver perspectives in treatment. Table 7-1 summarizes our discussion thus far.

Brink and Wood provide some helpful rules to follow in developing an appropriate level of question (Box 7-3).

**Box 7-3**

### Helpful rules in developing a research question

- At Level 1, examine a variable in one population.
- At Level 2, examine relationship between a minimum of two variables.
- If there is a cause or effect to be investigated, pose the question at Level 3.
- If the words "cause," "effect," or any of their synonyms appear in the question, eliminate these words or specify what they are and how they vary.
- All variables must be written so that they vary.
- At Level 3, there must be two variables that specify a cause and effect.
- If a Level 3 question is written, make sure it is both ethical and possible to manipulate the causal variable. If not, rewrite the question at Level 2.

### Hypotheses

As we previously indicated, experimental-type researchers frequently engage in studies that involve *hypotheses*. Neuman offers the following definition of a hypothesis as it relates to varying levels of research questions:

> A hypothesis is a proposition to be tested or a tentative statement of a relationship between two variables.[6]

Thus hypotheses are primarily developed for Level 2 and 3 questions. Experimental-type researchers often have a "hunch" about the expected distribution of a single variable for a Level 1 question; however, a statement about a single variable is not a hypothesis. By definition, a Level 1 question does not have the essential elements of at least two variables and a statement of expected relationship.

Earlier in this text we indicated that hypotheses were a researcher's best "hunch" about a phenomenon. As you may surmise, in the

**Table 7-1**

### Summary of the types of questions in experimental-type research

| Level | Stem | Level of abstraction | Design possibilities |
|---|---|---|---|
| 1 | What is...? <br> What are...? | Concepts and constructs | Survey <br> Exploratory <br> Descriptive <br> Case study <br> Needs assessment |
| 2 | What is the relationship...? | Relationships | Survey <br> Correlational/passive <br> Observation <br> Ex post facto |
| 3 | Why...? | Principles <br> Theories <br> Models | Experimental designs <br> Quasiexperimental |

experimental-type tradition the "guess" does not emerge from thin air. Rather, it is based on existing literature and theory and stems from the research question that guides the study.

Hypotheses serve several important purposes in experimental-type research. First, they form an important link between the research question and the design of the study. In essence, hypotheses rephrase the research question and turn it into a measurable statement. Second, hypotheses can identify the anticipated direction of the relationship. This information may not be contained in the question. Consider this research question, "What is the relationship between the attitudes of occupational therapy faculty and the number of students with disabilities admitted into occupational therapy education programs?" In this study the investigator may hypothesize that there will be an association between faculty attitudes toward inclusion and the number of students with disabilities admitted into programs. However, the direction of this expectation is not stated. If the investigator formulates a *directional hypothesis,* it may appear like this, "It is hypothesized that positive faculty attitudes will be associated with a greater number of students with disabilities." Notice that there is no statement of a hypothesis such as the one stated above, and it does not suggest or state an expected cause. Let us rename our Level 3 question. "To what extent do faculty attitudes influence the number of students with disabilities who are accepted into occupational therapy programs?" The researcher is interested in predicting admission rates as a result of faculty attitudes. The researcher may structure a project in which programs and faculty with positive attitudes are compared with programs

and faculty with unfavorable attitudes. If other variables are controlled and a design is developed in which causal relationships are ascertained, the following hypothesis may be stated:

> There will be a significant difference in admission rates between programs with and programs without positive faculty attitudes toward inclusion of students with disabilities.

A directional hypothesis may be stated as the following:

> There will be significantly less students admitted to programs with unfavorable faculty attitudes than to programs with favorable faculty attitudes toward inclusion.

As discussed later in this text, a third and critical purpose of hypotheses is that they set the stage, so to speak, for statistical analysis. Table 7-2 provides examples of hypotheses for each type of research question.

## Research queries in naturalistic inquiry

As previously discussed, there is a range of philosophical perspectives that inform inquiry within naturalistic research. Each perspective is rooted in a distinct philosophical tradition and approaches the task of framing the problem somewhat differently. However, there are similarities in approaches to problem development that are discussed here.

Researchers in the naturalistic tradition generally identify a topic and a broad problem

**Table 7-2** Examples of hypotheses by level of question

| Level | Question | Nondirectional hypothesis | Directional hypothesis |
|---|---|---|---|
| 1 | What is the pattern of use and reasons for nonuse of mobility aids among the elderly with ambulation difficulties? | No hypothesis is possible. | Expected distribution: Older adults with ambulation difficulties will use mobility aids with high frequency. |
| 2 | What is the relationship between the attitudes of faculty toward disability and the actual number of admissions of students with disabilities? | There will be an association between attitudes and the number of student admissions. | Positive faculty attitude will be associated with a greater number of admissions of students with disabilities. |
| 2 | What is the relationship between gender and depression in spousal caregivers of the elderly with physical disabilities? | The level of depression in female spouses will be different from the level of depression in male spouses. | Female spouse caregivers will be more depressed than male spouse caregivers. |
| 3 | To what extent do faculty attitudes influence the number of students with disabilities who are accepted in occupational therapy programs? | There will be a significant difference in admission rates between programs with and programs without positive faculty attitudes toward inclusion. | Significantly fewer students are admitted to programs in which faculty has unfavorable attitudes than those programs with faculty who has favorable attitudes toward inclusion. |
| 3 | What is the effect of psychoeducational counseling for family caregivers with depression? | The level of depression in family caregivers who attend psychoeducational sessions will differ from those who do not attend sessions. | Depression will be lower among caregivers who attend psychoeducational sessions than among those who do not attend. |

area or phenomenon from which a query is pursued. We use the term "query" to refer to a broad statement that identifies the phenomenon or natural field of interest. The phenomenon of interest may refer to symbolic patterns of interaction in a cultural group, the experience of disability, the meaning of pain, and so forth. The natural field in which the phenomenon occurs forms the basis for discovery from which more specific and limited questions evolve in the course of conducting the research. That is, as new insights and meanings are obtained, the initial problem statement and query become reformulated. Based on new insights and issues

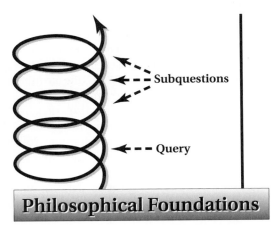

Subquestions

Query

**Philosophical Foundations**

the researcher assumes a "learning role" in which different cultural settings are interpreted and experienced firsthand. The information gathered bridges the world and culture of the researcher to that of the researched.[8] Once the ethnographer has identified a phenomenon and cultural setting, a query is pursued. Agar explained the process in this way:

> When you stand on the edge of a village and watch the noise and motion, you wonder, "Why are these people [here] and what are they doing?" When you read a news story about the discontent of young lawyers with their profession, you wonder, "What is going on here?"[7]

that emerge in the field, the investigator formulates smaller, concise subquestions that are then pursued. These smaller questions are contextual, or context-based, in that they evolve inductively within the study itself from the investigator's ongoing efforts to understand the broad problem area. This interactive questioning–data gathering–analyzing–reformulating of the questions represents the core action process of naturalistic inquiry. Let us examine three qualitative methods in the naturalistic tradition to determine how each develops a researchable query and engages in a process of formulation and reformulation.

## Classical ethnography

As the primary research approach in anthropology, ethnography is concerned with description and interpretation of cultural patterns of groups and the understanding of the cultural meanings people use to organize and interpret their experiences.[7] In this approach

As you can see, experimental-type questions and hypotheses stand in stark contrast to the interpretative-opened query posed by the ethnographer.

As the process of data gathering and analysis proceeds in tandem, specific questions emerge and are pursued. These questions emerge in the field as a consequence of what Agar labels as *breakdowns*, or disjunctions.[7] He describes this occurrence in this way, "A breakdown is a lack of fit between one's encounter with a tradition and the schema-guided expectation by which one organizes experience."[7] Put simply, a breakdown represents the difference between what the investigator observes and expects. These differences stimulate a series of questioning and further investigation. Each subquestion is related to the broader line of query and is investigated to resolve the breakdown and develop a more comprehensive understanding of the phenomenon in its entirety.

An ethnographic query, therefore, establishes the phenomenon, the setting of interest, or both. The query also sets up the thought-and-action processes necessary to understand the boundaries. To summarize, once a query has been posed, questioning occurs simultaneously with collecting information and making sense of it. One process drives the other. The interactive questioning, data gathering, and analytical processes result in the reformulation and refinement of the problem and the structuring of small subquestions. These subquestions are then pursued in the field to uncover underlying meanings and cultural patterns.

Health and human service professionals have used ethnographic methods, such as interviewing and participant observation (discussed more fully in subsequent chapters), to examine cultural variations in response to disability, adaptation, health services utilization, health care practices, and other related areas. The health or human service professional conducting ethnography may start with a general query such as, "How is pain expressed differently by men and women?" or "How are individuals with severe disabilities able to live independently, and what are their patterns of adaptation to community inclusion?"

## Phenomenology

The purpose of the phenomenological line of inquiry is to uncover the meaning of how humans experience phenomena through the description of those experiences as they are lived by individuals.[8] The first research step from this perspective is to identify the phenomenon of investigation. For example, being in pain, homeless, or sad may be phenomena that are relevant to the helping professions. From the articulation of the phenomenon, a research query is generated such as, "What is the meaning of being homeless for middle-aged women?" "What is the meaning of fear for persons with traumatic injury?" "What are the common elements in experiencing a feeling of well-being among poor, rural, elderly persons?" This approach is different from ethnography in that phenomenological queries focus on experience from the perspective of the individual and do not seek to understand a group or cultural patterns. However, similar to ethnography, the research begins with a broad query. Based on what the investigator knows through the action of conducting the research, subquestions and other inquiries are developed that further inform the meaning of experience for the individuals participating in the study.

## Grounded theory

Grounded theory is a method in naturalistic research that is used primarily to generate theory.[9] The researcher begins with a broad query in a particular topic area and then collects relevant information about the topic. As the action processes of data collection continue, each piece of information is reviewed, compared, and contrasted with other information. From this constant comparison process, commonalities and dissimilarities among categories of information become clear, and principles and, ultimately, a theory that explains observations is inductively developed. Thus queries that will be answered through grounded theory relate not to specific domains but to the structure of how the researcher wants to organize his or her findings (Box 7-4).

| Box 7-4 | **Examples of grounded theory queries that generate theory** |
|---|---|

- What theoretical principles characterize the experience of women who become homeless?
- What similarities and differences can be revealed among ways in which traumatically injured patients experience their acute care hospitalization?
- How do Native Americans residing in a rural New England community define and maintain their health?

| Box 7-5 | **Examples of grounded theory queries that modify theory** |
|---|---|

- How can the current theory of moral development be expanded or modified to explain the moral development of Native American children and adolescents?
- What is the relevance of current theory on career development in white, middle-class male children and African-American, middle-class female children?

As you can see, each query indicates that the research aim is to reveal theoretical principles about the phenomenon under study.

Grounded theory can also be used to modify existing theory or to expand on what is known in different ways. Queries related to these research objectives appear in Box 7-5.

In these two queries, grounded theory is structured to address current theory from a new and inductive perspective.

As you can see, ethnography, phenomenology, and grounded theory reflect distinct approaches in naturalistic inquiry. Queries developed from each design approach reflect a different purpose and a preferred way of knowing and are shaped by the particular resources available to the investigator.

## Differences in approaches

Table 7-3 summarizes what we have discussed and adds the category of integrated designs. As you may have surmised, integrated designs rely on query, question, or both and may order these

in diverse ways to accomplish the research purpose.

Consider an example that highlights the differences in approaches among the research traditions. Let us assume we want to study caregiving in the elderly population. There are many issues one can investigate under the broad rubric of caregiving. For example, if your purpose is to understand how caregiving affects psychologic well-being, you may pose a specific question such as, "What is the relationship between the cognitive status of impaired individuals and perceived health in caregivers of spouses with the diagnosis of dementia?" What type of question is this? If you guessed Level 2 in the experimental-type tradition, you are correct. This question narrows the area of concern of relationships between cognitive status of the individual with dementia and a specific caregiver outcome—perceived health. The investigator has isolated constructs based on a deductive thinking process and an orientation to knowing that favors experimental-type design. The constructs posed in the research question

| Table 7-3 | Form and function of question/query formulation across research traditions | | |
|---|---|---|---|
| | *Experimental-type* | *Naturalistic* | *Integrated* |
| Form | Focused question | Broad query | Both or either |
| Function | Define variables, population, and level of inquiry | Identify phenomena of interest and context | Both or either |

may have been identified from reading the research literature, from practice experience, or from federal funding initiatives that isolate self-efficacy and management as important constructs from which to understand caregiver experiences. The question lends itself to a design that involves interviewing a substantial number of caregivers to examine the stated relationships. The way the question is posed assumes that the investigator has the necessary fiscal resources and personnel to implement the research action processes that will answer the question.

In contrast, let us assume your purpose is to understand the experience of caregiving using an epistemologic framework based in a naturalistic tradition. In this case, a research query that is initially posed as a broad statement will be developed. For example, the query, "How do caregivers experience the act of caring for their spouses with dementia in the home?" identifies caregiving spouses in the home as the field of query and the personal and lived experience of caring as the particular phenomenon of interest. In such a study, relevant constructs will emerge based on uncovering and revealing the meaning of caregiving from the caregivers. The initial formulation of the

problem as "caregiver experience" assumes that the investigator does not know the range of such experiences. The investigator proceeds inductively, based on the framework that there are multiple caregiver experiences and realities that need to be discovered and understood. It is from understanding these realities that meaningful concepts, constructs, and relationships will emerge in the course of the study. In this case the monetary and personnel resources available to the investigator will determine the scope of the field that is investigated and the time engaged in field observation and the interview process.

An integrated study may pose both a concise question and query and conduct the studies sequentially or simultaneously.

## Summary

There are many ways to frame a research problem. Each approach to problem formulation and query/question development differs within the two traditions of research design. In experimental-type design, the question drives each subsequent research step. Refinement of a research question occurs before any action processes. Conciseness and refinement are critical to the conduct of the study and are the hallmarks of what makes the research question meaningful and appropriate. Experimental-type questions are definitive, structured, and derived deductively before one engages in research actions. In naturalistic inquiry, the query sets the initial boundaries for the study and is reformulated in the process of data collection and analysis.

Question refinement emerges from the action of conducting the research. The development of questions occurs inductively and emerges from the interaction of the investigator with the field or phenomenon of the study. Thus questions have quite different levels of meaning and implication for the conduct of the study in experimental-type design and naturalistic research. Research queries and subquestions are dynamic, ever changing, and derived inductively. Integrated studies use the strengths of both traditions to pose questions and queries that can reveal, describe, relate, or predict.

## Exercises

1. To test your understanding of the differences between levels of questioning in experimental-type designs, select a problem area in which you are interested. Frame the problem in terms of Level 1, 2, and 3 questions.

2. Using the problem area in exercise 1, formulate a broad query to pursue within a naturalistic design.

3. Review your different problem statements and specific queries or questions. Identify the different assumptions each make about level of knowledge, preferred way of knowing, and required resources to conduct the study. Use the tabular grid that follows to assist you.

4. Select three research articles in the literature and identify each research question or query. After you have identified them, characterize the nature of each using the tabular grid that follows.

**Exercise 3** **Chart to compare studies on level of knowledge, preferred way of knowing, and resources**

| Question/query | Assumption of level of knowledge | Preferred way of knowing | Required resources |
|---|---|---|---|
| 1. | | | |
| 2. | | | |
| 3. | | | |

## References

1. Brink PJ, Wood MJ: *Basic steps in planning nursing research: from question to proposal,* ed 3, Boston, 1998, Jones & Bartlett.
2. Gitlin LN, Levine R, Geiger C: Adaptive device use in the home by older adults with mixed disabilities, *Arch Phys Med Rehabil* 74:149-152, 1993.
3. Gitlow L: *Attitudes of occupational therapy faculty towards inclusion,* Minneapolis, Minn, 1997, Paper presented at the Society for Disability Studies.
4. McMurtry SL, McClelland RE: Trends in student-faculty rations and the use of non-tenured faculty in MSW programs, *J SW Education,* 33(3):293-306, 1997.
5. Chandler JM, Duncan PW, Sanders LY, Studenski S: The fear of falling syndrome, *Topics Ger Rehab* 11(3):55-63, 1996.
6. Neuman WL: *Social research methods: qualitative and quantitative approaches,* ed 3, Boston, 1997, Allyn Bacon.
7. Agar M: *Speaking of ethnography,* Newbury Park, Calif, 1986, Sage.
8. Farber M: *The aims of phenomenology: the motives, methods, and impact of Husserl's thought,* New York, 1966, Harper & Row.
9. Glaser B, Strauss A: *Grounded theory: strategies for qualitative research,* New York, 1967, Aldine.

# *Chapter* 8

# Language and thinking processes

**Key terms**    Bias
Conceptual definition
Context specific
Control
Dependent variable
Design
Emic
Etic

External validity
Independent variable
Internal validity
Intervening variable
Manipulation
Operational definition
Statistical conclusion validity
Variable

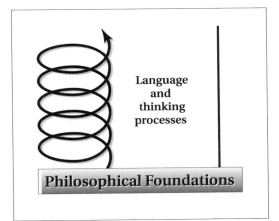

Language and thinking processes

**Philosophical Foundations**

We now are ready to explore the language and thinking of researchers who use the range of designs relevant to health and human service inquiry. As discussed in previous chapters, there are significant philosophical distinctions between experimental-type and naturalistic research traditions. Experimental-type designs are characterized by thinking and action processes based in deductive logic and a positivist paradigm in which the researcher seeks to identify a single reality through systematized observation. This reality is understood by reducing and examining its parts and observing the relationship among these parts. Ultimately the purpose of this research is to predict what will occur in one part of the universe by knowing and observing another part.

Dissimilar to experimental-type design, the naturalistic tradition is characterized by multiple ontologic and epistemologic foundations; but, as previously discussed, naturalistic designs share common elements that are reflected in their language and thinking processes. Researchers in the naturalistic tradition base their thinking in inductive and abductive logic and seek to understand context-embedded phenomena. Thus the notion of multiple realities and the attempt to characterize holistically the complexity of human experience are two elements that pervade naturalistic approaches.

Because experimental-type and naturalistic traditions are based in different philosophical foundations, their language and criteria for scientific rigor differ. Rigor is a term used in research that refers to procedures that enhance the scientific integrity of the research design. Let us first examine the language and thinking process of experimental-type design and then move to an analysis of the language and thinking processes of naturalistic research. (As you read this chapter, you may want to compare and contrast the two traditions and consider the application and integration of both.)

## Experimental-type language and thinking processes

Experimental research can be characterized as shown in Box 8-1. Within this tradition, there is consensus about the adequacy and scientific rigor of action processes. For example, all designs in experimental-type tradition share a common language and a unified perspective as to what constitutes an adequate *design*. Although there are many definitions of research design, each reflecting a different epistemologic perspective, all types of experimental-type research share a single and agreed upon meaning. In experimental-type research, design is the plan or blueprint that specifies and structures the action processes of collecting, analyzing, and reporting data to answer a research question. As Kerlinger states, design is "the plan, structure, and strategy of investigation conceived so as to obtain answers to research questions and to control variance."[1] In this definition, plan refers to the blueprint for action or the specific procedures used to obtain empirical evidence. Structure represents a more complex concept and refers to a model of the relationships among the variables of a study; that is, the design is structured in such a way as to enable an examination of a hypothesized relationship

| Box 8-1 | Characteristics of experimental-type research |
|---|---|

- Based in one epistemology
- Historically accepted as the "scientific method" for discovering "fact"
- Evaluated and described by a unified and an agreed-upon vocabulary that is well-established

among variables. The main purpose of the design is to structure the study so that the researcher can determine the extent to which one phenomenon (the independent variable) is responsible for change in another (the dependent variable).

The purpose of the design is to control variances or restrict or control extraneous influences on the study. By exerting such control, the researcher can state with a degree of statistical assuredness that study outcomes are a consequence of either the manipulation of the independent variable (as in the case of a true-experimental design) or the consequence of that which was observed and analyzed (as in the case of non-experimental designs). In other words the design provides a degree of assuredness that an investigator's observations are not haphazard or random but reflect a true and objective reality. The researcher is thus concerned with developing the most optimal design that eliminates or controls what researchers refer to as disturbances, variances, extraneous factors, or situational contaminants. The design controls these disturbances or situational contaminants through the implementation of systematic procedures and data collection efforts discussed in subsequent chapters. The purpose of imposing control and restrictions on observations of natural phenomena is to ensure that the relationships specified in the research question(s) can be identified, understood, and ultimately predicted.

To summarize, the design is what separates research from both the everyday types of observations and the thinking and action processes in which each of us engages. Design instructs the investigator to "do this" or "don't do that." It provides a mechanism of control to ensure that data are collected objectively, in a uniform manner, with minimal investigator involvement or bias. The important point to remember is that the investigator remains separate from and uninvolved with the phenomena under study and that procedures and systematic data collection provide mechanisms to control and eliminate bias.

## Sequence of experimental-type research

Let us review the sequence of thought and actions of experimental-type researchers to understand the central role of design. The design is pivotal in the sequence (Figure 8-1). It stems from the thinking processes of formulating a problem statement, a theory-specific research question, and hypotheses or expected outcomes, as well as conducting a literature review. In turn, the design dictates the nature of the action processes of data collection, the conditions under which observations will be made, and, most importantly, the type of data analyses and reporting that will be possible.

Recall our previous discussions on the essentials of research in which we illustrate how the problem statement identifies the purpose of the research and the broad topic the investigator wishes to address. The literature review then guides the selection of theoretical principles and concepts of the study and provides the rationale for a research project. This rationale is based on the nature of research previously conducted and the level of theory development for the phenomena under investigation. The experimental-type researcher must develop a literature review

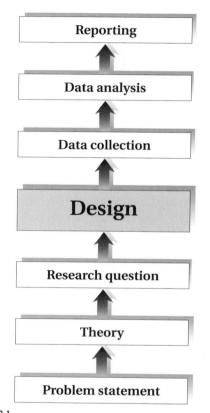

Figure 8-1 Sequence of experimental-type research.

rigor. Choice of the design is not only shaped by the literature and level of theory development, but it also depends on the specific question asked. There is nothing inherently good or bad about a design. Every research study and design has its own particular strengths and weaknesses. The adequacy of a design is based on how well the design answers the question that is posed.

## Structure of experimental-type research

Experimental-type research has a well-developed language that sets clear rules and expectations for the adequacy of design and research procedures. Table 8-1 summarizes the meaning of nine key terms used by researchers to structure designs within the tradition of experimental-type research.

***Concepts.*** A concept is defined as the words or ideas that symbolically represent observations and experiences. Concepts, in and of themselves, are not directly observable; rather, what they describe is observed or experienced. Concepts are "(1) tentative, (2) based on agreement, and (3) useful only to the degree that they capture or isolate something significant and definable."[2] For example, the terms "grooming" and "work" are both concepts that describe specific observable or experienced activities in which people engage on a regular basis. Other concepts, such as personal hygiene or sadness, have various definitions, each of which leads to the development of assessment instruments to measure the underlying concept.

***Constructs.*** Constructs are defined by Babbie as "theoretical creations based on observations but

in which the specific theory and measures that he or she will use in a study are discussed and supported as "the best." Furthermore, the type of research question asked must be consistent with the knowledge reported in the literature.

Thus the researcher develops a design that builds on both the ideas that have been formulated and the actions that have been conducted in ways that conform to the rules of scientific

| Table 8-1 | Key terms in structuring experimental-type research | |
|---|---|
| Term | Definition |
| Concept | Symbolically represents observation and experience |
| Construct | Represents a model of relationships among two of more concepts |
| Conceptual definition | Concept expressed in words |
| Operational definition | How the concept will be measured |
| Variable | Operational definition of a concept assigned numeric values |
| Independent variable | Presumed cause of the dependent variable |
| Intervening variable | Phenomena that have an effect on study variables |
| Dependent variable | Phenomenon that is affected by the independent variable or is the presumed effect or outcome |
| Hypothesis | Testable statement that indicates what the researcher expects to find |

which cannot be observed directly or indirectly."[3] A construct can only be inferred and may represent a model of a relationship between two or more concepts. For example, the construct of community function may be inferred from observing concepts such as grooming, personal hygiene, and work. However, the construct is not directly observable unless it is broken down into its component parts or concepts.

*Definitions.* There are two basic types of definition relevant to research design: conceptual definitions and operational definitions. A *conceptual definition,* or lexical definition, stipulates the meaning of a concept or construct with other concepts or constructs. An *operational definition* stipulates the meaning through observation or experience. Operational definitions

"define things by what they do." For example, the construct of self-care may be conceptually defined as the activities that are necessary to care for one's bodily functions, whereas it is operationally defined as observations of an individual engaged in bathing, dressing, and grooming.

*Variables.* A variable is a concept or construct to which numerical values are assigned. By definition, a variable must have more than one value even if the investigator is interested in only one condition. For example, if an investigator is interested in determining the self-care routine of persons with disabilities who are employed, both self-care routine and employment are variables. Although self-care routine may have multiple values, the investigator undertaking this inquiry is interested in only one of the potential values that may be attributed to employment status—that of being employed.

There are three basic types of variable: independent, intervening, and dependent. An *independent variable* "is the presumed cause of the dependent variable, the presumed effect."[4] The independent variable almost always precedes the dependent variable and has a potential influence on it. It is also sometimes referred to as the predictor variable. An *intervening variable* (also called a confounding or an extraneous variable) is a phenomenon that has an effect on the study variables but is not necessarily the object of the study. In the study of self-care routines of employed individuals with disabilities, employment status represents the independent variable, whereas self-care routine represents the dependent variable. Intervening variables in this study may include any other variable that potentially influences either the independent or dependent variable, such as family support, degree of disability, motivational status, and functional ability. A *dependent variable* (also called outcome and criterion) refers to the phenomenon that the investigator seeks to understand, explain, or predict.

*Hypotheses.* A hypotheses is defined as a testable statement that indicates what the researcher expects to find, based on theory and level of knowledge in the literature. A hypothesis is stated in such a way that it will either be verified or falsified by the research process. The researcher can develop either a directional or nondirectional hypothesis. In a directional hypothesis, the researcher indicates whether she or he expects to find a positive relationship or an inverse relationship between two or more variables. In a positive relationship, the researcher may hypothesize that the employed individual with a disability has greater self-esteem than the unemployed individual with a disability. An inverse relationship may involve a hypothesis similar to the following: An individual with a disability who remains employed will demonstrate less difficulty in performing self-care routines than the individual who is unemployed.

Let us summarize how these nine key terms are used. Research questions narrow the scope of the inquiry to specific concepts, constructs, or both. These concepts are then defined through the literature and are operationalized into variables that will be investigated descriptively, relationally, or predictively. The hypothesis establishes an equation by which independent and dependent variables are examined and tested.

## Plan of design

The plan of a design requires a set of thinking processes in which five core issues—bias, manipulation, control, validity, and reliability—are considered by the experimental-type researcher.

*Bias.* Bias is defined as the potential unintended or unavoidable effect on study outcomes. Many factors can cause bias in a study (Box 8-2).

Let us consider each source of bias. There are two major issues in instrumentation, bias resulting from inappropriate data collection procedures and bias resulting from inadequate questions. Assume you are a counselor working in a community mental health center and your

Box 8-2 **Possible sources of bias in a study**

- Selection of inappropriate instrumentation
- Sample selection process that favors a particular unintended group
- Improper training of interviewers
- Deviation from the plan and from structure of the design

supervisor, the agency administrator, is conducting a survey of worker satisfaction. To obtain information from employees, the supervisor decides to interview people. Knowing that this person is your superior, how likely are you to provide responses to job satisfaction questions, particularly knowing that your performance evaluation is next month? Using the same example, suppose this question is asked, "Don't you agree that this is a great place to work?" Certainly this question is poorly phrased; it implies a socially and politically correct response. Interview questions that are posed in a way that elicit a socially correct response or questions that are vague, unclear, or ambiguous introduce a source of bias into the study design.

Suppose that only the supervisor's social friends were selected as a sample to participate in the survey and are claimed to represent the agency population. Such a sample would not represent the overall level of job satisfaction for all employees. The characteristics of the sample serve as potential bias or influence on the outcomes of the study.

In this same study, if multiple persons collected information about job satisfaction but each asked questions differently, interviewer procedures will serve as a strong bias. Improper or uneven training of data collectors can bias the outcomes of a study.

Experimental-type designs are characterized by the elaboration of plans and procedures before conducting the study. Thus any deviation from the original plan for data collection and analysis may introduce bias. For example, suppose that the agency director decided to collect data regarding the level of job satisfaction of agency employees on Monday. Monday was selected because all employees were normally available. However, the data collection was accomplished on Tuesday because Monday was a holiday. On Tuesday, all home-based service providers were in the field and therefore were not surveyed for their degree of job satisfaction. This deviation in the plan could have significantly affected the study outcome since a large segment of the agency employee population would have been omitted from the study.

There are many causes of bias in experimental-type design. An essential part of planning a design is to introduce systematic procedures to minimize or eliminate as many sources of bias as possible.

***Manipulation.*** *Manipulation* is defined as the action process of maneuvering the independent variable so that the effect of its presence, absence, or degree can be observed on the dependent variable. To the extent possible, experimental-type researchers attempt to isolate the independent and dependent variables and then to manipulate or change conditions so that the cause-and-effect relationship between the variables can be examined. Goodman's study of the effects of two types of support groups on the well-being and perceived social support of the caregivers of persons with Alzheimer's disease illustrates the concept of manipulation. To determine which of two interventions promoted positive outcome, Goodman tested the subjects to ascertain their well-being and perceived social support before any intervention. They were randomly assigned (assigned on a chance-determined basis) to each intervention and then tested again after completing the intervention. The subjects were then asked to switch groups and participate in the intervention that they had not experienced. They were tested again to determine if changes in well-being and perceived social support had occurred. In this example, the independent variables, or interventions, were manipulated. By manipulating the circumstances under which a subject received the intervention, the investigator was able to examine the effect of each intervention and their combination on subject well-being and perceived social support. Goodman was able to evaluate the independent effects and the joint effects of each intervention.[5]

***Control.*** *Control* may be defined as the set of action processes that direct or manipulate factors to achieve an outcome. Control plays a critical role in experimental-type design. Controlling not only the independent variable but also other aspects of the research context, such as subject assignment and the experimental environment, the relationship among the study variables can be clearly observed. In experimental-type design, procedures to establish control are implemented to minimize the influences of extraneous variables on the out-

come or dependent variable. In Goodman's study, two basic methods of control were introduced, random group assignment and reversal of group assignment. By randomly assigning subjects to one group or the other, Goodman attempted to develop equivalence, or eliminate subject bias, caused by inherent differences that may occur in the two groups. For example, let us assume Goodman had not used random assignment but instead assigned the first 10 volunteers to the first group and the next 10 volunteers to the second group. It is possible that the first 10 subjects knew each other and entered the study first because they were highly motivated to seek help. On the contrary, suppose the last 10 subjects were somewhat less motivated to participate. Familiarity with other subjects and a high motivation to seek help (two factors inherent in the subjects assigned to group one) may influence the measures of well-being and perceived social support. By not using random assignment, the investigator may be at risk of developing groups that initially differ from each other. This initial difference will make it difficult to discern what effect, if any, the independent variable may have on the outcome.

Another method to enhance control is the development of a control group. For example, Goodman may have randomly assigned subjects to a third group that did not receive any intervention. By comparing subject scores of this control group with the two intervention groups, Goodman will have been able to determine whether changes in the dependent variable occurred as a consequence of the passage of time, were the result of the attention factor inherent in participation in a study, or were produced by the particular content of each group.

*Validity.* Validity is a concept that has numerous applications in experimental-type research. However, the concept as it applies to design refers to the extent to which your findings are accurate or reflect the underlying purpose of the study. Although many classifications of validity have been developed, four fundamental types of validity are discussed, based on Campbell and Stanley's initial work.[6] They are internal validity, external validity, statistical conclusion validity, and construct validity.

**Internal validity.** *Internal validity* refers to the ability of the research design to accurately answer the research question. If a design has internal validity, the investigator can state with a degree of confidence that the reported outcomes are the consequence of the relationship between the independent variable and dependent variable and not the result of extraneous factors. Campbell and Stanley identify seven major factors that pose a threat to the ability of a researcher to determine whether the observable is a function of the study or the result of external forces (Box 8-3).

To illustrate these threats to validity, consider a hypothetical example. Suppose you are conducting a study to determine the extent to which an acquired immunodeficiency syndrome (AIDS) prevention program has reduced behavior that increases the risk of developing AIDS in an adolescent population. Before the intervention, you test the subjects to determine the extent to which they exhibit risk behavior. You conduct a prevention program and retest the participants. The retest shows an amazing reduction in risk behavior, and you claim that your program is a success. In doing so, you are making a claim that a relationship exists be-

---

**Box 8-3** | **Seven threats to internal validity**

1. *History.* Effect of external events on study outcomes
2. *Testing.* Effect of being observed or tested on the study outcome
3. *Instrumentation.* Extent to which the instrument is accurate in its measurement and extent to which the instrument itself may be responsible for outcomes
4. *Maturation.* Effect of the passage of time
5. *Regression.* Effect of a statistical phenomenon in which extreme scores tend to regress or cluster around the mean (average) on repeated testing occasions
6. *Mortality.* Effect on outcome caused by subject attrition or dropping out of a study before its completion
7. *Interactive effects.* Extent to which each of these threats interacts with sample selection to influence the outcome of a study

---

tween your program (the independent variable) and risk behavior (the dependent variable). Furthermore, you are claiming that there is a causal relationship between the variables; that is, you claim that your program caused the reduction in behavior that increases the risk of developing AIDS.

Consider how each of the seven threats to internal validity affects your research outcomes. First, let us assume you have just learned that Arthur Ashe has held a news conference in which he announced he has tested positive for the human immunodeficiency virus (HIV). This announcement has come immediately after you first administered your test to your subjects but before the final testing occasion. It is possible that this historical event, rather than the independent variable, was the factor responsible for reducing risk behavior in your subjects.

However, assume that your subjects already knew about Arthur Ashe before beginning the study. Now consider the threat of testing to the validity of your claims. As a sensitive researcher, you have decided to measure risk behavior by observing a discussion group about sexual behaviors among adolescents. Each time you hear a risk behavior, you score it as such without informing your subjects. In the first testing situation, the adolescents appear to openly discuss their sexual decision making. However, you note that they are very aware of group norms and of being observed and stay well within the boundaries tacitly set by the group when discussing their personal behavior and views. In the second test, you note a large reduction in reported risk behaviors or in risky decision making expressed by the adolescents. Although it is possible that the prevention program is actually responsible for the reduction of risk behavior, there are also competing alternative explanations for the change. For example, in the first testing situation, the adolescents may have revealed what was normative and acceptable in the group rather than accurately representing their risk potential.

Another alternative for the observed reduction in risk behavior may be the result of the testing situation itself. Participants who are aware of what is being observed and recorded may answer more cautiously. In other words, the testing procedures may pose yet another threat to the internal validity of the design. The reduction in reported risk behaviors may be a function of participants actively changing or adjusting their behaviors or thoughts on the topic as a consequence of participating in a group discussion with peers. The test itself or mode of data collection may have influenced a change in behavior independent of the effect of participating in the intervention. Therefore it is difficult to determine whether change is a consequence of the test, a consequence of the intervention, or both.

This example also illustrates the threat to validity posed by instrumentation. In this example the instrumentation may not be measuring what was intended. Instead of measuring risk behavior, the instrumentation may be a more accurate indicator of group norms related to sexual decision making.

Another way in which instrumentation poses a threat to a study is through changes that may occur within interviewers over time or with the instrument itself. For example, if you are collecting data regarding weight or blood pressure, any deviation in the calibration of a scale or blood pressure cuff from one testing occasion to the next will pose a significant threat to the validity of the data that are obtained. Further, interviewer fatigue or any change in the way in which interviewers pose interview questions may cause deviation in responses that will affect the way in which the investigator will interpret the findings.

To illustrate the threat posed by maturation, let us assume that the AIDS prevention program just discussed is being conducted over a 1-year period. It is possible that the participants have matured in their thinking and have become more responsible in their decision making as a function of time rather than as a result of the prevention program.

The threat of regression frequently occurs when subjects with extreme scores are selected to participate in a study. In this example, assume adolescents who are sexually active participate in the study and therefore tend to report extremely risk behaviors. High scorers at the beginning of the program will tend to report lower scores at the end. This change in scores, however, may be a consequence of a statistical principle known as "statistical regression toward the mean" in which extreme scores tend to move toward the mean on repeated testing occasions.

Consider this scenario. Fifty participants began the AIDS prevention program, but only ten remained by the final testing period. It is possible that as a result of experimental mortality, those who remained in the study may be more committed to reducing risk behavior than those who dropped out. Thus mortality or selective attrition of subjects poses a threat to the interpretation of study findings.

Numerous interactive effects could also confound the accuracy of the findings. For example, consider that the selected sample for the study was a population of adolescents on probation. This group was highly motivated to report a change in their risk behavior (a sampling bias) and were also sensitive to being tested because of their judiciary status. The interactive effect of the sample bias and the testing condition may wreak havoc on claims that the outcome was a result of the prevention program.

**External validity.** *External validity* refers to the capacity to generalize findings and develop inferences from the sample to the study population. External validity answers the question of generalizability. Let us use the example of the AIDS study to explore the issue of external validity.

Assume that the investigator obtained a sample by asking for volunteers from a large group of adolescents between the ages of 12 and 18 years who were on probation in Philadelphia. The potential to generalize the findings from the sample to all adolescents on probation is limited by several important factors. First, the sample was a volunteer sample, making them potentially different from adolescents who did not volunteer. Second, the experiences of adolescents who live in large cities do not necessarily represent the experiences of adolescents in other geographic locations. Third, because the sample was voluntary, the researcher cannot know in what ways the sample may differ from the larger population, which includes those who refused participation or did not have the opportunity to volunteer. Finally, the investigator limits generalizability to a select population and will not be able to infer the experiences of the research sample to adolescents who are not on probation, who live in rural communities, and who may be sexually active and at risk. These factors represent some of the threats to external validity that may occur in a study. Even when a sample is randomly selected, there are threats to external validity (Box 8-4).[7]

These two threats exist as a result of the experimental condition, not the limitations of sample selection. Consider your own behavior when being watched in a simulated situation. Certainly you act differently than you would under similar but unobserved and nonsimulated conditions. (We discuss external validity in detail later in this text.)

Box 8-4

**Potential threats to external validity**

1. *Reactivity.* Extent to which the subjects are responding to the condition of being part of a study and thus do not represent the population from which they are selected
2. *Realism.* Extent to which the experimental conditions simulate actual life situations to which the population is exposed

The internal validity and external validity of a study are interrelated. As an investigator attempts to increase the internal validity of a study, the ability to make broad generalizations and inferences to a larger population decreases. That is, as more controls are implemented and extraneous factors are eliminated from a study design, the population to which findings can be generalized becomes more limited. Investigators try to enhance the internal validity of a study to ensure that valid and accurate conclusions can be drawn. Internal validity is the investigator's primary concern, although it may limit the degree of external validity of his or her findings.

**Statistical conclusion validity.** *Statistical conclusion validity* refers to the power of your study to draw statistical conclusions. One aim of experimental-type research is to find relationships among variables and ultimately to predict the nature and direction of these relationships. Support for relationships is contained in the action process of statistical analysis. However, selection of statistical techniques is based on many considerations. The expectation of making errors in determining relationships is built into the theory and practice of sta-

tistical analysis. The accuracy and potential of the statistics to support or predict a relationship among variables must be considered as a potential threat to the validity of a design.

Consider this example. Assume you want to ensure that you do not overestimate the effects of your AIDS prevention program on risk behavior. You select a statistic that will be less likely to find a false relationship when there is none. However, this decision increases the possibility that you may not find a significant relationship when, in fact, one exists. Thus your statistical testing may lead you to believe that no relationship exists when there is one or, conversely, to believe that there is a relationship when there is not one.

**Construct validity.** Construct validity addresses the fit between the constructs that are the focus of the study and the way in which those constructs are operationalized. As indicated earlier, constructs are abstract representations of what humans observe and experience. The method used to define and measure constructs accurately is in large part a matter of opinion and consensus. It is possible for several factors related to construct validity to confound a study. First, it is possible for a researcher to define a construct inappropriately. For example, although smiling may be one indication of happiness, if a researcher measured level of happiness exclusively by observing the frequency of smiling behavior, the full construct of happiness would not be captured. Poor or incomplete operational definitions can result from incomplete conceptual definitions or from inadequate translation of the construct into an observable one. Second, when a cause-and-effect relationship between two constructs is determined, it may be difficult to exclusively define each construct (referring to both the independent and dependent variables) and to isolate the effects of one on the other.

Consider the following example. You are an occupational therapist who is attempting to test a feeding program for persons with Alzheimer's disease. You design a program in which you choose certain foods and techniques to improve independent feeding. To ensure that your design can reveal cause and effect, you randomly select your sample and randomly assign them to the experimental group (which receives the program) and the control group (which does not receive the program). You measure feeding behavior by two methods, observation of independent feeding and volume of food consumed independently. You implement your feeding program with the experimental group and test all participants after the program to determine whether the experimental group scored higher on your measures of feeding than the group that did not receive the intervention. You conclude that your program was successful in improving independent feeding, because the experimental group performed significantly better than the group without the intervention. However, you begin to consider other confounding influences that cannot be separated from your two constructs—independent feeding and the experimental program. It is possible that the attention of the experimenter may have been responsible for the improvement in the experimental group, because eating is a social behavior and may change under different social conditions. Second, it is possible that food preferences influenced the response of the groups to their respective conditions. Interactive effects of being

observed and participating in an experiment (referred to as the attention factor or Hawthorne effect [8]) may also limit your capacity to isolate a causal relationship between the constructs.

***Reliability.*** Reliability refers to the stability of a research design. In experimental-type research, rigorous research is well-planned and executed when, if repeated under the same circumstances, the design yields the same results. Investigators frequently replicate or repeat a study in the same population or in different groups to determine the extent to which the findings of one study are true in a broader scope. To replicate a study, the procedures, measures, and data analytical techniques must be consistent, well-articulated, and appropriate to the research question. Reliability is threatened when a researcher is not consistent and changes a design in midstream or does not fully plan a sound design.

To summarize, design is a pivotal concept in the research process for experimental-type research in that it indicates both the structure and the plan of action. Designs are developed to eliminate bias and the intrusion of unwanted factors that may potentially confound findings and make them less credible. We have defined basic terms used in structuring a design: concepts; constructs; conceptual and operational definitions; independent, intervening, and dependent variables; and hypotheses. We have identified five primary considerations in the plan of a design: bias, control, manipulation, validity, and reliability. We have demonstrated how four types of validity threaten study outcomes: internal, external, statistical conclusion, and construct.

Experimental-type research is designed to minimize the threats posed by extraneous factors and bias through maximizing control over the research action process. In Chapter 9 we discuss how each type of design in the experimental-type tradition addresses these considerations in structuring and planning a design and in the variety of action processes that investigators use to increase control.

## Naturalistic language and thinking processes

We have already discussed some of the basic characteristics of naturalistic inquiry. Let us now examine these attributes and their implications for design.

## Purpose

Designs within the tradition of naturalistic research vary in purpose from developing descriptive knowledge to evolving full-fledged theories about observed or experienced phenomena. As discussed in earlier chapters, when no theory explains a human phenomenon or when the investigator believes that existing theory and explanations are not accurate, true, or complete, naturalistic designs are preferred because their structure is exploratory, revealing new insights and understandings without the imposition of preconceived concepts, constructs, and principles. Although the specific purpose of a study may differ, all naturalistic designs seek to describe, understand, or interpret daily life experiences and structures from the perspective of those in the field. As stated by Denzin and Lincoln, naturalistic inquiry has emerged through five phases of development to its current form of action-oriented social criticism in which grand narratives will be replaced by more local, small-scale theories fitted to specific problems and specific situations.[9] Thus naturalistic inquiry is becoming useful in examining and revealing phenomena that guide health and human service practitioners to address specific problems that emerge in the field.

Let us once again consider as an example Liebow's ethnography of street corner life as presented in his classic book, *Tally's Corner*.[10] In his work, Liebow is interested in understanding the nature of a street corner culture to which he does not belong. Although there has been extensive research on the population he has chosen to examine, these investigations have not characterized the group from the perspective of its members. Naturalistic method, in this case, ethnography, is the only way to reveal the complexity and richness of the culture. Liebow gains valuable insights because his informants speak for themselves and describe their life experiences.

## Context specific

As in *Tally's Corner*, to discover "new truth" rather than impose an existing frame of reference, the investigator must go to the setting where the human phenomena occur or must seek information from individuals who experience the phenomena of interest from their perspectives. Because of the revelatory nature of naturalistic research, this form of investigatory action is conducted in a natural context or seeks explanations of the natural context from those who experience it from the inside. Naturalistic research is therefore *context specific*, and the knowing derived therefrom is embedded in that context and does not extend beyond it. The designs in the tradition of naturalistic inquiry share this basic attribute of context specificity and knowledge grounded in or linked to the data that emerge from a particular field.

## Complexity and pluralistic perspective of reality

As a result of its underlying epistemology and its inductive and abductive approaches to knowing, naturalistic research assumes a pluralistic perspective of reality that characterizes complexity.

Let us consider this point in greater detail. One of the hallmarks of inductive reasoning, reasoning in which principles are extracted from seemingly unrelated information, is that the information can be organized differently by each individual who thinks about it. The end result of induction is the development of a complex relationship among smaller pieces of information, not the reduction of principles to their parts as in the case of deductive reasoning. It is therefore possible that the same information may have different meanings or that there may be pluralistic interpretations to different individuals. Adding abduction to this equation ensures that the information will be revisited and reanalyzed at several points, thereby sharpening and rendering the accuracy of the interpretation more credible and trustworthy.

For example, in the study by Maruyama on prison violence, the nature of violence was investigated in two separate institutional settings. The findings from each prison, although yielding some similarities, indicated cultural differences between the two prisons in the reported causes of violence and the inmates' interpretation of the meaning of that violence. The naturalistic design was able to reveal the pluralistic nature of prison violence while shedding light on the basic elements that were shared in both settings.[11]

## Transferability of findings

The findings from naturalistic design are specific to the research context; that is, it is not the desired outcome of naturalistic design to generalize findings from a small sample and apply this generalization to a larger group of persons with similar characteristics. You may ask, "Why bother doing it if you cannot use the research beyond the actual scope of the study?" The answer lies in the purpose of naturalistic research as a theory-generating tool. Naturalistic researchers use their methods and findings to generate theory and to reveal the unique meanings of human experience in human environments. Because the investigator assumes that no current knowledge adequately explains the phenomenon under investigation, the outcome of naturalistic design is the emergence of explanations, principles, concepts, and theories. This point is illustrated by Liebow in his claim:

> There is no attempt here to describe any Negro men other than those with whom I was in direct immediate association. To what extent this descriptive and interpretive material is applicable to Negro street corner men elsewhere in the city or in other cities or to lower class men generally in this society or any other society is a

matter of further and later study. This is not to suggest that we are dealing with unique or even distinctive persons and relationships. Indeed, the weight of the evidence is the other direction.[12]

In this passage, even though the researcher is highlighting the contextual limitations of the knowledge, he also is indicating that the principles revealed in his study may have relevance to other arenas. Further, he suggests that additional research is the appropriate means to ascertain the degree of fit, or what Guba calls the transferability of his findings to other similar populations and contexts.

Because phenomena are context bound and cannot be understood apart from the context in which they occur, naturalistic inquiry is not concerned with the issue of generalizability or external validity. Rather, the concern is with understanding the richness and depth within one context and with the capacity to retain unique meanings that are lost when generalization is a goal.[9] The development of "thick"[13] in-depth descriptions and interpretations of different contexts leads to the ability to transfer meanings in one context to another. In so doing, the researcher is able to compare and contrast contexts and their elements to gain new insights as to the specific context itself.

## Flexibility

In experimental-type research, the design provides the basic structure and plan for the thinking and action processes of the research endeavor. However, in naturalistic research, design is a fluid, flexible concept. Design labels such as ethnography, life history, and grounded theory suggest a particular purpose of the inquiry and orientation of the investigator. However, these labels do not refer to the specification of step-by-step procedures, a blueprint for action, or a predetermined structure to the data gathering and analytical efforts. Rather, a characteristic of naturalistic design is flexibility.[14] It is expected that the procedures and plans for conducting naturalistic research will change as the research proceeds. For example, Willoughby and Keating indicate in their study of caregivers of persons with Alzheimer's disease that, "Ongoing field notes kept by the researchers assisted in the development of key concepts and in suggesting the direction of later interviews."[15]

Not only do procedures change, but also the nature of the research query, the scope of the study, and the manner by which information is obtained are constantly reformulated and realigned to fit the emerging truths as they are discovered and obtained in the field. This flexibility is illustrated more fully in our discussions of gathering information and analytical actions.

## Language

A major shared concern in naturalistic inquiry is understanding the language and its meanings for the people who are being studied. This concern with language is not just relevant to the ethnographer who studies a cultural context in which the language used is different from that of the investigator. Even within the same cultural or language context, people use and understand language differently. It is through language, symbols, and ways of expression that the investigator comes to understand and derive meaning within each context.[16] The investigator engages in a rigorous and active analytical process to translate, so to speak, the meaning and structure of the context of those studied into those meanings and language structures represented in the world of the investigator. The investigator must be careful to accurately represent the meanings and intent of expression in this translation of analytical and reporting process.

## Emic and etic perspectives

Design structures vary as to their emic or etic orientation toward field experience. An *emic* perspective refers to the insider's or informant's way of understanding and interpreting experience. This perspective is phenomenological in that experience is understood as only that which is perceived and expressed by informants in the field. Data gathering and analytical actions are designed to enable the investigator to bring forth and report the voices of individuals as they themselves speak and interpret their unique perceptions of their reality. The concern with the emic perspective is often the motivator for naturalistic inquiry. For example, Krefting explains why she decided to study head injury from an ethnographic perspective and, in doing so, highlights the preference for an emic viewpoint shared by designs in this tradition:

> Until recently, the investigation of health problems was dominated by the outsider perspective, in which important questions of etiology and treatment are identified by the professions. Studies based on this perspective assume that professionals are the authorities on what wellness is and

that they alone know what questions ought be asked to investigate methods to promote and maintain wellness while preventing and treating illness. ...Ethnographic studies of the experience of illness and disability,...consider what these experiences look like from an insider's perspective.[17]

An *etic* orientation reflects the structural aspects or those that are external to a group; that is, the etic perspective is held by those who do not belong to the group being investigated but who select an analytical and epistemic lens through which to examine information. Unlike the emic perspective in which those who experience are considered to be most knowledgeable, the etic perspective assumes that those who do not experience a phenomenon can come to know it through structuring an investigation, selecting a theoretical foundation that expands beyond the group being examined, and, through that lens, conducting the interpretation of data.[18] Many investigators integrate an emic and etic perspective. Typically, fieldwork will start by using an emic perspective or a focus on the voices of individuals. Further along the fieldwork process, other pieces of information are collected and analyzed to place individual articulation and expression within a social structural or systemic framework. Although she started with an emic consideration, Krefting uses a range of data collection strategies to integrate her understandings with an etic viewpoint. She states that:

> While gathering data, I was able to review theory and check it for pertinence. There

was, then, a constant movement back and forth between the concrete data and the social science concepts that helped explain them.[17]

Some designs, such as phenomenology and life history, favor only an emic orientation. Read how Frank describes her preference for an emic perspective and the purpose of her life history approach:

The life history of Diane DeVries represents a collaborative effort, between the subject and researcher, to produce a holistic, qualitative account that would bear on theoretical issues, but that primarily and essentially would convey a sense of the personal experience of severe congenital disability. The life history, conceived in this way, emerged from a humanistic interest in presenting the voices of people often unheard, yet whose lives were otherwise studied, and acted upon, based on data that are decontextualized and fragmented from the standpoint of the individual.[19]

Because the investigator enters the field having bracketed, suspended, or let go of any preconceived concepts, the naturalistic researcher defers to the informant or experiencer as the knower. This abrogation of power by the investigator to the investigated is characteristic of all naturalistic designs to a greater or lesser degree. An extreme example of relinquishing control over the research process is illustrated by Maruyama's work. In the prison study, not only did the inmates function as the informants, but they also planned and conducted the research in its entirety.[11] (We discuss a variation of this collaborative research effort in our discussion of endogenous research later in this book.)

Where the investigator stands regarding an emic or etic perspective shapes the overall design that is chosen and the specific data collection and analytical actions that emerge within the context of the field.

## Gathering information and analysis

Finally, analysis in naturalistic designs relies heavily on qualitative data and is an ongoing process that is interspersed throughout data-gathering activities. Data gathering and analysis are interdependent processes. As one collects information or datum, the investigator engages in an active analytic process. In turn, the ongoing analytic activity frames the scope and direction of further data collection efforts. This interactive, iterative, and dynamic process is characteristic of all designs within the tradition of naturalistic inquiry and is explored more fully later in this text.

To summarize, the purpose of naturalistic inquiry and the nature of the concept of design in this tradition are vastly different from experimental-type research. The language and thinking processes that characterize naturalistic design are based on the notion that knowing is pluralistic and that knowledge derives from understanding multiple experiences. Thus the thinking process is inductive and abductive, the action processes are dynamic and changing, and they are carried out within the context where the phenomena of interest occur. The outcome of these thinking and action processes is the generation of theory, principles, or concepts that explain human experience in human environments and capture its complexity and uniqueness.

Within any one type of naturalistic design, there are also variations in the way in which the investigator implements the 10 essentials. Designs vary from informant-driven and no structure to researcher-driven and more structure.

As indicated by Denzin and Lincoln, the nature of qualitative inquiry has evolved over the past several decades in its form, scope, and purpose.[9] Naturalistic inquiry is continuing to evolve in its standards, vocabulary, and criteria for design adequacy and is becoming a well-respected tradition in its own right as it is increasingly used to answer questions about health and human service practice.

## Summary

Experimental-type and naturalistic traditions each have a distinct set of language and thinking processes. Experimental-type researchers approach their studies with intact theory and a set of procedures. Procedures are developed and followed to eliminate the potential for factors other than those studied to be responsible for the study findings. Dissimilarly, naturalistic language and thinking processes are flexible, fluid, and changing. As the investigator proceeds throughout the research design, the aim of capturing complexity from the perspective of the individuals or phenomena studied is actualized through systematic but dynamic interaction between collecting and analyzing information.

## Exercises

1. Select a research article from a journal that uses an experimental-type design. Identify the independent variable or variables, the dependent variable or variables, and any intervening variables that may be confounding the study.

2. Identify the conceptual definitions and the operational definitions in the article that you selected.

3. Using the same article, determine (a) threats to validity of the study, (b) how the investigator minimized bias and enhanced control and validity, and (c) ethical issues that shaped the design.

4. Select a research article that uses naturalistic inquiry. Identify and provide evidence of the eight elements of the researcher's thinking process:
- Purpose of research
- Context of research
- Pluralistic perspective of reality
- Concern with transferability
- Flexibility
- Concern with language
- Emic and etic perspectives
- Interactive/analytic process

5. Using the same article, determine some of the ethical issues that shaped the investigator's behavior in the field.

*References*

1. Kerlinger FN: *Foundations of behavioral research,* ed 2, New York, 1973, Holt, Rinehart, & Winston.
2. Wilson J: *Thinking with concepts,* Cambridge, Mass, 1966, Cambridge University Press.
3. Babbie E: *The practice of social research,* ed 6, Belmont, Calif, 1991, Wadsworth.
4. Polansky NA: *Social work research: methods for the helping professions,* Chicago, 1975, University of Chicago Press.
5. Goodman C: Evaluation of a model self help telephone program: impact of natural networks, *Social Work* 35:556-562, 1990.
6. Campbell DT, Stanley JC: *Experimental and quasi-experimental design,* Chicago, 1963, Rand McNally.
7. Neuman WL: *Social research methods: qualitative and quantitative approaches,* ed 3, Boston, 1997, Allyn Bacon.
8. Perrow C: *Complex organizations: a critical essay,* ed 2, New York, 1979, Random House.
9. Denzin NK, Lincoln YS: *Handbook of qualitative research,* Thousand Oaks, Calif, 1994, Sage.
10. Liebow E: *Tally's corner,* Boston, 1967, Little Brown.
11. Maruyama M: Endogenous research: the prison project. In Reason P, Rowan J, editors: *Human inquiry: a sourcebook for new paradigm research,* New York, 1981, John Wiley & Sons.
12. Guba EG: Criteria for assessing the trustworthiness of naturalistic inquiries, *Educ Commun Technol J* 29:75-92, 1981.
13. Geertz C: Thick description: toward an interpretative theory of culture. In *The interpretation of cultures: selected essays,* New York, 1973, Basic Books.
14. Anastas JW, MacDonald ML: *Research design for social work and the human services,* New York, 1994, Lexington.
15. Willoughby J, Keating N: Being in control: the process of caring for a relative with Alzheimer's disease, *Qualitative Health Res* 1:27-50, 1991.
16. Hodge R, Kress G: *Social semiotics,* Ithaca, NY, 1988, Cornell University Press.
17. Krefting L: Reintegration into the community after head injury: the results of an ethnographic study, *Occup Ther J Res* 9:67-83, 1989.
18. Headland TN, Pike KL, Harris M: *Emics and etics: the insider/outsider debate,* Newbury Park, Calif, 1990, Sage.
19. Frank G: Life history model of adaptation to disability: the case of a congenital amputee, *Soc Sci Med* 19:639-645, 1984.

# PART III

## *Design approaches*

Now that we have delved into the thinking processes of research, we are ready to examine its structure. The structure of research refers to the design elements used by researchers to answer queries and questions. In Part III, we present diverse approaches to design that are used to conduct research in experimental-type, naturalistic, and integrated inquiries.

# Chapter 9

# Experimental-type designs

**Key terms**  Counterbalance designs
Factorial designs
Manipulation
Non-experimental designs
Pre-experimental designs
Quasi-experimental designs
Randomization
Solomon four-group designs
True-experimental designs

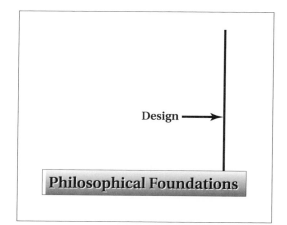

Design ⟶

**Philosophical Foundations**

Using the language introduced in Chapter 8, we are ready to examine the characteristics of designs in the experimental-type research tradition. Designs in this tradition have traditionally been classified as true experimental,

quasi-experimental, pre-experimental, or non-experimental. As the language of this tradition implies, it is the experiment that is the criterion by which all other methodologic approaches are judged. Of all the experimental-type designs, the true-experimental design offers the greatest degree of control and internal validity; therefore it is used to reveal causal relationships between independent and dependent variables.

Before we begin discussing experimental-type designs, it is important to recognize that every design in the experimental-type tradition has merit and value. The merit and value of a design is based on how well the design answers the research question and the level of rigor that the investigator brings to the plan and conduct of the inquiry. This view of research differs from the perspective of many experimental-type researchers who present true experiment as the design of choice and suggest that other designs are deficient or limited.[1,2] However, we believe that a design in the experimental-type tradition should be chosen because it fits the question, level of theory development, and setting or environment in which the research will be conducted. True experimentation is the best design to use to predict causal relationships, but it may be inappropriate for other forms of inquiry and research in health and human service settings. In other words, not all research questions seek to predict causal relationships between independent and dependent variables.

## True-experimental designs

Let us begin our discussion of designs in the experimental-type tradition with the true-experimental design. To express the structural relationships of designs in this tradition, we use Campbell and Stanley's notation system, which has been widely adopted by researchers. Stanley and Campbell used the following symbols to diagram design: $X$ for independent variable, $O$ for dependent variable, and $R$ for random sample selection.[3]

We also find it helpful to use the symbol $r$ to refer to random group assignment. As you will see in this and subsequent chapters, it is often difficult and frequently inappropriate or unethical for health and human service professionals to select a sample from a larger pre-defined population based on random selection (referred to as $R$ in Campbell and Stanley's format); rather, typically in health and human service research, subjects enter studies on a volunteer basis. Such a sample is one of convenience in which subjects are then randomly assigned to either the experimental or the control group. The addition of $r$ denotes this important structural distinction.

| $R$ | $O$ | $X$ | $O$ |
|-----|-----|-----|-----|
| $R$ | $O$ |     | $O$ |

*True-experimental designs* are perhaps best known by beginning researchers and laypersons. True-experimental design refers to the classic two-group design in which subjects are randomly selected and randomly assigned ($R$) to either an experimental or control group condition. Before the experimental condition, all subjects are pretested or observed on a dependent measure ($O$). In the experimental group, the independent variable or experimental condition is imposed (*X*), and it is with-held in the control group. After the experimental condition, all subjects are posttested or observed on the dependent variable (*O*).

In this design the investigator expects to observe no difference between the experimental and control groups on the dependent measure at pretest. In other words, subjects are chosen randomly from a larger pool of potential subjects and then assigned to a group on a chance-determined basis; therefore subjects in both groups are expected to perform similarly. On the other hand, the investigator anticipates or hypothesizes that differences will occur between experimental and control group subjects on the posttest scores. However, this expectation is expressed as a *null hypothesis,* which states that no difference is expected. In a true-experimental design, the investigator always states a null hypothesis that forms the basis for statistical testing. Usually in research reports, however, the alternative hypothesis is stated (i.e., that of an expected difference). If the investigator's data analytical procedures reveal a significant difference between experimental and control group scores, he or she can fail to accept the null hypothesis with a reasonable degree of certainty. In failing to accept the null hypothesis, the investigator accepts with a certain level of confidence that the independent variable or experimental condition (*X*) caused the outcome observed at posttest time in the experimental group. In other words, the investigator infers that the difference at posttest time is not the result of chance but is caused by participation in the experimental condition.

There are three major characteristics of the true-experimental design (Box 9-1).

**Box 9-1** | **Three characteristics of true-experimental design**
- Randomization
- Control group
- Manipulation of an independent variable

Let us consider each of these characteristics.

## Randomization

*Randomization* occurs at the sample selection phase or at the group assignment phase. If random sample selection is accomplished, the design notation appears as presented earlier (*R*). If randomization occurs only at the group assignment phase, we represent the design as such (**r**):

| | | | |
|---|---|---|---|
| *r* | *O* | *X* | *O* |
| *r* | *O* | | *O* |

This variation has implications for external validity. A true-experimental design that does not use random sample selection is limited in the extent to which conclusions can be generalized to the population from which the sample is selected. Because subjects are not drawn by chance from a larger identified pool, the generalizability or external validity of findings is limited. However, such a design variation is common in experimental research and can still be used to reveal causal relationships within the sample itself.

The random assignment of subjects to group conditions based on chance is essential in true experimentation. It enhances the probability that subjects in experimental and control groups will be theoretically equivalent on all major dependent variables at the pretest occasion. Randomization, in principle, equalizes subjects or makes subjects in both experimental and control groups comparable at pretest time. Any influence on one group theoretically affects the other group as well, since no order was used to obtain or assign the sample to experimental or control groups. An observed change in the experimental group at posttest time then can be attributed with a reasonable degree of certainty to the experimental condition.

Randomization is a powerful technique that increases control and eliminates bias by neutralizing the effects of extraneous influences on the outcome of a study. For example, the threats to internal validity by historical events and maturation are theoretically eliminated. Based on probability theory, such influences should affect subjects equally in both the experimental and control groups. Without randomization of subjects, you will not have a true-experimental design.

## Control group

We introduced the concept of control in Chapter 8. Here we extend our discussion to refer to the inclusion of a control group. The control group allows the investigator to see what the sample will be without the influence of the experimental condition or independent variable. A control group theoretically performs or remains the same relative to the independent variable at pretest and posttest occasions, since the control group has not had the chance of being exposed to the experimental condition. Therefore the control group represents the characteristics of the experimental group before being changed by participation in the experimental condition.

The control group is also a mechanism that allows the investigator to examine what has been referred to as the attention factor, Hawthorne effect, or halo effect."[4] These three terms each refer to the phenomenon of the subject experiencing change as a result of simply participating in a research project. For example, being the recipient of personal attention from an interviewer during pretesting and posttesting occasions may influence how a subject feels and responds to interview questions. A change in scores in the experimental group may occur then, independent of the effect of the experimental condition. Without a control group, investigators are not able to observe the presence or absence of this phenomenon and are unable to judge the extent to which differences on posttest scores of the experimental group reflect experimental effect, not additional attention.

Interestingly, this attention phenomenon was discovered in the process of conducting research. In 1934, a group of investigators were examining productivity in the Hawthorne automobile plant in Chicago. The research involved interviewing workers. To improve productivity the investigators recommended that the lighting of the facility be brightened. The researchers noted week after week that productivity increased after each subsequent increase in illumination. To confirm the success of their amazing findings, the researchers then dimmed the light. To their surprise, productivity continued to increase even under this circumstance. In reexamining the research process, they concluded that it was the additional attention given to the workers through the ongoing interview process and their inclusion in the research itself that caused an increased work effort.[5]

## Manipulation

In the true-experimental design, the independent variable is manipulated either by having it present (in the experimental group) or absent (in the control group). *Manipulation* is the ability to provide and withhold the independent variable that is unique to the true experiment.

According to Campbell and Stanley, true experimentation theoretically controls for each of the seven major threats to internal validity (see Chapter 8). However, when such a true-experimental design is implemented in the health care or human service environment, certain influences may remain as internal threats, thereby decreasing the potential for the investigator to support a cause-and-effect relationship. For example, the selection of a data collection instrument in which there is a learning effect based on repeated testing could pose a significant threat to a study, regardless of how well the experiment is structured. It is also possible for experimental mortality to affect outcome, particularly if the groups become nonequivalent as a result of attrition from the experiment. The health or human service environment is complex and does not offer the same degree of control as a laboratory setting. Therefore in applying the true-experimental design to the health or human service environment, the researcher must carefully examine how each threat to internal validity is or can be resolved.

## Variations of experimental designs

There are many design variations of the true experiment that have been developed to enhance its internal validity. For example, to assess the effect of the attention factor, a researcher may develop a three-group design. In this structure, subjects are randomly assigned to an experimental condition, an attention control group that receives an activity designed to equalize the attention that subjects receive in the experimental group, or a silent control group that receives no attention other than that obtained naturally during data collection efforts. Silent control groups can also refer to the situation in which information is collected on subjects who have no knowledge of their own participation. For example, extracting information from medical records or other such artifacts on a group who remains unaware may provide the researcher with an understanding of how subjects in their study compare with those who are not, at least along key demographic and medical characteristics. Let us examine four basic design variations of the true experiment.

### Posttest-only designs

Posttest-only designs conform to the norms of experimentation in that they contain the three elements of random assignment, control group, and manipulation. The difference between classical true-experimental design and this variation is the absence of a pretest. The basic design notation for a posttest-only experiment is:

| $R$ | $X$ | $O$ | | $r$ | $X$ | $O$ |
|-----|-----|-----|-----|-----|-----|-----|
| $R$ |     | $O$ | *or* | $r$ |     | $O$ |

In a posttest-only design, a leap of faith is taken, so to speak, in that groups are considered equivalent before the experimental condition as a result of random assignment. Theoretically, randomization should yield equivalent groups. However, the absence of the pretest makes it impossible to determine whether random assignment successfully achieved equivalence between the experimental and control groups on the major dependent variables of the study. There are a number of variations of this basic design. For example, the researcher may add other posttest occasions or different types of experimental or control groups. Posttest-only designs are most valuable when pretesting is not possible or appropriate but the research purpose is to seek causal relationships.

## Solomon four-group designs

*Solomon four-group designs* represent more complex experimental structures than those previously discussed. They combine the true-experiment and the posttest-only designs into one design structure. The strength of this design is that it eliminates the potential influence of the test-retest learning phenomenon by adding the posttest-only two-group design to the true-experimental design. This design is noted as:

| | | | |
|---|---|---|---|
| *GROUP 1: R* | *O* | *X* | *O* |
| *GROUP 2: R* | *O* | | *O* |
| *GROUP 3: R* | | *X* | *O* |
| *GROUP 4: R* | | | *O* |

As shown in this notation, group 3 does not receive the pretest but participates in the experimental condition. Group 4 also does not receive the pretest but serves as a control group. By comparing the posttest scores of all groups, the investigator can evaluate the effect of testing on scores on the posttest and interaction between the test and the experimental condition. The key benefit of this design is its ability to detect interaction effects. An interaction effect refers to changes that occur in the dependent variable as a consequence of the combined influence or interaction of taking the pretest and participating in the experimental condition.

Let us consider an example to illustrate the power of the Solomon four-group design and the nature of interaction effects. Suppose you want to assess the effects of an acquired immuno-deficiency syndrome (AIDS) information training program (independent variable) on the sexual risk-taking behaviors (the dependent variable) of adolescents. You can pretest groups by asking questions about sexual activities and levels of knowledge regarding behavioral risks of developing AIDS. You can expose one group to the experimental condition that involves attending an educational forum led by their peers. On posttesting you discover that levels of knowledge increased and that risk behaviors decreased in subjects who received the experimental program. However, you cannot determine the effect of the pretest itself on the outcome. By adding group 3 (the experimental condition without a pretest), you can determine whether the change in scores is as strong as when the pretest is administered (group 1). If group 2 (control) and group 3 (experimental) show no change but experimental group 1 does, this change is a consequence of an interaction effect of the pretest and the intervention. If there is a change in experimental groups 1 and 3 and some change in control group 2 but none in control group 4, there may be a direct effect of the intervention or experimental condition plus an interaction effect. This design allows the investigator to determine the strength of the independent effects of the intervention and the strength of the effect of pretesting on outcomes. If the groups that have been pretested show a testing effect, statistical procedures can be used to correct it, if necessary.

As you can see, the Solomon four-group design offers increased control and the possibility of understanding complex outcomes. However, because it requires the addition of two groups, it is a costly and time-consuming alternative to the true-experimental design and is not frequently used in health and human service inquiry.

## Factorial designs

*Factorial designs* offer even more opportunities for multiple comparisons and complexities in analysis. In these designs the investigator evaluates the effects of either two or more independent variables ($X_1$ and $X_2$) or the effects of an intervention on different factors or levels of a sample or study variables. The interaction of these parts, as well as the direct relationship of one part to another, is examined.

Let us assume you are interested in examining the effects of an exercise program on older adults. Specifically, you want to determine the extent to which two levels of health status (good and poor) influence three quality-of-life areas for participants. In this case the first independent variable that is manipulated assumes two values: participation in an exercise experimental group or participation in a nonexercise control group. The other independent variable that is not ma-

nipulated (health) also has two values (good and poor). The dependent variable or outcome measure (quality of life) has three factors (e.g., activity level, overall satisfaction, and sense of well-being). This study represents a factorial design in which the independent variables have two factors or levels and the dependent variable has three levels. This structure is referred to as a *2 X 2 X 3* factorial design, as displayed in Figure 9-1. This design will allow you to examine the relationship between different levels of health and specific quality of life indicators for two different conditions—one in which subjects exercised and one in which they participated in a nonexercise control group. This design will also enable you to examine not only direct relationships but interactive relationships as well. You can determine the combined effects of two or more variables that may be quite different from each direct effect. For example, you may want to examine whether the less healthy exerciser benefits more on the activity indicator of quality of life than the less healthy nonexerciser. To statistically evaluate all of the possible contrasts in this design, you will need to have a very large sample size to ensure that each cell or block (see Figure 9-1) contains an adequate number of scores for analysis. Of course, you can develop more complex factorial designs in which both independent and dependent variables have more than two levels. However, with more complexity, increasingly large sample sizes are necessary to ensure that there are sufficient numbers in each variation to permit analysis.

## Counterbalance designs

*Counterbalance designs* are often used when more than one intervention is being tested and

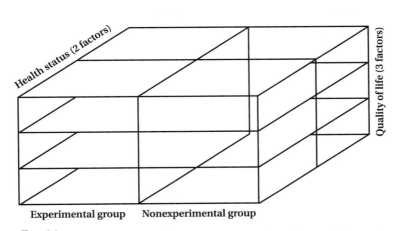

**Figure 9-1** Factorial design: investigating state of quality of life in elderly participants in experimental exercise program.

when the order of participation is manipulated. This design allows the investigator to determine the combined effects of two or more interventions and the effect of order on study outcomes. Although there are many variations, the basic design is:

| R | O | $X_1$ | O | $X_2$ | O |
|---|---|-------|---|-------|---|
| R | O | $X_2$ | O | $X_1$ | O |

Note the subscript numbers on the independent variables. The reversal of the conditions is characteristic of counterbalance designs in which both groups experience both conditions but in different orders. This reversal is called crossover. In a crossover study, one group is assigned to the experimental group first and to the control condition later; the reverse order is assigned for the other group. Measurements will occur before the first set of conditions, before the second set, and after the experiment. Such a study would allow you to eliminate the threats to internal validity caused by the interaction of the experimental variable and other aspects of the study.

Goodman's study of the psychosocial effects of two different interventions for caregivers of individuals with Alzheimer's disease is an example of a counterbalance study. Goodman randomly assigned her sample to one of two conditions, lecture only and peer telephone network, and then reversed their assignment. Testing occurred at three intervals: just before the experiment, after participation in condition one, and after the experiment. Goodman was not only able to ascertain the effects of each program on a single group, but she was also able to compare groups over time in each of the conditions.[6]

To summarize, true-experimental designs must contain three essential characteristics: random assignment, control group, and manipulation. The classic true experiment and its variations all contain those elements and thus are capable of producing knowledge about causal relationships among independent and dependent variables. The four design strategies in the true-experimental classification are appropriate for an experimental-type research question in which the intent is to predict and reveal a cause. Each true-experimental type controls the influences of the basic threats to internal validity and unwanted or extraneous phenomena that can confound a causal study and invalidate causal claims. There are three criteria for using a true-experimental design or its variation: sufficient theory to examine causality; a causal question; and conditions and ethics that permit randomization, use of a control group, and manipulation.

## Quasi-experimental designs

Although true experiments have been upheld as the ideal or prototype in research, there are many reasons why such designs may not be appropriate, as we have indicated throughout this book. First, in health and human service research, it may not be possible, appropriate, or ethical to use randomization or to manipulate the introduction and withholding of an experimental intervention. Second, all inquiries do not ask causal questions. There are other design options that do not contain the three elements of true experimentation that are frequently used by health and human service researchers to generate valuable knowledge. Even though the language of the experimental-type tradition implies that these designs are "missing something," we suggest that these designs are not inferior; rather, they produce different interpretations and uses than true experimentation. The deci-

sion to use *quasi-experimental designs* should be based on the level of theory, type of research question asked, and constraints of the research environment.

According to Cook and Campbell, who wrote the seminal work on quasi-experimentation, these designs can be defined as:

> ...experiments that have treatments, outcome measures, and experimental units, but do not use random assignment to create comparison from which treatment-caused change is inferred. Instead, the comparisons depend on nonequivalent groups that differ from each other in many ways other than the presence of the treatment whose effects are being tested.[7]

The key to the effective use of quasi-experimental designs lies in the claims made by the researcher about the findings. Because random assignment is absent in quasi-experimentation, the researcher has one of two choices: (1) he or she can make causal claims while acknowledging the alternative explanations for these claims and design limitations, or (2) he or she can avoid making causal inferences when they are unjustified by the design.

As discussed by Campbell and Cook, designs belonging to this category have two of the three experimental elements: control group and manipulation. Two basic design types that fit the criteria for quasi-experimentation are discussed in Box 9-2:

### Box 9-2 Quasi-experimental designs
- Nonequivalent control group
- Interrupted time series

## Nonequivalent control group designs

In nonequivalent control group designs, there are at least two comparison groups, but subjects are not randomly assigned to these groups. The basic design is structured as a pretest and posttest comparison group, as presented in this notation:

$$\begin{array}{ccc} O & X & O \\ \hline O & & O \end{array}$$

It is also possible to add comparison groups or to alter the testing sequence. Let us consider an example in which you want to test the effectiveness of an innovative mental health program for depression, but it is not possible to use randomization. You arrange for a community mental health center to use the experimental intervention for 1 month. You find another community mental health center in which the population is comparable and assign the comparison condition (conventional intervention) to that group. As with true-experimental design, you pretest and posttest all subjects and then compare group scores. If the group scores for the experimental condition are significantly different, there is strong support for the value of the innovative program. However, once again, because of the multiple threats to internal validity, most likely you will not use this design to support cause but to explain the comparative changes in each of the study groups; that is, you can indicate that the changes after the intervention in the experimental group were significantly greater than the changes in the comparison group.

## Interrupted time series designs

Interrupted time series designs involve repeated measurement of the dependent variable both before and after the introduction of the independent variable. There is no control or comparison group in this design. The multiple measures before the independent variable control for the threat to internal validity based on maturation and other time related changes. A typical time series design is depicted as:

$$\begin{array}{cccccc} O_1 & O_2 & O_3 & X & O_4 & O_5 & O_6 \end{array}$$

Although the number of observations may vary, it is suggested that no less than three occur before and after the independent variable is introduced. The investigator is particularly interested in evaluating the change in scores between the observation that occurs immediately before the introduction of the intervention ($O_3$) and the observation that follows the intervention ($O_4$). Any sharp change in score compared with the other measures may suggest that the intervention had an effect. The investigator must evaluate changes in scores in terms of the scoring patterns that occurred both before and after intervention. For example, if there is a trend for scores to increase at each testing occasion, even a sharp difference between $O_3$ and $O_4$ may not reflect a change because of the introduction of the intervention. Because of the absence of the control group and randomization, this design cannot strongly support a causal relationship between the independent and dependent variables. In this type of design, however, the series of premeasures theoretically controls threats to internal validity except for the threat of history. Maturation, testing, instrumentation, regression, and attrition are considered threats that may occur between all measures and thus are detectable and controlled by repeated measurements. However, in this design, it is extremely important to choose a form of measurement in which there is no learning effect or threat of testing.

In the health and human service context, a time series design is often used when the experimental intervention is a stimulus the researcher may not be able to manipulate but has knowledge of its introduction. In other words, the intervention or experimental program may be a naturally occurring event in which it is possible to document performance of the dependent variable before and after the event's occurrence. For example, let us assume a hospital announces a plan to implement a new employee benefits program to enhance job satisfaction. The effects of this program on job satisfaction can be determined by taking a quarterly survey of employees for 1 year before the introduction of the new program. The same survey can be used quarterly after employee participation in the new benefits program. In this way, the hospital will have four data points regarding employee satisfaction before the program's introduction that can be compared with four data points after its implementation. This strategy will allow for such extraneous factors as staff turnover, fluctuations in patient census, and other considerations to be tracked over time to account for their effect on job satisfaction. This type of design is extremely useful in answering questions about the nature of change over time.

A combination of nonequivalent groups and time series design is a quasi-experimental design that can be considered appropriate for answering causal questions. In this combination, some of the potential bias attributable to nonequivalent groups is limited by multiple measures, whereas the time series design is strengthened by the addition of a comparison group.

To review, quasi-experimental designs are characterized by the presence of a control group and manipulation, but they do not contain random group assignment. Although there is no control group in the time series and single-subject designs, control is exercised through multiple observations of the same phenomenon both before and after the introduction of the experimental condition. In nonequivalent group designs, the control is built in through the use of one or more comparison groups. We suggest that quasi-experimentation is most valuable when the investigator is attempting to search for change over time or when a comparison between groups and the constraints of the health or human service environment are such that random assignment is not appropriate, ethical, or feasible.

## Pre-experimental designs

*Pre-experimental designs* are those in which two of the three criteria for true experimentation are absent. In pre-experiments, it is possible to describe phenomena or relationships. However, the outcomes of the study do not support claims for a causal relationship because of inadequate control and the potential of bias. Pre-experimental designs can be of value to answer descriptive questions or to generate pilot, exploratory evidence, but the investigator using these designs cannot consider causal explanations. There are numerous pre-experimental designs, all of which are variations on the following three designs (Box 9-3).

**Pre-experimental designs**

- One-shot case study
- Pretest-posttest design
- Static group comparison

## One-shot case study

In the one-shot case study, the independent variable is introduced and the dependent variable is then measured in only one group:

$$X \quad O$$

Without a pretest or a comparison group, the investigator can answer the question, "How did the group score on the dependent variable after the intervention?" As you can see, a cause-and-effect relationship between the two variables cannot be supported because of the seven threats to internal validity.

## Pretest-posttest design

Similarly, the pretest-posttest design is also valuable in describing what occurs after the introduction of the independent variable:

$$O \quad X \quad O$$

This design can answer questions about change over time in that the pretest is given before the introduction of the independent variable. If subjects are tested before the intervention and after the intervention, a change in scores on the dependent variable can be reported but cannot be attributed to the influence of the independent variable. Threats to internal validity, if one were to attempt to infer cause

using this design, include maturation, history, testing, instrumentation, experimental mortality, and interactive effects.

## Static group comparison

In static group comparison, a comparison group is added to the one-shot case study design:

$$\underline{X \_ \_ \_ \underline{O}}$$
$$O$$

This design, as in other pre-experimental structures, can answer descriptive questions about phenomena or relationships but is not considered a desirable choice for causal studies. Let us assume we want to test an intervention that is designed to reduce depression in young adults. The investigator who uses the static group comparison will select two nonequivalent groups, such as two groups of persons with depression receiving treatment in two different community mental health centers. One group will receive the intervention and one will not. A posttest measuring level of depression will be administered to both groups and then compared. This design can answer the following question with a fair degree of certainty, "How did the experimental group compare with the comparison group on the measure of depression?" Because random assignment did not occur, it is difficult to infer cause. Furthermore, there is minimal control in that the level of depression in either group was unknown before the introduction of the experimental condition. Some researchers consider the comparison group score as a pretest measure, since it is feasible that the group that did not receive intervention approximated the pretest condition of the group receiving the intervention. Introducing a static comparison group offers more control over extraneous factors than the one-shot case and pretest-posttest designs. However, we caution against its use to make statements concerning causal relationships between the independent and dependent variables.

In review, pre-experimental designs may be valuable in answering a descriptive question. However, the absence of two of the three major conditions for true experimentation makes these designs an inappropriate choice if your pursuit is prediction and causal inference. If you attempt to answer predictive or causal questions with these designs, the basic seven threats to internal validity limit effective checks against bias.

## Non-experimental designs

*Non-experimental designs* primarily rely on statistical manipulation of data rather than mechanical manipulation and sequencing. By definition, non-experimental designs are those in which none of the three criteria for true experimentation exist. These designs are most useful when testing a concept or construct or relationship among constructs that naturally occur. Any manipulation of variables is done *post hoc* through statistical analysis. Here we describe the three designs (Box 9-4) that are frequently used in health and human service research.

| Box 9-4 | Non-experimental designs |
|---|---|

- Surveys
- Passive observation
- *Ex post facto* designs

## Survey designs

Survey designs are primarily used to measure characteristics of a population. Through survey designs, it is possible to describe population parameters, as well as to predict relationships among these characteristics. Typically, surveys are conducted with large samples. Questions are posed through either mailed questionnaires or telephone or face-to-face interviews. Perhaps the most well-known survey is the U.S. Census, in which the government administers mailed surveys and conducts selected face-to-face interviews to develop a descriptive picture of the characteristics of the population of the United States.

The study of job satisfaction of occupational therapy faculty conducted by Rozier et al. is an example of how a survey design was used in health care to describe a population and to predict factors that may lead to job satisfaction.[8] The investigators mailed questionnaires to program directors of schools of occupational therapy and asked the directors to distribute these instruments to faculty. Responses from 538 faculty member yielded information about demographic characteristics and job satisfaction. Through statistical analysis of the data, descriptive and predictive conclusions were developed.

The advantages of survey design are that the investigator can reach a large number of respondents with relatively minimal expenditure, numerous variables can be measured by a single instrument, and statistical manipulation during the data analytical phase can permit multiple uses of the data set. Disadvantages may include how the action processes of the survey design are structured. For example, the use of mailed questionnaires may yield a low-response rate, compromising the external validity of the design. Face-to-face interviews are time-consuming and may pose reliability problems. There are many books on how to design a survey study by mail, by telephone, or face-to-face that should be consulted if this type of design is pursued.[9,10]

## Passive observation designs

Passive observation designs are used to examine phenomena as they naturally occur and to discern the relationship between two or more variables. Often referred to as correlational designs, passive observation can be as simple as examining the relationship between two variables, (e.g., height and weight), or it can be as complex as predicting scores on one or more variables from knowledge of scores on other variables. As in the case of the survey, variables are not manipulated but are measured and then examined for relationships and patterns of prediction. In the survey just described by Rozier et al., the investigators examined the relationships among multiple variables and predicted the degree of teaching satisfaction with respondent scores on four other variables.[8]

## Ex post facto designs

*Ex post facto* designs are considered to be one type of passive observation design. However, in *ex post facto* designs (literally translated as "after the fact"), the phenomena of interest have already occurred and cannot be manipulated in any way. *Ex post facto* designs are frequently used to examine relationships between naturally occurring population parameters and spe-

cific variables. For example, let us assume you are interested in understanding the effects of coronary bypass surgery on morale and resumption of former roles for men and women. Coronary bypass surgery is the event that the researcher cannot manipulate, but it can be examined for its effects after its occurrence. Fortune and Hanks used an *ex post facto* survey design to examine the differing career patterns among male and female social workers. Through a survey about their job history and gender, 520 recent graduates of schools of social work answered questions about gender differences in salary and career opportunity in the field of social work.[11]

In review, non-experimental designs have a wide range of uses. The value in these designs lies in their ability to examine and quantify naturally occurring phenomena, so that statistical analysis can be accomplished. In this category of design the investigator therefore does not manipulate the independent variable but examines it in relation to one or more variables for descriptive or predictive purposes. These designs have the capacity to include a large number of subjects and to examine events or phenomena that have already occurred. Because random selection, manipulation, and control group are not present in these designs, investigators must use caution when making causal claims from the findings. As in the quasi-experimental and true-experimental situation, the researcher is still concerned with potential biases that may limit the internal validity of the design. The researcher tries to control the influence of external or extraneous influences on the study variables through the implementation of systematic data collection procedures, the use of reliable and valid instrumentation, and other techniques that are discussed in later chapters. The researcher also increases the generalizability of a study or its external validity by using random sample selection procedures when appropriate and feasible to ensure representation and minimize systematic sampling bias.

## Criteria for selecting appropriate and adequate designs

As discussed in this chapter, there is a strong belief among researchers that the true-experimental design represents the only structure that is appropriate and adequate. However, each design in the experimental-type tradition has its strengths and limitations. The true experiment is the best design for testing theory and making causal statements. However, if causality is not your purpose or if the design structure does not fit the particular environment in which the research is to be conducted, it is not an appropriate or adequate design choice.

It is often difficult to apply strict experimental conditions to a field setting. For example, although subjects may be randomly assigned to a group, it may not be possible to obtain the initial list of subjects for a random sampling process, or it may be unethical to withhold a type of treatment (or experimental intervention) from a service consumer. Although clinical drug trials or testing of new technologies often obtain the degree of control necessary for true-experimental conditions, research on the social and psychologic dimensions of health and human service work often pose a different set of issues and challenges for the researcher. These challenges make it essential for the investigator

to be flexible in the use of design so that a research strategy appropriate to the question and to the level of theory, purpose, and practical constraints can be selected and rigorously applied.

To illustrate the value of each type of design within the experimental-type tradition, apply the concepts in this chapter to an example that you may encounter in your practice. Suppose you are employed in a hospital in the rehabilitation unit. You have just read about a new computer intervention that seems to enhance the cognitive recovery of persons with traumatic brain injury. You order the program and recruit a group of patients to use it. To determine the extent to which the program works (which you have defined as significant improvement in cognitive function), you select an instrument to measure cognitive function (operationalizing your concept of cognitive improvement), and then you test a sample of 10 patients with the same instrument after their use of the computer intervention. This type of inquiry is an *XO* design (pre-experimental) in which the computer program is the independent variable and cognitive performance is the dependent variable. The mean score for your sample was within normal limits, with a normal dispersion of scores around the mean. From this design, you have answered the question, "How did subjects score on a test of cognitive performance after their participation in a computer intervention?" Although these data are valuable to you in describing your sample, you still have not answered the question about whether the program "works." There are multiple threats to internal validity that interfere with your ability to make a causal inference between variables with any degree of assuredness. You therefore decide to build on this study by adding a pretest. In the next study you pretest your new sample, introduce the computer intervention, and then posttest the sample. This type of study is an *OXO* design (also pre-experimental). Because the subjects have greatly improved from the pretest to the posttest, you conclude that your program has worked. However, can you really come to this conclusion? What about the effects of sampling bias, maturation, and history on your sample? You realize that even though you have stronger evidence for the value of the program, the design that you have selected has answered the question, "To what extent did the subjects change in cognitive function after participating in the experimental condition?"

For your next sample, you add a control group so that your research structure is now a quasi-experimental design and looks like this:

| *O* | *X* | *O* |
|---|---|---|
| *O* | | *O* |

When the experimental group improves more than the control group, you now are convinced that your program works. However, can you make that claim? What about sampling bias and other interactive effects that might confound your study? From this design, you can answer the question, "Which group made more progress?" This type of design provides fairly strong support for the value of your program, but it cannot yet be used to make causal claims.

For your next project, you add random group assignment to your design so that you are conducting a true experiment. Your design looks like this:

| *r* | *O* | *X* | *O* |
|---|---|---|---|
| *r* | *O* | | *O* |

Because your experimental group has improved significantly more than the control group, you can now make the claim, with reasonable certainty, that the program works. You have used true experimentation to test the efficacy of the computer intervention in your sample. However, can you advise your colleague to use this intervention for his or her clients? The answer of course is a resounding "maybe." Because you did not randomly select your sample, the capacity to generalize your findings beyond your own experiment is limited. We are often faced with the desire to generalize, but practical restraints of conducting practice research will not allow us to randomly select our sample, as discussed in detail later in the text.

Suppose you were interested in examining the extent to which the cognitive intervention produced outcomes that were satisfactory to family members, once your client is discharged. You may then select a non-experimental survey design to examine the level of satisfaction, and you may include predictor variables, such as length of time in treatment and degree of family support, inform future use and success with this intervention.

As you can see, each design has its values and limitations not only related to claims that can be made about the knowledge generated but about practical and ethical issues as well. The key to doing rigorous and valued research with experimental-type designs is to clearly state your question; select a design that can best answer the question given the level of theory development, the practical considerations, and the purpose in conducting the study; and report accurate conclusions.

Now that you are aware of experimental-type designs and techniques for enhancing the strength of these design, you still may wonder how to select a design to fit your particular study question. Begin by asking yourself the important guiding questions listed (Box 9-5).

What do each of these questions really ask you to consider? In question 1, the issues of validity are raised. When a design is selected, it is essential that the project be internally consistent, construct valid, and capable of providing the level of answer that the question seeks. Question 2 also speaks to validity but addresses issues of control and structure as well. This question guides the researcher to consider what extraneous influences can potentially confound the study and what ways maximum control can be built into the design. Question 3 summarizes the issues raised in the previous questions by guiding the researcher to be most rigorous in planning control and minimizing bias. External validity and sampling are the focus of question 4. The answer to this question should be the development of a design that allows as broad a generalization as possible without threatening internal validity. Finally, in question 5, the researcher is reminded of practical and ethical concerns that shape the design.

If the questions are answered successfully, the criteria for adequacy of experimental-type designs have been addressed. However, keep in mind that design considerations within the experimental-type tradition are more than just knowing the definitions of design characteristics. Knowledge of these design possibilities is your set of tools, which you can apply and modify to fit the specific conditions of the setting in which you are conducting research. Developing a design within the tradition of experimental-type research in the health and human service field is a creative process. You must use your knowledge of the language and thinking processes, the basic elements of design, and the issues of internal and external validity to develop a study that fits the particular environment and question that you are asking. Table 9-1 provides a summary of the characteristics of each major category of experimental-type design.

## Examining outcomes of intervention

Over the past 10 years, the term "outcomes" has increasingly appeared in the literature. Essen-

---

### Box 9-5   Guiding questions to select a design

1. Does the design answer the research question? Is there congruence between the research question(s) and hypotheses and the design?
2. Does the design adequately control independent variables? Are other extraneous independent variables present that may confound the study?
3. Does the design maximize control and minimize bias?
4. To what extent does the design enhance the generalizability of results to other subjects, other groups, and other conditions?
5. What are some of the ethical and field limitations of the research question that influence the research design?

**Table 9-1** — **Summary of design characteristics**

|  | Experimental | Quasi-experimental | Non-experimental | Pre-experimental |
|---|---|---|---|---|
| Randomization | Yes | No | No | No |
| Control group | Yes | Maybe | Maybe | No |
| Manipulation | Yes | Maybe | No | Yes |

tially, health and human service professionals are being asked to show accountability by demonstrating that their interventions actually produce desired outcomes. As you may have surmised, the most ideal design for attributing outcomes to professional intervention is true-experimental design or a variation thereof. However, as we have also discussed, structuring true experimentation may be difficult at best and unethical at worst. Thus each professional must be adept at selecting a design that examines the extent to which his or her intervention influenced outcome. The use of non-experimental designs, which rely on statistical manipulation of data, has become increasingly popular. Whereas a causal link between intervention and outcome cannot be asserted with certainty, changes and descriptive understandings of outcomes can be informative to the professional and explain what has followed an intervention, even when quasi-experimental or pre-experimental designs are used. A full discussion of outcomes research is beyond the scope of this book. However, we encourage you to pose research questions about your practice and select the design that best and most practically answers these questions.

## Summary

In this chapter we examined the range of experimental-type designs from true experi-

mental to nonexperimental. We have shown how each design varies in its level of control, randomization, and manipulation of variables. Also, we have shown how field conditions and other practicalities influence the actual implementation of any one type of design. The basic elements of design structures in the experimental-type tradition have been described in full recognition of its many variations. Furthermore, new applications of experimental designs are being advanced with the advent of outcomes research and field-based intervention studies.

## Exercises

1. Select an experimental-type research article and identify the dependent and independent variables. Diagram the design using $X O$ notation.

2. Develop research questions and designs using the $X O$ notation to illustrate: (a) true-experimental design, (b) quasi-experimental design, (c) pre-experimental design, and (d) non-experimental design.

3. Identify up to three potential ethical and field limitations of each research design developed in exercise 2.

### References

1. Kerlinger FN: *Foundations of behavioral research,* ed 2, New York, 1973, Holt, Rinehart, & Winston.
2. Currier DP: *Elements of research in physical therapy,* Baltimore, 1984, Williams & Wilkins.
3. Campbell DT, Stanley JC: *Experimental and quasi-experimental designs for research,* Chicago, 1963, Rand McNally.
4. Perrow C: *Complex organizations: a critical essay,* ed 2, New York, 1979, Random House.
5. Roethlisberger FJ, Dickson WJ: *Management and the worker,* Cambridge, Mass, 1947, Harvard University Press.
6. Goodman C: Evaluation of a model of self help telephone program: impact of natural networks, *Soc Work* 25:556-562, 1990.
7. Cook TD, Campbell DT: *Quasi-experimentation: design and analysis for field settings,* Boston, 1979, Houghton Mifflin.
8. Rozier C, Gilkeson G, Hamilton BL: Job satisfaction of occupational therapy faculty, *Am J Occup Ther* 45:160-165, 1991.
9. Czaja R, Blair J: *Designing surveys: a guide to decisions and procedures,* Thousand Oaks, Calif, 1996, Pine Forge Press.
10. Fink A (series editor): *The survey kit,* Thousand Oaks, Calif, 1995, Sage.
11. Fortune AE, Hanks LL: Gender inequities in early social work careers, *Soc Work* 33:221-226, 1988.

# Chapter 10
# Naturalistic inquiry

**Key terms**    Critical theory
Endogenous research
Ethnography
Grounded theory
Heuristic research
Life history
Participatory action research
Phenomenology

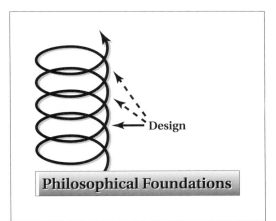

Design

**Philosophical Foundations**

 Using the language and thinking processes intro- duced in Chapter 8, we are ready to explore naturalistic inquiry in detail. In this chapter we select eight basic designs to illus- trate the different ways in which naturalistic researchers tackle the complexity of social ex-

perience and organize the 10 thinking and action essentials of the research process.

As indicated earlier in this text, a principle that is shared by researchers using different types of naturalistic designs is that phenomena occur or are embedded in a context, natural setting, or field. The term fieldwork refers to the basic activity that engages all investigators in this tradition. In conducting fieldwork the investigator enters the natural setting without the intent of altering or manipulating conditions. The purpose is to observe, understand, and come to know, so that theory may be described, explained, and generated. However, how investigators come to know, describe, and explain phenomena differ among designs. Although each design shares the basic language and thinking processes explored in Chapter 8, each is based in its own distinct philosophical tradition. As such, these designs differ in three basic aspects (Box 10-1).

In this chapter, we provide an overview of the basic framework of eight designs: endogenous, participatory action, critical theory, phenomenology, heuristic, life history, ethnography, and grounded theory. Table 10-1 compares and contrasts these naturalistic designs along three dimensions: research purpose, sequence of research essentials, and level and nature of investigator involvement. (We discuss the actual action

processes of conducting naturalistic inquiry in subsequent chapters in this text.) You will notice that in all naturalistic designs, the sequence of essential thinking and action processes is not fixed and therefore cannot be prescribed. Now, let us discuss the selected designs.

## Endogenous research

*Endogenous research* represents the most open-ended approach to research in this tradition. In this approach, research is "conceptualized, designed and conducted by researchers who are insiders of the culture, using their own epistemology and their own structure of relevance."[1] The unique feature of this design is the nature of investigator involvement. The investigator relinquishes control of a research plan and its implementation to those who are the subjects of the inquiry. The subjects are primary investigators or co-investigators who work independently or with the investigator to determine the nature of the study and how it is to be shaped. It is the subjects and investigators who make decisions about and participate in the building and testing of information as it emerges.

Endogenous research can be organized in a variety of ways and may include the use of any research strategy and technique in the naturalistic or experimental-type tradition or in the integration of the two. Endogenous research is a naturalistic design because of its paradigmatic framework; that is, the investigator views knowledge as emerging from individuals who know the best way of obtaining that information. As Argyris and Schon point out, this approach is based on a proposition developed by Kurt Lewin:

| Box 10-1 | Three differences in naturalistic designs |

- Purpose of the research
- Sequence and use of the 10 essentials
- Nature of investigator involvement

**Table 10-1**  **Basic framework of eight naturalistic designs**

| Design strategy | Purpose | Sequence | Investigator involvement |
|---|---|---|---|
| Endogenous | To yield insider perspective through involvement of subject as researcher | Variable | Determined by subjects/informants |
| Participatory action | To generate knowledge to inform action | Variable | Inclusive team of investigators and participants |
| Critical theory | To understand experiences experiences for social change | Variable | Investigator directed |
| Phenomenology | To discover meaning of lived experience | Narrative | Listener/reporter |
| Heuristic | To reveal personal and lived experience | Variable | Investigator and informant |
| Life history | To yield biographical experience | Narrative | Investigator directed |
| Ethnography | To understand culture | Prescribed | Investigator directed |
| Grounded theory | To generate theory | Prescribed | Investigator directed |

Causal inferences about the behavior of human beings are more likely to be valid and enactable when the human beings in question participate in building and testing them. Hence it aims at creating an environment in which participants give and get valid information, make free and informed choices (including the choice to participate), and generate internal commitment to the results of their inquiry.[2]

This design gives "knowing power" exclusively to the persons who are the subjects of the inquiry and is characterized by the absence of any predefined truths or structures. Because endogenous research is conducted by insiders, there are no external principles that guide the selection of thought and action processes in the study itself. Because the researcher's involvement is determined by the individuals who are the subjects of the investigation, the researcher may participate as an equal partner or not at all or somewhere in between these two levels.

Let us look at a classic example of endogenous research on prison violence. Maruyama entered the prison environment as a collaborator and participant observer rather than as the research consultant, an important characteristic of endogenous research. As a collaborator, Maruyama deferred to the subjects of the investigation to determine the degree of investigator involvement. Two teams, composed of prisoners who had no formal education in research methods, held a series of group meetings and created purposes and plans of action that were important and meaningful to each group. Maruyama describes the research in this way:

A team of endogenous researchers was formed in each of the two prisons. The overall objective of the project was to study interpersonal physical violence (fights) in the prison culture, with as little contamination as possible from academic theories and methodologies. The details of the research were left to be developed by the inmate researchers.[1]

The prisoners chose both experimental-type interview techniques and a form of qualitative data analysis to characterize the violence in the environments in which they were insiders. Maruyama found that the prisoners were not only able to collect extensive and meaningful data, but they were also capable of conducting sophisticated conceptual analyses of their data set. The findings from a study "owned" and conducted by insiders will yield very different results from one in which a researcher enters the prison environment as a stranger to ask questions regarding the reasons and nature of violence. From this study, violence was explicated in the language of the inmates, and the findings clearly displayed the cultural nature of violence in each prison. Consider how different the findings may have been if an investigator went to a group of inmates and asked questions about the reasons prison violence occurs. The endogenous methodology not only gave the inmates a voice, but it also revealed insights that may never have been uncovered by techniques in which the investigator takes an authoritative position in the project.

The concerns of the investigator in this type of research design include how to build and work with a team, how to relinquish control over process and outcome, and how to shape the group process to move the research team along in the study of themselves.

## Participatory action research

*Participatory action research* is a broad term that refers to different kinds of action research approaches. These varied approaches to action research each reflect a different epistemologic assumption and methodologic strategy. All, however, are founded in the principle that those who experience a phenomenon are the most qualified to investigate it. Similar to endogenous research, participatory action research involves individuals as full participants in the designing, conducting, and reporting of the research. However, the purposes and strategies of action research, as well as the nature of investigator involvement, differ significantly from endogenous research. As implied in the name, the purpose of action research is to generate knowledge to inform action. Researchers using a participatory framework usually work with groups or communities experiencing issues related to societal control, oppression, or dominance.

Action research was first coined in the 1940s by Kurt Lewin, a social psychologist. He blended experimental-type approaches to research with programs that addressed critical social problems. In this approach, social problems served as the basis for formulating a research purpose, question, and methodology. Each research step was connected to or involved with the particular organization, social group, or community that was the focus of inquiry. More recently, others have expanded this approach to inquiry. This design is now used in planning and enacting solutions to community problems or service dilemmas.[3]

Action research is based on four principles or values (Box 10-2). Let us examine each one. The principle of democracy means that action research is participatory; that is, all individuals who are stakeholders in a problem or issue and its resolution are included in the research process. The principle of equity ensures that all participants are equally valued in the research process, regardless of previous experience in research. Liberation suggests that action research is a design that is aimed at decreasing oppression. Finally, the principle of life enhancement positions action research as a systematic strategy that promotes "the expression of full human potential."

Action research employs thinking and action processes from either the experimental or naturalistic traditions or the integration of the two. There is not a prescribed or uniform design strategy. Nevertheless, action research is consistent with naturalistic forms of inquiry in that all research occurs within its natural context. Also, most action research relies on action processes that are characteristically interpretive in nature.

Let us examine the sequence in which the 10 research essentials are followed in an action research study. Action research is best characterized as cyclical, beginning with the identification of a problem or dilemma that calls for action, moving to a form of systematic inquiry, and culminating in planning and using the findings of the inquiry. Each step is informed or shaped by the participants of the study. Let us examine a particular study, the purpose of which was to establish community programs to enhance the transition of adolescents with special health care needs from high school to work or higher education. Using the principles of action research, the investigators first identified the stakeholders involved in this issue. They included adolescents and their parents, educators, health care providers, employers, and policy makers. To ensure that the research plan reflected the underlying principles of democracy and equity, the investigators convened a group made up of representatives from each of the stakeholder groups. This group became the core participatory researchers. These participatory researchers and the two investigators discussed the research problem and structured the research method. Focus groups were identified as the primary data collection method. Therefore all members of the team were trained in this particular approach. Focus groups of each of the stakeholder groups examined the service needs perceived by each group. Each focus group was facilitated by two members of the participatory team. Data were collected and analyzed by the participatory team. The findings were reported by the team to planning groups that were made up of the same stakeholder groups. A comprehensive service plan was developed, implemented, and evaluated by the participatory action team.[5] As you can see by this example, all members of the team were valued and contributed equally to the design, implementation, analysis, and application of the research.

---

**Box 10-2** **Four principles of action research**

- Democracy
- Equity
- Liberation
- Life enhancement

---

## Critical theory

As implied by the name, *critical theory* is not a research method but a world view that suggests both an epistemology and a purpose for conducting research. Whether critical theory is a philosophical, political, or sociologic school of thought has been debated in contemporary literature. In essence, critical theory is a response to postenlightenment philosophies and positivism in particular. Critical theorists "deconstruct" the notion that there is a unitary truth that can be known by using one way or method. We suggest that critical theory is a movement that is best understood by philosophers. Because critical theory is inspired by so many diverse schools of thought, including those informed by Marx, Hegel, Kant, Foucault, Derrida, and Kristeva, just to name a few, it is not a unitary approach. Rather, it represents a complex set of strategies that are united by the commonality of sociopolitical purpose.

Critical theorists seek to understand human experience as a means to change the world. The common purpose of researchers who approach investigation through critical theory is to come to know about social justice and human experience as a means to promote social change.

Critical theory was born in the Social Institute in the Frankfurt School in the 1920s. As the Nazi party gained power in Germany, critical theorists moved to Columbia University and developed their notions of power and justice, particularly in response to the hegemony of positivism in the United States. With a focus on social change, critical theorists came to view knowledge as power and the production of knowledge as "socially and historically deter-mined."[6] Derived from this view is an epistemology that upheld pluralism or a coming to know about phenomena in multiple ways. Furthermore, knowing is dynamic, changing, and embedded in the sociopolitical context of the times. According to critical theorists, there is not one objective reality that can be uncovered through systematic investigation.

Critical theory shares other principles in naturalistic inquiry, such as a view of informant as knower, the dynamic and qualitative nature of knowing, and a complex and pluralistic world view. Furthermore, critical theorists suggest that research crosses disciplinary boundaries and challenges current knowledge generated by experimental-type methods. Because of the radical view posited by critical theorists, the essential step of literature review in the research process is primarily used as a means to understand the *status quo*. Thus the action process of literature review may occur before the research, but the theory derived is criticized, deconstructed, and taken apart to its core assumptions. The hallmark of critical theory is, however, its purpose of social change and empowerment. Critical theory relies heavily on interview and observation as methods by which data are collected. Strategies of qualitative data analysis (discussed in detail in Chapter 18) are the primary analytical tools used in critical research agendas.

Consider this example. Suppose you are interested in understanding the relationship between clients who are substance abusers and formal service providers and the influence of this relationship on the outcome of therapeutic interventions. Using a critical theory perspective, the researcher will first review the literature critically.

Of particular importance for the critical theorists is an examination of the underlying assumptions that reflect a power imbalance based on race, class, and gender differences between client and practitioner. In critical theory this imbalance is presumed to have an effect of disempowering the client while elevating the status, control, and power of the service provider. Second, a range of strategies based in naturalistic inquiry will be used to explore the relationship from the perspectives of both clients and providers. Third, the understanding derived from the research will be used to promote social change with a particular focus on advancing social justice and equality for clients or oppressed groups.[7]

## Phenomenology

The specific focus of phenomenological research is everyday experience and an interpretation of the meaning of those experiences for individuals. *Phenomenology* differs from other forms of naturalistic inquiry in that phenomenologists believe that meaning can be understood only by those who experience it. In other forms of naturalistic inquiry, the research attributes meaning to experience in the analytical phases of the inquiry. In contrast, phenomenologists do not impose an interpretive framework on data but look for it to emerge from the information they obtain from their informants. Phenomenological research is further anchored in the principle that the methods by which we share and communicate experience is limited. "The phenomenon we study is ostensibly the presence of the other, but it can only be the way in which the experience of the other is made available to us."[8]

The primary data collection strategy is the telling of a biographical story with emphasis on eliciting the experience as it relates to time, body, and space, as well as other persons. For example, in eliciting experience, the phenomenologist will ask questions similar to, "What is it like to be a patient with breast cancer?" "What was the day like when you learned of your diagnosis?" "What is it like to live with breast cancer?" "What is it like to tell others about your diagnosis?" The elicitation of these types of experiences differs from a life history approach in that in phenomenology the informant interjects the primary interpretation and analysis of experience into the interview.

How do phenomenologists use literature review? Literature review is framed with the phenomenological principle of the limits of communication. Thus the literature may be used to illustrate the constraints of our understanding of human experience or to corroborate the communication of the other. It may also support the experiences that emerge from informants. Let us assume you are conducting a phenomenological research study on the experience of aging. You will recruit a small number of individuals for study participation (e.g., 10 to 15) and engage in lengthy discourse with each about life experiences and the meanings each attributes to his or her lived experience. You may examine the research and clinical literature on aging to ascertain the commonalities of what is being communicated. You may also use the literature to suggest a rationale for using phenomenological methodology, or you may draw on different theoretical perspectives to inform you of the context of the experiences that emerge.

In phenomenological research, involvement by the researcher is limited to eliciting life experiences and hearing and reporting the perspective of the informant. Active interpretive involvement during data collection is not part of the investigator's role.[9,10]

## Heuristic research

*Heuristic research* is another important design in the naturalistic tradition. According to Moustakas, heuristic research is an "approach which encourages an individual to discover, and methods which enable him to investigate further by himself."[11]

Heuristic research is a design strategy that involves complete immersion of the investigator into the phenomenon of interest and self-reflection of the investigator's personal experiences. The investigator engages in intensive observation of and listening to individuals who have experienced the phenomenon, as well as records their individual experiences. The meanings of those experiences are interpreted and reported. The premise of this approach is that knowledge emerges from personal experience and is revealed or known to the investigator through his or her own experience of the phenomenon. Thus investigator involvement in this type of design is extensive and pervades all areas of inquiry, from the formulation of the query to the collection of data from the investigator as an informant.

Moustakas provides an example of heuristic research. When his daughter became ill, he experienced his own loneliness and realized that health care professionals revealed, by their behavior, that they did not understand the nature of loneliness in persons who were sick. Moustakas therefore engaged in an extensive project where he examined his own loneliness, listened to the stories of hospitalized children, and examined the literature on loneliness to further reveal the meaning of the concept. In this design the literature served as another form of data. It was not used as a source for defining the concept of loneliness before the field was entered.[11]

As you can see from this example, heuristic research is conducted by an individual for the purpose of discovery and understanding of the meaning of human experience. The research involves total emersion in the experience of humans as a way of understanding their perspectives. The experiences of the researcher and information derived from a literature review are considered primary and critical sources of data. Note the sequence and blurring of the essentials where the literature review is a source of data and is synthesized with other data sources. The name, heuristic, suggests that this form of inquiry serves as a foundation for further inquiry into the human experience that it describes.

## Life history

*Life history* is another important design in naturalistic inquiry. Life history is an approach that can stand by itself as a legitimate type of research study, or it can be an integral part of other forms of naturalistic inquiry, such as ethnography. This approach is a part of the traditions of naturalistic inquiry because of its focus on examining the social, cultural, and political context of individual lives. Similar to other designs such as phenomenology, the investigator is primarily concerned with eliciting life experiences and with how individuals themselves interpret and attribute meanings to these experiences. As its name suggests, the aim of life history research is to reveal the nature of the "life process traversed over time."[12] The assumption is that individual lives are unique. These unique life processes are important to examine to understand the context in which people live their lives. Researchers using a life history approach therefore focus on one individual at a time. A study may be composed of just one individual or a few individuals.

There are many diverse purposes for using a life history approach. For example, a life history can be used to explicate the impact of major sociopolitical events on individual lives[13] or the processes of personal adaptation to disease or chronic illness. Depending on the aim of inquiry, life history researchers sequence the essential action processes and use literature in different ways. Investigators who attempt to analyze the value of theory in explaining the complexity of a human life may begin with literature review and use it as an organizing framework, whereas researchers who seek new theoretical or unique understandings may conduct literature review at different junctures in the research thinking and action processes.

Life history research involves a particular methodologic approach in which the sequence of life events are elicited and the meaning of those events are examined from the perspective of the informant and within a particular sociopolitical and historical context.[13] In eliciting events the researcher seeks to uncover and characterize marker events, or "turnings."[15] These are defined as specific occurrences that shape and change the direction of individual lives.

Typically, researchers rely heavily on unstructured interviewing techniques. The research may begin with asking an informant to describe the sequence of life events from childhood to adulthood. Based on a time line of events, the investigator asks questions to elicit the meanings of these events. Participatory and nonparticipatory observation may also be combined with the interview as data collection strategies in order to examine meanings and understand how life is lived. Whereas life history relies mostly on the person who tells his or her story, the investigator shapes the story in part by the types of questions that are asked. For example, the researcher may ask more detailed questions about a particular life event than is initially offered by the participant. This probing by the researcher structures, in effect, the telling of the story to fit the interests or concerns of the researcher.

Consider an example from Frank's research. Frank was interested in understanding disability and how individuals adapt to life-altering conditions. She identified a woman who had congenital quadriplegia; she used the life history approach to characterize adaptation and the unique meanings of disability to the life course of this individual. Through in-depth interviews, Frank was able to uncover not only the chronology of life events but also the symbolic and practical meanings of these events to her informant. Analysis of "turnings" allowed Frank to examine the types of experience that were most influential in determining the future direction of the informant's life and her adaptive style.[15] The experience of this individual provided invaluable insight to the sociocultural world of individuals with disabilities and the interface of that world with able-bodied individuals.

Life history studies can be retrospective or prospective. In health and human service research, the majority of life history studies are retrospective in their approach; that is, informants are asked to reconstruct their lives and reflect on the meaning of past events.

## Ethnography

*Ethnography* is a research method primarily derived from the discipline of anthropology, although it is informed by many schools of thought.[16-21] It is a term that is often used to refer to any type of research involving field activity. Although different forms of naturalistic inquiry use fieldwork as a basis for data collection, not all fieldwork represents ethnography.[22]

The intent of ethnography is to understand the underlying patterns of behavior and meanings of a culture. Because there are so many definitions of culture, we use a broad meaning that represents a synthesis of the most common elements found in the literature. In this book we define culture as the set of explicit and tacit rules, symbols, and rituals that guide patterns of human behavior within a group. The ethnographer, as an "outsider" to the cultural scene, seeks to obtain an "insider" perspective. Through extended observation, immersion, and participation in the culture, the ethnographer seeks to discover and understand rules of behavior.[16] Data are collected through several primary methods: (1) interview and observation of those who are willing to inform the researcher about behavioral norms and their meanings, (2) researcher's participation in the culture, and (3) examination of meaning of cultural objects and symbols. Insiders who willingly engage with the investigator are called informants. Informants are the investigator's "finger on the pulse of the culture," without which the investigator will not be able to achieve full understanding. Although the results of ethnography are specific to the culture being studied, some ethnographers attempt to contribute to a broad theory of universal human experience through this important naturalistic methodology.

Ethnography begins by using techniques to gain access to a context or cultural group. The investigator characterizes the context or "social scene"[16] by observing the environment in which the culture operates. Equipped with an understanding of the cultural context, the ethnographer uses participant observation, interview, and examination of materials or artifacts to obtain data. Through field notes, audiotape recordings, videotape recordings, or a combination thereof, qualitative data are logged.[23] Analysis of the data is ongoing and moves from description to explanation, to revealing meaning, to generation of theory. Impressions and findings are verified with the insiders and reported once the findings are determined to accurately represent the culture. Reflexive analysis, or the analysis of the extent to which the researcher influences the results of the study, is an active component of the research process.[22,24] (These processes are described in more detail in subsequent chapters.)

We classify ethnography as a naturalistic design because of its reliance on qualitative data collection and analysis, the assumption that the researcher is not the knower, and the absence of *a priori* theory, or a theory imposed before entering the field. In this design, investigator involvement is significant and guides the sequence and conduct of the 10 essential thinking and action processes. It is the investigator who makes the decisions regarding the who, what, when, and where of each observation and interview experience. The belief that knowledge can be generated about the "other" without the viewpoint of the investigator influencing the study is a different philosophical approach from heuristic and endogenous designs. Furthermore, ethnography is a design that is capable of moving beyond description to reveal complex relationships, patterns, and theory.

Within the past 10 years, a contemporary ethnography has emerged, which departs from some of the basic assumptions and design elements of classical ethnography. As Gubrium and Holstein describe, "Where the older ethnography cast its subjects as mere components of social worlds, new ethnography treats them as active interpreters who construct their realities through talk and interaction, stories, and narrative....What is 'new' about this is the sense that participants are ethnographers in their own right."[25] The new ethnography challenges the basic assumptions held by classical ethnographers, such as investigator objectivity and objective presentation of the social setting.[26] The new concern is how best to represent the participants' own perspectives and their ways of explaining their lives. The focus is on the interpretive practices of people themselves, or how people make sense of their lives as reflected in their own words, stories, and narratives. These concerns are similar to those of the phenomenological and life history approaches. Ethnography is changing in other ways as well. For example, Ulichny discusses a critical ethnography

in which ethnographical thinking and action processes are applied to social change. The purposes and action processes of contemporary ethnography are becoming much more diverse, in contrast to classical ethnography. However, one key element continues to bound all forms of ethnography—the examination of cultural and social groups and underlying patterns and ways of experiencing a social context.

In health and human services, research based on ethnographical principles is becoming a widely accepted approach. Investigators use ethnography to obtain an insider's perspective on the meaning of health and social issues as a basis from which to develop meaningful health care and social service interventions or as a basis on which to promote policy and social change. Ethnography has also been used to understanding various service environments. One example is the ethnography of a nursing home conducted by Savishinsky. Several data collection strategies, including interview and participant observation, were used to describe the culture of the nursing home and the meaning of life in that setting. Through analysis and synthesis of the perspectives of residents and staff, Savishinsky was able to identify ways of changing that environment to improve the quality of life of the residents.[27]

## Grounded theory

*Grounded theory* is defined as "the systematic discovery of theory from the data of social research."[20] It is a more structured and investigator-directed strategy than the previous naturalistic designs that we have discussed. Primarily, its purpose is to develop and verify theory.

Developed by Glaser and Strauss, grounded theory represents the integration of a quantitative and qualitative perspective in thinking and action processes.[21] The primary purpose of this design strategy is to evolve a theory or, as the name implies, ground a theory in the context in which the phenomenon under study occurs. The theory that emerges is intimately linked to each datum of daily life experience that it seeks to explain.

This strategy is similar to the designs we have discussed in its use of an inductive process to derive concepts, constructs, relationships, and principles to understand and explain a phenomenon. It is distinguished from other naturalistic designs by its use of a structured data-gathering and analytical process named the constant comparative method. In this approach, each datum is compared with others to determine similarities and differences. Glaser and Strauss and others have developed an elaborate scheme by which to code, analyze, recode, and produce a theory from narratives obtained through a range of data-collection strategies.

Let us briefly consider an example of the constant comparative method. In a study of homeless middle-aged women, Butler used constant comparison in combination with other strategies to develop her analysis. Initially she examined the data set to induce categories of data that were repeated throughout the experiences of the women who served as her informants. As she analyzed each datum, either an experience, articulation, or observation, she compared it with the data in the existing categories to determine similarities and differences between new and previously obtained information. If it fit, the datum was coded with an ex-isting code. If it did not, a new category or subcategory was developed.[28]

The purpose of the constant comparative method is not only to reveal categories but also to explore the diversity of experience within categories, as well as to identify links among categories.

Glaser and Strauss also suggest that grounded theory strategies are capable of generating and verifying theory.[21] A query using a grounded theory approach begins with broad descriptive interests and through data collection and analysis moves to discover and verify relationships and principles.

## Summary

In this chapter we examine eight designs and show how they differ in their purpose, sequence, and investigator involvement. As you can see, naturalistic designs are flexible in the degree to which the investigator participates in the formulation of the design, data collection, and interpretive analysis. Moreover, the sequence of the 10 essential thinking and action processes is diverse, and boundaries among these processes, which are clearly delineated in experimental-type designs, may be blurred in naturalistic inquiry.

With this introduction to some of the more frequently used designs within the naturalistic tradition, you may want to explore each in greater depth. We recommend the bibliography for sources that address each design, its use, and its conduct.

## Exercises

1. To understand the different purposes of naturalistic designs, identify a broad topic or problem area. Formulate at least four distinct research queries that lead to four different designs that have been discussed in this chapter.

2. Go to a public place and determine how you would conduct a study using classical ethnography to determine public behavior patterns. Determine how you would conduct the study using heuristic research.

3. Plan a study using a naturalistic design to discover the health beliefs of a chronically ill, older Asian population living in an urban community. Plan a study using a naturalistic design with Asian children who are chronically ill and living with their families. How would your strategies differ?

### References

1. Maruyama M: Endogenous research: the prison project. In Reason P, Rowan J, editors: *Human inquiry: a sourcebook of new paradigm research*, New York, 1981, John Wiley & Sons.
2. Argyris C, Schon DA: Participatory action research and action science compared: a commentary. In Whyte WF, editor: *Participatory action research*, Newbury Park, Calif, 1991, Sage.
3. Whyte WF, editor: *Participatory action research*, Newbury Park, Calif, 1991, Sage.
4. Stringer ET: A*ction research: a handbook for practitioners*, Thousand oaks, Calif, 1996, Sage.
5. DePoy E, Gilmer D: *Adolescents with special health care needs in transition: an action research project*, Indianapolis, Ind, 1997, paper presented at the American Public Health Association annual Conference.
6. Tierney W: *Culture and ideology in higher education*, New York, 1991, Praeger.
7. Nencel L, Pels P: *Constructing knowledge: authority and critique in social science*, Newbury Park, Calif, 1991, Sage.
8. Darroch V, Silvers RJ: *Interpretive human studies: an introduction to phenomenological research*, Washington, DC, 1982, University of American Press.
9. van Manen M: *Researching lived experience: human science for an action sensitive pedagogy*, Albany, NY, 1990, State University of New York Press.
10. Douglas J, editor: *Understanding everyday life*, London, 1970, Routelage & Kegan Paul.
11. Moustakas C: Heuristic research. In Reason P, Rowan J, editors: *Human inquiry: a sourcebook of new paradigm research*, New York, 1981, John Wiley & Sons.
12. Rabin AI, Zucker RA, Emmons RA, et al: *Studying persons and lives*, New York, 1990, Springer-Verlag.
13. Mkhonza S: Life histories as social texts of personal experiences in sociolinguistic studies: a look at the lives of domestic workers in Swaziland. In Josselson R, Lieblich A, editors: *Interpreting experience: the narrative study of lives*, Newbury Park, Calif, 1995, Sage.
14. Langness LL, Frank G: *Lives: an anthropological approach to biography*, Novato, Calif, 1981, Chandler & Sharp.
15. Frank G: Life history model of adaptation to disability: the case of a congenital amputee, *Soc Sci Med* 19:639-645, 1984.
16. Spradley JP: *Participant observation*, New York, 1980, Holt, Rinehart & Winston.
17. Sperber D: *On anthropological knowledge*, Cambridge, Mass, 1987, Cambridge University Press.
18. Levi-Strauss C (Jacobson C, Schoepf BG, translators): *Structural anthropology*, New York, 1960, Basic Books.

19. Agar M: *Speaking of ethnography,* Newbury Park, Calif, 1986, Sage.
20. Geertz C: *The interpretation of cultures: selected essays,* New York, 1973, Basic Books.
21. Glaser B, Strauss A: *The discovery of grounded theory,* New York, 1967, Aldine.
22. Bogden RC, Biklen SN: *Qualitative research for education,* Boston, 1992, Allyn Bacon.
23. Lofland J, Lofland L: *Analyzing social settings: a guide to qualitative observation and analysis,* ed 2, Belmont, Calif, 1984, Wadsworth.
24. Ulichny, P: When critical ethnography and action collide, *Qualitative Inquiry* 3(2):139-168, 1997.
25. Gubrium J, Holstein J: Biographical work and new ethnography. In Josselson R, Lieblich A, editors: *Interpreting experience: the narrative study of lives,* Thousand Oaks, Calif, 1995, Sage.
26. Agar, MH: *The professional stranger: an informal introduction to ethnography,* ed 2, San Diego, 1996, Academic Press.
27. Savishinsky JS: *The ends of time: life and work in a nursing home,* New York, 1991, Bergen & Garvey.
28. Butler S: *Homeless women,* Seattle, 1991, University of Washington (unpublished dissertation).

# Chapter 11

# Case study designs

**Key terms**   Case study
Celeration line
Multiple-case design
Single-case design
Time series design
Triangulation

**What is a case study?**
**Structure of case studies**
**Design sequence**
**Summary**

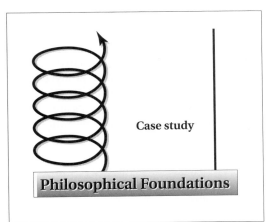

Case study

**Philosophical Foundations**

In the past, case study designs have been viewed as inferior to group or nomothetic designs (discussed in Chapter 9). However, the value and flexibility of case study designs are increasingly recognized by researchers and practitioners. Case study designs represent a methodology that can be quite complex.[1] In this chapter we examine case study methodology and suggest guidelines for its use.

## What is a case study?

Let us begin to understand case methodology by examining the definition advanced by Yin, who defined *case study* as the following:

> An empirical inquiry that…investigates a contemporary phenomenon within its real life context; when the boundaries between phenomenon and context are not clearly evident; and in which multiple sources of evidence are used.[2]

It is usually assumed that case study is a design in which a single subject is investigated. However, this element of case study designs does not even appear in Yin's classical definition. The view that all case studies are investigations that focus on a single person is misleading. Rather, case study designs may involve multiple persons or units. The key element of case study design as illuminated by Yin is that it is an approach that is used to investigate a single phenomenon. A single phenomenon may be composed of a single subject, a single part, or many subparts. For example, an investigator may be interested in a single family as the "case." Because a family is composed of more than one individual, case study design may involve more than one person, where all of the individuals make up one unit of analysis—the family.

Yin's definition does not limit case study to a particular research tradition or design strategy; that is, a case study approach does not exclu-

sively belong to experimental-type or naturalistic research. Rather, the approach is flexible; it can be conducted in either research tradition, or it can integrate both traditions. The purpose of a case study can be to describe phenomena, examine relationships, or make predictions.

Furthermore, a critical element of case study research is its reliance on multiple methods of data collection to capture the complexity of a case. *Triangulation,* or collecting information using different strategies to examine a phenomenon, is a basic strategy in case study designs.[2] In keeping with the flexibility of case study research, one can gather information using experimental-type or naturalistic techniques or their combination. These four basic characteristics of case study are summarized in Box 11-1.

## Structure of case studies

There are many variations of case study designs that are labeled as single-subject, single-system, or *N* of 1 single-case experimental trial (*N* refers to the size of the sample). A case study approach is useful in the following circumstances: (1) when it is not possible or desirable to randomize, (2) when it is not possible or desirable to study a particular population as a group with similar characteristics, (3) when it is desirable to determine intervention outcomes or change in a behavior over time as a consequence

**Box 11-1** **Characteristics of case study designs**

- Flexibility
- Used by either experimental-type or naturalistic traditions
- Multiple purposes
- Multiple data collection methods

of one or multiple interventions, or (4) when it is desirable to obtain pilot information in a cost-efficient way. Moreover, case study is an excellent theory-generating tool, since the findings of a single case can be theoretically explained and then tested through other types of design strategies.

To understand the different approaches to case study designs, we use Yin's description of its structural components. Yin classifies case studies into four categories (Figure 11-1).

Let us examine each type. Holistic case studies are those in which the unit of analysis is viewed as one global phenomenon. For example, if we were to select a family as a case, a holistic, single-case study approach will examine the function of the entire family as a single unit. In contrast, in embedded case studies, the cases are conglomerates of multiple subparts or are subparts placed within larger contexts. This

type of case study would be the design of choice for the investigator who is attempting to determine the dynamics among individuals that may potentially provoke family violence.

Assume you are interested in the phenomenon of family violence. The investigator who believes that family violence is a cultural phenomenon may select a holistic single-case study design to analyze the response of the total family to cultural sanctions for violence. The family is observed and tested as a whole. In the embedded approach, individual members of the family are observed and tested as subparts of the single family case. When considering holistic versus embedded designs, the investigator must examine the nature of the phenomenon that is of interest. Does the unit of analysis naturally have occurring parts that will reveal relevant information? If yes, then an embedded approach is used. Does the "whole" provide the most informative approach? If yes, then a holistic approach is used.

Now that you understand a holistic versus embedded approach, let us consider the differences between single- and multiple-case designs. In a *single-case design,* only one study of a single unit of analysis is conducted. In a *multiple-case design,* more than one study of single units of analysis is conducted. It logically follows, therefore, that the holistic single-case study is conducted only once on one case. The holistic multiple-case study examines several global units of analysis more than once. Likewise, an embedded single-case study focuses on multiple parts of a single case using only one case. On the other hand, an embedded multiple-case study examines more than one case in which each case contains many subparts.

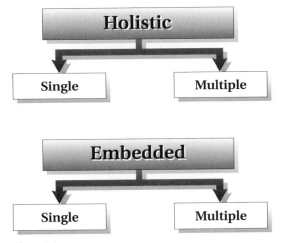

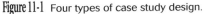

**Figure 11-1** Four types of case study design.

The decision to conduct a single- or multiple-case study depends on several considerations. First, the aim of the research must fit the structure that is selected. Multiple-case studies enable the investigator to examine the same phenomenon across several different cases. It is somewhat analogous to the concept of replication in group (or nomothetic designs). Thus if an investigator wants to repeat a study to strengthen theory or test the findings of a single case on other cases, then a multiple-case study approach is preferred. However, if the purpose of the research is to generate theory, explication of an atypical phenomenon, or describing the progress of an individual over time, then a single-case study approach is warranted. Let us assume you are a hospice social worker who is working in the homes of clients with acquired immunodeficiency syndrome (AIDS). In your client group, you find one individual who seems unusual in her ability to cope with terminal illness. To further understand this individual and to discover the factors that contribute to coping strategies, you conduct a single-case study. This "deviant" case study approach can illuminate distinctions in coping strategies. However, if you are interested in characterizing the experience of persons with AIDS in their communities, it may be more appropriate to select a multiple-case study design. The reason an investigator would select a multiple-case study design instead of a more traditional group design lies in the definition of case study designs. Case study, whether single or multiple, is ideal for describing persons in-depth and over time in their contemporary context without sacrificing or reducing the complexity of human experience.

## Design sequence

Assume you plan to conduct a case study and have decided on its basic structure; that is, you have determined whether you will use a holistic or embedded, single- or multiple-case approach. Deciding on the basic structure is one of the first thinking processes involved in implementing a case study design. The second thinking process involves determining the sequence of the design.

There are many types of case study design sequences that can be used, depending on the purpose of the study. Each design sequence has a specific strength and weakness. Some design sequences are more consonant with the naturalistic research tradition in which the sequence is flexible and may change in the process of collecting and analyzing information. Alternatively, the design sequence may be linear and fixed, similar to experimental-type designs.

Let us examine some of the more frequently used case study designs of the experimental type. There are many different strategies to single-subject research. Each strategy is based on the premise that the individual serves as his or her own control. Bloom and Fischer refer to the elements in single-subject design as phases.[3] They note that phases consist of distinct parts of intervention research, beginning with the baseline phase in which no intervention occurs, proceeding to the intervention phase, and then ending with the follow-up phase. Of course, many variations of these phases, including multiple intervention and follow-up phases, can be found in the research literature. Single-subject case study design has a notation system similar to experimental-type design. However, different symbols are used. Rather than denoting the phases with *X* and *O,* case study uses *A* and *B; A* depicts the observation, and *B* indicates the intervention or independent variable. The most basic design is called the *AB* design, where *A* represents the baseline phase and *B* represents the intervention phase. Although this type of design cannot predict, it can explain what happens during an intervention. During the baseline period *(A),* repeated measures are obtained on specified variables. It is suggested that the investigator obtain as many measurements as possible, or from six to nine observation points, to establish a stable baseline. However, the number of measurements may vary depending on whether the observed behavior is stable. If, for example, observed scores are highly variable, many repeated measures may be necessary to detect a baseline pattern of behavior. It is important to establish a baseline pattern before introducing the intervention phase.

After a baseline pattern has been established, the intervention is introduced, followed by repeated measurement. The *A* phase represents the measures that form the "control" measures. The *B* phase represents the measures that are obtained after intervention. The *B* phase are compared with those of the *A* phase. It is recommended that a similar number of observations be obtained in both the *A* and *B* phases to examine the stability of change over time. After the *AB* assessments, the investigator plots each score and performs a visual analysis to detect a change in the pattern of scoring between the *A* and *B* phases. Typically, a *celeration line* is drawn through the baseline data to facilitate visual inspection of observed scores. This line represents the best fit of the baseline

data points. The same line is then drawn along the data points in phase *B* to determine whether there is an difference in the direction and placement of scores.

There are many variations on the *AB* design, such as the *ABA* and *ABAB* designs. In the *ABA* design, there is a baseline period *(A),* followed by an intervention period *(B),* which is then followed by the withdrawal of the intervention *(A).* In the *ABAB* design, the previous sequence is followed and then the intervention is reapplied. There are many variations of these two design sequences. For example, each *B* phase may involve different therapeutic strategies. The structure of the *ABA* design is stronger than a simple *AB* sequence when there are questions regarding the extent to which change is produced as an outcome of an intervention.

The *time series design,* another type of single-subject design, is used to follow one subject over time. Suppose you want to determine if an innovative intervention with a chronically depressed population decreases levels of depression. Because you are unable to test a group of subjects, you select a single-subject design. For the first three sessions, you administer a depression inventory. You then conduct the intervention and follow up with three administrations of the same instrument. If, based on visual inspection, you observe a difference between the observed scores immediately preceding and immediately after the intervention, you can surmise that a change occurred and that this change may be a consequence of the intervention. With this type of design, you cannot claim that the intervention is the cause of the improvement. However, you have demonstrated that a change occurred. You have some evidence to support the need for further investigation to determine the effectiveness of the intervention.

Now, let us examine the nature of data collection in single-case designs. As suggested by Yin, multiple data collection strategies strengthen the credibility of findings in case study research. Ideally, the use of several measures at both baseline and follow-up phases should be used. Let us consider an example. Suppose you are interested in ascertaining the extent to which a group approach improved the socialization skills of nursing home residents. You select an embedded single-case study. The unit of analysis is the group in which the subparts are the participants. To test socialization before the initiation of the group, you establish a counting system to measure the amount or extent to which interaction occurs among the participants of the group. You complete this measure on six occasions to obtain a baseline. Additionally, to ascertain the quality or nature of the interaction, you also observe the participants and record field notes at regular intervals. You continue data collection using the two strategies throughout the intervention and after its termination. Your results therefore inform you about the change in the frequency of contacts from preintervention to postintervention, as well as the quality or nature of the interactions.

Data analysis of experimental-type case study designs is controversial. Although many consider it inappropriate to use statistical techniques to analyze single-subject data, other researchers disagree. Those who suggest that group analyses are not appropriate call our attention to sampling logic. For most statistical analysis techniques, an underlying assumption is that a sample is selected to represent a population and that every effort is made to minimize bias that can be introduced through inadequate sampling. Because group sampling logic (discussed in Chapter 13) does not guide the selection of a case, statisticians suggest that the use of group analysis techniques is contraindicated. On the other end of the spectrum, investigators may subject multiple-case studies to group analyses. These investigators argue that group analysis of multiple cases is analogous to meta analysis, where investigators aggregate the findings of replicated studies and conduct secondary analysis of the data, even though the studies are not originally planned as part of the larger investigation. Our position is that each of these perspectives are neither right nor wrong. The choice to use group analytic techniques for case study designs needs to be explicated, and a clear rationale for doing so should lie in the purpose and nature of the research question and the investigator's view of knowledge. We suggest, however, that analytical strategies such as descriptive statistics, visual presentation of changes in quantitative measures, and inductive analyses of narrative information are the most useful analytical tools in case study designs, and we urge investigators to consider these techniques before others in which the fit between design and analytical strategy may be tenuous.

A major concern in case study research is generalizability. There is a limitation to the external validity of a case study. However, its limited external validity is in part overcome by the ability to generalize findings to theory, through replication, or the repetition of systematic single-subject studies and the evaluation of each of these efforts as a whole.

## Summary

Case study represents an approach to systematic inquiry that can incorporate an experimental-type design, a naturalistic-type design, or a combination of the two. The approach is particularly helpful when little is known about a phenomenon and when aggregating or grouping responses across subjects does not allow sufficient insight into the phenomenon of interest. A variety of design structures and sequences are available to the researcher. Also, multiple data collection methods can be used. The ability to use different design structures, methodologies, and data collection approaches makes the case study a flexible research approach. A case study approach is useful under a variety of circumstances, especially to explicate in-depth understandings of a phenomenon, to examine change over time in one or more individuals, or to examine a theoretical construct.

## Exercises

1. Find a research study that uses a case study approach. Identify its underlying structure using Yin's classification scheme. Redesign the study using a different structural approach. Compare and contrast the strengths and weakness of each structure.

2. Choose a setting in which a health or human service might be delivered. The setting can be an outpatient department, a senior center, a community organization, or another context. Design a case study that examines the delivery of a service in that setting.

### References

1. Stake RE: *The art of case study research*, Thousand Oaks, Calif, 1995, Sage.
2. Yin RK: *Case study research: design and methods*, (Revised edition), vol 5, Newbury Park, Calif, 1989, Sage.
3. Bloom, Fisher: *Evaluating practice: guidelines for the accountable professional*, Englewood, Calif, 1982, Prentice Hall.

# PART IV
## *Action processes*

Now that you have grasped the vocabulary and general thinking processes across the research traditions, we are ready for action. In Part IV we focus on the way in which researchers implement or put design strategies into action. Each chapter introduces specific research action processes of naturalistic inquiry and experimental-type research. You will learn diverse and varied ways to implement and put into action four processes as follows:

● Bounding your study and obtaining individuals, concepts, or other phenomena to study (Chapters 12-14)
● Collecting information or data using a range of strategies (Chapters 15-17)
● Analyzing and interpreting information or data (Chapters 18-20)
● Reporting and using information and conclusions (Chapter 21)

As you read about each action process, keep in mind that there are five factors that affect the selection of an action process. These are:

● Philosophical or epistemological framework of the research
● Investigator's specific research purpose
● Nature of the research question or query
● Particular type of design
● Resources available and practical limitations or challenges of the environment in which the research occurs

# Setting the boundaries of a study

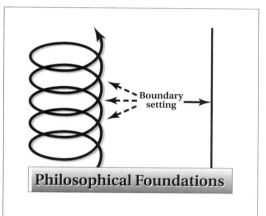

Assume you have a research problem and an appropriate design that matches your research purpose and question or query. You are ready to consider how individuals will be selected for your study and how particular concepts or phenomena will be defined and identified. Selecting research participants and identifying concepts and phenomena are one of the first action processes that set or establish the boundaries or limitations of a study. This chapter provides an overview of the importance and ethics of setting boundaries in studies.

## Why set boundaries to a study?

Setting limits or boundaries as to what and who will be in a study is an action that occurs in every type of research design, whether it is the experimental-type or naturalistic tradition. A researcher sets boundaries that limit the scope of the investigation to a specified group of individuals, phenomena, or set of conceptual dimensions. Why is it important to set boundaries or limitations of a study? Consider a study that uses a survey design to describe the health and social service needs of parents of children with disabilities. It would be impossible from a monetary and practical point of view to interview every person who falls into that category in the United States. As the researcher, you will need to make some decisions as to who you should specifically interview and how. One consideration may be to limit the survey to particular geographic locations. Another way of limiting the study may be to consider only certain types of disabling conditions Limiting the number of parents of children with disabilities who are selected for study participation is an example of setting a boundary by restricting the characteristics of the person who will be studied.

Studies are also necessarily limited or bounded by identifying particular data collection strategies and concepts that will be considered. Let us assume you are interested in the historical development of the profession of physical therapy. It would not be feasible, timewise, to examine every historical detail or written document to understand the sociopolitical and health care context of professional growth of physical therapy. In this case you need to determine criteria for selecting historical documents to examine and identify the key historical events in which professional activity emerged. Deciding which historical documents to examine is an example of limiting your study by specifying the boundaries of the concept and time period that will be explored. There are numerous ways to limit the scope of a study. As discussed in previous chapters on the thinking processes of research, an investigator actively bounds a study based on five interrelated considerations (Box 12-1). Most obviously, your philosophical approach or the particular research tradition you are using to develop your study will set the backdrop from which all action decisions will be made. A deductive, experimental-type study will tightly bound the study to preidentified concepts and a highly specified population. The purpose of the study, the particular research question, and the design will also shape the ex-

**Box 12-1  Considerations in setting study boundaries**

- Researcher's philosophical framework
- Study purpose
- Research question
- Research design
- Access to the object(s) of inquiry (participants), investigator's time frame, and monetary limitations

tent to which concepts, phenomena, and populations are delimited. For example, an intervention study that tests the effectiveness of a particular home care service in producing a specified outcome will need to carefully match the intent of the intervention with the subject group who will be recruited. Thus highly specified criteria as to who can participate will be required. On the other hand, a broad inquiry as to the experience of caring for a person with acquired immunodeficiency syndrome (AIDS) may cast a wide net and set few restrictions as to who can participate in the study. Finally, your access to the target population of interest or the phenomenon to be studied is another consideration as to how a study is bounded. Limited resources, such as monetary and time restrictions, will likely yield a study design that is tightly delimited.

Thus there are both practical and theoretical considerations in bounding the context of either an experimental-type or a naturalistic form of inquiry. Practically speaking, it will be impossible to observe every speech event, personal interaction, or activity in a particular natural setting. You must bound the study by making purposeful selections as to what will be observed and who will be interviewed.[1, 2]

In experimental-type designs, *boundary setting* is a process that occurs before entering the field or beginning the study. Boundaries are set in three ways: (1) specifying the concepts that will be operationally defined, (2) defining the population that will be studied, and (3) developing a sampling plan.

In naturalistic designs, boundary setting occurs throughout the research process. Initial boundary setting begins by first defining the do-

main of interest and the point of access from which to enter that domain. This domain may be geographic, as in the selection of a community in which to study health perceptions. The domain may be a group of individuals, such as the selection of persons with traumatic brain injury living in the community. The domain may be a particular experience, such as trauma, dialysis, and chronic health problems. In the context of the defined domain, a selection process occurs as to who should be interviewed and when, what scenes or events to observe, and which materials or artifacts to review. This selection process occurs or unfolds in the course of performing fieldwork. Setting boundaries is therefore an ongoing process that moves the researcher from a broad to a more narrow focus in most but not all forms of naturalistic inquiry. The process of data collection, analysis, and further data collection (see Chapter 18) can be understood as a process of redefining and refining the boundaries of the phenomenon being studied.

Bounding a study is a purposeful action process in both research traditions. The inclusion or exclusion of people, concepts, events, or other phenomena has considerable implications for knowledge development. As you set the limits of your study, you must reflect on your actions and understand the implications of your decisions. The consequences of the bounding actions taken by the researcher are often described in a proposal or report as "limitations" of the study. As you read research articles in the professional journals, take a close look at how the authors recruit individuals into the study, define the primary concepts, and explain the limitations of their study. The consequences of limiting a study may be made more clear by examining the way in which a sample or study group is identified. For example, let us assume an investigation is interested in symptom reporting among older men and women. The exclusion of a particular group of individuals, such as different ethnic groups, from study participation will limit the ability of the researcher to generalize findings of the study to these other groups. This limitation is a consequence of the way in which the researcher bounds the study population at the start of the project.

## Involving humans in research

One of the most important ways a researcher sets limits in a study is determining who will be included and, consequently, who will be excluded from participating in the study. The *inclusion and exclusion criteria* that are developed by an investigator will reflect the underlying purpose of the research endeavor and the research question.

Experimental-type researchers usually establish detailed criteria before recruiting individuals into a study. These criteria are highly specified and are used to develop a sampling and recruitment plan. Let us assume you are planning a study that reflects a Level 2 question. You plan to investigate the level of functional ability in older adults with chronic health conditions and the relationship of their functional ability to depression over two points in time—1 month and 12 months after hospitalization for acute illness. First, the purpose of the study limits the inquiry to examining two concepts—function and disability. Second, the purpose also limits the study to examining these concepts in a particular

group, specifically those with an acute health episode. Your inclusion criteria will specify the age, gender, ethnic group, level of physical function, level of cognitive status, and type of disabling conditions of the participants you seek to involve. Your criteria for excluding people may involve certain health conditions, living arrangements, and geographic locations. For example, you may want to include individuals with a hip fracture but not those who also have terminal cancer or heart disease. You will use both types of criteria, those that include and those that exclude, to establish a plan to sample and recruit individuals into your study. (Sampling plans are described in greater detail in the next chapter.) However, for the purposes of this example, let us assume you will use a sample of convenience. Doing so will involve identifying and recruiting any individual who fits your criteria and who has been discharged from three area hospitals. Your next effort will involve a way of identifying appropriate study subjects and a mechanism to involve them in your study. You will want to make certain that your sampling and recruitment procedures are systematically followed to ensure that bias is not introduced into your study; that is, you will want to make certain that every person who is truly eligible for your study has an opportunity to be identified and asked to participate. One recruitment strategy may involve asking discharge coordinators at each participating hospital to screen individuals, using the criteria of your study as they leave the hospital. You will develop a simple form that can be easily implemented by the discharge coordinator. For each person identified by the coordinator, you will want to gain permission to contact him or her and ask his or her willingness to participate in your study.

This may sound simple. However, suppose the coordinator is busy one week and is unable to screen patients who are being discharged, or assume the coordinator does not refer some patients who fit the study criteria because they are perceived as uncooperative. These two instances, which are not uncommon occurrences in field studies of the experimental type, introduce bias to the recruitment process. Selecting individuals for this type of study will require constant vigilance by the investigator over the implementation of these recruitment procedures.

In experimental-type designs there is a high level of specificity in bounding the study. In contrast, usually only broad inclusion and exclusion guidelines are established before engaging in fieldwork in naturalistic designs. However, the extent to which boundaries are established depends on the particular type of naturalistic design. For example, in a phenomenological study the researcher may bound a study only by identifying the type of experience that is of interest to the researcher. The only criterion for participating in the study may simply be that an individual has experienced the phenomenon of interest. Other factors, such as age, gender, or race, may not be specified or used as criteria to include or exclude individuals from the study. Likewise, in a large-scale ethnography, only the context or natural setting may be initially specified or bounded, whereas the participation of individuals in the natural context may not be restricted—at least initially. In a focused life history, however, individuals are selected for study participation who meet specific criteria, and these are specified before engaging in fieldwork.

Involving humans in health and social service research and establishing participation criteria have important ethical considerations that must be fully understood and carefully thought out by the researcher. When writing a proposal to carry out a research study, whether experimental-type or naturalistic, the researcher must address the ethical concerns of involving humans and clearly identify how he or she intends to address three critical issues (Box 12-2).

## Full disclosure

Researchers from all traditions are bound by certain ethical practices when involving humans in their studies. Any person who participates in a study, whether it be participatory action research or single-subject design, has the absolute right to full disclosure of the purpose of the study. Full disclosure means that the investigator must clearly share with the informant, subject, or research participant the types of interviews, observations, and other data collection procedures that will occur and the scope and nature of the person's involvement. Full disclosure does not mean, however, that conditions that may adversely affect the study must be shared. However, any potential risk to a subject must be identified and a plan for remediation must be offered to every subject. Although sharing study procedures may be a straightforward matter in

**Box 12-2  Ethical considerations for involving humans in research**

- Need for full disclosure of study purpose
- Need to ensure confidentiality of all information obtained
- Need to ensure that study participation is voluntary

experimental-type research, disclosure can create many difficulties for the naturalistic form of inquiry. Since all of the procedures are clearly articulated and determined before entering the field, the researcher conducting an experimental-type study can identify in layperson's terms the purpose and scope of the data collection effort. In naturalistic designs, most of these decisions are made in the field and evolve over time. Researchers who work in this tradition must solve this dilemma in creative, thoughtful, and ongoing ways. There is much discussion in the literature regarding the approaches to remaining ethical and preserving the integrity of the methodology. All researchers must struggle over the best way to describe the study truthfully without revealing specific hypotheses or introducing biased perspectives that may shape the informant's responses during the study.

## Confidentiality

The investigator must ensure that information shared by a respondent is kept confidential. *Confidentiality* means several things. First, no one other than the research team can have access to the respondent's information unless those who have access to the data are identified to the participants before their participation. Second, the information cannot be linked to the person's identity. This is an important consideration, especially in studies that focus on political or sensitive topics such as AIDS research, teenage pregnancy, crime, or drug dealing. An investigator ensures confidentiality in several ways. The name of the respondent is removed from the actual information that is obtained; that is, the identity of the respondents in your study

must be protected. Usually investigators assign identification numbers to individuals who are interviewed. This action presents some difficulty for studies that primarily use observation as the principal data collection effort. Ensuring confidentiality can be difficult when using audiotapes and videotapes as data collection sources. In these instances the investigator does not usually transcribe names that are taped. He or she establishes procedures for coding and storing tapes in locked filing cabinets or offices with restricted access, as well as establishing procedures for destroying tapes at the conclusion of the study.

Confidentiality of research participants must also be protected when results are reported. In reporting findings from a case study or naturalistic design, usually the names of individuals are changed so that there is not a direct way of linking the person's identity to the information he or she provides. Most experimental-type studies report findings that reflect summative scores or outcomes of an aggregate of individuals, presenting less challenge for this research tradition.

Researchers who investigate controversial topics must carefully plan how information will be stored and reported. Studies about drug trafficking or substance abuse, for example, may obtain information that may be of interest to the legal system. Investigators can refuse to turn over documentation but run the risk of being called into court to testify.

## Voluntary participation

When humans are involved in studies, their participation must be strictly voluntary. Individuals have the right to participate or not to participate. Also, an individual who initially agrees to participate in a study has the right to withdraw from the study or refuse to answer a particular question or participate in a particular procedure. Withdrawal or refusal presents sticky methodologic problems for the investigator. The researcher needs to be concerned with the reasons individuals choose to withdraw from a study. For example, is withdrawal the result of the demands of the study procedures? Is the research team offensive in any way? Is withdrawal based on the individual, perhaps a change in health status or relocation to another geographic region? Reasons for a withdrawal from a study may have implications for understanding study results and may affect the ability to generalize the outcomes to other groups. It is important to track the reasons for withdrawal or for study refusal to enable the investigator to determine the differences between participants and nonparticipants.

Refusal to answer a question leads to what is technically called "missing data" in experimental-type research. Missing data can be a big problem in this research tradition since it limits the types of statistical analyses that can be used and the inferences that can be derived from the data. One question typically refused in experimental-type studies is the subject's level of income. Missing data on this variable make it difficult to summarize the socioeconomic status of research participants. Missing information in naturalistic studies is less of a problem. The refusal to answer a question is, in itself, an indicator of the salience of that particular topic or area, and it becomes, in essence, a type of data that can be analyzed. However,

missing an observation, such as an important community event, may be more problematic for the naturalistic inquirer. Adjustments in data collection may need to occur to overcome this issue, such as prolonging engagement in the field or obtaining information about the event from newspaper reports, community meetings, and personal interviews.

## Institutional Review Board procedures

The involvement of humans in research is usually overseen by a government-mandated board of experts that must be established at each institution involved in the research process. Before beginning a research study, you must write a brief proposal that describes in detail your plans for involving humans. This proposal must be submitted for review to a designated office of research or to an official board that is usually called either an Institutional Review Board (IRB) or a Human Subjects Board. Most academic settings have an IRB; however, only a few health and human service settings have established research committees. If you are located in a setting that does not have an established board, you may need to form a partnership with a university or hospital that can review your protocol. This is particularly important when seeking funding to support your research effort. All federally funded research studies must be approved by an official IRB. However, in most institutions, any research study—funded or not, small or large scale—must be reviewed by a committee to examine the nature of human involvement.

The purpose of the IRB or Human Subjects Board is to evaluate whether a research protocol may adversely affect study participants. The IRB addresses the issue of whether the research itself justifies the involvement of humans. The IRB evaluates the procedures that will be used to enroll humans in the study to make certain that participation is voluntary, that confidentiality will be ensured, and that there is full disclosure of study procedures.

Assume you are a rehabilitation clinician and plan to evaluate the relationship between client self-report of functional ability and observation of actual performance. You plan to evaluate the patients you see in the rehabilitation setting. Although this idea is not necessarily unethical, you must carefully consider how you will introduce the study to your clients. You must set up procedures to ensure that patients understand several points. First, they must understand that their participation in the study is strictly voluntary; in other words, it is their decision to participate. Second, they need to understand that a decision not to participate will not affect the type of intervention they will receive. Third, if they decide to participate, they can also choose to discontinue participation at any point in the study with no consequences for other medical and social services that they are eligible to receive. The IRB will review your procedures to make certain they are ethical and not coercive. You will not be able to begin your study until you have received approval of these procedures from the IRB.

Most IRBs have three levels of review: full, expedited, and exempt. A full review involves a formal examination of an investigator's research protocol by members who have been officially appointed by an institution. The composition of board members is mandated to include a con-

sumer representative and a member with scientific expertise in the protocols that are being reviewed. The board can be composed of as many as twenty individuals or as few as five, depending on how the institution has set up its IRB. A study that involves what is called a vulnerable population must receive a full review. *Vulnerable populations* refer to individuals who may not be able to represent themselves or who may be at particular risk when participating in a research study. Examples of vulnerable populations include infants, children, pregnant women, prisoners, mentally incompetent individuals, or persons addicted to substances. Additionally, research involving human immunodeficiency viral (HIV) testing, AIDS, investigational drugs, or medical devices also require a full board review. In a full board review, all members read the research protocol, discuss its merits and weaknesses, and vote to either approve (with changes or no changes to recruitment and consent procedures) or disapprove it.

An expedited review involves an evaluation of a research protocol by a subcommittee selected from the IRB membership. Studies that receive an expedited review do not involve vulnerable populations, do not test invasive techniques, or represent minimal risk to individual participants. Examples of studies that can have an expedited review include those that collect data from individuals who are 18 years of age or older using noninvasive procedures that are routinely used in practice, studies that use existing data, or research on group behavior where the investigator is not manipulating behavior. The previous example of the study in rehabilitation is appropriate for an expedited review.

Exempt status means that a study protocol is exempt from formal review from either the full board or its subcommittee. Although it is usually necessary to inform the IRB of the intent to conduct the research, no further review is necessary. Examples of studies that are exempt from formal review procedures include those involving normal educational practices or the use of educational tests or research involving the collection or study of existing data, documents, and records, as long as these sources are publicly available or the information is recorded in such a manner that the individuals cannot be identified. An example of the latter situation is a retrospective study involving chart review or hospital census data from the last 10 years of individuals who suffered strokes and their level of functional status at discharge.

In submitting your procedures to an IRB, there are six consideration that need to be addressed (Box 12-3).

**Box 12-3  Six considerations in an IRB review**

- Describe the characteristics of the humans who will participate in the study.
- Describe any potential risks and benefits of study participation.
- Describe procedures to ensure confidentiality.
- Describe data collection sources and procedures.
- Describe plans for recruitment and procedures for obtaining informed consent.
- Describe procedures for protecting against or minimizing potential risks.

## Informed consent

The ethical issues of conducting research have only recently been a focus of national concern. On July 12, 1974, the National Research Act was signed. This Act created a commission to delineate the ethical issues and guidelines for the involvement of humans in behavioral and biomedical research. This Act and its subsequent activities were an outgrowth from the revelations during the Nuremberg war crime trials of the devastating human experiments that were conducted by medical scientists during the Holocaust. Other tragic abuses of human subjects involved in research have occurred in the United States. The Tuskegee experiments in the 1940s are the most notable. These experiments involved poor rural African-American men who were diagnosed with syphilis. Investigators withheld known effective treatment from these men to observe the natural course of the disease process.

Three important principles emerged as a consequence of reviewing these extreme research cases and have been articulated in the Belmont Report.[3] The first ethical principle identified in this report is the importance of distinguishing the boundaries between research and clinical practice. This differentiation is perhaps more clear in health and human service research than in other types of science research. However, it is important to distinguish between daily or traditional practice versus systematic efforts to evaluate new approaches and service interventions. The second principle identified in the Belmont Report describes three ethical considerations: respect for persons, beneficence, and justice. The third ethical consideration, respect, suggests that individuals should be treated as autonomous individuals who are capable of personal choice and self-determination. Related to this notion is the mandate that individuals who are not autonomous or vulnerable, such as the person with reduced cognitive capacity, must be protected. The second ethical consideration, beneficence, specifies that research will "do no harm" and will "maximize" benefits and "minimize possible harm" to individuals. The third ethical consideration, justice, specifies that people should be treated equitably; that is, research that poses a risk should not be conducted on vulnerable populations.

These principles are embodied or applied to the conduct of research by the requirement to use *informed consent.* Informed consent is an official statement developed by the researcher that informs study participants of the purpose and scope of the study. Although the specific wording and format of informed consents varies widely, most contain the following basic elements (Box 12-4).

Important elements of informed consent include a description of the procedures in which you are asking the person to participate and assurance that participation is voluntary. Also, you need to specify whether there are any known risks to participation in the study; if so, what are they and what measures should be taken if any occurs? In proposing a study you need to consider the elements to include in your informed consent and the procedures you will use to introduce it to study participants. A consent form must be read before collecting any information from a person. Usually, the form is signed by the participant and the interviewer or investigator and a copy is made for the participant to keep. A written consent is

| Box 12-4 | Typical elements of informed consent |

- Statement of purpose of study in layperson's terms
- Description of study procedures (e.g., number of interviews, length of interviews)
- Disclosure of any risks or discomforts from study participation
- Statement describing how confidentiality will be ensured
- Statement describing the right of refusal and voluntary consent
- Description of benefits of participation
- Signature of study participant, interviewer, and researcher
- Name of institute and telephone number of the investigator

not required for every type of study. For example, in conducting a mail survey, the act of returning the survey to the investigator is considered an indication of the respondent's consent to participate. Likewise, in a telephone survey the act of agreeing to answer questions over the telephone is a sign of volunteering or consenting to the study.

Obtaining consent, whether written or verbal, from participants is somewhat straightforward in experimental-type research that involves individuals who are not cognitively impaired. The researcher knows exactly who is eligible to participate in the study and can review informed consent before asking a set of standardized questions. It can be more difficult in naturalistic inquiry, especially when data collection involves observing different events where you cannot predict who will be attending or involved in the setting. Researchers using a naturalistic approach must be creative and thoughtful as to the best and most ethical way of handling consent.

The research of Bluebond-Langer, a medical anthropologist, illustrates the different approaches ethnographers must consider in addressing ethical dilemmas.[4] She used several different procedures for obtaining consent in her study of children with leukemia and their parents. Her study posed several challenges. First, it involved a vulnerable, protected population—children. Second, it involved data collection over time at different sites, in the physician's office, clinical settings, and hospitals. Third, it involved children who were dying and parents who were grieving. She first obtained consent from the parents by approaching them during their visits to the clinic. When she observed the same families admitting their children to the hospital, she reintroduced the study. Any parent who appeared uncomfortable or told someone else that he or she would rather not participate was dropped from the study. As she describes, "I would never take any statement of consent as final, since I felt that the parents needed a way of getting out of the study any time they desired."[4] She also asked each child for permission to speak with him or her about thoughts and feelings each time she approached him or her. These procedures not only ensured protection of participants but it also led the children and their parents to trust the researcher. She believed that mutual trust and understanding were established very early in the study and were constantly reinforced.

## Subjects, respondents, informants, or participants

Are individuals who are involved in a study the subjects, respondents, informants, or participants?[5] These four terms refer to the individuals who agree to become part of a research study. Each term reflects a different way that an individual participates in a research study and a different type of relationship that is formed between the individual and the investigator. In experimental-type research, individuals are usually referred to as subjects, a term that denotes their passive role and the attempt of the investigator to maintain a removed and objective relationship. In survey research, individuals are often referred to as respondents, because they are asked to respond to very specific questions. In naturalistic inquiry, individuals are usually referred to as informants, a term that reflects the active role of informing the investigator as to the context and its cultural rules. Participants can refer to those individuals who enter a collaborative relationship with the investigator and who contribute to decision making about the research process and who inform the investigator about themselves. This term is often used in endogenous and participatory action research. Although there are no specific rules to guide the use of these terms, you should select the one that reflects your preferred way of knowing and the role that individuals play in your study design.

## Summary

This chapter has examined the action process of setting boundaries in a study. Setting boundaries represents one of the first action processes that occurs in experimental-type research. In naturalistic inquiry, boundary setting occurs throughout the data collection and analytical action phases and is an on-going process. Boundary setting refers to the act of determining selection criteria for study participants, study concepts, or study phenomena. The degree to which a study is bounded will depend on your preferred way of knowing, research purpose, question or query, and practical considerations such as monetary and time constraints. It is important to recognize that there is nothing inherently superior about any one boundary-setting approach. The strengths and limitations of a boundary-setting technique depend on its appropriateness and adequacy in how well it fits the context of the particular research problem.

Appropriateness is defined as the extent to which the method of boundary setting fits the overall purpose of the study, as determined by the research problem and the structure of the research design. For example, it would be inappropriate to use a random sampling technique when your purpose is to understand how individuals interpret their experience of illness. In this case, the purposeful selection of individuals who can articulate their feelings may provide greater insight than the inclusion of a sample with predetermined characteristics. Purposeful selection to bound the study facilitates understanding, which is the underlying goal of the study.

Adequacy is defined as the extent to which the boundary setting yields sufficient data to answer the research problem. In experimental-type designs, adequacy is determined by sample size. In naturalistic designs, adequacy is determined by the quality and completeness of the information and the understanding obtained in the selected domain. Saturation in the field, such as obtaining repetitive information, is a cue that the boundary has been obtained and the investigator has achieved a complete understanding of the context. Thus appropriateness and adequacy are two criteria that can be applied to boundary-setting decisions.

One crucial way in which studies are bounded is developing inclusion and exclusion criteria for the involvement of human participants. The involvement of humans in studies raises important ethical considerations that are addressed by IRBs and through the process of informed consent. The way in which an IRB conducts its review and the way informed consent is handled will differ among studies depending on the purpose, question or query, and design of the research. Consideration of the ethical issues and the actions that are put into place to recruit humans are critical components of the research process.

## Exercises

1. Identify a research article that tests an experimental intervention. Describe how the authors recruit individuals into the study and how they handle informed consent. Identify three ethical considerations in conducting the study.

2. Identify a research article that reports findings from an ethnographic study. Describe how the authors identify informants and handle informed consent. Identify three ethical considerations in the study.

*Continued*

## Exercises

3. Plan a study that involves the participation of cognitively impaired adults. Identify ethical considerations in conducting an experimental-type design and compare it with the ethical considerations in conducting a naturalistic design. Identify solutions for each type of design.

### References

1. Agar MH: *The professional stranger: an informal introduction to ethnography*, ed 2, San Diego, 1996, Academic Press.
2. Rubin HJ, Rubin IS: *Qualitative interviewing: the art of hearing data*, Thousand Oaks, Calif, 1995, Sage.
3. The National Commission for the Protection of Human Subjects of Biomedical and Behavioral Research: *The Belmont Report: ethical principles and guidelines for the protection of human subjects of research*, Washington, D.C., 1979, The Commission.
4. Bluebond-Langner M: *The private worlds of dying children*, Princeton, NJ, 1978, Princeton University Press.
5. Subjects, respondents, informants and participants (editorial), *Qualitative Health Res* 1:403-406, 1991.

# Chapter 13

# Boundary setting in experimental-type designs

**Key terms**

Cluster sampling
Convenience sampling
Effect size
External validity
Nonprobability methods
Population
Probability sampling
Purposive sampling
Quota sampling

Sample
Sampling error
Sampling frame
Simple random sampling
Snowball sampling
Statistical power
Stratified random sampling
Systematic sampling
Target population

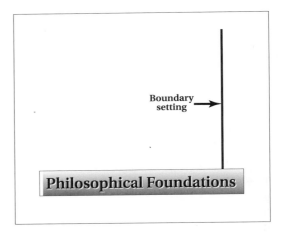

Boundary
setting →

**Philosophical Foundations**

As discussed in Chapter 12, setting boundaries in experimental-type designs is one of the first action processes that occurs. In boundary setting the primary concern in this research tradition is selecting a group of study participants or subjects who adequately represent the population that is the target of the study. Let us examine how researchers who use the range of experimental-type designs approach the action process of selecting individuals for study participation.

In experimental-type design the boundary setting action process is basically deductive. First, the researcher begins with a clear idea of who he or she wishes to study. The study group of interest to the investigator is called a *population*. A population is defined as a group of persons, elements, or both that share a set of common characteristics that are predefined by the investigator. The researcher must clearly define the characteristics of the population that includes the individuals to be studied. Second, a set of procedures are chosen from which a subset or sample is selected from the population that will participate in the study. The individuals from the population who actually participate in the study are called a sample. A *sample* is a subset of the population. The process of selecting a subgroup or sample is called sampling.

## Sampling process

The main purpose of sampling is to select a subgroup that can accurately represent the population. The intent is to be able to accurately draw conclusions about the population by studying a smaller group of elements (sample). The problem for the experimental-type researcher is how best to select a sample that is representative of an entire population. Accurate representation is critical to allow findings from the study sample to be generalized to the larger group (population) from which the sample is drawn.

Sampling designs or procedures have been developed to increase the chances of selecting individuals or elements that will be most representative of the larger population from which they are drawn. The more representative the sample, the more assured the researcher will be that the findings from the sample also apply to the population. The extent to which findings from a sample apply to the population is called *external validity*. Most researchers conducting experimental-type designs maximize external validity by using one of the sampling procedures discussed in this chapter.

Investigators follow many different action processes to draw a sample from a population. There are five steps to the sampling process (Box 13-1). Each step is described in this chapter.

The first step in sampling involves the careful definition of a population. As we indicated earlier, a population is defined as the complete set of elements that share a common set of characteristics. Examples of elements are persons, households, communities, hospitals, or outpatient settings. The element is the unit of analysis included in the population, regardless of its type. For example, in a study of the

---

**Box 13-1** **Five steps in sampling**

- Define population by specifying:
  Inclusion criteria
  Exclusion criteria
- Develop sampling plan:
  Probability or nonprobability
- Determine sample size
- Implement sampling procedures
- Compare critical values of sample to population

management practices of hospitals, the investigator is interested in the hospital as a whole, rather than the people in it. The hospital is the unit of analysis, and the sample is a specified number of hospitals. In a study of the characteristics of older persons admitted to hospitals in the summer months, each patient is the unit of analysis, and the sample is the set of individuals selected for the study.

The investigator defines or chooses the characteristics or parameters of the elements of a population that are important in a study. Let us assume you are interested in studying the needs of parents caring for children with chronic illness. The first step will be to identify the specific characteristics of the population you are interested in examining. Suppose you decide to include parents caring for children between the ages of 3 and 8 years of age who have been diagnosed with cystic fibrosis and who are currently hospitalized. You may also decide to exclude cases in which both parents do not reside together, are both unemployed, and in which there is more than one other sibling in the home. By establishing these inclusion and exclusion criteria, you have defined a target population from the universe of parents caring for a child with a chronic illness. In some instances the target population is an "ideal" group only because such a population cannot be accessed by the investigator. However, in this chapter we define the *target population* as the group of individuals or elements from which the investigator is able to select a sample. Each element of the target population may possess other characteristics than those specified by the investigator. However, each element must fit three criteria (Box 13-2).

**Box 13-2 Criteria for elements of a target population**

- Must possess all of the characteristics that the investigator has identified as inclusion criteria
- Must not possess any of the characteristics that the investigator has defined as exclusion criteria
- Must be available, at least in theory, for selection into the sample

How do investigators using experimental-type designs identify a population? First, the research question guides the investigator. Second, the researcher uses the literature to clarify and provide support for establishing population parameters. For example, if an investigator is interested in persons with chronic mental illness, there is a vast body of literature that provides clear descriptions and definitions of this broad category of individuals. An astute investigator may choose a well-accepted source, such as the DSM-IV, for a definition of chronic mental illness to structure parameters based on this knowledge.[1]

The literature also helps identify those characteristics that the investigator may want to exclude from the targeted population. In the same example, persons may be excluded from the target population if they possess a primary physical diagnosis along with a psychiatric diagnosis or if the mental illness is a secondary consequence of a traumatic head injury.

Let us consider another example. Assume you are interested in understanding the daily routines of persons with quadriplegia. The first step will be to define the population characteristics of the group you want to study. Some guiding questions you should ask are shown in Box 13-3.

**Questions to guide identifying a population**

- Should I include both men and women in the study?
- Should all persons with quadriplegia be included regardless of functional level?
- In what type of setting should the persons included in the study reside—community, independent living center, or institutional setting?
- In which geographic location should they live? What ages, ethnic groups, or occupational groups should be included?
- What family styles should be included?
- Should persons with additional diagnoses be excluded?

Reading how other researchers bound their studies is helpful in answering these questions. Your answers will lead to the development of specific criteria by which to include and exclude individuals. Additionally, to answer these questions you will need to consider your purpose in conducting the study and your research question. Finally, you will need to refer to the clinical and research literature for definitions of terms such as quadriplegia and functional level.

Defining a population is an important step in sampling and must be carefully and thoughtfully done. Santiago et al. illustrate two different ways of defining a target population that lead to different sets of findings.[2] One study of the homeless and mentally ill population specified that a person was homeless "if residing on the streets, in automobiles, or in shelters or missions, at the time of their entrance into the study."[2] A second study extended the inclusion criteria to those individuals who lived in a household in the past 3 months but who previously met the homeless criteria for the first study. By opening up the selection criteria, the investigators obtained significant differences in the gender balance between the two studies.

The second step in boundary setting in experimental-type design involves drawing a sample through the use of a sampling plan. There are two basic categories of sampling plans, probability sampling and nonprobability sampling. Table 13-1 provides an overview of the commonly used sampling plans we discuss in this chapter.

## Probability sampling

*Probability sampling* refers to those plans that are based on probability theory. The two basic principles of probability theory as applied to sampling are: (1) the parameters of the population are known, and (2) every member or element has an equal probability or chance of being selected for the sample.

The important point is that the probability of each element included in the study is known and greater than zero. By knowing the population parameters and the degree of chance that each element may be selected, an investigator can calculate the sampling error. *Sampling error* refers to the difference between the values obtained from the sample and the values that actually exist in the population. It reflects the degree to which the sample is actually representative of

| Table 13-1 | Summary of commonly used sampling plans | |
| --- | --- | --- |
| | *Probability sampling* | *Nonprobability sampling* |
| | • Parameters of a population are known. | • Parameters of a population are not known. |
| | • Sampling frame is used. | • No sampling frame is available. |
| | • Every member/element has same probability of being selected for sample. | • Probability of selection is not known. |
| | **Examples:** | **Examples:** |
| | • *Simple random sampling*<br>Table of random numbers is used to randomly select sample. | • *Convenience sampling*<br>Available individuals enter study. |
| | • *Systematic sampling*<br>Sampling interval width is determined and individuals are selected | • *Purposive sampling*<br>Individuals are deliberately selected for study. |
| | • *Stratified random sampling*<br>Subjects are randomly selected from predetermined strata that correlate with variables in study. | • *Snowball/network sampling*<br>Informants provide names of others who meet study criteria. |
| | • *Cluster sampling*<br>Successive random sampling of units is used to obtain sample. | • *Quota sampling*<br>Individuals who are unlikely to be represented are included. |

the population. The larger the sampling error, the less representative the sample is of the population and the more limited is the external validity of the study. The purpose of probability sampling is to reduce sampling error and to increase the external validity of a study. To determine sampling error, we can derive a calculation called the "standard error of the mean." This statistic reflects the standard deviation of the sampling distribution and is designated in statistical terms as $SE_m$. Let us assume you want to draw a sample of 50 older adults with cancer from a larger population of older patients with cancer and then test them using a life satisfaction measure. Then assume you want to draw another sample of 50 older adults and then a third sample, and so forth. If you compute the mean

for each sample, you will have what is called a sampling distribution of means. Theoretically, the distribution of these means should be in a normal shape (Chapter 19). However, the means will most likely vary among the samples, simply as a result of chance error. You will then calculate the standard deviation of each mean. The standard deviation of the sampling distribution is known as the standard error of the mean. In actuality, however, you will not draw several samples from the population to derive the standard error of the mean. There is a formula that can be used with one sample to estimate this statistic. Also, the larger the sample, the smaller the standard error of the mean. Likewise, the less the variability in a population, the smaller the standard error of the mean.

Sampling error may be caused by either random error or systematic bias. Random error refers to those errors that occur by chance. Not much can be done about random error at the sampling stage of the research process except to calculate the standard error of the mean. On the other hand, systematic error or bias reflects a basic flaw in the sampling process and is characterized by scores of subjects that systematically differ from the population. Sampling plans based on probability theory are designed to minimize systematic error.

To use probability sampling, the investigator must be able to develop a *sampling frame* from which individuals or elements are selected. A sampling frame is defined as a listing of every element in the target population. Examples of sampling frames include the white or yellow pages of the telephone book, a complete list of hospitals in a specific region, and other similar lists. Defining a sampling frame can be a simple or complicated process. A simple approach involves defining the sampling frame as those population members who the investigator can easily access. A more complex approach involves developing a sampling frame to ensure that the total population can be accessed by the investigator. This approach can involve extensive time and money. For example, in a study of reasons for attrition from the field of occupational therapy, Bailey developed her sample from two sampling frames. She used a roster of respondents who were members of the American Occupational Therapy Association (AOTA) and who had indicated in a member survey that they were not working. She also used a roster of occupational therapists who had allowed their membership in the professional association to lapse.[3]

Because only AOTA members were considered, the sampling frame was composed of only those occupational therapists with a membership. Thus the target population for Bailey's study was occupational therapists who were AOTA members but who were not working in occupational therapy positions. Figure 13-1 illustrates the relationship among population, target population, sampling frame, and sample.

There are four basic sampling procedures that can be used to select individuals or elements from a sampling frame (Box 13-4).

**Box 13-4** **Four sampling procedures**

- Simple random sampling
- Systematic sampling
- Stratified random sampling
- Cluster sampling.

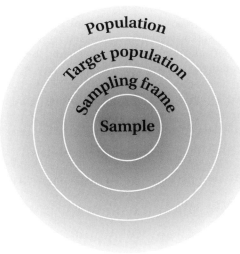

**Figure 13-1** Levels in sampling process.

## Simple random sampling

*Simple random sampling* (SRS) is the simplest method used to enhance the representativeness of a sample. The term, random, does not mean haphazard. Rather, it means that theoretically every element in the population has an equal chance of being included in the sample. Theoretically, if elements are chosen by chance, they also have an equal chance to be exposed to all conditions to which all other members in the population are exposed. This random nature of selection therefore precludes the possibility of the sample being selected because of a special trait that is uncommon in the target population or of being exposed to an influence that does not theoretically affect the total population. Returning to Bailey's study, a sample was randomly selected from the two rosters provided by AOTA, ensuring that each individual who met the criteria for inclusion had an equal chance of being selected for the study.[3]

Most researchers who want to attain a large sample size use a table of random numbers to determine which elements should be included in the sample (Box 13-5).

The table, only a small portion of which is displayed below, is carefully constructed through computer-generated programs to ensure a random listing of digits that appear with the same frequency.

Let us assume you plan to survey all full-time, nonsupervisory nurses in a selected hospital (target population). You will obtain a complete listing of nurses (the sampling frame) who fit the study criteria. You will assign a unique number to each nurse on the list . If there are 150 nurses, the list will run from 001 to 150. Because the numbers contain three digits, you will select the random numbers in sets of three. To use the table, you begin by randomly selecting a starting point and then establishing a plan as to how to move through the table. Let us assume that you decide to start from the third column from the left and one row down (925) and proceed to read down each row. Numbers outside the range of the numbers assigned to the nurses on the list (e.g., numbers greater than 150) are ignored. Therefore the first two numbers, 925 and 623, are outside the range and do not yield a selection. Moving to the top of the fourth row, numbers 143 and 007 reflect number assignments of nurses in the sampling frame. You will thus proceed through the table as such until the total number of nurses needed for the study has been selected.

Random sampling can be done with or without replacement. Using a table of random numbers involves replacement because it is possible to select a number more than once. Random sampling without replacement can be as simple as drawing sample member names from a hat that contains all the names listed on a sampling frame. Let us consider what may happen with smaller numbers in the sampling

| Box 13-5 | Subset from a table of random numbers | | | | | | |
|---|---|---|---|---|---|---|---|
| 345 | 687 | 798 | 143 | 203 | 107 | 654 | 176 |
| 241 | 267 | 925 | 007 | 115 | 003 | 409 | 115 |
| 076 | 861 | 623 | 351 | 090 | 065 | 190 | 325 |

frame when random sampling without replacement is used. Suppose we have ten persons in our sampling frame and we wish to select three persons for our sample. Before any subject is selected, the chances are 1 in 10 that an individual will be chosen. However, once the first name is chosen and not replaced in the pool, the next individual has a 1 in 9 chance of being selected. As you can see, the rule of equal chance for selection is violated. However, if we replace the name of the subject who was selected for the subsequent two selections, the chance for sample selection remains 1 in 10. Replacement ensures the same probability of chance of selection for each element throughout the selection process.

## Systematic sampling

SRS can often be time-consuming and difficult to complete when one is drawing a large sample. *Systematic sampling* offers a simpler method to randomly select elements. It involves determining a sampling interval width based on the needed sample size and then selecting every Kth element from a sampling frame. For example, let us assume you want to survey a sample of 200 health care professionals from a total population of 1000. First, a sampling fraction (the interval width), 200:1000, or 1 in 5, is derived. Second, a random number between 1 and 5 will be selected to determine the first person in the sampling frame. Every fifth person from this starting point will be selected for inclusion in the sample (i.e., 8th, 13th, 18th, and so on). A number from the table of random numbers can also be used to determine the starting point. If the sampling fraction is not a whole number, the decimal is usually rounded upward to the next largest whole number. When this sampling approach is used, it is critical that the sampling frame represents a random listing of names or elements and that there are no hidden biases, purposes, or cyclical arrangements of the elements. For example, suppose by chance every tenth health professional on the list has just entered the practicing arena. If we used a sampling interval of five and started with the fifth person, we will select only novice practitioners. This will introduced systematic bias in our sample and increase the sampling error.

## Stratified random sampling

Systematic sampling and SRS treat the target population as a whole. In *stratified random sampling* the population is divided into smaller subgroups or strata. Elements are then chosen from each stratum. This sampling plan is a more complex approach to sampling than either simple or systematic sampling. Stratified random sampling enhances sample representation and lowers sampling error on a number of predetermined characteristics by increasing the homogeneity and by decreasing the variability in each subgroup. The more homogeneous a population, the fewer the number of elements needed to enhance representation and the lower the error in generalizing from part to whole. The Nielsen polls are an example of a complex definition of sampling frames and samples. The researchers clearly specify a multiplicity of characteristics that typify the television-watching population in the United States. Because this population is diverse, it is separated into strata based on characteristics such as geographic location, socioeconomic status, age, and gender.

The proportion of each subgroup or stratum in the total population is then determined. Sample subjects are drawn from each stratum in the same proportions that are represented in the population. Proportionate stratified sampling is frequently used when it is known that a given characteristic appears disproportionately or unevenly in the population. If we used SRS or systematic sampling, we may not obtain a sample that represents the proportions of various characteristics as they exist in the population.

Consider how a researcher may use this technique. Suppose in our population of persons with quadriplegia, only 20% are women. The researcher will split the sampling frame into two strata representing each gender. As a result, 20% of the sample from the female group and 80% from the male group will be selected. This selection process will ensure that gender is proportionately represented in the chosen sample. Without stratification, it is likely that the gender balance of the sample will not match the population. Characteristics are chosen for stratification based on the assumption that they will have some effect on the variables under study. In the previous example, gender may be actually associated with daily routines. Thus it will be important to ensure that a comparison between men and women can be made with regard to daily activity. In Bailey's study of attrition in occupational therapy, the sampling frame was stratified into three groups: members of AOTA who were not working in occupational therapy positions but were interested in returning to the field, members of AOTA who were not working in occupational therapy positions but were not interested in returning to the field, and persons who had allowed their membership to AOTA to expire.[3] By strati-fying the sampling frame, Bailey was able to examine differences for attrition that were related to the variable of "intention" to return.

## Cluster sampling

*Cluster sampling*, also referred to as multistage or area sampling, is another subject selection plan that involves a successive series of random sampling of units. With cluster sampling the investigator begins with large units, or clusters, in which smaller sampling units are contained. This technique allows the investigator to draw a random sample without a complete listing of each individual or unit. For example, in testing a rehabilitation intervention for persons with a cerebrovascular accident in inpatient rehabilitation settings, the researcher will first list the geographic regions of the United States. Using simple random selection procedures, geographic regions will be selected from this list. In each selected region the investigator will obtain a complete listing of the free-standing rehabilitation hospitals and make a random selection among these units. In each selected hospital the investigator will randomly select participants from a list of individual patients.

## Nonprobability methods

In experimental-type design, probability sampling plans are preferred to other ways of obtaining a sample, particularly when the research goal is to generalize from sample to population or, in other words, to increase the external validity of the study. Probability sampling plans provide a degree of assurance that selected members will represent those who are not selected. These methods are often used in health and human service research for needs assessments, survey designs, or large-scale funded research projects. However, random methods are often impractical because using them requires the researcher to have considerable knowledge about the characteristics and size of the population, access to a sampling frame, access to a large number of elements, and the ability to ethically omit elements from the study. Therefore in health and human service research, various forms of nonprobability sampling techniques are effectively used for experimental-type designs.

In *nonprobability sampling*, nonrandom methods are used to obtain a sample. These methods are used when the parameters of the population are not known or when it is not feasible or ethical to develop a sampling frame. If you are unable to use probability sampling in your research, does that mean that your project is flawed? Not at all. The key to using nonprobability sampling is to attain the greatest degree of representation as possible and to clearly identify to your readers the limitations of your findings. For example, in a study of attitudes of allied health students toward persons with disabilities, Estes selected a sample from two universities using a nonrandom process. In their discussion, they indicate that the generalization of findings to other student groups needs to be substantiated by further study in which larger sample sizes and additional university settings are tested. The investigators clearly identified their sample selection procedures and, in the discussion, point out the application of the findings, as well as the limitations and implications for further replication.[4]

There are four basic nonprobability sampling methods (Box 13-6).

| Box 13-6 | **Four nonprobability sampling methods** |
|---|---|
| | ● Convenience |
| | ● Purposive |
| | ● Snowball |
| | ● Quota |

## Convenience sampling

*Convenience sampling*, also referred to as accidental, volunteer, or opportunistic sampling, involves the enrollment of available subjects as they enter the study until the desired sample size is reached. The investigator establishes inclusion and exclusion criteria and selects those individuals who fit these factors and volunteer to participate in the study. Examples of convenience sampling include interviewing individuals in a physician's office or enrolling subjects as they enter an outpatient setting.

## Purposive sampling

*Purposive sampling*, also called judgmental sampling, involves the deliberate selection of individuals by the researcher based on predefined criteria. In the example of the study of persons with quadriplegia, you may decide to purposely choose only those who are college educated and able to articulate their daily experiences. In this way you purposely select individuals to represent insight into the daily routines of a larger group, or you may ask clinical staff which of their patients with quadriplegia are representative or typical of the clients in their site.

## Snowball sampling

*Snowball sampling*, or networking, involves asking subjects to provide the names of others who may meet study criteria. This type of sampling is often used when researchers do not have access to a population. For example, in their study of how women addicts cope with the issue of AIDS, Suffet and Lifshitz used a snowball sample. They asked the counselors in the agency from which they selected their sample to "nominate" informants who, in turn, were also asked to identify additional informants. In this way, Suffet and Lifshitz were able to access a population that would otherwise have been difficult to find.[5]

## Quota sampling

This technique is often used in market research. The goal of *quota sampling* is to obtain different proportions of subject types who may be underrepresented by using convenience or purposive sampling methods. In quota sampling, parameters of a population and their distribution in the population are known. The researcher then purposively selects a sample that is representative of the population in that elements are selected to display parameters in the same proportions exhibited in the population.

Let us consider an example. Suppose you are interested in testing the effects of a model day-care intervention on the functional level of persons with schizophrenia living in the community. Because schizophrenia represents different types of syndromes, you first determine the proportions of varying types of schizophrenia in your population. You then find that gender and age are distributed differently in

each type. To ensure that your nonrandom sample is as representative of your population as possible, you will set up a matrix of diagnoses, ages, and genders and select your sample by filling each cell in the same proportions that are exhibited in your population.

## Comparison of sample and population

We began by saying that the major reason for sampling is to ensure representativeness and the ability to generalize from sample findings to the target population. The power of probability sampling is that population estimates can be made based on statistical theory. Five steps are involved in determining whether findings from the sample are representative of the population (Box 13-7).

These steps are briefly reviewed so that you can become familiar with this process.

The first step involves a statement of the hypothesis of no difference (null hypothesis) between the population and the sample being compared. This null hypothesis implies that the values obtained in the sample, for example, on a depression scale are the sample values that would have been obtained had depression been mea-

---

**Box 13-7 Steps to compare sample to population**

- State hypothesis
- Select level of significance
- Compute calculated statistical value
- Obtain a critical value
- Accept or fail to accept null hypothesis

sured in other samples drawn from the same population. Second, the researcher selects a level of significance or the probability that defines how rare or unlikely the sample data must be before the researcher can fail to accept the null hypothesis. If the significance level equals 0.05, the researcher is 95% confident that the null hypothesis should not be accepted. Failure to accept the null hypothesis means that, with a degree of certainty, there is a difference between the sample and the population. Third, a statistical value is computed using a statistical formula. Fourth, the statistical value is compared with a critical value. Most statistical texts have tables of critical values to which the researcher can refer. The critical value indicates how high the sample statistic must be at a given level of significance to fail to accept the null hypothesis. If the sample value is greater than the critical value, the null hypothesis can be rejected, and the researcher will conclude that a significant difference exists between sample and population. In many instances the researcher wants to accept the null hypothesis, as in the case when he or she wants to demonstrate that sample values mirror or represent the population from which it was selected. In other cases the researcher wants to reject a null hypothesis when he or she wants to demonstrate that a particular intervention changed the sample significantly from the values represented in the population.

## Determining sample size

Determining the number of participants in the study or the size of the sample is a critical issue and one with which new investigators often have difficulty. A common suggestion you may receive is to obtain as many subjects as you can afford. However, a large sample size is not always the best policy and is often unnecessary. The size of your sample can influence the type of data collection techniques, procedures for recruitment, and the costs involved in conducting the study. Although few published research articles discuss the rationale for the size of the sample for a study, you should have a reason for the number you choose. A defense of your sample size is particularly important when you submit a proposal to a funding agency requesting funds to conduct the study. In the proposal you will need to provide justification for the number of subjects that will be included in your study. How do researchers determine the appropriate size of a sample?

The number of elements in a sample is determined once the population and sampling frame have been identified. The determination of sample size may be based on the proportion of units from the population that are necessary to conduct statistical testing. The number of subjects needed to test a hypothesis is directly related to the issue of what is called *statistical power*. This term refers to the probability of identifying a relationship that exists or the probability of rejecting the null hypothesis when it is false or should be rejected. Assume you are testing the outcome of a new intervention. Without sufficient power to detect a difference between experimental and control group outcomes, there will be no use in conducting the study. You want to ensure an adequate number of subjects in the study to have the power to determine whether the intervention made a difference in the study outcomes.

There are basically four considerations in determining the size of your sample (Box 13-8).

| Box 13-8 | Considerations in determining sample size |
| --- |

- Data analytical procedures that will be used
- Statistical level of significance (usually chosen at 0.05 or 0.01 level)
- Statistical power (.80 acceptable)
- Effect size

Statistical power refers to the probability that a statistical test will detect a significant difference if one exists. An 80% power level is considered the minimum level of acceptability. If a power analysis is calculated and it is lower than 80%, the researcher runs the risk of a Type II error (described in Chapter 19) or the inability to detect significance if one exists. If power is low, it is not wise to conduct the study. Cohen has advanced the technique of power analysis.[6] He indicates that four factors must be considered in a power analysis: significance level, sample size, effect size, and power. If three of the four are known, the fourth can be calculated. Significance level and sample size are straightforward. The investigator sets both of these parameters before data collection. Cohen has developed tables indicating power levels for different sample sizes, significance levels, and effect sizes.

*Effect size* refers to the strength of differences in the sample values that the investigator expects to find. For example, consider a study that tests the benefits of a low-impact aerobic exercise program for the elderly. Let us assume that based on empirical evidence from literature reviews or data from small-scale or pilot studies, the investigator hypothesizes that there will be a large effect of the program on muscle strength and a minimal-to-moderate effect on cardiovascular fitness. If the difference between values in experimental and control group subjects is large, only a few subjects will be needed in each group to detect such differences. If the effect size is small, a large sample size will be necessary to detect differences.

The number in the sample is also determined by the number of units in the sampling frame. Practical considerations, such as time and financial support for conducting the research, may also provide guidelines on the number of units to be included in the sample.

## Summary

We have said that the object of boundary setting in experimental-type designs is twofold—to complete the study in a timely, cost-effective, and manageable manner, and to use the findings about the subset (sample) to inform us about the larger group (population) from which the sample was selected. We present a number of probability and nonprobability methods that can be used to select a sample from a population. Probability sampling procedures are used to ensure that a sample reflects or is representative of the larger population. Nonprobability methods are used when it is not possible to identify a sampling frame or when random selection is not feasible or desirable. Although this four-step process sounds simple, many decisions have to be made along the way. There are many texts available that provide in-depth discussion of each procedural step and the statistical theory of the sampling plans just discussed. Furthermore, you should be aware that an investigator may use variations and combinations of these sampling plans, depending on the nature of the research question and the resources available to the investigator.

When probability sampling is used, it is wise to consult a statistical expert to ensure that the sampling plan maximizes representation.

Experimental-type designs increase external validity by achieving representativeness of the sample through probability sampling. However, in health and human service research, it is frequently not practical or ethical to use probability sampling techniques. The state of the field is such that most researchers use nonprobability methods to obtain their sample. However, even with limited external validity, studies that are well-planned and in which conclusions are consistent with the level of knowledge that the sampling can yield are extremely valuable.

## Exercises

1. Find a research article that uses probability sampling. Describe the sampling plan.

2. Find a research article that uses nonprobability sampling. Describe the sampling plan and then compare it with the article in exercise 1 that uses probability sampling.

3. Develop a sampling plan for a study on lifestyles of adults who are hospitalized for chronic heart disease. First, identify population parameters, and then suggest how best to obtain a representative sample of that population.

4. Discuss how you may obtain a random sample of children, given the regulation that participation in research must be consented to by a child's legal guardian.

## References

1. American Psychiatric Association: *Diagnostic and statistical manual (DSM,IV)*, ed 4, Washington, DC, 1995, American Psychiatric Press.
2. Santiago JM, Bachrach LL, Berren MR, et al: Defining the homeless mentally ill: a methodological note, *Hosp Community Psychiatry* 39:1100-1102, 1989.
3. Bailey D: Reasons for attrition from occupational therapy, *Am J Occup Ther* 44:23-29, 1990.
4. Estes J, Deyer C, Hansen R, et al: Influence of occupational therapy curricula on students' attitudes toward persons with disabilities, *Am J Occup Ther* 45:156-165, 1991.
5. Suffet F, Liftshitz M: Women addicts and the threat of AIDS, *Qualitative Health Res* 1:51-79, 1991.
6. Cohen J: *Statistical power analysis for the behavioral sciences*, New York, 1977, Academic Press.

# Chapter 14

# Boundary setting in naturalistic designs

**Key terms**
Confirming case
Deviant case
Disconfirming case
Gaining access
Homogeneous selection
Maximum variation
Theory-based selection
Typical case

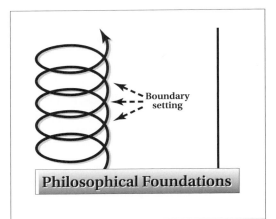

Boundary setting

**Philosophical Foundations**

Let us now look at the way in which a researcher engages in the action process of setting boundaries when conducting a study using naturalistic designs. In naturalistic research, setting boundaries is a dynamic, inductive process. It is an action process that is flexible and fluid and one that occurs over a prolonged period of engagement in fieldwork. Because the basic purpose of naturalistic research is exploration, understanding, description, and explanation, the researcher does not often know the boundaries of the inquiry or the conceptual domains before undertaking the study. Indeed, the very point of the study may be to develop the characteristics that bound or define a group of persons or explicate a particular concept. Thus naturalistic researchers often find that the boundaries emerge from the process of data collection and ongoing analysis. For example, the bounding of a particular concept or set of constructs may not occur until the formal analysis and reporting phases of the study. Nevertheless, a researcher must start somewhere and make decisions as to what to observe, who to talk with, and how to proceed in the field. How are such decisions made?

## Ways of setting boundaries

Researchers working in the traditions of naturalistic inquiry must consider bounding their study along a number of dimensions. These dimensions include the geographical location or physical setting, the cultural groups, the range and nature of experiences that will be examined, the particular concepts that will be explored, the artifacts that will be examined, and the ways in which individuals are involved.

### Geographical location

Let us consider the classical ethnography, *Tally's Corner,* written in 1967 by Elliot Liebow as an example. In his work, Liebow conducted an ethnography to "gain…a clear, first-hand picture of lower class Negro men especially street corner Negroes."[1] Thus the boundaries of the research were not clearly delineated by characteristics of the group of "street corner Negroes," because the researcher did not know who these people were. Rather, the research was initially bounded by the geographical location of a neighborhood in which the men lived, worked, and "hung out." As the study proceeded, Liebow noted that his data collection took him beyond the initial geographical boundaries to "courtrooms, jails, hospitals, dance halls, beaches, and private houses."[1] Liebow initially set boundaries for entry into the study and then expanded and modified these boundaries as the study proceeded. This process is characteristic of boundary setting in naturalistic inquiry.

In *Tally's Corner,* for example, the geographical location initially formed the boundary because the query sought to understand the lives and experiences of African-American men who frequented urban street corners. Likewise, in Gubrium's study of life at a nursing home, the facility of Murray Manor established the initial boundaries of the study. Gubrium conducted all of his observations in this facility. He implicitly chose not to observe prior home life of residents or examine interactions that occurred outside the nursing home setting. By focusing or delimiting the study to the world within the nursing home, he achieved a rich or thick description of the multiple social worlds of patients and staff.[2]

### Cultural groups

In other naturalistic studies, cultural groups may form the initial boundary of the study. A culture may be loosely defined as the customs and tacit knowledge held by individuals who belong to a group, or the culture may be identified by the location in which it exists. For example, assume you want to study family interactions and the impact of caregiving among Cuban Americans, a cultural group that is highly concentrated in Florida and in the southern region of the United States. Let us assume you begin your study in one region of Florida but are uncertain of the impact of southern values and culture of the United States on interaction patterns. You may want to expand or redefine the boundary of your study to include other geographical locations with Cuban-American communities. As a researcher collects information about a cultural group, he or she may refine the boundaries of the study to obtain a fuller understanding of the group.

## Personal experience

In studies that focus on the exploration of a particular experience, the phenomenon immediately sets the boundaries as to what will be examined; that is, the boundaries of the inquiry lie within the realm of the particular experiences described by the individuals. For example, in phenomenologic studies the goal is to understand the experiences of a small set of individuals from their own perspectives. A phenomenologic researcher who wishes to describe the experience of a parent who has a child with a terminal illness may choose to interview and observe that parent. The boundary of the study and thus the understanding derived from it applies only to the individual's lived experience; but, once again, the researcher must begin somewhere and make a selection decision as to which individual or individuals to interview who possess the specific characteristic of having a child

with the illness. The selection process may be purposeful in that the researcher makes the judgment as to which parent may be a reasonable informant based on the scope or depth of his or her particular experiences.

For example, Wiseman, in a phenomenologic study of the experience of loneliness, identified the domain of concern as the phenomenon of loneliness among university students.[3] To explore the different meanings of this experience, she selected four students who had scored high on a loneliness trait scale. Her study demonstrated that even though these students had similar scoring patterns on a standardized test, their experiences of loneliness and the meanings attributed to this psychological state varied greatly. Wiseman's study was delimited by the conceptual domain of loneliness.[3] The study purpose shaped other bounding decisions, such as who was selected for study participation.

## Concepts

As in the previous example, some forms of inquiry explore a particular concept. Thus it is the particular concept that initially bounds the scope of the study in these types of inquiry. Wiseman's study was limited to the exploration of one concept—loneliness.[3] The study expanded our understanding of the dimensions and nature of loneliness by identifying the range of different meanings.

In other types of naturalistic inquiry the investigator casts a wide net, so to speak, and is interested in understanding underlying values or beliefs that guide behaviors.[4] In these forms of inquiry, the concepts of interest may not be immediately identified and may emerge only in the course of the study as a consequence of the analytical process. For example, Gitlin et al. were interested in discovering the meanings attributed to mobility aids and other special assistive devices for persons with a first time strokes.[4] The concepts that explicated particular meanings were uncovered from an analysis of interviews with 102 individuals who had a diagnosis of stroke. Concepts, such as social "stigma," "biographic management," and "continuity of self," emerged as important analytical domains that explained the dimensions of meanings associated with device use. Each of these concepts had been defined and developed by other researchers involved in disability studies. Gitlin et al. did not initially bound the study to these conceptual domains; these concepts emerged as important focal points in the analytical phase of the study.[4]

Some studies, however, begin by setting conceptual boundaries. For example, a study by DePoy using a Delphi technique sought to define the concept of "mastery" in occupational therapy practice.[5] The investigator wanted to know what is meant by being "good" at clinical practice. In the first part of a two-part study, DePoy used a nonprobability purposive sampling process to select a group of experts who could define mastery. These experts nominated masters who were then interviewed to obtain their unique experiences as master clinicians. However, even though a sample of experts provided the initial data, the boundary was the concept of mastery, not the individuals who contributed to its definition. In the second part of the study, DePoy expanded the boundary to the practice arena and examined how mastery was demonstrated by the three masters who were nominated by the expert respondents. The concept of mastery derived from part one of the study was examined in the practices of these three informants through an extensive unstructured interview with each informant. DePoy made no claim of external validity but suggested that the model of mastery that was developed (i.e., the domain of the study) should be tested for its relevance to other domains of practice.

Let us examine another example of naturalistic research to further understand the process of setting conceptual boundaries. In his study of the culture of a nursing home, Savishinsky was originally interested in describing the behavioral responses of nursing home residents to pet therapy. He states:

> The approach that I took began with two concepts at the very heart of pet therapy—companionship and domesticity. In the broadest terms, I came to realize that the study had to be a cultural and not just a behavioral one....It had to look at meanings and not simply actions.[6]

As you can see, the initial boundaries of the study—that of observing actions during pet therapy—became modified and expanded as the study proceeded to the nursing home culture as a whole, including not only behavioral patterns but also meanings embedded within that culture.

## Involving research participants

Involving research participants is perhaps the most critical approach to boundary setting in naturalistic inquiry. It is often believed that researchers who engage in naturalistic inquiry simply select any individual, based on convenience or his or her availability for study participation. This belief is a misconception and simplistic understanding of the actions undertaken by researchers to involve participants. There is nothing haphazard about selecting participants in naturalistic inquiry. The use of a convenience strategy is one important approach but not the only one used by researchers working from these multiple traditions. As in experimental-type designs, selecting individuals is a purposeful action process, and the investigator must be acutely aware of the implications of his or her selection decisions. Selection decisions stem from either the investigator's theoretical perspective or the study purpose and research query; or it is informed by judgments or interpretations that emerge in the course of fieldwork.

There are important differences between the two primary research traditions—experimental-type and naturalistic inquiry—in involving humans in research. Understanding these differences provides a basis from which to further grasp the decision-making process used by naturalistic researchers. You may recall from Chapter 13 that the concern in identifying subjects in experimental-type research is representativeness. Generally, the more subjects involved in a study, the better the chances of achieving representation and detecting group differences or patterns. In comparison, the concern in naturalistic inquiry is the selection of individuals who have the potential for illuminating a particular concept, experience, or cultural context. The number of participants in a study is not as important to the investigator as the amount of exposure to participants and opportunities to explore phenomena indepth.

Hence the investigator develops selection strategies that ensure richness of information and indepth understandings. The concern is not with selecting individuals who represent a population; rather, naturalistic inquiry is typically characterized by a small number of study participants with whom the investigator has repeated exposures and multiple occasions to observe and interview. Decisions as to who to interview or observe and when to interview in the course of the study are thus based on this principle. Although some researchers label the approaches used in naturalistic inquiry as sampling techniques, we prefer to call them strategies for involving individuals. As we discuss in Chapter 13, sampling techniques are based on the premise of representation and randomization. Therefore using this term in naturalistic inquiry is misleading and does not capture the intent of the decision-making process within these traditions.

The way in which individuals are selected for study participation will depend on the purpose and design of the study. Individuals may be involved differently at distinct points in the fieldwork process. This variability is the case especially for large ethnographic studies or forms of naturalistic inquiry that occur over a long period and that focus on a broad domain of concern. In any case, researchers working from the traditions of naturalistic inquiry use a wide range of strategies for involving participants, and these strategies emerge within the context of carrying out fieldwork. Occasionally, probability or nonprobability sampling techniques may be integrated into naturalistic studies when these approaches are appropriate and fit the structure of the study purpose and design. These types of strategies have typically been used in large ethnographic studies and after the investigator has identified particular patterns that warrant further explication through the use of these sampling approaches. These sampling techniques can be used by the ethnographer to determine the representativeness of the particular concept or domain of concern within the cultural group, community, or context.

Patton and others have suggested many distinct strategies that can be used separately or in combination for involving individuals in naturalistic inquiry.[7-10] The following six strategies are commonly used to identify informants. (Some of these strategies are discussed in Chapter 13 and involve nonprobability techniques, such as convenience, purposive selection, and snowball techniques.)

## Maximum variation

*Maximum variation* is a strategy that involves seeking individuals for study participation who are extremely different along dimensions that are the focus of the study; that is, in using this strategy the researcher attempts to maximize variation among the broadest range of experiences, information, and perspectives of study participants. Maximizing differences and variability challenges the researcher and is an attempt to involve a universe of vast experiences. From different experiences, the researcher attempts to identify common patterns that cut across variations. For example, let us assume you are interested in understanding and developing a theory of adaptation to life-altering disabilities. A grand theory needs to be based on adaptation to many different types of disabilities and involve an examination of individuals from vastly different life circumstances. The investigator will want to maximize variation of disabling conditions and experiences to ensure that a theory of adaptation captures all possible life worlds.

## Homogeneous selection

In contrast to maximum variation, *homogeneous selection* involves choosing individuals with similar experiences. This approach reduces variation and thereby simplifies the number of experiences, characteristics, and conceptual domains that are represented among study participants. This approach is particularly useful in focus group methodology or when group interview techniques are used.

## Theory-based selection

*Theory-base selection* involves selecting individuals who exemplify a particular theoretical construct for the purposes of expanding understanding of the theory. Wiseman's study is an example of a theoretical approach to participant involvement. In that study, individuals were selected who demonstrated the state of loneliness. Through in-depth interviewing using a phenomenological approach, the investigator was able to elucidate the properties of the theoretical construct. In other words, participants were purposely selected based on a set of experiences that would contribute to a more in-depth examination of the phenomenon of loneliness. One way the investigator could expand upon this study would be to introduce a second phase of data collection. In this second phase the investigator could purposely select individuals who did not experience loneliness. This technique would be an example of using disconfirming cases to elucidate the phenomenon under study.

## Confirming and disconfirming cases

*Confirming and disconfirming cases* are strategies in which the investigator purposely searches for an informant who will either support or challenge an emerging interpretation or theory of the investigator. The investigator is concerned with expanding an initial understanding of the phenomena by identifying exceptions or deviations. The investigator must modify or broaden his or her initial understanding to account for such variations. In this way the researcher engages in a process of elaborating and expanding on an understanding that accounts for all phenomena. Based on this expanded understanding, concepts, theories, or interpretations are developed. Assume you are interested in developing a theory of parental caregiving of children with a disability. You may begin your inquiry with in-depth interviews of parents with children who are severely disabled. As you develop guiding concepts, you may choose to verify them by interviewing a few parents who have never had a child with a disability. These interviews will offer contrasts and will either confirm or highlight the experiences of families of children with disabilities.

## Extreme or deviant case

In the extreme or *deviant case*, the researcher selects a case that represents an extreme example of the phenomenon of interest. You may recall the life history by Frank. Frank was interested

in understanding the sociocultural context of adaptation to disability. To explore adaptation, she selected an individual who had a severe congenital quadriplegic disability. Thus every aspect of life for this person was different from an able-bodied individual. The case provided a basis for understanding lifelong adaptations.

## Typical case

In contrast to the severe case, an investigator may choose to select a *typical case*. A typical case is one that typifies a phenomenon or represents the average. Let us assume you want to gain insight into the experiences of graduate students in health profession schools. You may begin by identifying a few students who typify that experience. Based on the information you gather, your next selection strategy may be to choose an atypical or deviant case.

## How many study participants?

How many participants do you need to interview or observe in research involving naturalistic inquiry? There are no specific rules in naturalistic inquiry that assist the researcher in selecting the number of persons needed in a study. The concern in naturalistic inquiry is not with the number of individuals as with the types of opportunities for in-depth observation and interviewing. There are some guidelines, however, that can be used to determine the number of participants to include in a naturalistic study. If the intent is to examine an experience that has been shared by individuals, a homogeneous strategy should be used to obtain study participants. Given that one is minimizing variation, only a small number of individuals (e.g., 5 to 10) will be necessary to include in the study. The small number of participants provide a "representative picture" of the phenomenon or focus of the study. In contrast, if the intent is to examine approaches to family caregiving of patients with dementia and to develop a theoretical understanding of caregiver management techniques, you may want to maximize variation in experiences and approaches to derive the broadest understanding of this activity. Thus a large number of caregivers (e.g., 20 to 50 individuals) will be required, each representing different life circumstances and stages of caregiving. Note that the term "representation" in naturalistic inquiry does not imply external validity. Rather, it speaks of developing an understanding of what may be typical of or common to a group.

## Process of setting boundaries and selecting informants

The process of boundary setting in naturalistic research follows several principles (Box 14-1).

| Box 14-1 | **Five guiding principles in boundary setting** |
|---|---|

- Inductive process is used.
- Each selection decision informs the next.
- Boundaries are adjusted throughout fieldwork.
- Range of selection strategies are used to select individuals, events, artifacts, concepts.
- Boundary setting occurs until redundancy or saturation is achieved.

Boundary setting begins with the investigator determining an entry point into the inquiry. The actual point of entry into the study is often referred to as *gaining access*.[12] Frequently, an investigator will seek introduction to a group through one of its members. This member acts as a facilitator or bridge between the life of the group and investigator. From that entry point, which could be but is not limited to establishing rapport with other group members, examining a concept, or observing a location in which a culture lives and performs, the researcher collects information or data to describe the boundaries. Once a researcher has gained initial access, other issues of access emerge. For example, although the researcher may be initially accepted into a cultural group or community, it may take a prolonged period before participants will share intimate information. Thus gaining access refers not only to the process of entering the physical location where the researcher plans to conduct fieldwork, but it also includes gaining entry to the level of information and personal experiences that frame the purpose of the study. Gaining access is not necessarily an easy action process, and much literature has been written on this important research action. The approach to gaining entry will differ depending on the context and whether the investigator is a member or stranger of the context. (Some of these issues are discussed in greater detail in Chapter 17.)

In the process of discovery and within the context of the field, the researcher continually makes boundary decisions as to whom to interview, what to observe, and what to read. There may be an overwhelming number of observational points and potential individuals to interview. Selection decisions are based on the specific questions the researcher poses throughout the research process and the practicalities of the field, such as who is available or willing to be interviewed or observed.

Boundary setting begins inductively, and as concepts emerge and theory development proceeds, the researcher assumes a more deductive way of selecting observations, individuals, or artifacts. For example, observational points may be chosen to ensure representation of that which is observed. Let us assume you are interested in understanding how patients feel about their hospital experiences. As part of your study, you will purposely select different observational times throughout the day and night to ensure representation of time.

Throughout fieldwork, the researcher is actively determining which sources will help the most in understanding the particular question to derive a complete perspective of the culture, practices, or experiences of the group or single individual. Thus once in the field the investigator uses other techniques and approaches to establish the boundaries of the study. For example, to understand certain practices, an ethnographer may seek a key actor or informant to represent the group. This individual is selected because of his or her strategic position in the group or because he or she may be more expressive or able to articulate that which the researcher is interested in knowing. Throughout Liebow's study, four key informants continued to provide substantial insights used as the basis of analysis, although many other men participated in the study. The selection of such informants was purposive and based on the judgment of the investigator.[1]

One strategy in ethnography is to begin broadly. The investigator initially samples, so to speak, what is immediately accessible or in view.

As fieldwork and interviewing proceed, questions and observational points become increasingly focused and narrowed. The investigator may use a snowball or chain approach to identify informants, search for extreme or deviant cases, or purposely sample diverse individuals or situations to increase variation.

The process of selecting and adding pieces of information through interview, observation, and review of literature and artifacts, as well as analyzing them for discovery and description of the boundaries of the phenomenon being examined, is called domain analysis.[4] Understanding the domain is critical in naturalistic inquiry. The intent is to understand, indepth, specific occurrences within the domain of the study. Thus the domain must be clearly understood to ensure that findings or interpretations are meaningful. Although no claim is made about the representativeness of a domain, in naturalistic inquiry principles are suggested that may be relevant to other settings. Thus naturalistic boundary setting is unlike boundary setting in experimental-type design in which the purpose is to maximize representation and external validity. In naturalistic inquiry, selection processes are used to obtain a "thick description" (i.e., detailed or rich data) of a particular domain, allowing the investigator to examine the transferability of principles of one domain to another.[13]

## Summary

Boundary setting in naturalistic research is an ongoing and active process that is part of and emerges inductively from data collection. Research is undertaken not only to address a research problem but also to promote further understanding and descriptions of the boundaries of the research. The researcher is constantly making decisions and judgments about who should be interviewed and when and what to observe. The investigator uses a range of selection strategies in a study. The selection strategy used to choose an individual to interview, event to observe, or artifact to review is based on the specific focus of the investigator. These strategies may include both probability and nonprobability techniques or many others that have been developed specifically for naturalistic inquiry (i.e., selection of typical or deviant cases). Although initially a boundary may be defined globally, the investigator delimits the nature of the group, phenomenon, or concept under investigation through domain analysis. In naturalistic inquiry, boundary setting occurs inductively in which the domain is revealed through ongoing data collection and analysis.

## Exercises

1. To understand boundary setting in naturalistic inquiry, select a public place, such as a shopping mall or a restaurant. Spend at least 1 hour observing, and determine patterns of human behavior in the location. As you observe, record how and why you select to focus on specific elements of the location. Reflect on the range of strategies you use. What did each strategy provide in terms of understanding the setting?

2. After leaving the location in exercise 1, write a list of events and behaviors that you believe will be important to observe on another occasion to confirm your emerging understanding.

## Exercises

3. Develop a research plan to examine the experience of being a health professional under a managed care facility. Identify three strategies for involving study participants, and provide a rationale for using each approach.

### References

1. Liebow E: *Tally's corner,* Boston, 1967, Little, Brown.
2. Gubrium J: *Living and dying at Murray Manor,* New York, 1975, St Martin's Press.
3. Wiseman H: The quest for connectedness: loneliness as process in the narratives of lonely university students. In Josselson R, Lieblich A (editors): *Interpreting experience: the narrative study of lives,* Thousand Oaks, Calif, 1995, Sage.
4. Gitlin LN, Luborsky M, Schemm R: Emerging concerns of older stroke patients about assistive devices in rehabilitation, *The Gerontologist* 38(2):169-180, 1998.
5. DePoy E: Mastery in clinical occupational therapy, *Am J Occup Ther* 44:415-420, 1990.
6. Savishinsky JS: *The ends of time,* New York, 1991, Bergen & Garvey.
7. Patton MQ: *Qualitative evaluation and research methods,* ed 2, Newbury Park, Calif, 1990, Sage.
8. Kuzel AJ: Sampling in qualitative inquiry. In Crabtree BF, Miller WL: *Doing qualitative research,* Newbury Park, Calif, 1992, Sage.
9. Gilchrist VJ: Key informant interviews. In Crabtree BF, Miller WL: *Doing qualitative research,* Newbury Park, Calif, 1992, Sage.
10. Marshall C, Rossman GB: *Designing qualitative research,* Newbury Park, Calif, 1989, Sage.
11. Frank G: Life history model of adaptation to disability: the case of a congenital amputee, *Soc Sci Med* 19:639-645, 1984.
12. Spradley J: *Participant observation,* New York, 1980, Holt, Rinehart & Winston.
13. Geertz C: *The interpretation of cultures: selected essays,* New York, 1973, Basic Books.

*Continued*

# Chapter 15

# Collecting information

**Key terms**    Artifact review
Closed-ended question
Hawthorne effect
Interviews
Observation
Open-ended question
Probes
Questionnaires
Secondary data analysis
Unobtrusive methodology

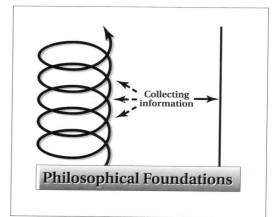

Collecting information

**Philosophical Foundations**

You now have an idea as to the strategies for involving individuals, events, observations, and artifacts in your study. Now let us explore the different strategies you can use to collect information or data. This chapter provides an overview of the action process of information gathering to answer research questions or queries. A number of strategies are discussed, some of which are used strictly by one or the other major research tradition. (The subsequent chapters examine the specific approaches used by each of the research traditions.)

In experimental-type research, data collection is a distinct action phase that represents the crossroads between the thinking process of question formation, development and implementation of design, and the action process of analysis. Strategies for data collection involve actions that are pertinent to the research problem and consistent with the design. In turn, the types of data that are collected and the methodologic approach used to obtain information shape both the type and nature of the analytical process and the understandings and knowledge that can emerge.

In naturalistic inquiry, gathering information stems from the initial query. However, it is embedded in an iterative, abductive approach that involves ongoing analysis, reformulation, and refinement of the initial query.

## Principles of collecting information

Three basic principles characterize the process of collecting information within the different research traditions (Box 15-1).

First, the aim of collecting information or data, regardless of how it is done, is to obtain information that is both relevant and sufficient to answer a research question or query. Second, the choice of a data collection or information gathering strategy is based on four major factors: the researcher's paradigmatic framework, the nature of the research problem, the type of de-

> **Box 15-1** **Three principles for collecting information**
> - Information needs to be relevant and sufficient to answer the question or query.
> - Selection of collection strategies needs to be purposeful.
> - Use of single or combination of strategies must enhance validity or trustworthiness.

sign, and the practical limitations or resources available to the investigator (Table 15-1). Third, although a collection strategy reflects the researcher's basic philosophical base, a specific procedure, such as observation or interview, may be shared by researchers from either a naturalistic or an experimental-type study. Many researchers find it useful to collect data and information with more than one procedure or technique to answer more fully a question or query. The use of multiple collection techniques is called triangulation of method and is useful for increasing the accuracy of information.[1] (We discuss this technique in subsequent chapters.)

In general the action process of data and information collection uses one or more of the following strategies: (1) watching, listening, and recording; (2) asking; and (3) obtaining and examining materials. As summarized in Table 15-2, each one of these strategies can be structured, semistructured, or open-ended, depending on the nature of the inquiry. Also, each strategy can be used in combination with the other. Let us examine each strategy.

| Table 15-1 | **Factors influencing choice of collection strategy** | |
|---|---|---|
| | *Factor* | *Specific issue* |
| | Paradigmatic framework | Relationship of investigator to that which is being investigated |
| | Research problem | Question or query |
| | Design type | Naturalistic or experimental-type |
| | Practical limitations | Time<br>Money<br>Access to research population |

| Table 15-2 | **Summary of collection methods** | | |
|---|---|---|---|
| | *Method* | *Structured* | *Unstructured* |
| | Watching and listening | Checklists<br>Rating scales | Participatory<br>Nonparticipatory |
| | Asking | Closed-ended | Open-ended<br>Guided questioning |
| | Artifact | Coding schemes | Open-ended observation |

## Watching, listening, and recording

One important data and information gathering strategy is engaging in the process of systematic observation. The process of *observation* includes three interrelated activities: watching, listening, and recording data. The way in which one watches and listens may range in approach from being structured to unstructured, participatory to nonparticipatory, narrow focus to broad, and time limited to fully immersed.[2] In the experimental-type tradition, observation is usually time limited and structured. Criteria to watch, listen, and record are selected *a priori* to gathering data, and the data are recorded along a structured measurement system. Checklists may be used that indicate the presence or absence of a particular behavior or object under

study. Phenomena other than those specified before entering the field are ignored or remain outside the investigator's interest. Rating scales may also be used to record observations in which the investigator rates the observed phenomenon on a scale ranging on a predetermined point system. (We discuss rating scales in more detail in Chapter 16.)

In naturalistic designs, watching, listening, and recording take on an inductive, participatory quality. The investigator broadly defines the field of observation (e.g., a nursing home), and then moves to a more focused observational approach (e.g., particular units, staff-resident interactions) as the process of collecting and analyzing information from previous observations unfolds.

Let us examine the concept of intelligence to illustrate different observational approaches. In experimental-type studies, intelligence testing relies, in large part, on the use of a structured instrument that involves paper-and-pencil tests and a tester observing a subject's performance in a laboratory setting. Measurements are obtained on dimensions that have been predefined as composing the construct of intelligence. However, in a naturalistic approach, rather than using predefined criteria, the investigator may watch and listen to persons in their natural environments to reveal the meaning of intelligence in a particular culture. Each approach has its value in addressing specific types of research problems. Structured observation of intelligence will be appropriate for the investigator who wishes to compare populations or individuals, measure individual or group progress and development, or describe population parameters on a standard indicator of intelligence. On the other hand, naturalistic observation of intelligence will be useful to the researcher who is attempting to develop new understandings of the construct.

## Asking

Health and human service professionals routinely ask questions to obtain information. In research, asking is a systematic and purposeful aspect of a data collection plan. As in observation, asking questions can vary in structure and content from unstructured and open-ended to closed-ended or fixed-response questions that use a predetermined response set. An example of an *open-ended question* is, "How have you have been feeling this past week?" In contrast, an example of a structured or *closed-ended question* is, "In this past week, how would you rate your health: excellent, good, adequate, fair, or poor?" Naturalistic research relies more heavily on open-ended types of asking techniques, whereas experimental-type designs tend to use structured, fixed-response questions. Focused, structured asking is used to obtain data on a specified phenomenon, whereas open-ended asking is used when the research purpose is discovery and exploration.

When you are asking, questions can be posed through either interview or questionnaire.

## Interviews

*Interviews* are conducted through verbal communication, may occur face-to-face or by telephone, and may be either structured or unstructured. Interviews are usually conducted with one individual. However, sometimes group interviews are appropriate, such as those conducted with couples, families, and work groups. Group interviews of five or more individuals involve a focus group methodology in which the interaction of individuals is key to the information the investigator wishes to obtain.[3] An audiotape of the group interview is transcribed, and the narrative (along with investigator notes) forms the information base, which is then analyzed.

Structured interviews involve a written document in which maximum researcher control is imposed on the content and sequencing of questions. Each question and its response alternatives are developed and placed in sequential order before an interview is conducted. Interviewers are instructed to precisely ask each question precisely as it is written. Most questions are closed-ended or fixed; that is, subjects select one response from a predetermined set of answers. Closed-ended questions vary with regard to the type of response alternatives (Box 15-2). Each response set forms a different type of scale, as discussed in this chapter.

In a structured interview, the investigator may use a few open-ended questions. Responses are examined, coded, and, in effect, changed into a closed-ended response set on a *post hoc* analytical basis; that is, the investigator develops a numerical coding scheme based on the range of responses obtained and assigns a code to each subject. The numerical response is then analyzed.

Unstructured interviews are primarily used in naturalistic research and exploratory studies in experimental-type designs. The researcher initially presents the topic area of the interview to a respondent and then uses probing questions to obtain information. The interview may begin with an explanation of the study purpose and a broad statement or question such as, "Could you please describe your day as a patient in this hospital?" Other probing questions emerge as a consequence of the information provided from this initial query. *Probes* are statements that are neutral or do not bias the subject to respond in any particular way. Probes are used to encourage the respondent to provide more information or elaborations. A probe, such as, "Tell me more about it," or simply repeating a question, encourages a respondent to discuss an issue or elaborate on an initial response. Unstructured interviews are sometimes used by quantitative researchers in pilot studies to uncover domains and response codes for inclusion in a more structured interview and question format.

## Questionnaires

*Questionnaires* are written instruments and may be administered face-to-face, by proxy, or through the mail. Similar to interviews, questionnaires vary as to whether questions are structured or unstructured. (The process of developing questionnaires is examined in Chapter 16 as part of the discussion on measurement in experimental-type research.)

Each way of asking—structured or unstructured—has strengths and limitations that the researcher must understand and weigh to determine the most appropriate approach. There is not one best way of collecting information. The strengths and limitations (Boxes 15-3 and 15-4) must be evaluated in terms of the researcher's purpose.

---

**Box 15-2 Response alternatives for closed-ended questions**

- Dichotomous (yes or no)
- Multiple choice
- Rank order questions (Guttman scale)
- Four or more graded responses (Likert-type scale)

---

**Box 15-3 Strengths of structured questioning**

- Honest responses can be obtained.
- Large cohort can answer questions in short period.
- Responses can be compared across groups.
- Statistical analysis can be conducted to describe and compare responses.

**Box 15-4** Limitations of structured questioning

- Researcher is uncertain how respondents interpret or understand the questions.
- Issues relevant to respondents may not be captured.
- Respondent answers may or may not reflect socially desirable responses.

Let us consider a study conducted by Atchison et al. that illustrate these strengths and limitations. In this study the investigators were interested in understanding the attitudes, knowledge, and fears of occupational therapists regarding human immunodeficiency virus (HIV) and acquired immunodeficiency syndrome (AIDS). The investigators chose to ask about these fears by using a structured questionnaire format that had been previously used with nursing students. Respondents had to rate their agreement with items on a 5-point Likert scale (strongly agree, agree, uncertain, disagree, strongly disagree). This type of asking limited the response of subjects to these five options. Any other comments or explanations were considered extraneous and were not recorded.[4]

Now let us consider a different way of asking respondents about HIV and AIDS. Using an open-ended, face-to-face interview approach, a researcher may obtain more in-depth and relevant information that may not have been included in a structured questionnaire. Further, the complexity of responses to HIV and AIDS can be retained and become the focus for analysis. Some of the advantages of using open-ended asking are listed in Box 15-5.

**Box 15-5** Strengths of open-ended questions

- Highly sensitive issue can be explored.
- Nonverbal behaviors can be captured and analyzed.
- Issues salient to respondent can be identified.
- Meaning of questions to respondent can be identified.

The limitations of an open-ended questioning approach in the study are listed in Box 15-6.

**Box 15-6** Limitations to open-ended questions

- Respondents may not want to directly address sensitive issues.
- Extensive time is required to conduct interviews and analyze information.
- Responses across groups cannot be readily compared.

As you can see, both types of asking have their merits and limitations, depending on the research purpose, phenomena to be studied, and study population.

## Obtaining and examining materials

There are numerous reasons why researchers use existing data. First, existing data may be accessible where direct observation and interview data are not. Second, the use of existing materials eliminates the attention factor, or the *Hawthorne effect*.[5] This effect refers to a change in a respondent's answer as a consequence of participating in the research process itself. Third, using existing data allows the researcher to view phenomena in the past and over time, which may not be possible with a primary data collection strategy that occurs at one time point. Finally, existing materials are valuable in obtaining data in sensitive inquiries, where informants may not want or be able to share their experiences.

In experimental-type design, securing and examining materials are structured by criteria before the research field is entered. In naturalistic inquiry, the selection of materials to observe or examine emerges as a consequence of the investigative process. There are three distinct approaches to obtaining and examining existing materials: (1) unobtrusive methodology, (2) secondary data analysis, and (3) artifact review.

## Unobtrusive methodology

*Unobtrusive methodology* involves the observation and examination of documents and objects that bear on the phenomenon of interest.[6] It is a methodology that is nonreactive; that is, there is minimal investigator effect in the research setting. For example, to estimate the alcohol consumption of a neighborhood, the investigator may search trash cans and count empty alcohol containers. This approach can be used to confirm information obtained from another source. In this example, the researcher may have searched trash cans as a way of confirming information obtained during a face-to-face interview on alcohol consumption. Examples of written materials that investigators may use for analysis are listed in Box 15-7.

| Box 15-7 | Examples of sources of written data |
| --- | --- |

- Diaries or personal journals
- Medical records
- Clinical notes
- Historical documents
- Minutes from meetings
- Letters
- Newspapers, magazines, and professional journals

In *secondary data analysis,* the researcher reanalyzes one or more existing data sets.[7] For example, a health care researcher may examine patient medical records to obtain data or may combine the data of two studies for subsequent analysis. A social work researcher may examine process recordings as a basis for understanding therapeutic interaction in family therapy. The purpose of a secondary analysis is to ask different questions of the data from the data set analyzed in the original work. There are several large national health and social service data sets that researchers use for secondary data analysis. The census tracts, National Health Interview Surveys, National Health Care Data Set, Medicare and Medicaid data, Annual Housing Survey, and court report recordings are important sources for secondary analysis in health and human service research.

## Artifact review

*Artifact review* is a technique primarily used to ascertain the meanings of objects in research contexts. For example, archaeologists examine ruins to learn about ancient cultures. Artifact review in health and human service research may include the examination of personal objects in a patient's hospital room or client's home to determine interests and preferred ways of arranging the environment as a basis for intervention planning.

## Summary

We have described three basic principles that guide the action process of obtaining information: (1) collecting relevant and sufficient information for the research question or query; (2) choosing an information gathering or data collecting strategy that is consistent with the research question, epistemologic foundation, design, and practical constraints of the research effort; and (3) recognizing that methods can be shared across traditions. We discuss the three categories of collecting information in all designs: watching, listening, and recording; asking questions; and examining materials. You are now ready to examine some of the specific data collection strategies in experimental-type design and gathering information in naturalistic design that are discussed in the following chapters.

## Exercises

1. Assume say you want to study the level of function of individuals with spinal chord injuries immediately after hospitalization. Identify and describe two data collection strategies you may use. Evaluate the strengths and limitations of each.

2. Conduct a brief interview with an older adult. Ask the person how he or she rate his or her health on a five-point scale

## Exercises

(excellent, very good, good, fair, poor). Ask the person to describe why he or she rated his or her their health in that way. Compare and contrast the type of information you obtained by asking a structured and an unstructured question.

### References

1. Morse JM: *Qualitative nursing research,* Rockville, Md, 1989, Aspen.
2. Patton M: *Qualitative evaluation and research methods,* ed 2, Newbury Park, Calif, 1990, Sage.
3. Kreuger R: *Focus groups: a practical guide for applied research,* Newbury Park, Calif, 1988, Sage.
4. Atchison DJ, Beard BJ, Lester LB: Occupational therapy personnel and AIDS: attitudes, knowledge and fears, *Am J Occup Ther* 44:212-217, 1990.
5. Roethlisberger FJ, Dickson WJ: *Management and the worker,* Cambridge, Mass, 1947, Harvard University Press.
6. Webb EJ, Campbell DT, Schwartz RD, et al: *Nonreactive measures in the social sciences,* Boston, 1981, Houghton Mifflin.
7. Stewart DW: *Secondary research: information sources and methods,* Newbury Park, Calif, 1984, Sage.

*Continued*

*Chapter* **16**

# Measurement in experimental-type research

| **Key terms** | Continuous variable | Random error |
|---|---|---|
| | Discrete variable | Ratio |
| | Guttman scale | Reliability |
| | Interval | Scales |
| | Likert-type scale | Semantic differential scale |
| | Measurement | Systematic error |
| | Nominal | Validity |
| | Ordinal | |

**Measurement process**
**Levels of measurement**
    Nominal
    Ordinal
    Interval
    Ratio
**Types of measure**
    Likert-type scale
    Guttman scale
    Semantic differential
**Confidence in instruments**
    Reliability
    Validity
    Practical considerations
**Instrument construction**
**Administering the instrument**
**Summary**

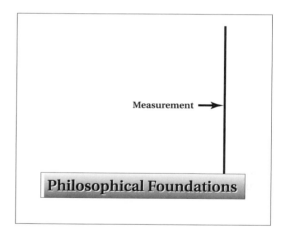

Measurement →

**Philosophical Foundations**

In experimental-type designs, the purpose of data collection is to learn about an "objective reality." As we indicate in previous chapters, the investigator is considered separate and removed from that which is known. There is strict adherence to a data collection protocol. A protocol refers to a

194

series of procedures and techniques designed to remove the influence of the investigator from the data collection process and ensure a nonbiased and uniform approach to obtaining information. These data are made more "objective" by the assignment of numerical values, which are submitted to statistical procedures to test relationships, hypotheses, and population descriptors. These descriptions are viewed as representing objective reality. Therefore in experimental-type research, the process of quantifying information or measurement is a primary concern. The investigator must develop instruments that are reliable and valid or have a degree of correspondence to an objective world or truth.

In this chapter we discuss the critical issues related to the measurement process. These include instrumentation and issues of reliability and validity.

### Measurement process

*Measurement* can be defined as the translation of observations into numbers. It is a vital action process in experimental-type research, which links the researcher's abstractions or theoretical concepts to concrete variables that can be empirically or objectively examined. In experimental-type research, concepts must be made operational; in other words, they must be put into a format such as a questionnaire or interview schedule that permits structured, controlled observation and measurement. The measurement process involves a number of steps that include both conceptual and operational considerations (Figure 16-1).

The first step in the measurement process involves conceptual work by the researcher.

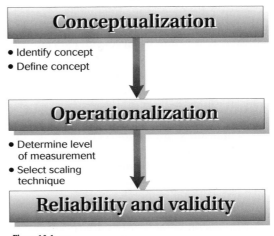

Figure 16-1 Measurement process.

The researcher must identify and define what is to be measured. This step involves asking, "How shall I conceptualize the phenomenon I wish to study?" or "How shall I define these concepts in words?" For example, basic concepts such as attitude, depression, anxiety, self-mastery, or adaptation have been defined in many different ways in the research literature. Once the researcher identifies a concept, such as anxiety, depression, etc., the literature is then reviewed to decide on an appropriate definition.

The second step in the measurement process involves developing an operational definition of the concept. This operational consideration of measurement involves asking, "What kind of an indicator shall I use as a gauge of this concept?" or "How shall I classify and/or quantify what I observe?" A measure is an empirical representation of an underlying concept. Because, by definition, a concept is always unobservable, the strength of the relationship between an indicator and an underlying concept is critical. This relationship is referred to as validity. Also, it is important for the indicator to measure consistently the underlying concept. The consistency of a measure is referred to as its reliability. The greater the reliability and validity, the more desirable the instrument. Reliability and validity are two fundamental properties of indicators. Researchers engage in major efforts to evaluate the strength of reliability and validity to determine the desirability and value of a measure. (These terms are discussed in greater detail later in this chapter.)

The action process of information gathering in experimental-type research begins with identifying concepts. This step is followed by developing conceptual and operational definitions of these concepts. Based on these definitions, specific indicators (scales, questionnaires, rating forms) are specified or developed. These indicators represent the source of information or data that will be collected.

## Levels of measurement

The first step in developing an indicator involves specifying how a variable will be made operational. This action process involves determining the numerical level at which the variable will be measured. The level of measurement refers to the properties and meaning of the number assigned to an observation. There are four levels of measurement: nominal, ordinal, interval, and ratio. The level of measurement leads to different types of mathematical manipulations. In other words, determining how a variable is measured has a direct bearing on the type of statistical analysis that can be performed. The deci-

sion regarding the level of measurement is a critical component of the measurement process.

Several principles are used to determine the level of measurement of a variable. The first principle is that every variable must have two qualities. One quality of a variable is that it is exhaustive of every possible observation; that is, the variable should be able to classify every observation in terms of one or more of its attributes. A simple example is the concept of gender, which has been classically defined as either a male or female attribute. These two categories represent the full range of attributes for the concept of gender. Another quality of a variable is that the attributes or categories must be mutually exclusive. For example, there can be only a male or female attribute.[1]

The second principle is that variables can be characterized as being either discrete or continuous. A *discrete variable* is one with a finite number of distinct values. Again, gender is a good example of a discrete variable. Gender, as classically defined, has either a male or female value. There is no in-between category. A *continuous variable,* on the other hand, has an infinite number of values.[2] Age and height are two examples of continuous variables in that they can be measured along a numerical continuum of years, months, days, or in inches and feet. It is possible to measure a continuous variable using discrete categories such as the classification of the age variable as young, middle aged, or old or the height variable as tall, medium, or short. Discrete and continuous structures represent the natural characteristics of a variable. These characteristics have a direct bearing on the level of measurement that can be applied. Let us examine each level in greater detail.

## Nominal

The simplest or lowest level of measurement is *nominal*. It involves classifying observations into mutually exclusive categories. The word nominal means name; therefore at this level of measurement, numbers are used, in essence, to name attributes of a variable. This level merely names or labels attributes, and these attributes are not ordered in any particular way. For example, your telephone number, the number on your sports jersey, or the number on your social security card is used to identify you as the attribute of the variables "person with a telephone," "an athlete," and "a taxpayer." All are examples of nominal numbers.

Variables at the nominal level are discrete. For example, we may classify individuals according to their political or religious affiliation, gender, or ethnicity. In each of these examples, membership in one category excludes membership in another, but there is no order to the categories. One category is not higher or lower than another. Box 16-1 provide examples of mutually exclusive categories.

For data analysis, the researcher assigns a numerical value to each nominal category. For example, "male" may be assigned a value of 1, whereas "female" may be assigned a value of 2. The assignment of numbers is purely arbitrary, and no mathematical functions or assumptions of magnitude or ranking are implied or can be performed. Many survey analyses, conducted by telephone, mail, or face-to-face, use nominal level questions. The intent of these surveys is to describe the distribution of responses along these discrete categories. For example, a survey may provide answers to questions such as how many men versus women have low back pain, or

**Box 16-1 Examples of nominal-type variables**

- Yes or no
- Male or female
- Democrat, republican, or independent
- Caucasian, African American, Hispanic, or Asian

how many African Americans have health care insurance compared with Caucasians.

## Ordinal

The next level of measurement is *ordinal*. This level involves the ranking of phenomena. Ordinal means order and thus can be remembered as the numerical value that assigns an order to a set of observations. Variables that are discrete and conceptualized as having an inherent order at the theoretical level can be operationalized in a rank order format. Variables operationalized at this level have the same properties of nominal categories in that each category is mutually exclusive of the other. In addition, ordinal measures have a fixed order, so that the researcher can rank one category higher or lower than another. For example, income may be ranked into categories, such as 1=poor, 2=lower income, 3=middle income, 4= upper income. Using this ordinal variable we can say that middle income is ranked higher than lower income, but we can say nothing about the extent to which the rankings differ. The assignment of a numerical value is symbolic and arbitrary as in the case of nominal variables, because the distance or spacing between each category is not numerically equivalent. However, the numbers imply magnitude;

that is, one is greater than the other. Because there are no equal intervals between ordinal numbers, mathematical functions such as adding, subtracting, dividing, and multiplying cannot be performed. The researcher can merely state that one category is higher or lower, stronger or weaker, or greater or lesser. Many scales that are useful to health and human service researchers are composed of variables measured at the ordinal level. For example, the concept of self-rated health is ranked from 1= very poor to 5=excellent. Although the numbers imply a state of being in which 5 is greater than 1, it is not possible to say how much greater the distance is.

## Interval

The next level of measurement shares the characteristics of ordinal and nominal measures but also has the characteristic of equal spacing between categories. This level of measurement indicates how much categories differ. *Interval* measures are continuous variables in which the 0 point is arbitrary. Although interval measures are a higher order than ordinal and nominal measures, the absence of a true 0 point does not allow statements to be made concerning ratios. However, the equidistance between points allows the researcher to say that the difference between scores of 50 and 70 is equivalent to the difference between scores of 20 and 40. Examples of a true interval level of measurement include Fahrenheit and Celsius temperature scales and intelligence quotient (IQ) scales. In each of these cases there is no absolute 0, but there is equal distance between mutually exclusive categories.

In the social and behavioral sciences, there is considerable debate as to whether behavioral scales represent interval levels of mea-surement. Typically, such scales have a Likert-type response format in which a study participant responds to one of four to seven categories such as strongly agree, agree, uncertain, disagree, or strongly disagree. Researchers who accept this type of scaling as an interval measure argue that the distance between strongly agree and agree is equivalent to the distance between disagree and strongly disagree. Others argue that there is no empirical justification for making this assumption and that the data generated should be considered ordinal. In the actual practice of research, many investigators assume such scales are at the interval level to use more sophisticated and powerful statistical procedures that are only possible with interval and ratio data. You should be aware that this debate continues to be a controversial matter among experimental-type researchers.

## Ratio

*Ratio* measures represent the highest level of measurement. Such measures have all the characteristics of the previous levels and, in addition, have an absolute 0 point. Income is an example of a ratio measure. Instead of classifying income into ordinal categories, as in the previous example, it can be described in terms of dollars. Income is a ratio measurement because it is possible for someone to have an income of 0 and we can say that an income of $40,000 is twice as high as an income of $20,000.

Table 16-1 summarizes the characteristics of each level of measurement. Experimental-type researchers usually strive to measure a variable at its highest possible level. However, the level of measure is also a reflection of the researcher's concepts. If, for example, political af-

**Table 16-1** | **Characteristics of levels of measurement**

|  | Nominal | Ordinal | Interval | Ratio |
|---|:---:|:---:|:---:|:---:|
| Mutually exclusive categories | X | X | X | X |
| Fixed ordering |  | X | X | X |
| Equal spacing |  |  | X | X |
| Absolute 0 |  |  |  | X |

filiation, gender, or ethnicity are the concepts of interest, nominal measurement may be the most appropriate level, because magnitude does not apply to these concepts.

## Types of measures

Now that we have discussed the properties of numbers, let us examine the different methods by which data are collected and transformed into numbers. We begin with a discussion of specific types of measures that are frequently used in experimental-type research.

*Scales* are tools for the quantitative measurement of the degree to which individuals possess a specific attribute or trait. Box 16-2 lists examples of scales that are frequently used by health and human service professionals in research.

Scaling techniques measure the extent to which respondents possess an attribute or personal characteristic. There are three primary scaling formats used by experimental-type researchers: Likert approach to scales, Guttman scales, and semantic differential scales.[10] Each has its merits and disadvantages. The researcher who is developing a scale needs to make basic formatting decisions about response set structure, whereas the researcher selecting an already existing scale must evaluate the format of the measure for his or her project.

**Box 16-2** | **Examples of useful scales**

- Dyadic Adjustment Scale
  (a measure of marital adjustment)[3]
- Self-Rating Anxiety Scale
  (a measure of clinical anxiety)[4]
- Family Adaptability Cohesion Scale[5]
- State-Trait Anxiety Scale[6]
- Session Evaluation Questionnaire[7]
- CES-D Depression Scale[8]
- SF-36 (a measure of health status)[9]

*CES-D,* Center for Epistemological Studies; *SF,* short form.

## Likert-type scale

In the *Likert-type scale,* the researcher develops a series of items (usually between 10 and 20) worded favorably and unfavorably regarding the underlying construct that is to be assessed. Respondents indicate a level of agreement or disagreement with each statement by selecting one of several response alternatives (usually five to seven). Researchers may combine responses to the questions to obtain a summated score, examine each item separately, or summate scores on specific groups of items to create subindexes. In developing a Likert-type format the researcher must decide how many response categories to allow and whether the categories should be even or odd in number. Even choices force a positive or negative response, whereas odd numbers allow the respondent to select a neutral or middle response. The Dyadic Adjustment Scale[3] is an example of a Likert-type scale with several different even-numbered response formats. The first set (22 separate items) has six response categories that range from always agree, agree a lot, agree a little, disagree a little, disagree a lot, to always agree. The instructions read:

> Most persons have disagreements in their relationships. Please indicate the approximate extent of agreement or disagreement between you and your partner for each item on the following list.

The Family Adaptability and Cohesion Scale (FACES-III),[5] on the other hand, is an example of a scale that measures family function, allowing a neutral response by structuring responses into five ordinal categories: almost never, once in a while, sometimes, frequently, and almost always. The "sometimes" category is the middle response and receives a score of three.

Likert-type scaling techniques are frequently used by social science researchers. They provide a closed-ended set of responses while still giving the respondent a reasonable range of latitude. Likert-type scales, as indicated earlier, may be considered ordinal or interval, depending on what is being measured and on the desired data analytical procedures to be selected. A disadvantage of Likert-type scaling is that there is no way of ensuring that respondents have the same understanding of the magnitude of each response.

## Guttman scale

The *Guttman scale* is referred to as unidimensional or cumulative.[1] The researcher develops a small number of items (four or seven) that relate to one concept. The items form a homogeneous or unitary set and are cumulative or graduated in intensity of expression. In other words, the items are hierarchically arranged so that endorsement of one item means an endorsement of those items below it, which are expressed at less intensity. Knowledge of the total score is predictive of the individual's responses to each item. Let us consider a series of items developed by Stouffer (Box 16-3).[11] Stouffer was interested in measuring tolerance toward a man who admits he is a communist.

In this series you can see that if a person answers "no" to items one, two, and three, he or she is most tolerant. On the other hand, a person who answers "yes" to all three questions is the least tolerant. Another person who answers "no" to item two will probably answer "no" to item one. Thus in the Guttman ap-

---

**Box 16-3 Examples of a Guttman scale**

1. Assume this admitted communist wants to make a speech in your community. Should he be banned from speaking?
2. If some people in your community suggest that a book he wrote favoring government ownership should be taken out of your public library, would you favor removing the book?
3. Suppose he is a clerk in a store. Should he be fired?

proach to scaling, items are arranged according to the degree of agreement or intensity.

## Semantic differential

The *semantic differential* approach to scaling is usually used for psychological measures to assess attitudes and beliefs.[12] The researcher develops a series of rating scales in which the respondent is asked to give a judgment about something along an ordered dimension, usually of seven points. Ratings are bipolar in that they specify two opposite ends of a continuum (good-bad, happy-sad). The researcher sums the points across the items. The Session Evaluation Questionnaire[7] is an example of a semantic differential scale. The scale measures two constructs, depth and smoothness, related to clients' perceptions of clinical counseling sessions in which they have participated. The scale also measures two postsession mood constructs, positivity and arousal. The scale includes 24 items, 12 each for the 2 sections. One item related to the session reads:

The session was:
    Bad—Good
One postsession item reads:
    Right now, I feel:
    Happy—Sad

The respondent is instructed to place an X in the space that most accurately depicts his or her feelings. Semantic differential scaling is most useful when natural phenomena can be categorized in opposite or contrary positions. However, it limits the range of responses to a linear format.

## Confidence in instruments

In selecting a scale or other type of measurement, the researcher is concerned about two issues. The first issue is whether the instrument consistently or reliably measures a variable. The second issue is whether the instrument represents an adequate or valid measure of the underlying concept of interest.

## Reliability

*Reliability* refers to the extent to which you can rely on the results obtained from an instrument. You will want to be assured that if you were to measure the same variable in the same person in the same situation over and over again, your results would be the same. More formally, reliability refers to the degree of consistency with which an instrument measures an attribute. Reliability is an indicator of the ability of an instrument to produce similar scores on repeated testing occasions that occur under similar conditions. The reliability of an instrument is important to consider to ensure that changes in the variable under study represent observable variations and not those resulting from the measurement process itself. If an instrument yields different scores each time the same subject is tested, the scale will not be able to detect the "objective" value or truth of the phenomenon that is being examined.

It is easy to understand the concept of reliability when you consider a physiological measure such as a scale for weight. If you weigh an individual on a scale, you can expect to derive the same weight on repeated measures if that subject stepped on and off the scale several times without doing anything to alter his or her weight between measurements. Instruments, such as a weight scale or blood pressure cuff, must be consistent to assess an accurate value that approximates a "true" physiological value for an individual. Let us consider another example. Suppose you are interested in measuring the level of depression in a group of inpatients who are in an experimental intervention program. You will want to determine whether depression scores decline after participation in the program. You will need to administer a depression scale before beginning the program and after its conclusion. Thus it will be important that the depression measure you select is reliable. If the measure is reliable, any change in depression scores that are observed after the intervention will indicate a "true" alteration in level of depression rather than a variation on a scale.

However, there is always some error in measurement. A scale may not always be completely accurate. Take, for example, a tape measure that is not precisely held at the same place for each measure. This error is random in that it occurs by chance, and the nature of the error may vary with each measurement period. Reliability represents an indication of the degree to which such random error exists in a measurement. A formal representation of *random error* in measurement is expressed by examining the relationship among three components: (1) the "true" score that is unknown ($T$), (2) the observed score ($O$) that is derived from an instrument or other measurement process, and (3) an error score ($E$). An observed score will be a function of the "true" score and some error. This tripartite relationship can be expressed as:

$$O = T + E$$

As we can see in this equation, the smaller the error term, the more closely $O$ (the observed score) will approximate $T$ (the "true" value). The standardization of study procedures and instruments serves to reduce this random error term. In a questionnaire, for example, a question that is clearly phrased and unambiguous will increase its reliability and decrease random error.

Consider an example. Suppose you want to know whether your client is feeling depressed. You ask, "How do you feel today?" The client answers, "Fine," and then begins to weep. Obviously the client and you do not have the same question in mind, even though you both heard the same words. If you ask the client, "Do you feel depressed today?" you may more likely obtain the desired information. Although both questions mean the same to you, the second question eliminates room for interpretation by the client. The client understands exactly what you are asking and gives the answer that you seek.

The same holds for measurement. Reduction of ambiguity decreases the likelihood of misinterpretation and thus error. Also, the longer the test or the more information collected to represent the underlying concept, the more reliable the instrument will become. Let us once again consider the example of depression. If your client answers that he or she is not depressed but breaks down in your clinic and weeps, you may experience some cognitive dissonance. However, if you administer a scale to the client that asks multiple questions, all of which measure aspects of depressive behavior, you may be able to obtain a more accurate picture of your client's mood.

Because all measurement techniques contain some random error (error that occurs by chance) reliability can exist only in degrees. The concept of reliability is thus expressed as a ratio between variation surrounding $T$ (a "true" score) and variation of $O$ (an observed score):

$$r = \frac{T}{O}$$

Because we can never know the "true" score, reliability represents an approximation to that "objective" reality.

Reliability is expressed as a form of a correlation coefficient that ranges from a low of 0 to a high of 1.00. The difference between the observed coefficient and 1.00 tells us what percent of the score variance can be attributed to error. For example, if the coefficient is 0.65, then 0.35 reflects the degree of inconsistency of the instrument. On the other hand, 65% of the observed variance is measuring an individual's "true" or actual score.

To assert reliability, experimental-type researchers frequently conduct statistical tests. These tests of reliability (Table 16-2) focus on three elements: stability, internal consistency, and equivalence. The choice of a test depends on the nature and intended purpose of the instrument.

**Stability.** Stability is concerned with the consistency of repeated measures. Test-retest is a reliability test in which the same test is given twice to the same subject under the same circumstances. It is assumed that the individual should score the same on the test and retest. The degree to which the test and retest scores corre-

| Table 16-2 | Tests of reliability | | |
|---|---|---|---|
| | *Stability* | *Internal* | *Equivalence* |
| | Test-retest | Split half | Interrater |
| | | Cronbach's | Alternate |
| | | alpha | forms |
| | | Kuder- | |
| | | Richardson | |
| | | formula | |

late or are associated is an indication of the stability of the instrument and its reliability. This measure of reliability is often used with physical measures and paper-and-pencil scales. The use of test-retest techniques is based on the assumptions that the phenomenon to be measured remains the same at two testing times and that any change is the result of random error. Usually physiological measures and equipment can be tested for stability in a short time period, whereas paper-and-pencil tests are retested in a 2-week to 1-month time period. This approach of measuring reliability is not appropriate for instruments in which the phenomenon under study is expected to vary over time. For example, in the measurement of mood or any other transitory characteristic, we anticipate variations in the "true" score at each repeated testing occasion. Thus a test-retest approach is not an appropriate way of indicating stability.

***Tests of internal consistency.*** These tests are also referred to as tests of homogeneity and are primarily used with paper-and-pencil instruments. In these tests the issue of consistency is internally examined in relation to a composite score. In the split-half technique, instrument items are split in half and a correlational procedure is performed between the two halves. In other words, the scores on one half of the test are compared with the scores on the second half. The higher the correlation or relationship between the two scores, the greater the reliability. Tests are split in half by comparing odd-numbered with even-numbered responses, by randomly selecting half of the items, or by splitting the instrument in half (e.g., questions 1 through 10 are compared with questions 11 through 20). This technique assumes that a person will consistently respond throughout a measure and therefore demonstrate consistent scores between the halves.

Cronbach's alpha or Kuder-Richardson formula ($K-R\,20$) are two statistical procedures often used to examine the extent to which all the items in the instrument measure the same construct. The statistic generated is a correlation coefficient between the values of 0 and $+1.00$ in which a 0.80 correlation is interpreted as adequate reliability. An 80% correlation basically means that the test is consistent 80% of the time and that error may occur 20% of the time. A score close to $+1.00$ is most desirable; such a score indicates minimal error and maximum consistency.

*Equivalence.* There are two tests of equivalence: interrater reliability and alternate forms. The interrater reliability test involves the comparison of two observers measuring the same event. A test is given to one subject but scored by two or more raters, or the same rater observes and rescores an event on two different occasions. The total number of agreements between raters is compared with the total number of possible agreements and multiplied

by 100 to obtain the percent of agreement. Eighty percent or more is considered to be an indication of a reliable instrument. As in the other tests of reliability, a higher score is most desirable.

Consider the following hypothetical data (Table 16-3). There are four potential chances for agreement, yet only two actual agreements occur among the raters. Thus agreement occurred in the ratio of 2 to 4 (2/4), or 1 to 2 (1/2). Therefore the interrater reliability in the example is 50% ($1/2 \times 100 = 50$).

The alternate or parallel forms test involves the comparison of two versions of the same paper-and-pencil instrument. In this case two equivalent forms of one test are administered to one subject on the same testing occasion. The use of this technique depends on the availability of two equivalent versions of a form.

## Validity

An indicator or measure must not only be reliable, but it must also be valid. *Validity* addresses the critical issue of the relationship between a concept and its measurement. It asks whether what is being measured is a reflection of the underlying concept. Figure 16-2 diagrams three different degrees of validity and highlights how instrumentation ($A_1$) only approximates the un-

**Table 16-3** Interrater reliability

| Rater 1 | Rater 2 |
|---------|---------|
| 30 | 35 |
| 25 | 25 |
| 31 | 32 |
| 33 | 33 |

derlying concept (*A*). The closer an instrument comes to representing the "true" definition of the concept, the more valid the instrument.

Take, for example, the theoretical concept of intelligence and the traditional indicator of adult intelligence, the Wechler Adult Intelligence Scale.[13] Researchers have argued whether this test actually measures what it purports to and whether it is valid for different cultures and populations. Because researchers can only approximate a perfectly valid instrument, as in relia-bility, validity is a question of degree and may vary with the intended purpose of the instrument and the specific population for which it is developed or intended. Thus the Wechler Adult Intelligence Scale may be a valid measure of intelligence as it has been traditionally defined for white, middle-class Americans but an invalid measure of intelligence for, as an example, Mexican Indians.

Unlike reliability, the validation of an instrument occurs in many stages, over time, and with many different populations. Thus a scale that assesses problem solving that is validated with college students may need further validation before being used with middle-aged and older persons. Also, a scale that is valid is necessarily reliable, but the opposite may not be true. In other words, a scale may reliably or consistently measure the same phenomenon on repeated occasions, but it may not actually measure what it is intended to assess. Thus validation of an instrument is extremely critical to ensure some degree of accuracy in measurement.

Where reliability is a measure of the random error of the measurement process itself, validity is a measure of *systematic error,* or nonrandom error. Systematic error refers to a systematic bias or an error that consistently occurs. For example, a weight scale that systematically weighs individuals 5 pounds heavier than an accurate scale is an example of systematic error and an invalid measurement. A measure that systematically introduces error indicates that it is a poor indicator of the underlying concept it intends to represent. Validity is thus inversely related to the amount of systematic error present in an instrument; the smaller the degree of systematic error, the greater the validity of the instrument.

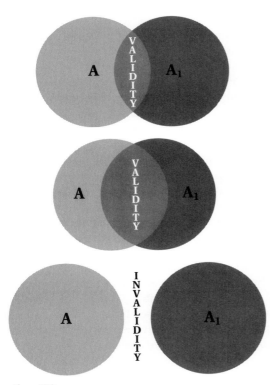

**Figure 16-2**  Three degrees of validity.

There are three basic types of validity that examine the degree to which an indicator represents its underlying concept: content, criterion, and construct.

***Content validity.*** Content validity is sometimes referred to as face validity. It is considered the most basic form by which an instrument is validated. This type of validity addresses the degree to which the indicator reflects the basic content of the phenomenon or domain of interest. Ideally the steps to obtain content validity include (1) specification of the full domain of a concept through a thorough literature search, and (2) adequate representation of domains through the construction of specific items.

If all domains are known to the investigator, a sampling of items that reflects each domain can occur. The problem with content validity is twofold. First, for most concepts of interest to health and human service professionals, there is no agreed-upon acceptance of the full range of content for any particular concept. Take, for example, such concepts as poverty, depression, self-esteem, or physical function. These concepts have been defined and conceptualized in many different ways. There is no unified understanding of the domains that constitute any one of these concepts. Second, there is no agreed-upon "objective" method for determining the extent to which a measure has attained an acceptable level of content validity. One way of obtaining some degree of assuredness of content validity is to submit constructed items or drafts of a scale for review by a panel of experts. This review process can be repeated until agreement has been obtained as to the validity of each item. However, this process does not yield a coefficient or other statistical indicator to discern the degree of agreement or the extent to which an instrument is content valid.

***Criterion validity.*** This type of validity involves demonstrating a correlation or relationship between the measurement of interest and another instrument or standard that has been shown to be accurate. There are two types of criterion validity: concurrent and predictive.

**Concurrent validity.** In concurrent validity, there is a known standardized instrument or other criterion that also measures the underlying concept of interest. It is not unusual for researchers to develop instrumentation to measure concepts, even if prior instrumentation already exists. Assume you are interested in developing your own measure of self-esteem. To establish concurrent validity, you will administer your instrument along with an already accepted and validated instrument measuring the same concept to the same sample of individuals. The extent of agreement between the two measures, expressed as a correlation coefficient, will tell you whether your scale is accurately measuring the same construct measured by the validated scale. The problem, however, is that this form of validity can only be used if another criterion exists. Also, this form is only as good as the validity of the selected criterion.

**Predictive validity.** Predictive validity is used when the purpose of the instrument is to predict or estimate the occurrence of a behavior or event. For example, this type of validity can be used to evaluate whether an instrument designed to assess risk of falls can predict the incident of falling. Agreement between the instrument and the criterion (a fall or an established assessment of the risk of falling) is indicated by a correlation coefficient.

***Construct validity.*** Construct validity represents the most complex and comprehensive form of validation. Construct validity is used when an investigator has developed a theoretical rationale underlying the test instrument. The researcher moves through different steps to evolve supporting evidence of the relationship of the test instrument to related and distinct variables. Construct validity is based not only on the direct and full measurement of a concept but also on the theoretical principles related to the concept. Therefore the investigator who attempts construct validity must consider how the measurement of the selected concept relates to other indicators of the same phenomenon. The researcher who is developing a measure of depression will therefore base a set of expectations of the measurement outcome on sound theory about the nature of depression. If the instrument is a self-report of depression that is based in cognitive behavioral theory, the researcher will hypothesize that certain behaviors and thoughts, such as lethargy, agitation, appetite changes, self-effacing thoughts, and melancholia, will frequently be found in subjects who score as clinically depressed. Thus the relationship of the scale score to other expected relationships will be measured as an indicator of construct validity.

There are many complex approaches to construct validity. The validation of a scale is ongoing in which each form (content, criterion, and construct) builds on the other and occurs in a progressive or sequential fashion.

## Practical considerations

In addition to the issues of reliability and validity, two other practical considerations influence the selection of a data collection technique. First, the nature of the research question dictates which method is appropriate. For example, if you are interested in surveying how professionals use theory in their practice, a closed-ended questionnaire can be developed. If you are interested in determining the accuracy of self-report of performance in self-care for older clients with serious mental illness, an interview and observation of performance may be appropriate.

Second, the nature of the sample also determines the appropriateness of the data collection procedure. Such factors as level of education, socioeconomic background, verbal ability, and cognitive status influence the selection of a data collection method. For example, college students are familiar with a self-administered, fixed-format questionnaire. However, this format may not be appropriate with the present cohort of elderly persons who may be visually impaired or unfamiliar with completing such questionnaires. For this population, a face-to-face interview may be more appropriate. Also, questionnaires will not be appropriate with children whose logical way of thinking cannot be captured in this format. The characteristics of a sample also determine the appropriate length of an interview or contact time with the investigator. For example, an individual with an attention deficit may not be able to attend to an interview that lasts longer than 20 minutes.

## Instrument construction

Now let us examine the basic steps involved in constructing an instrument. In health and human service research, the investigator often finds that measures have to be newly constructed to fit the study purpose. The development of a new measure in experimental-type research should always include a plan for testing its reliability and some level of validity (i.e., as content, at the very minimum) to ensure a level of accuracy and rigor to the study findings. Some investigators combine previously tested and established measures with newly constructed ones to test their relationships and relative strengths in the study.

The development of new instrumentation is, in itself, a specialty in the world of experimental-type research. We have introduced the basic components of the measurement process and have provided some principles for ensuring that your items are reliable. However, constructing an instrument and its components is a major research task (Box 16-4). It is best to seek consultation.

**Box 16-4 | Basic steps in instrument construction**

- Review the literature for relevant instrumentation.
- Identify the theory from which to develop a new instrument.
- Specify the concept or construct to be operationalized into an instrument.
- Conceptually define the full range and content of the concept.
- Select an instrument format.
- Translate the concept into specific items or indicators with appropriate response categories.
- Test the instrument.

There are many different sources of error that interfere with the reliability and validity of an instrument. We list six considerations in the development of an instrument and its administration (Box 16-5).

**Box 16-5 | Considerations in instrument development**

- Format or design of the instrument
- Clarity of the instrument
- Social desirability of the questions
- Variation in administration
- Situational contaminants
- Response set biases (all "yes" or all "no" responses)

For more detailed information on instrument construction, we refer you to the bibliography, in which we have listed texts that are specifically devoted to this topic.

## Administering the instrument

In many cases, as in small studies or in studies using written response instruments, administering the instrumentation is a function of distributing a paper-and-pencil assessment to subjects or directly observing the phenomena of interest. However, it is not unusual to engage in a project where more than one researcher is obtaining information. The influence of the data collector can potentially confound the findings. Let us consider how.

Assume you and another investigator are studying perceived quality of life in a nursing home environment. You both have a set of questions with a closed-ended response set to be answered by the subjects. You begin your interview with a "thank you" statement and then ask the questions, whereas the other interviewer discusses the respondent's poor health status before beginning the interview schedule. In your data analysis, you find that the subjects interviewed by you tend to be more satisfied with their lives than those interviewed by the other investigator. Is it be possible that the second investigator influenced the subjects by discussing potentially depressing issues before administering the instrumentation? This scenario highlights the importance of training for data collectors. Training is essential to ensure that data collection procedures are the same for all data collection action processes and to reduce bias that can be introduced by investigator differences. Establishing a strict protocol for administering an interview and training interviewers in that protocol will result in standardization of procedures to ensure that "objective measurement" will occur.

## Summary

Data collection instruments for experimental-type designs vary along several dimensions (Box 16-6).

The purpose of data collection is to ensure minimum researcher obtrusiveness through the systematic and consistent application of procedures. The researcher minimizes systematic and random errors through validation and reliability testing, respectively. Other procedures are developed to ensure consistency in obtaining data (Box 16-7).

Reliability and validity represent two critical considerations when a data collection instrument is selected. When experimental-

| Box 16-6 | **Characteristics of data collection instruments** |

- Structure (open or closed)
- Level of measurement
- Objectivity (reliability and validity)

| Box 16-7 | **Procedures for enhancing consistency** |

- Establish testing procedures and protocols.
- Establish when and how subjects are contacted.
- Establish a script by which to describe the study.

type research is conducted, the researcher's first preference is the selection of instruments that have demonstrated reliability and validity for the specific populations or phenomena the investigator wishes to study. However, in health and human service research, as in other substantive or content areas (e.g., gerontology), there are a limited number of developed instruments to measure the range of relevant researchable concepts. Because of the lack of reliable and valid instruments, some professional organizations such as the American Occupation Therapy Foundation have placed a high priority on funding research that is directed at the development of instruments.

## Exercises

1. Develop at least five questions on a Likert-type scale to measure job satisfaction among your peers. Ask at least three of your peers to respond to the questions. Ask each to indicate the clarity of the questions. Do you need to revise the questions? Did the questions appear to measure what you intended?

2. Using job satisfaction as your construct, develop a Gutman scale and a semantic differential scale. What are the advantages and disadvantages of each? Ask your peers to respond to these questions, and compare the responses.

3. With a peer, observe a child in a playground and attempt to independently determine his or her age. Record the criteria used to make your judgment. Compare your impressions with those of your peer to determine the extent of interrater reliability between the two of you.

*References*

1. Kerlinger F: *Foundations of behavioral research,* New York, 1973, Holt, Rinehart & Winston.
2. Miller D: *Handbook of research design and social measurement,* Newbury Park, Calif, 1991, Sage.
3. Spanier GB: Measuring dyadic adjustment: new scales for assessing the quality of marriage and similar dyads, *J Marriage Fam* 38:15-28, 1976.
4. Zung WK: A rating instrument for anxiety disorders, *Psychosomatics* 12:371-379, 1971.
5. Olson DH, Portner J, Lavee Y: FACES-III. In *Family social science,* Minneapolis, 1985, University of Minnesota.
6. Spielberger CD, Jacobs G, Russel S, et al: Assessment of anxiety: the state-trait anxiety scale, *Adv Personality* 2:159-187, 1983.
7. Stiles WB, Snow JS: Counseling session impact as seen by novice counselors and their clients, *J Counseling Psychol* 31:3-12, 1984.
8. Radloff LS: The CES-D scale: a self report depression scale for research in the general population, *Appl Psychol Measurement* 1:385-401, 1977.
9. Stewart AL, Ware JE, (editors): *Measuring functioning and well-being: the medical outcomes study approach,* Durham, 1992, Duke University Press.
10. DeVellis RF: *Scale development: theory and applications,* Newbury Park, Calif, 1991, Sage.
11. Stouffer SA: *Communism, conformity and civil liberties,* New York, 1955, Doubleday.
12. Osgood CE, Suci GJ, Tannenbaum PH: *The measurement of meaning,* Urbana, Ill, 1957, University of Illinois Press.
13. Wechsler D: *The measurement of adult intelligence,* ed 4, New York, 1958, Psychological Corp.

# Chapter 17

# Gathering information in naturalistic inquiry

**Key terms**  Audit trail
Field notes
Gaining access
Investigator involvement
Life history
Member check
Peer debriefing
Reflexivity
Saturation
Triangulation

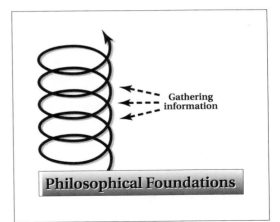

Gathering
information

**Philosophical Foundations**

Let us shift worlds and perspectives and examine the actions of researchers engaged in gathering information in naturalistic forms of inquiry. Gathering information involves a set of investigative actions that are quite divergent in purpose, approach, and process from experimental-type research. In naturalistic inquiry, knowledge is "mind dependent" in that it emerges from and is embedded in the shared understandings and interactions of individuals. The overall purpose of gathering information in naturalistic inquiry is to uncover multiple and diverse perspectives and underlying patterns that structure the context or field experience. The investigator gathers sufficient information that leads to description, discovery, understanding, interpretation, meaning, and explanation of the rich mosaic of daily life experiences. As you know by now, there are many distinct perspectives that compose the rubric of naturalistic inquiry. Thus there is wide variation in the information gathering approaches of researchers conducting naturalistic inquiry. For example, in semiotics the focus of data collection is on discourse, symbol, and context.[1] In classical ethnography the focus of data collection may be broader than semiotics and include verbal exchanges, behavioral patterns, and physical objects.[2]

## Four principles

Although the process of gathering information differs across the types of naturalistic inquiry, there are four basic principles that tend to be shared: (1) the nature of involvement of the investigator; (2) the inductive, abductive process of gathering information, analyzing information, and gathering more information; (3) the time commitment in the field; and (4) the use of multiple data-collection strategies. Let us begin our discussion by examining these four principles that guide the action of data gathering.

## Investigator involvement

In experimental research the investigator implements a set of procedures that remove himself or herself from informal or nonstandardized interactions with study participants. However, naturalistic inquiry is based on *investigator involvement* and active participation with people and other sources of information, such as artifacts or written historical documents. The quality of data that are collected from people is often dependent on the investigator's ability to develop trust, rapport, and mutual respect with those being studied. The level and nature of the investigator's involvement with people and other sources of information will depend, however, on the specific type of naturalistic study that is pursued. Table 17-1 outlines the diverse roles of investigators in collecting information from study participants among the different types of naturalistic inquiry.

In most forms of naturalistic inquiry, but particularly in classical ethnography, life history, grounded theory, and heuristic designs, the process of eliciting stories, personal experiences, and the telling of events is based on a strong relationship or bond that forms between the investigator and informant. Some researchers characterize this bond as a collaborative endeavor or partnership between investigator and informant. In these approaches to inquiry, the primary instrument for gathering trustworthy information from study participants is the investigator. As Fetterman describes:

> The ethnographer is a human instrument. Relying on all its senses, thoughts, and feelings, the human instrument is a most sensitive and perceptive data-gathering tool.[3]

| | | | | | | |
|---|---|---|---|---|---|---|
| **Table 17-1** Investigator involvement in gathering information from study participants | | | | | | |
| *Endogenous* | *Participatory action* | *Phenomenologic* | *Heuristic* | *Life History* | *Ethnography* | *Grounded theory* |
| ● Variable<br>● Flexible<br>● Depends on study team decisions | ● Variable<br>● Flexible<br>● Depends on study team decisions | ● Active listener | ● Fully partici-patory | ● Active listener | ● Fully parti-cipatory | ● Fully partici-patory |

The investigator as a data-gathering instrument is a logical extension of the primary contention of naturalistic inquiry. This position, which is shared by many but not all forms of naturalistic inquiry, maintains that the only way to "know" about the "lived" experiences of individuals is to become intimately involved and familiar with the life situations of those who experience them. The extreme of this position is found in heuristic inquiry in which the investigator attempts to live the same experience as that which is being investigated. In phenomenological research the investigator develops rapport with study participants but engages in active listening to understand the experiences of others. In ethnography the researcher, as the primary data-gathering instrument, strives for intimate familiarity with the people in the study. By engaging in an active learning process through watching, listening, participating, interviewing, and reviewing materials, the investigator enters the life world of others and uncovers what it means to live those experiences.

In endogenous and participatory action research the level of investigator involvement in data collection varies depending on the way in which the study team chooses to proceed. In these forms of naturalistic inquiry the investi-gator tends to serve more as a facilitator of the research process and may or may not be directly involved in the various data-collection strategies that are implemented by the team of participants.

It is important to note that it is not uncommon in naturalistic forms of inquiry to employ others in the data-gathering process. This strategy is particularly useful in studies involving multiple field sites or when the volume of interviews to be conducted is high and requires assistance from others. In these cases the investigator and data gatherers form a team and work together to develop a common interview style to ensure similarity and consistency in the use of techniques for building rapport, as well as for probing and eliciting responses. The team must also work together to share field impressions, notes, and emerging analytical categories and themes.

## Gathering and analyzing information

The act of gathering information also involves an analytical process, another principle of naturalistic inquiry; that is, collecting data is closely linked with the act of analysis in that one action directly informs another. Once immersed in the field, the investigator evaluates the information obtained through observation, examination of artifacts in taped interviews, and participation in activities. These initial analytical efforts detail the who, what, when, and where aspects of the context that, in turn, is used to further define and refine subsequent data-collection efforts. The dynamic process of ongoing data gathering, analysis, and more data gathering can be graphically represented by the spiral as shown in the graphic used in this text. In the spiral, as analysis and data collection are refined, the investigator moves from a broad conception of the field to a more in-depth, richer, and "thick" understanding and interpretation of multiple field "realities."[4]

## Time commitment in the field

The amount of time spent immersed in a field setting varies greatly across the types of naturalistic inquiry. In some studies, understanding a natural setting can take a lot of time because of the complexity of the initial query and the context that is being studied. In any type of naturalistic inquiry, however, the investigator must become totally immersed in the setting or involved with the phenomenon of study. Immersion means that the investigator must spend sufficient time in the field to ensure that a complete description is produced. In ethnographic research, spending time "hanging out," so to speak—interviewing, observing, and participating—has traditionally been called "prolonged engagement" in the field. Prolonged engagement is essential to ensure that the investigator reaches an in-depth understanding of the particular cultural group of focus.

But how much time is necessary? The amount of time spent in the field may vary from a few months to 9 months to 2 years. The amount of time varies depending on the nature of the initial query and its scope, the availability of resources that support the investigator in the endeavor, the amount of time available to the investigator, and the specific design strategy that is followed. Assume, for example, you want to examine the initial meanings attributed to the diagnosis of breast cancer among young women in their 20s. This approach represents a rather focused query that will require, perhaps, only a few months of interviewing women in this age group who have recently learned of their diagnosis. Even if you plan to observe physicians interacting with these patients, your observations will be confined to this early treatment phase. On the other hand, assume you want to examine the experiences of women as they move through the stages of biopsy, diagnosis, surgery, chemotherapy, and the uncertainty of the future. Compared with the first approach, this query is broader in scope and will require following a group of women over time. It may require up to 9 months or 1 year of the investigator's time to interview women at each of these different stages, as well as to conduct interviews with their significant others and physicians to understand the full impact of the sequence of events.

Whether the investigator spends a short or long time in the field, he or she must determine the point at which sufficient information has been obtained. When sufficient information has been obtained, the investigator leaves the field and engages in a final interpretative process that involves writing one or more final reports. The point at which sufficient information is obtained is sometimes referred to as "saturation." There are several considerations that will indicate when an investigator has obtained saturation. Examples of saturation include when the investigator is no longer puzzled or surprised by events or by what people say in the field, or when the investigator can predict behaviors or outcomes, or when information becomes redundant when compared with what has already been collected and learned by the investigator. When the investigator begins to hear the same story or can predict what a respondent is going to say, it is time to leave the field. (Saturation is discussed in greater detail later in this chapter.)

## Multiple data-gathering strategies

In most naturalistic forms of inquiry the investigator draws on and combines a variety of data-collection strategies. Different strategies are designed to derive information from numerous sources. All sources of information are analyzed to ensure that they support an interpretative scheme and set of conclusions. More than one data-collection strategy is used even if a query is small in scope.

There are many different data-gathering strategies that can be used by investigators. (Some of the more frequently used approaches are discussed in greater detail later in this chapter.) In most types of naturalistic inquiry the investigator may not know exactly which strategy he or she will use before entering the field. The decision to use a particular approach to collecting information occurs as the research progresses. In the course of doing fieldwork, the investigator must decide which data-collection technique to use and at which point during fieldwork it should be introduced.

There is not a standard approach that will indicate which strategy should be used and when it should be introduced across the different forms of naturalistic inquiry. Data collection decisions are specific to the research query, preferred way of knowing by the investigator, and context-specific opportunities that emerge in the process of being in the field. For example, in a phenomenological study some investigators prefer to interview respondents first and then review written documents, journals, medical records, or other materials. In this type of study, it is considered critical to initially listen in an interview to the emotions and feelings as they are naturally expressed by individuals who are asked to reflect on their experiences. It is thought that reading the literature or other written documents before the interviewing process may introduce analytical frames that may prevent attentive listening to the experiences of individuals. In contrast, some ethnographers prefer to initially "hang out" in the field and use the data-collection strategy of observation before introducing interviewing or other collection strategies. Still other ethnographers initially conduct open-ended interviews with key informants and then engage in participant observation. Other strategies, such as videotaping, standardized questionnaires, or review of documents, may be introduced at subsequent stages of fieldwork.

In summary, the hallmark of gathering information for the naturalistic researcher is that this action process occurs in a natural context. Data-gathering actions are designed to examine the natural context and all that occurs within it. The critical components of these actions tend to differ, based on the particular form of inquiry. Usually, the investigator is actively involved in the context over a prolonged time period to ensure sufficient immersion in the phenomena under study. However, the level of investigator involvement varies depending on the form of inquiry. In all forms of naturalistic inquiry, multiple strategies are used to obtain information in an ongoing and integrated data-collection and analytical process. These basic components or guiding principles in data gathering yield interpretations and understandings of phenomena that are embedded in specific natural contexts and complex interrelationships. The complexity of phenomena is preserved by the very nature of the data-gathering process. Let us examine how these principles are implemented and how naturalistic inquiry actually works.

## The process

What is the process of conducting fieldwork or gathering information? Although the process has been variably defined, we borrow the structure suggested by Shaffir and Stebbins and view it as involving four interrelated parts or considerations: context selection and "getting in the field," "learning the ropes" or obtaining meanings of the setting, "maintaining relations," and "leaving the field."[5] Although these actions appear to represent distinct phases or research steps, the process is truly integrated; each component overlaps and shapes the other.

### Context selection and getting in the field

The first decision about data collection in naturalistic research is where or in what context information should be obtained. The researcher must bound the study by depicting a context

that is either conceptual or locational (see previous discussions in Chapters 12 and 14). Because naturalistic research focuses on the natural research context, as well as what happens in it, selection of a context is an important factor in gathering data. The context may be the private lives of famous people, the interrelationships of a surgical team, the world of hospice specialists, or the meanings of caregiving to Hispanic families. Context selection may sound simple, but there are several important considerations. First, the specification of a context must be practical or realistic to study. For example, how realistic is it to propose an inquiry to study the private lives of famous people? Will you be able to gain access to such individuals? Will these people choose to participate in this type of study since agreement will jeopardize their privacy?

Second, in bounding a study to a particular context, the researcher must be careful not to limit the focus and thus the opportunity to obtain a full picture of the phenomenon under investigation. For example, let us assume you want to study how children with learning disabilities learn to cope with and adapt to their differences. Identifying the classroom as the main context of the investigation may be too narrow. It may enable you to identify and describe the strategies that children use in that context, but it may not enable you to understand the full range of adaptive mechanisms that are used in learning in other contexts and how these mechanisms are obtained. In another example, let us assume you are interested in studying the interrelationships and behaviors of a surgical team. You initially plan to examine the interactions of the surgical team during surgery. However, observations of this context may be too limiting. It may not yield a complete understanding of the interprofessional relationships that inform interactions in the specific context of surgery. Perhaps examining professional behaviors in other contexts, such as in the cafeteria, at staff meetings, or in social engagements, may provide important insights.

Consider one more example. Assume you are interested in examining the functional capacities of persons with traumatic brain injuries. If the context for the study is functional capacity in a clinical setting, the informant may be maximally functional in this particular setting. The investigator who does not expand the context to include other environments may not discover the functional incapacity that the person with traumatic brain injury often exhibits in less structured settings. It is important to recognize that identifying the context of a naturalistic study will depend, in part, on the nature of the query, the design strategy, and the characteristics of the persons being studied.

Once the context for the research endeavor is identified, the investigator must gain access to it. This is not as simple as it may sound. *Gaining access* to the context of the study requires strategizing, negotiating with key individuals who may serve as gatekeepers, and perhaps renegotiating once initial entry has occurred. In some cases the investigator may already be a part of the natural context. For example, assume you are a student and want to understand the process of becoming a health professional. As a student in health care, you are actually an "insider" of this particular context. Although access is not a problem, there are other aspects to fieldwork that will be challenging. As an "insider," you will have to work hard to understand how your knowledge and pre-

vious experiences influence the information you gather and interpret. Consider, for example, the study by DePoy and Archer of the culture of a nursing home. In this research effort, Archer was employed as an occupational therapist in the nursing home in which the study was conducted. She also functioned as the primary data collector. Because of her familiarity with the setting, she had no difficulty gaining entry and conducting observations. She was a familiar and trusted member of the context. Although this was an advantage, Archer had to work hard to ensure that she did not impose her previously conceived notions of that setting on the information she gained. She had to understand how her "insider" status influenced her data-collection and analytical actions.[6]

If the investigator is an "outsider," access must be obtained. Mechanisms for gaining access have been extensively discussed in the literature, particularly by ethnographers. How the researcher gains access into a context can influence the entire course of the research process. What does gaining access entail? It involves obtaining permission to enter and become part of the social or cultural setting. Investigators may use different strategies, depending on the nature of the context and their initial relationship to it. Formal introduction to an informant by another, slowly building rapport through participation, and gift giving are just a few of the techniques used by investigators to successfully enter a field. Let us assume you want to conduct a study in a medical setting. To gain access, initially it will be important to discuss the nature of your study with the directors of the departments you wish to include. This will be followed by a more formal introduction to medical personnel in staff meetings.

Gaining access can take time and hard work. You need to be clear as to how you intend to be involved in the context and the implications of your study for the participants. The basic considerations in gaining access are listed in Box 17-1.

An important consideration in obtaining access is the way in which the intent of your study is presented to participants. The researcher must decide on the extent to which the research activity is revealed to those being observed or interviewed. Although disclosure of the purpose and scope of the research must be made clear to those informants who provide initial access, the specifics of the research activity may remain vague to others who are either observed or interviewed at different times in the course of fieldwork. The extent of overt or covert research activities varies in any type of inquiry and from study to study and has important ethical concerns for researchers.

The other aspect of disclosure of research purpose is to ensure your informants that the information they provide will remain confidential. Stearns discusses this issue for physicians in her descriptive study of the way in which health management organizations (HMOs) structure the professional relationship between physician and patient:

> Only a few physicians refused to allow me to tape the interview. However, many expressed concerns that the interview remain confidential. This concern as well as their hesitancy to be interviewed meant that I had to be especially careful not to reveal who I had interviewed or what they had said. Confidentiality of physician (and other) responses was thus of great concern in the research.[7]

**Box 17-1** **Considerations in gaining access**

- Presenting study to participants
- Ensuring confidentiality
- Minimizing impact of investigator on natural context

Another consideration in gaining access is the impact of the investigator on the investigated. Whether the researcher is initially an insider or outsider, his or her presence may change the nature of the field and how people present and live their experiences. The reactive effects of the investigator's presence on the phenomenon being observed is a major methodologic dilemma for this type of research.

Liebow, in his study of African-American men who frequented urban street corners, describes the effect of his presence:

> All in all, I felt I was making steady progress. There was still plenty of suspicion and mistrust, however. At least two men who hung around Carry Out—one of them the local numbers man—had seen me dozens of times in close quarters but kept their distance and I kept mine.[8]

## Learning the ropes

Once initial entry into the context has been made, the investigator must gain access to different informants, personal stories and experiences, or types of observations. Thus gaining access remains an ongoing process that involves continued negotiation and renegotiation with members of the site or the individual or groups of individuals that are the focus of the study. This ongoing access process is part of the active work of doing fieldwork and has been referred to as "learning the ropes,"[5] "obtaining meanings," or obtaining an "intimate familiarity"[9] with the setting or study phenomena. In classical ethnography this process may appear as if the investigator is simply "hanging out." However, a range of data-gathering strategies that include watching and listening, asking questions, recording, and examining materials is brought into play to learn meanings within a setting. These strategies are purposely chosen, combined, and integrated and are all part of the unfolding process of learning about the field. The choice of strategy depends on the ebb and flow of the fieldwork situation and the particular issue on which the investigator is focused. Any data-gathering strategy is designed to move the investigator from being an outsider to an insider capable of understanding and experiencing the meanings of symbols, language, and behavior within the setting. The movement from outside to inside involves a reflexive process in which the investigator is constantly comparing and analyzing pieces of information. Data-collection strategies are designed to reveal the unknown and examine phenomena that the investigator does not understand or finds puzzling.

Let us assume you are studying families who are experiencing stress as a result of their efforts to provide daily care to a loved one with dementia. As you interview a particular family, you are certain that the family will soon choose nursing home placement for the individual with dementia. You become surprised to learn, however, that institutionalization has never been considered by the family. This example represents what Agar refers to as a "rich point."[2] A rich point represents a problem in your understanding and is the point at which you learn that your as-

sumptions are not adequate to explain how things are working. Rich points reflect the active work of the investigator that bridges the distance between his or her world and the world of the people who are the focus of the study. Learning the ropes involves using different data-collection strategies that give rise to these rich points.

## Data-gathering strategies

There are many different information-gathering strategies that are used in naturalistic inquiry. The three main strategies introduced in Chapter 15—watching and listening, asking, and examining materials—have a different purpose and structure when used in naturalistic inquiry than when used in experimental-type designs.

### Watching and listening

The process of watching and listening is often referred to as observation. In naturalistic research, observation occurs within the natural context or field. In this data-collection strategy the investigator can be either a passive observer or a participant. Passive observation involves the investigator situating himself or herself in the field or particular activity and simply observing that which occurs. On the other hand, active involvement or participation in combination with observation is defined by Lofland and Lofland as "...the process in which the investigator establishes and sustains a many-sided and relatively long term relationship with a human association in its natural setting for the purpose of developing a scientific understanding of that association.[9]

In participant observation the investigator is not a passive observer but actively engages in the research context to come to know about it. The investigator begins with broad observations to describe what is seen and then narrows the focus to discover the meaning of what has been described. In descriptive observation it is often helpful to think of the investigator as a video camera that records what it sees as it scans the boundaries of the research setting. This technique reminds the researcher that description, not interpretation, is the first step in participant observation.

Participant observation is based on the assumption that an important way of learning about a context and group of people is to participate with them in their daily activities and personally experience and observe what transpires. Participant observation has many behaviors in common with what we do in newly encountered social situations. All of us participate and observe in social situations. However, as a researcher engaged in participant observation, he or she seeks to become explicitly aware of the way things are. The researcher remains introspective and examines the "self" in the situation and his or her experiences as both the insider participating in the event and the outsider observing the actions.

Krefting describes why and how she used participant observation for her study on individuals with brain injury and their family members:

> The second fieldwork strategy was participant observation in which I, as the researcher, was both engaging in and observing the scene. In participant observation I recorded my own actions, the behaviors of others, and aspects of the

sociocultural situation. Participant observation is a particularly valuable strategy in cases of head injury, because what people say is not always reflected in what they do. In this study, I engaged in participant observation in three ways. First, I attended various meetings of family support groups and related social events. Second, I attended treatment sessions, either at schools or at day treatment centers. Third, I spent time with head-injured people and their families: together we went shopping, ate in restaurants, and visited neighbors. I made no attempt to interview professionals: my goal was to experience life from the perspective of a head-injured person.[10]

Gubrium summarizes the advantages of this approach:

> The goal is to wind up with a depiction of "the way it is," as it were, in a particular setting. ...we can represent the meanings of a setting in terms more relevant to our subjects than other methods permit. "I've been there," the participant observer likes to put it, "seen what actually happens, and this is the way it is.[11]

In one of his early ethnographies on nursing homes, Gubrium describes the multiple roles he assumed over several months as a participant observer:

> ...I took many roles, ranging from doing the rather menial work called "toileting" by people there to serving as gerontologist at

staff meetings. I attempted to spend sufficient time in the setting to establish trust, to interact with as many people as possible, and to observe the varied facts of life at Murray Manor in their natural states. [preface][12]

Some types of designs or fieldwork situations warrant less participation in the observation process. Nonparticipatory observation can be used to obtain an understanding of a natural context without the influence of the observer. For example, Runcie suggests that a student may observe the patterns of activity in a public location without interfering in the action as a basis for understanding the time and action cycle that occurs. To contrast participation with nonparticipation, Runcie suggests that the observer make himself or herself known to the persons in the location and observe the differences in the action.[13] The nonparticipant observer may record field notes while watching and listening or may choose to log observations after leaving the scene. Each has its advantages. Recording while watching may call attention to the observer, who will be more participatory in the setting. However, waiting to recall descriptions relies too much on memory.

During the fieldwork process, watching and listening tend to move from broad, descriptive observations to a narrow focus in which the observer looks for not only more descriptive data but also for specific understandings of the meanings of what he or she has observed. The degree of participation in the context and the extent of immersion vary throughout fieldwork and are based on the nature of the inquiry, access to the setting, and practical limitations.

## Asking

Asking in the form of interviewing as a method of data collection is another essential strategy that is used in most types of naturalistic inquiry. Often, asking information from key informants is the first primary data-collection strategy in phenomenology, ethnography, and grounded theory approaches. The investigator may use an asking strategy to obtain an example of a social interchange to clarify or verify the accuracy of observations or to obtain the informant's experience with and view of the phenomenon under study. Asking, unlike observation, involves direct contact with persons who are capable of providing information. Thus to collect data by asking, the researcher must establish a relationship appropriate to the level of involvement with the informant.

Asking can take many forms in naturalistic research, from an informal, open-ended conversation to focused or long, in-depth interviews.[14] The timing of the interview in the research process, the purpose of the asking, and the nature of the relationship with the informant all influence the type of asking the investigator chooses.

The most common form of asking in naturalistic design is unstructured, open-ended interviewing. This type of interviewing is particularly important in the beginning stages of fieldwork when the investigator is trying to become familiar with the language of the group and everyday occurrences. As Krefting describes, interviewing individuals with brain injuries and their family members was her first data-collection strategy and one that she continued to use throughout the fieldwork:

The first [form of data collection] was extensive nonstructured interviews with disabled persons, their families, and their friends. All interviews were taped with informed consent. I conducted over 80 interviews, which ranged from 1 to 4 hours.[10]

The open-ended interview may consist of informal conversation recorded by the investigator, or it may consist of face-to-face twosomes or small groups in which the investigator sets the context for the interview and the informants offer their knowledge.

Among the most common face-to-face interviews are the ethnographic interview[15] and life history.[16] In ethnographic interview the investigator seeks to understand culture through talking with insiders in the culture. The investigator not only attends to the content of the interview but also examines the structural and symbolic elements of the social exchange between the investigator and the informant. Contemporary ethnographic interview acknowledges that meanings may be changed and made within the context of the interview itself.[14-17]

*Life history* is a form of ethnographic interview that chronicles an individual's life within a social context.[18] The investigator elicits information not only on the important events or "turnings" in an individual's life but on the meaning of those events within the sociocultural context. This form of interviewing can also be an independent design structure.

Common forms of group questioning include focus groups and interviews with social units, such as families that contain more than one individual. In a focus group the investigator sets the parameters for the conversation. The participants, usually a group of 6 to 12 individuals, address the topic by responding to guiding probes or questions posed by the investigator. This approach is used when it is believed that the interactions and group discussions will yield more meaningful understanding than single, independent interviews.[19] Interviews with small social units are also useful in observing group dynamics and symbolic meanings exchanged among group members. In cultural descriptions, questioning social units can be most valuable in understanding the structural groups of a society. This form of interviewing can also be an independent design structure.

Although the use of structured questionnaires is primarily used in experimental-type designs, it is occasionally incorporated into certain naturalistic inquiries. Investigators have found that structured or even semistructured questionnaires can provide important insights into specific questions that emerge in the course of conducting fieldwork. The use of a standardized instrument or structured questionnaire also enables the investigator to determine the distribution of a particular phenomenon. Let us assume you are conducting a study of the meaning of breast cancer among young women. In open-ended interviewing you detect the possibility that many of the women are depressed. Some of their recurring statements suggest evidence of depressive symptomatology. To test your hunch or emerging hypothesis, you decide to administer a standardized depression scale. The scores that result provide an additional source of data that may or may not support your initial impressions. Also, the use of the scale will enable you to determine the distribution of depression among the study group.

The use of a structured set of questions or standardized scale represents a purposeful and focused approach to asking. This approach is introduced only in naturalistic inquiry when the investigator has been in the field for some time and has developed rapport and "learned the ropes."

## Four components of asking

There are four interrelated components of an asking strategy: access, description, focus, and verification.

*Access.* Asking begins with access. The investigator initially wants to meet and select one or more individuals who can articulate information about the people or phenomenon that is the focus of the study. You may ask who would be willing to speak to a stranger about himself or herself, events and personal experiences, and feelings. It is important to know the reasons someone is willing to speak to you so that you have a context to understand what they relate. Sometimes the first key informant is someone who is formally or informally designated by the cultural group to speak to an outsider. Other times the informant may be a person who is considered a deviant within the cultural group or a person who has nothing to lose by "hanging out" with a stranger. In other cases the informant may represent the person with the most knowledge, experience, or seniority in a group. In any case the investigator initially seeks to speak to a number of persons who can orient him or her to the context or field of inquiry. As the research progresses, the researcher may want to select specific individuals to be interviewed who possess distinct knowledge that is important to gain for the study.

For example, in her study of homeless, middle-aged women, Butler entered the field with broad criteria for selecting informants. These criteria included those willing to speak with her over a 3-month period and those willing and able to articulate their experiences. Much of her time was spent "hanging out" and establishing rapport with informants. Once a level of rapport and confidence was established, she was able to apply more purposeful and structured interviewing approaches.

In the ethnographic study of urban black men by Liebow, access was initially gained through "hanging out" on the street corner where men were likely to congregate. Liebow describes his first entree into the social scene as one that occurred serendipitously. On his first day in the field, he noticed a commotion and immediately went to the site where it was occurring. As a result of being there, Liebow was able to introduce himself into the culture of the street corner.[8]

*Description.* Once access is obtained, the initial goal of asking is to describe. Description begins with asking broad questions that become more focused as trends, recurrent patterns, and themes emerge. Frequently the investigator begins the asking process with a broad probe such as, "Tell me about...." In the study by Liebow, asking began informally when he invited a man whom he had met on the street corner to have coffee. Liebow clarified his task as a researcher and "...sat at the bar for several hours talking over coffee."[8]

*Focus.* Based on emerging descriptive knowledge, the researcher's asking becomes more focused and probing. Asking questions requires intense listening, a show of respect, and great interest in each aspect of what the informant is saying. The investigator wants to ask questions that yield answers that are detailed and that go into depth about what the person is feeling, thinking, and doing. If an informant shows disinterest or boredom with the interview, the investigator knows the questions are not salient or do not focus on the aspects of the experience or phenomenon important to the interviewee. There are several points to consider in developing an open-ended or semistructured interview in which you want to focus on details and elicit rich description (Box 17-2).

***Verification.*** As the investigator gains an understanding of the context, asking strategies serve the purpose of verifying impressions and clarifying details of the setting. Verification is the process of checking the accuracy of impressions with informants.

Throughout fieldwork, the interview process may occur in one session, several sessions, or many sessions. It is usually combined with one or more of the other primary data-collection strategies of observation and review of existing materials. Of no surprise, the decision about length and frequency of using asking strategies is dependent on the nature and scope of the query, the purpose of the interviews, and the practical limitations that influence the conduct of the study.

## Examining materials

Examining materials such as records, diaries, journals, and letters is another essential data-collection strategy in contemporary naturalistic research. This is particularly the case in health and human service research where written records, such as charts, progress notes, or minutes, are routinely maintained as a natural part of the context.

Similar to watching, listening, and asking, review of materials usually begins with a broad examination of items. Then the investigator moves to a more focused evaluation to explore recurring themes and emerging patterns. Knowledge about what materials are available may occur at any point in the research process. It is not unusual to plan to examine objects and records at the beginning of a project. Let us assume that you are interested in determining the extent to which a behavioral program for persons with mental retardation improves social behavior in sheltered work environments. You may begin by observing workplace behavior. However, there are times throughout the day when you cannot observe. You may examine

**Box 17-2** | **Guidelines for obtaining rich description**

- Do not use questions that yield "yes" or "no" responses.
- Ask informants for examples to explain their statements.
- Obtain more details from the examples by asking specific follow-up questions.
- Use follow-up questions such as, "Is this how it always happens?" "How typical is this for you?" "What would have happened if...?" "How did you feel when...?"

progress notes written by the sheltered workshop staff as a way of obtaining additional information about behavior. These notes may help you understand behavioral patterns at different times of the day, as well as the perceptions of staff. Their perceptions will be analyzed in light of your own observations and the other forms of information you obtain.

To access written documents, the investigator must obtain appropriate consent, even if he or she is an insider. For nonobtrusive data collection, consent may not be desirable or possible. The primary aim of nonobtrusively collecting information will be to keep the research role covert. Consider the researcher who is asked to evaluate the impact of a community-based intervention that is designed to decrease drug use in a particular neighborhood. One indicator of drug use in the area is the presence of drug paraphernalia, such as vials and needles, that are strewn, especially in a small, centrally located park. Examining the contents of the trash and the grounds of the community park may shed light on substance abuse patterns. The community members may be reluctant to report drug abuse behaviors. These observations may provide the most accurate way to determine the impact of the intervention. Positive changes in the environment may provide an important source of evidence that the intervention is having an impact.

Krefting describes the range of materials she used as a data-collection strategy:

> The third fieldwork strategy was a review of pertinent nontraditional documents. These included human interest stories from local newspapers, newsletters from the National Head Injury Foundation and state organizations, brochures describing new treatment programs, and personal documents provided by informants. These personal documents were perhaps the richest source of data. One such document was a diary that had been kept for 2 years. Used as a memory prompt, it detailed all the major events in the informant's life. I also read several testimonials, or what people called head injury stories, prepared by the informants, and even the lyrics of a song describing the head injury experience.[10]

## Recording information

While in the field, there are several different strategies an investigator can use to record the information that is obtained by watching and listening, asking, or reviewing materials. Recording information is an important aspect of collecting information. The record of information serves as a data set that is analyzed by the investigator in the process of doing fieldwork and then more formally after leaving the field. An investigator must decide how he or she will record information while watching and listening, asking, and reviewing material. Usually, multiple recording strategies are used in fieldwork. The decision about which strategy to use is based on the purpose of the study and the resources of the investigator. Let us examine three primary mechanisms for recording information.

### Field notes

*Field notes* are a basic way in which investigators record information. This type of recording has been a popular topic in the research literature on naturalistic inquiry and has been described in many ways. Usually, field notes have two basic components: recordings of events, observations, and occurrences, and recordings of the investigator's own impressions of events, personal feelings, hunches, and expectations. Some investigators separate these two components. They maintain one set of field notes that carefully document major field activities and events. In a separate notebook, they keep a running account or personal diary of their own feelings and personal dilemmas encountered in the field. There are numerous formats that are suggested in the literature for recording descriptive field notes. According to Spradley, a matrix design can be used to examine the interaction of persons, places, and objects.[21] Other formats are equally useful. Lofland and Lofland suggest recording description and bracketing impressions and interpretation within the context of the description.[9] We have found it useful to use a stenographer's pad on which the left side is used to describe and the right is used to record the investigator's immediate thoughts, impressions, hunches, or questions as the observation or interview occurs. The ability to separate a description from interpretation is important.

Krefting describes her approach to field notes in this way:

>...I prepared field notes using the short-note technique of recording data immediately after concluding interviews. These notes contained my perceptions regarding the interviews and the activities observed. General impressions of interviews, particularly of the participants' moods, were noted, as was interactive data. ...I kept a field log, or diary, that recorded the thoughts, feelings, ideas and hypotheses generated by my contact with informants. This log also contained my questions, problems, and frustrations concerning the overall research process.[10]

There has also been discussion in the literature as to when to record field notes. This decision is an important consideration in doing fieldwork and will depend on the nature of the inquiry. Some investigators find it useful to keep a pencil and pad available at all times during participant observation activities. Bluebond-Langner, in her study of children dying of leukemia, initially found it useful to "hang out" in the hallways of the hospital with pad in hand to record as she observed staff and children interacting.[22] This action differentiated her from the medical staff in such a way that was acceptable to patients and staff. Other investigators find the act of recording while participating in an event too intrusive and recommend that documentation occurs at the conclusion of the day and in privacy. If the investigator waits until the end of the day, however, he or she runs the risk of depending on long-term memory and losing details that may later prove to be important. Bluebond-Langner found it best to record her interactions with children immediately after each contact rather than during her visits or at the end of the day.

Field notes are only one way of recording information and are used in conjunction with other mechanisms.

## Audiotape

Audiotaping is a fundamental data-recording strategy in naturalistic inquiry that is primarily used when conducting face-to face interviews. It is especially important to use audiotaping when conducting an open-ended interview. In such interviews, informants provide long, detailed accounts that are usually difficult for the investigator to write verbatim. When using an audiotape, it is important to test the equipment before an interview to make certain that it will adequately record both your voice and that of the respondent. Sometimes it is best to use a microphone. Also, you should plan to have a back-up tape recorder in case there is equipment failure during the interview. You need to plan for every contingency so you do not run the risk of losing data.

Let us assume you audiotape an interview. Your next step will be to carefully label the tape and make a back-up. You will need to transcribe the audiotape. Transcription is an important step that involves typing the entire audiotape in a word processing file. In transcribing, you will need to decide if every utterance should be recorded, such as "uh hum" or laughter. You will need to decide how pauses and silences will be noted in the transcript. Transcription takes time; it is estimated that every hour of dense interview can take 6 to 8 hours of transcribing. After transcribing an audiotape, you need to compare the written record with the tape to ensure accuracy. Finally, you will want to listen to the tape to examine the nuances in vocalization, as well as read the transcript to analyze the narrative.

There are several considerations in using audiotapes. First, you need to consider whether audiotaping will be intrusive in your field setting and prevent informants from expressing private thoughts. Second, when using an audiotape, informants must be informed that their conversations with you are being recorded. In most cases, obtaining consent from study participants is not a problem. However, if you are studying issues that are highly sensitive, such as sexual practices of teenagers or drug use among business men, there may be concerns expressed by informants. You will need to explain your plan for maintaining confidentiality and decide who will have access to the audiotapes and where the tapes will be kept. Also, it is important to inform research participants that they can request that audiotaping cease at any point in the interview process. The third consideration in using audiotapes is their analysis. In the beginning phases of fieldwork, it is important to immediately transcribe tapes after completing an interview. Reviewing these early tapes informs the initial development of analytical categories, subsequent data-collection efforts, and type of follow-up questions that need to be pursued.

## Videotape

Videotaping is another data-recording strategy that is being increasingly used in naturalistic inquiry.[23] Videotaping is particularly useful in studies that focus on interactions between individuals, such as a study on health professional and patient interactions or when observations of both nonverbal and verbal behaviors are the focus of the research study. In participant observation the investigator is involved with both nonverbal and verbal exchanges and may have difficulty monitoring the details of actions. Videotaping enables the investigator to record such details of behaviors that may not be detected at the time of the observation. With videotaping, the investigator obtains a permanent record that can be viewed and reviewed multiple times.

As in audiotaping, there are many considerations and decisions that need to be made when using videotaping. Obviously, familiarity with the equipment and the ability to manage it efficiently in the field setting is important. Also, the issue of reactivity needs to be considered. Do individuals monitor their behavior because of the camera? There are different strategies that investigators use to reduce discomfort and reactivity. Some investigators recommend that the camera be introduced into the field environment before recording the events that are of interest. Setting up the camera but not turning it on for several occasions can reduce fear or reluctance of participants to be videotaped. Another consideration is the angle of the setting and the behaviors that are captured by the camera. The videotape may capture only a set of activities that are performed in front of the lens and thus other movements and exchanges that occur simultaneously but outside its range of vision will be lost.

As in audiotaping, the investigator must carefully review each videotape many times. Initial review of a videotape helps inform the investigator as to how to proceed in the field and which questions to pursue. After leaving the field, formal analysis of the videotapes may proceed frame by frame if the investigator has the appropriate equipment. The use and analysis of tapes can become quite complex, time-consuming, and expensive. It can be used in combination with other techniques, such as participant observation, interviewing, and audiotaping.

## Accuracy in data collection

At this point, you may be asking how an investigator involved with naturalistic inquiry becomes confident that the information he or she has obtained is accurate and reflects empirical reality. This concern has been labeled by Guba and Lincoln as the issue of trustworthiness.[24] After all, the investigator wants to obtain information that correctly captures the experiences, meanings, and events of the field. How are we to know if the final interpretation is not simply a fabrication of the investigator or a reflection of his or her own personal biases and presuppositions? There are a number of techniques that are used in naturalistic inquiry that are designed to enhance the truth value of the data collection and initial analytical efforts of the investigator.

## Multiple data gatherers

One technique used in naturalistic inquiry is the involvement of two or more investigators in the data-gathering and analytical process. The old adage, "Two heads are better than one," is also true in naturalistic inquiry. If possible, it is useful for two or more investigators to observe and record their own field notes independently. This technique checks the accuracy of the observations; more than one pair of eyes and ears are examining and recording the same context. Careful training of both observers is essential to ensure that skilled recording and reporting are accomplished by each observer and that all investigators understand the purpose and intent of the study.

Consider an investigator who is studying the culture of a group of hospitalized adolescents. The purpose of such a study may be to determine the norms of the culture as they emerge within the boundaries of the hospital unit. Using the technique of multiple observers, two or more investigators will keep field notes independently of one another and will initially analyze these data independently. The investigators will then meet to compare notes and impressions and reconcile any differences through in-depth discourse about the data set. Not only are multiple observers used, but accurate data collection is also enhanced by multiple analyzers.

## Triangulation

Another technique that increases the accuracy of information gathering is called *triangulation*.[22] Triangulation of data collection refers to using more than one strategy to collect information that bears on the same phenomenon. For example, the use of observation with interviewing, examination of materials, or both is characteristic of triangulation in traditional naturalistic research. More recently, quantitative measures and analytical techniques such as content analysis have also been introduced to provide the meaning of a phenomenon from a different angle. In triangulating the investigator collects information from different sources to derive and validate a particular finding. The investigator may observe an event and combine observations with written materials to develop a comprehensive and accurate description.

## Saturation

*Saturation* is another way in which the investigator ensures rigor in conducting a naturalistic study. Saturation refers to the point at which an investigator has obtained sufficient information from which to obtain an understanding of the phenomenon. As previously discussed, when the information gathered by the investigator does not provide new insights or understandings, it is a signal that saturation has been achieved. If you can guess what your respondent is going to do or say in a particular situation, you have probably obtained saturation. As in the case of *Tally's Corner,* Liebow's prolonged engagement in the field ensured that the investigator obtained a point of saturation.[8]

However, lengthy immersion in the field may not be practical for service provider researchers who perhaps have limited time and funds to support such an endeavor. DePoy and Archer, for example, were constrained by time and money in collecting data in the nursing home study.[6] They therefore had to use other strategies such as triangulation to heighten the accuracy and rigor of their understandings and interpretations. They also used random observation as a strategy to ensure saturation. In this technique an investigator randomly selects times throughout the investigative period to increase the likelihood of obtaining a total picture of the phenomenon of interest. DePoy and Archer, for example, selected random times during the week, including morning, afternoon, and night, to observe. In this way they approximated full immersion in the culture of the nursing home. Through random observation, it is theoretically possible to sample the total cycle of the phenomenon of interest.

## Member checks

*Member checks* is a technique whereby the investigator checks out his or her assumptions with one or more informants. In the DePoy and Archer study, once the theme of "disconnectedness" emerged from the data set, it was verified with informants by asking them if the investigators' interpretations were accurate. Similarly, Wuerst and Stern verified the meanings that they extracted from their data with the participating families.[25] This type of affirmation decreases the potential for the imposition of the investigator's bias where it does not belong. This technique is important and is used throughout the data-collection process to confirm the truth value or accuracy of the investigator's observations and interpretations as they emerge. The informants' ability to correct the vision of their stories is critical to this technique.

The importance of routinely using member checks is highlighted by Frank's life history of a congenital amputee. In this study, Frank observed several self-care activities of Diane De-Vries, a woman with quadrilateral limb deficiencies. After recording her impressions, Frank asked Ms. DeVries to read the description and comment. Diane DeVries responded to Frank's written observations:

> Just a few technical corrections. I have a stool which enables me to get from the floor back up to my chair. At that time, my bed just happened to have been on the floor. I can get in and out of any bed— from wc (wheelchair) to bed and reverse— from bed to floor (not falling out! HA) but not the reverse.
>
> I balance a glass between my face and arm—if it were my shoulder I would die of thirst. Picture that, and you'll see what I mean. No one needs to place it there. I

can pick up a glass, cup, or can and drink it myself.

> I **do** and **can** brush my teeth. I place the brush in my mouth and move it with both arms—for the uppers—with my right arm and tongue for everywhere else. No, I cannot floss.
>
> Doors. I can **open** any door as long as I can get to the doorknob, which I turn with my arm and chin. I cannot close a door behind me (except, of course, for a sliding door).[26]

This passage provides great insight into the spirit and personality of Ms. DeVries. It also indicates the gross inaccuracies of the investigator's observational impressions. Some of Frank's initial observations, such as the transfer from chair to bed, were obviously serendipitous. In other words, her observation did not reflect the daily routine DeVries typically followed; thus Frank's conclusions were inaccurate. Frank increased the credibility of her understandings of self-care performance and adaptation to disability by having her informant check and correct the accuracy of her account.

## Reflexivity

Although investigator bias cannot be eliminated, it can be identified and examined in terms of its impact on data-collection processes and interpretative accounts. *Reflexivity* refers to the process of self-examination. In reflexive analysis the investigator examines his or her own perspective and determines how this perspective has influenced not only what is learned but also how it is learned. Langer, in a report on her phenomenological study of the experience of being a woman with HIV or AIDS, reflects on and evaluates her own perspective. "I do not know what it is [like]to be HIV positive, to have AIDS. I know something of what it is to care for someone who has HIV/AIDS in my role as nurse practitioner, health professional. What strikes me are the first four letters of 'health'—H-E-A-L. How do I do that when I know so little? Late at night, after the day is done, feelings and thoughts flood in, as I reflect on what I have learned, how I am taught by my patients."[26]

Through reflection, investigators evaluate how understanding and knowledge are developed within the context of their own thinking processes. Frank, for example, honestly described her biased and initial perspective as she entered into a study of the life of Diane DeVries. She first met DeVries as a student at UCLA in 1976 and explains:

> As I observed this woman,...I imagined that she lived at home with her parents and would probably never marry or have sexual experiences. In other words, the question arose, "What kind of life could such an individual have in our society?[27]

This initial broad query reflected Frank's limited understanding of the lives of individuals with disabilities. Through the life history approach, Frank's query became reformulated to a quest to understand the process of adaptation to severe congenital disability and how that adaptational process reflected the individual's own sense of cultural normalcy as a member of American society.

A personal diary or method of noting personal feelings, moods, attitudes, and reactions to each step of the data-collection process is a critical aspect of the process in naturalistic inquiry. These personal notes form the backdrop from which to understand how a particular meaning or analysis may have emerged at the data-collection stage. Fetterman suggests that keeping a personal diary is an effective quality-control mechanism.[28]

As an insider in the social scene of the nursing home, Archer consistently assessed how her relationship to the residents and staff influenced her focus and her interpretation of the data.[6]

Krefting's ethnography of 21 persons with moderate head injuries highlights the significance of personal diary keeping as an analytical component to fieldwork. In this study, Krefting used a variety of data-collection strategies, including nonstructured interviews, participant observation, and review of artifact materials to examine the life experiences of persons disabled by head injury and the life experiences of their family members. A major theme that emerged as a life-organizing perspective for persons with brain injury and their family members was the process of concealment. In the following passage, Krefting discusses how her personal notes reinforced the theme of concealment and solidified this component of her analysis:

> At first I believed that the experience of head injury was "not all that bad," as I noted in my field diary. What I mistook for the real experience was one largely concealed by the disabled persons and their

families. It took many months for them to reveal some of the more meaningful but tragic aspects of their lives.[10]

## Audit trail

Another way to increase rigor is to maintain an *audit trail* as the researcher proceeds analytically. Lincoln and Guba suggest leaving a path of thinking and action processes so that others can clearly follow the logic and manner in which knowledge was developed. In this approach the investigator is responsible not only for reporting results but for explaining how the results are obtained. By explaining the thinking and action processes of an inquiry, the investigator allows others to agree or disagree with each analytical decision and to confirm, refute, or modify interpretations.

## Peer debriefing

One technique to ensure that data analysis represents the phenomena under investigation is the use of more than one investigator as a participant in the analytical process. Throughout a co-investigated study, researchers frequently conduct analytical actions independent of one another to determine the extent of their agreement. Synthesis of analysis and examination of areas of disagreement shed additional understandings on the research query. In the case where only one investigator engages in a project, he or she will often ask an external analyzer to function in the capacity of a co-investigator. In some cases a panel of experts or advisors is used to evaluate the analytical process. This form of *peer debriefing* provides an opportunity for the investigator to reflect on other possible competing interpretations offered in the peer review process and in this way strengthens the legitimacy of the final interpretation. Wuerst and Stern used peer debriefing at multiple time intervals throughout their study to modify and affirm their interpretations.[23]

## Summary

The main purpose of the action process of data collection in naturalistic inquiry is to obtain information that incrementally leads to the investigator's ability to reveal a story, a set of descriptive principles or understandings, hypotheses, or theories. Each piece of information is a building block that the investigator inductively collects, analyzes, and puts together to accomplish one or more of the purposes just stated. One can think of a funnel in which the researcher begins with a broad query that gradually narrows as data collection proceeds and the context becomes clearer to the investigator.

In naturalistic research, data collection and analysis go hand in hand, and data collection continues to unfold dynamically as analysis reveals further direction for information gathering. The investigator is the main vehicle for data collection, although his or her involvement may vary among design strategies. To enhance the accuracy of data collection, multiple observers and triangulation of collection methods are two action processes often used by naturalistic investigators.

The action process of data collection for the naturalistic researcher involves the use and combination of three basic methods to gather information: watching and listening, asking, and examining materials. Watching and listening occurs in the form of observation and ranges on a continuum from full to no participation in the context that is being observed. Asking also varies in structure, with interviewing as the primary asking process in naturalistic design. Examination of materials occurs in an inductive way and is intended to reveal patterns related to the phenomena under study. Naturalistic data collection occurs along with analysis and moves from broad information gathering to more focused collection of information. The combination of these approaches is critical to obtain breadth and depth of analysis.

As descriptive data are collected to illuminate the answer to what, where, and when, the next step in the process is to focus data-collection efforts based on the ongoing analytical process. The process of information collection continues with why and how questions. In ethnography this effort is called thick description,[4] or focused observation,[20] in which meanings are sought.

Focused observation hones in on examining the patterns and themes that emerge from descriptive information. The investigator may choose to examine one pattern at a time or may focus on more than one. The investigator narrows the scope of inquiry to themes and the interaction between patterns and themes while remaining open to further discovery. In general, collection strategies provide information that answers the where, who, how, when, and why questions. Answers to these five questions yield description, understanding of the context, occurrences within the context, and timing.

## Exercises

1. Select a public place, such as a shopping mall, outpatient clinic, or public transportation station. Use nonparticipatory observation and then participatory observation to determine behavioral patterns that characterize the human experience in each setting. Compare your experiences using both forms of observation and what you learned from each.

2. Conduct an open-ended interview with a colleague to obtain an understanding of career choices and his or her career path. What other information-gathering techniques can you use to understand this phenomenon?

3. Select a research article that uses naturalistic inquiry. Identify the information-gathering techniques used and determine the ethical issues involved for each technique.

### References

1. Hodge R, Kress G: *Social semiotics,* Ithaca, NY, 1988, Cornell University Press.
2. Agar MH: *The professional stranger: an informal introduction to ethnography,* ed 2, San Diego, Calif, 1996, Academic Press.
3. Fetterman DL: A walk through the wilderness: learning to find your way. In Shaffir W, Stebbins R, editors: *Experiencing fieldwork: an inside view of qualitative research,* Newbury Park, Calif, 1991, Sage.
4. Geertz C: *Interpretation of cultures,* New York, 1973, Basic Books.
5. Shaffir W, Stebbins R, editors: *Experiencing fieldwork: an inside view of qualitative research,* Newbury Park, Calif, 1991, Sage.
6. DePoy E, Archer L: The meaning of quality of life to nursing home residents: a naturalistic investigation, *Topics Geriatr Rehabil* 7:64-74, 1992.
7. Stearns CA: Physicians in restraints: HMO gatekeepers and their perceptions of demanding patients, *Qualitative Health Res* 1:326-348, 1991.
8. Liebow E: *Tally's corner,* Boston, 1967, Little, Brown.
9. Lofland J, Lofland L: *Analyzing social settings: a guide to qualitative research,* Belmont, Calif, 1984, Wadsworth.
10. Krefting L: Reintegration into the community after head injury: the results of an ethnographic study, *Occup Ther J Res* 9:67-83, 1989.
11. Gubrium J: Recognizing and analyzing local cultures. In Shaffir W, Stebbins R, editors: *Experiencing fieldwork: an inside view of qualitative research,* Newbury Park, Calif, 1991, Sage.
12. Gubrium, J: *Living and dying at Murray Manor,* New York, 1975, St Martin's Press.
13. Runcie JF: *Experiencing social research,* Homewood, Ill, 1976, Dorsey Press.
14. McCraken G: *The long interview,* Newbury Park, Calif, 1988, Sage.
15. Spradley JP: *The ethnographic interview,* New York, 1979, Holt, Rinehart & Winston.
16. Merton RK, Fiske M, Kendall P: *The focused interview: a manual of problems and procedures,* New York, 1956, Free Press.
17. Van Maanen J, editor: *Qualitative methodology,* Newbury Park, Calif, 1983, Sage.
18. Langness LL, Frank G: *Lives: an anthropological approach to biography,* Novato, Calif, 1981, Chandler & Sharp.
19. Krueger R: *Focus groups: a practical guide for applied research,* Newbury Park, Calif, 1988, Sage.
20. Butler S: *Homeless women* (dissertation), Seattle, 1991, University of Washington.
21. Spradley JP: *Participant observation,* New York, 1980, Holt, Rinehart & Winston.
22. Bluebond-Langner, M: *The private worlds of dying children,* Princeton, NJ, 1978, Princeton University Press.
23. Bottorff, Joan L: Using videotaped recordings in qualitative research. In Morse JM: *Critical issues in qualitative research methods,* Thousand Oaks, Calif, 1994, Sage.
24. Guba EG: Criteria for assessing the trustworthiness of naturalistic inquiries, *Educ Commun Technol J* 29:75-92, 1981.
25. Wuerst J, Stern PN: Empowerment in primary health care: the challenge for nurses, *Qualitative Health Res* 1:80-99, 1991.
26. Langner SR: The experience of being a woman with HIV/AIDS. In Munhall PL (editor): *In women's experience,* New York, 1995, National League for Nursing Press.
27. Frank G: Life history model of adaptation to disability: the case of a congenital amputee, *Soc Sci Med* 19:639-645, 1984.
28. Fetterman DL: *Ethnography step by step,* Newbury Park, Calif, 1989, Sage.

# Chapter 18
## Preparing data for analysis

**Key terms**    Codebook
Database management
Data reduction
Memoing
Narrative
Raw data file
Transcription
Variable label

**Approaches in experimental-type research**
**Approaches in naturalistic inquiry**
**Summary**

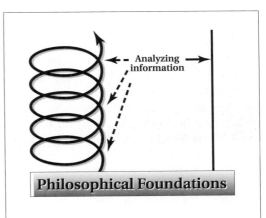

Thus far we have discussed the different strategies researchers use to collect information. Once you begin the data-gathering process, you will quickly obtain a massive amount of information. In experimental-type research, even a small survey study may yield over 100 variables for analysis. In naturalistic inquiry, a 1-hour interview may yield up to 50 pages of single-spaced type. Organizing all this information, whether it takes numerical or narrative form, is an important action that is not usually discussed or written by researchers. Most researchers learn to manage data by participating in the process as mentored students. However, there are definite actions in which researchers across both traditions engage to prepare information for analysis that can be described and learned. This chapter discusses the action process of preparing and managing information in the research traditions.

## Approaches in experimental-type research

If you are conducting an experimental-type study, you will be primarily interested in obtaining a quantitative understanding of phenomenon. Your data will be numerical. The analysis of these numbers will be an action process that is performed after completing all data collection. At the conclusion of the action process of collecting data, you will have numerical responses to your questionnaires, interviews, and observations. Consider a somewhat small study involving a survey of 100 students in a college of health professions. Assume the survey is designed to examine student satisfaction with the quality of health profession education. The survey will likely include a number of background questions such as the sex, level of education, financial assistance, marital status, and living arrangement of students. The survey will also include some type of scale that measures satisfaction with education, as well as a series of questions about other aspects of college life. As you will see, this type of study may have

from 50 to 100 items or variables that will be measured. In a study involving 100 students, this may represent a total of 10,000 data points that will be submitted to statistical analysis. Even in a small study, the amount of information obtained can be enormous and require the assistance of computer technology.

After collecting all this information, what does the researcher do next? The primary action process for experimental-type researchers is to prepare and organize the data for statistical analysis. The researcher follows six basic steps to prepare the numerical information for entry into a computer program from which statistical analysis will proceed (Box 18-1).

First, the researcher must examine each interview or data collection form to check for missing information, double-coded responses, or unclear demarcations of responses. This information reflects possible interviewer errors that must be corrected before entering the numerical values into a computer program.

Second, the researcher must label each variable on the data-collection instrument using

---

**Box 18-1** | **Steps in preparing data for statistical analysis**

- Check data collection instrument for accuracy and completeness of information
- Label each variable on instrument
- Assign variable labels to computer locations
- Develop codebook and control file
- Enter data using double verification or other quality control procedures
- Clean raw data files
- Develop summative scores

a convention specified by the statistical package used. For example, Statistical Package for the Social Sciences (SPSS) is a popular, menu-driven, statistical computer program that runs on a personal computer. In SPSS, *variable labels* must not exceed eight characters, and the first character cannot be a number or a symbol. The labeling of a variable is usually logical and straightforward.

Third, the researcher must also decide the order in which the variables will be entered into a data-entry computer program. Most researchers use the convention of placing each observation along an 80- to 120-column format (Table 18-1).

Usually each subject or research participant is assigned a unique identification number that is located in the first 10 columns of a line or row, depending on the length of the case identifier. If there is more than one line of data for a case, the subject identification number is repeated for each row of data. In Table 18-1 each number represents a response to a data-collection

instrument, in this case a closed-ended questionnaire. These numbers are often referred to as a raw data set and form the foundation from which the experimental-type researcher performs statistical manipulations. A data set merely consists of all the numbers obtained through data collection, which are organized in the data-entry program according to the format designed by the researcher. Data are usually entered in the order in which the items are sequenced on the data-collection form.

In Table 18-1, for example, the first column on each line refers to the subject's group assignment (i.e., experimental or control group). Columns 02 through 04 refer to the personal identification number. Column 05 indicates the subject's gender (1 = male; 2 = female). Column 06 is blank, and 07 refers to the line number.

Fourth, the researcher establishes a computer-based control file that consists of a list of the variable labels. Also, a written record is generated that is usually referred to as a *codebook* or data-definition record. This written

| Table 18-1 | Example of raw data set |
|---|---|
| 10291 | 1782312333828288384234343501293124224 |
| 10291 | 2221132000021231 |
| 10291 | 301924302    010212212736572524761 |
| 20822 | 1572122211272931888398479389842654746 |
| 20822 | 26341523465200123543654151425342563426234323 |
| 20822 | 368013223    654272342546546545212 |
| 12311 | 2234212352364246525641564265346235 |
| 12311 | 181223555251661726355527435441325423 |
| 12311 | 381726357    647652763674500000000 |
| 21071 | 183211221125356456253341324324342323 |
| 21071 | 21224244242424423131332252525251111122344 |
| 21071 | 318723648    723461987234687112333 |

record is a hard copy of the variable labels and the range or values they represent. The fifth step involves entering the numerical values into a computer-based program by a scanner, if you have the technology, or by manual entry. Although there is a variety of data-entry programs, they are basically similar. For small data sets (e.g., those under 50 variables), data entry can be conducted using a spreadsheet or *database management* program such as Lotus 1-2-3, Microsoft Excel, FoxPro, or Microsoft Access, to name just a few of the more commonly used programs. For large data sets, it is preferable to use a computer-based program that has been specifically developed for the purpose of entering data. Most data-entry computer programs enable the investigator to check for out-of-range codes, and some programs provide double verification. These are important quality-control features. Wild and out-of-range codes refer to errors in entering data in which characters or numbers entered in the program do not reflect the possible numerical scores assigned to the variable. For example, let us assume the only response to a question regarding marital status is 1 for not married or 2 for married. The data-entry operator, however, inadvertently types a 3. The data-entry program will signal the operator that an error has been made. Double verification refers to the process of entering the same set of data into the computer program on two separate occasions. The program checks each numerical entry against itself. The program either alerts the key operator when a discrepancy between two entries occurs, or it allows the operator to inspect the two entries visually to determine discrepancies. When this occurs, the keyed responses must be manually

checked against the original hard copy of the instrument to determine the correct value.

The sixth step involves a process of "cleaning" the data that have been entered into the computer. Cleaning data is an action process whereby the investigator checks the inputted data set to ensure that all data have been accurately transcribed from the data-collection instrument to the computer-entry program. This action step is essential to determine the extent of missing information, to ensure that each response has been correctly coded, and to confirm that no errors were made in entering the numerical scores into the computer. For example, if the age of a subject was entered in a data-entry program as 27 years rather than the true age of 57, this error would certainly skew understanding of the mean age and the range of ages represented in the study sample. In the chapter on data collection, we discuss the possibility of having either random or systematic errors. Data entry represents a possible source of random error.

Researchers use many techniques to clean data. One important way to inspect the data for errors is computing the frequencies of responses for each variable in the data set. For example, assume you use a scale to ascertain the level of dependence in basic activities of daily living. The possible responses for each self-care item range from 4 for completely independent to 1 for completely dependent. When you compute the frequencies for each self-care item, you discover that "bathing" has two responses with a value of 5. You will immediately know by inspecting the frequencies that the data are not correct. You will need to identify the subject identification numbers of the two individuals with the out-of-range values; you will need to manually check their interview forms to determine the source of the error. The error may have been inadvertently made by the interviewer or operator.

In addition to checking frequencies, some researchers manually check a random number of lines of data against the original hard copy of the data-collection instrument. Still others use the above methods in combination with printing *raw data files* sorted both by line and subject identification numbers. These printouts allow the researcher to visually inspect for misaligned data, as well as wild and out-of-range codes.

As you can see, there are a number of ways of ensuring quality data and minimizing the possibility of random error at this stage of the research process. At the minimum it is important for the investigator to conduct a careful and systematic examination of the raw data set and the initial frequencies of key variables. Although this examination is often a time-consuming task, it minimizes random error and increases the accuracy of the data set. You should not perform any statistical manipulations until the data have been thoroughly cleaned and are error free.

The final action to prepare data for analysis involves reducing the vast quantity of information to general categories, summated scores, or single numerical indicators. As you can see from the small excerpt of a larger data set (see Table 18-1), most studies generate an enormous amount of information. One of the first statistical actions taken by experimental-type researchers is to summarize information. Index development and descriptive statistical indicators, such as the mean, mode, median, standard deviation, variance, and other statistically derived values, reduce and summarize individual responses and scores. This summary process is often referred to as *data reduction* and is discussed in greater detail in Chapter 19. These scores are submitted to other types of statistical manipulations to test hypotheses and make inferences and associations.

Before the popular use of desktop computers, only huge data sets were analyzed on mainframe computers. However, in the past decade, superior hardware and software have made computerized data analysis available to most researchers. There are many statistical analytic programs on the market, some more user-friendly than others and some more capable of complex computations. Among the most popular and powerful are SPSS, (McGraw-Hill, New York) and SYSTAT (Systat, Evanston, Ill.). SPSS is a software program that can run many types of statistical computations on large data sets. It is based on BASIC, a computer programming language; the user must know exact commands to successfully use it. SYSTAT is another powerful program and is menu driven. In SYSTAT the user may select a statistical computation from a menu; he or she is then prompted with a series of branches to perform the next step. Each program has its advantages and disadvantages. There are many other statistical programs, and we advise that you carefully select one that fits your data analytical needs with the assistance of a statistician. Even with the use of computers, it is necessary to have a conceptual understanding of the range of available statistics.

Quantitative approaches to the analysis of data are well developed (see Chapter 19). Each statistical test has been developed and refined as computer technologies and the field of mathematics have advanced. There are clear and explicit rules as to when, how, and under what circumstances specific statistical analyses can be used. Because data must fit specific criteria for any analytical technique, you must be concerned with how you intend to measure concepts. As discussed in Chapter 16, the measurement process will determine the type of data you will obtain and, subsequently, the type of analyses you can perform.

## Approaches in naturalistic inquiry

If your research involves naturalistic inquiry, your approach to data management, data cleaning, and data reduction and analysis is different from that used in experimental-type research. First, you will be primarily interested in obtaining a qualitative understanding of phenomenon. Your data will be primarily *narratives* but can also include other types of data, such as artifacts or video frames of nonverbal behaviors. Second, the process of analysis will be on-going and linked to the process of collecting information. The integration of the actions of data collection and analysis is a critical aspect of naturalistic designs and is referred to as the interactive process. Third, you will be managing the information you obtain as you conduct fieldwork and engage in the process of collecting information.

The analytical strategies employed by researchers who use naturalistic inquiry are varied and explored in Chapter 20. Most, but not all, analytical strategies are designed to transform the volumes of interview transcripts, audiotapes, videotapes, fieldnotes, and other written and observational information into meaningful categories, taxonomies, or themes that explain the meaning and underlying patterns of the

phenomenon of interest. Other analytical strategies are designed to explicate the essence of personal experiences as told to the investigator. As discussed in previous chapters, the information gathered in the different forms of naturalistic inquiry is not numerical but rather verbal and nonverbal manifestations that have been transcribed from a variety of information gathering techniques and sources.

As shown in Chapters 15 and 17, there are many sources of data in naturalistic inquiry and, likewise, many different analytical strategies. Furthermore, each data source and analytical approach requires a somewhat different approach to managing the information that is gathered. For example, information that is derived from audiotapes is usually transcribed into written text or narrative. On the other hand, data involving videotape are visually examined and usually marked in terms of frames for repeated reviewing and interpretation. The most frequent approach to analysis, however, involves the written word or narrative; thus the transcription of audiotapes from interviews or fieldnotes is an important aspect of most types of designs involving naturalistic inquiry.

Let us examine the process of managing the voluminous amount of narrative information that is obtained in a naturalistic study. *Transcription* is the first step in analyzing narrative and involves transforming an audiotape into a verbatim written record. Transcription can be a time-consuming activity. You can expect an average of 6 to 10 hours of typing for each hour of interview tape, depending on the clarity of the tape, the density of the interview, and the typist's familiarity with the task. Explicit directions need to be given to a typist on how to handle the components of the audiotape. For example, you may wish to record the number and length of pauses, silences, laughter, or repetitive phrases such as "uh huh." The decision as to what to transcribe will depend on the purpose of the study. After the completion of a transcription, you must check its accuracy; you will want to ensure that the typed version accurately represents the audiotape verbatim. In checking the transcription, you will also need to resolve misspellings and missing sections attributed to poor taping. After cleaning the transcription, the investigator must immerse himself or herself in the data; that is, the transcription must be read multiple times to begin the analytical process. In the initial stages of any type of fieldwork, most investigators transcribe all audiotapes. As fieldwork progresses, however, the investigator may transcribe a random selection from each audiotape or a sample for complete transcription.[1] Random selection is particularly useful for large-scale projects, such as in the tradition of classical ethnography, where the investigator increasingly selects which audiotaped interviews are to be transcribed as the study unfolds.

The following short excerpt (Box 18-2) is taken from more than 100 pages of narrative derived from a transcription of a 2-hour audiotape. The audiotape was generated by a focus group discussion involving six occupational therapists who were practicing in rehabilitation hospitals in Pennsylvania.[2] In the focus group, therapists were asked to review a case vignette that involved an older man in rehabilitation after experiencing a cerebrovascular accident (CVA). Therapists were specifically asked to discuss the process by which they would select and provide instruction to this patient in the use of assistive devices.

**Box 18-2** Excerpts from transcript

- Ms. K: I personally would probably start off trying to figure out where his left upper extremity was and its recovery and seeing if I could work with that to get it more functional first versus whether I would go ahead right away and start issuing the suction things that would stabilize so that he could use his right hand.
- Mr. S: The things that struck me are that, one, he had a stroke. So I started going through a list of equipment that he might use. But then a 67-year-old Italian gentleman from south Philadelphia starts to put other things in my mind. The fact that he lives alone made an impression, and that he had been a butcher. That starts to generate ideas for me.
- Ms. V: You can sort of generally think for the most part that he was within functional limits in other perceptual cognitive areas. I guess from looking at the diagnosis end, that he is a right CVA and he does have a neglect. I would want to really assess his perceptual cognitive deficits a little further, especially in light of a nonfunctional left upper extremity, at that. So looking at the component end, I would want to further examine those areas.
- Ms. P: Sensation! Also because it does not mention [in the vignette] anything about any sensation at all. It would be extremely important with neglect.

These excerpts represent precoded, corrected versions of the transcript and illustrate one type of data in naturalistic inquiry. Consider this transcript and the other types of data that could have been collected from in-depth interviews and personal field notes. Think about all these written words; you can quickly obtain an appreciation of the volume of information that is generated in this type of research. These written forms of data can quickly become voluminous, and the researcher must set up multiple files that are cataloged to facilitate cross-referencing and easy access to its bits and pieces.

Transcription is only one aspect of preparing data for analysis. It is also critical to establish a system to organize information. On the most basic level, you will need to establish a log of each tape and the date of its recording. As you begin to identify categories of information, you will need to establish a system for easy retrieval of key passages that reflect these categories. It is also important to keep track of coding and analytical decisions as you read and review materials. Researchers use a variety of organizational schemes, depending on their personal style and preferences and the scope and needs of the research project. Some researchers use note cards and hand-code collected information. Others prefer to use word processing programs or computer-assisted coding programs such as Nudist, Zyindex, or Ethnograph. In experimental-type research, computer-based statistical programs are a necessity and have facilitated the development of more sophisticated statistical tests. In naturalistic inquiry, computer-based coding programs assist the investigator in organizing, sorting, and manipulating the arrangement of materials to facilitate the analytical process. Obviously, the programs cannot develop an analytical scheme or engage in the interpretative process. Nothing can replace the need for the investigator to be immersed and intensely involved in reading and coding the narrative. Word processing programs and specially designed qualitative software packages only enable the researcher catalog, store, and rearrange large sets of information in different sorted files more efficiently. Even when computer assistance is used, many investigators also depend on index cards or loose-leaf notebooks with tabs to separate and identify major topics and emerging themes. Some investigators establish multiple copies of narratives and cut and paste materials to organize and reorganize each written segment into meaningful segments.

In any case, researchers usually maintain a codebook in the form of index cards, word processing files, or a notebook that summarizes the codes that are used to describe major passages and themes and their location in a transcript. An index or codebook system can be developed in many different ways (Table 18-2).

In this example, a code, its definition, and its line location in the transcript are recorded. The excerpt from this codebook reflects three broad analytical categories (medical, individual, and situational) that emerged from the focus group study. In each category there are subcodes. For example, the category of "individual" considerations involved up to 14 different subcategories, such as self-care, previous roles, and future roles. The listing of the location of each code in the transcript provides a quick guide to the text. The text can then be sorted by codes, and smaller files can be created that reflect any category of interest (Table 18-3).

**Table 18-2** | Excerpt from codebook for focus group transcripts (as it relates to Table 18-3)

| Code | Definition | Line location |
|------|-----------|---------------|
| MED | Medical factors | 1282 |
| (DIAG) | 1. Diagnosis | |
| (FUNCT) | 2. Function | |
| (HS) | 3. Health status | |
| (PERC) | 4. Perceptual | |
| INDV | Individual factors | |
| | 1. Background characteristics | |
| (AGE) | a. Age | 1284 |
| (GEND) | b. Gender | |
| (SES) | c. Socioeconomic status | |
| (ETHN) | d. Ethnicity | 1284 |
| (REL) | e. Religion | |
| (ROLE) | 2. Role | |
| | a. Past | 1287 |
| | b. Present | |
| | c. Future | |
| SITUAT | Situational factors | |
| (LIV) | 1. Living situation | 1286 |
| (COM) | 2. Community | 1285 |
| DEC-MAK | Decision-making process | |
| | 1. Reference of order to thoughts | 1281-1282 |
| | 2. Reflection | 1288 |

**Table 18-3** | Excerpt from focus group transcript with preliminary analytical codes

| Line | Codes |
|------|-------|
| | *MED: DIAG* |
| | *INDV: AGE/GEND/ETHN/ROLE* |
| | *SITUAT: LIV/COM* |
| | *DEC-MAK:* |
| 1281 | The things that struck me are that, one, |
| 1282 | he had a stroke. So I started going through |
| 1283 | a list of equipment that he might use. But then |
| 1284 | a 67-year-old Italian gentleman from |
| 1285 | south Philadelphia starts to put other things in |
| 1286 | my mind. The fact that he lives alone made an |
| 1287 | impression, and that he had been a butcher. That |
| 1288 | starts to generate ideas for me. |

As part of the information gathering and storing process, the researcher may keep personal notes and diarylike comments and insights that provide a context from which to view and understand field notes at each stage of engagement in the field. In most forms of naturalistic inquiry the investigator is an integral part of the entire research process. It is through the investigator and his or her interaction with informants in the field that knowledge emerges and develops. Thus these personal comments are critical to the investigator's self-reflections, which occur as part of the analytical process. There are chapters and books written on taking field notes and their use in data collection and analysis.[3]

As the investigator reflects on his or her own feelings, moods, and attitudes at each juncture of data collection and recording, he or she can begin to understand the lens through which he or she interprets the cultural scene or slice of behavior at that point in time in the fieldwork. The organization of these notes and their emergent interpretations is an important technique. The investigator can develop questions to guide further data collection and to explain observations as they occur. Summarizing or *memoing*[3] as one proceeds in the analysis also produces what has been called an audit trail.[5] An audit trail indicates the key turning points in an inquiry in which the researcher has uncovered and revealed new understandings or meanings of the phenomenon of interest. This trail can be reviewed by others as a way of determining the credibility of the investigator's interpretations.

## Summary

Managing the information collected in a study is an important research task, but one that is not often explicitly discussed in the research literature. Techniques for effectively organizing information for its analysis tend to be learned through mentorship opportunities. Nevertheless, data management represents a potential source of random error in both naturalistic inquiry and experimental-type research and therefore warrants careful consideration.

Researchers in experimental-type research proceed in a series of actions to manage and prepare data for statistical analysis. As in all previous research steps, the approach in experimental-type research is linear; it follows data collection and proceeds statistical testing. In contrast, in naturalistic inquiry, analysis is an on-going and integral part of data collection actions. Likewise, the management of data and its cleaning and reduction into meaningful interpretative categories occur iteratively—first as part of data collection and then as part of a more formal analysis and report-generation process. In naturalistic inquiry, researchers use diverse approaches to manage information and its analysis. Consider the diverse philosophical traditions that make up this research approach. In keeping with these traditions, researchers pursue multiple ways of storing, managing, and preparing information for on-going analysis and final report writing.

## Exercises

1. Contact two researchers at a university who work in the experimental-type tradition. Through interviewing, determine their data management arrangements, data entry programs, and types of codebooks that are used.

*Continued*

## Exercises

2. Repeat exercise 1 with two researchers who use naturalistic inquiry.

3. Compare and contrast the different styles of managing information in and across the research traditions.

*References*

1. Agar MH: *The professional stranger: an informal introduction to ethnography,* ed 2, San Diego, 1996, Academic Press.
2. Gitlin LN, Burgh D, Durham D: *Factors influencing therapists' selection of adaptive technology for older adults in rehabilitation: legacies and lifestyles for mature adults,* Philadelphia, 1992, Temple University.
3. Sanjek R (editor): *Fieldnotes: the makings of anthropology,* Ithaca, NY, 1990, Cornell University Press.
4. Glaser B, Strauss A: *The discovery of grounded theory: strategies for qualitative research,* Chicago, 1967, Aldine.
5. Guba EG: Criteria for assessing the trustworthiness of naturalistic inquiry, *Educ Commun Technol J* 29:75-92, 1981.

# Chapter 19

# Statistical analysis for experimental-type research

**Key terms**

Associational statistics
Descriptive statistics
Dispersion
Frequency distribution
Inferential statistics
Interquartile range
Level of significance
Mean
Median
Measures of central tendency

Mode
Nonparametric
Parametric statistics
Range
Standard deviation
Statistics
Sum of squares
Type I error
Type II error
Variance

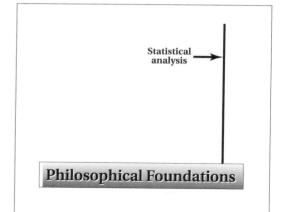

Statistical analysis

**Philosophical Foundations**

Many newcomers to the research process often equate *statistics* with research and express fear of this research phase. Hopefully, you understand that conducting statistical analysis is simply one of a number of important action processes in experimental-type research. You do not have to be a mathematician or memorize mathematical formulas to engage effectively in this research step. Statistical analysis is based on a logical set of principles that you can learn. In addition, you can always consult a statistical book for formulas and required calculations. Obviously, there are innumerable texts on statistical manipulations, and you can specialize in this area of the research process. Furthermore, there are hundreds of different statistical procedures that can be used to analyze data. The primary objective of this chapter is to familiarize you with three levels of statistical analyses and the logic of choosing a statistical approach. Our purpose is to provide an orientation to some of the basic principles and decision-making processes in this action phase rather than describe any one particular statistical test. We refer you to user-friendly books by Kachigan[1] and Huck et al,[2] in particular, and the reference list for other texts that discuss the range of available statistical analyses.

## What is statistical analysis?

Statistical analysis is concerned with the organization and interpretation of data according to well-defined, systematic, and mathematical procedures and rules. The term "data" refers to information obtained through data collection to research questions such as: How much? How many? How long? How fast? In statistical analysis, data are represented by numbers. The value of numerical representation lies, in large part, in the clarity of numbers. This property cannot always be exhibited in words. For example, let us assume you visit your physician, and he or she indicates that you need a surgical procedure. If the

physician says that most patients survive the operation, you will want to know what is meant by "most." Does it mean 58 out of 100 patients survive the operation or 80 out of 100? Numerical data provide a precise language to describe phenomena. As tools, statistical analyses provide a method to systematically analyze and draw conclusions to tell a story. Statistical analysis can be a stepping stone used by the experimental-type researcher to cross a stream from one bank (the question) to the other (the answer).

By now you can see that there are no surprises in the tradition of experimental-type research. Statistical analysis in this tradition is guided by all the previous steps of the research process, including the level of knowledge development, research problem, study design, number of study variables, level of measurement, sampling procedures, and sample size. Each of these steps logically leads to the selection of appropriate statistical actions.

Statistical analyses can be categorized into one of three levels: descriptive, inferential, or associational. Each level of statistical analyses corresponds to the particular level of knowledge about the topic, the specific type of question that is asked by the researcher, and whether the data are derived from the population as a whole or are a subset or sample.

*Descriptive statistics* make up the first level of statistical analysis and are used to reduce large sets of observations into more compact and interpretable forms.[3] If study subjects represent the entire population, descriptive statistics will be primarily used; however, descriptive statistics are also used to summarize the data derived from a sample. Description is the first step of any analytical process. The investigator will descriptively examine the data before proceeding to the next levels of analysis.

The second level of statistics is inference making. *Inferential statistics* are used to draw conclusions about population parameters, based on findings from a sample.[4] The concern is with tests of significance to generalize the population from which the sample is drawn. Inferential statistics are also used to examine group differences within a sample. If the study subjects represent a sample, both descriptive and inferential statistics can be used. There is no need to use inferential statistics when analyzing results from an entire population. There will be no sampling error in this case and no need to draw inferences, since every element of the population is represented in the study.

*Associational statistics* make up the third level of statistical analysis. These statistics refer to a set of procedures that is designed to identify relationships between multiple variables and to determine whether knowledge of one set of data allows the investigator to infer or predict the characteristics of another set. The purpose of these multivariate types of statistical analyses is to make causal statements and predictions. Table 19-1 summarizes the primary statistical procedures associated with each level of analysis.

Table 19-2 summarizes the relationship among the level of knowledge, type of question, and level of statistical analysis. Let us examine the purpose and logic of each level of statistical analysis in greater detail.

**Table 19-1** Summary of primary tools of each level of statistical analysis

| Level | Purpose | Selected primary statistical tools |
|---|---|---|
| Descriptive statistics | Data reduction | Measures of central tendency<br>　Mode<br>　Median<br>　Mean<br>Measures of variability<br>　Range<br>　Interquartile range<br>　Sum of squares<br>　Variance<br>　Standard deviation<br>Bivariate descriptive statistics<br>　Contingency tables<br>　Correlational analysis |
| Inferential statistics | Inference to known population | Parametric statistics<br>Nonparametric statistics |
| Associational statistics | Causality | Multivariate analysis<br>　Multiple regression<br>　Discriminant analysis<br>　Path analysis |

## Level 1: Descriptive statistics

Consider all the numbers that are generated in a research study such as a survey. Each number provides information about an individual phenomenon but does not provide an understanding of a group of individuals as a whole. Recall our discussion in Chapter 16 of the four levels of measurement (nominal, ordinal, interval, and ratio). Large masses of unorganized numbers, regardless of the level of measurement, are not comprehensible and cannot in themselves answer a research question.

Descriptive statistical analyses provide techniques to reduce large sets of data into smaller sets without sacrificing critical information. The data are more comprehensible if summarized into a more compact and interpretable form. This action process is referred to as data reduction and involves the summary of data and their reduction to singular numerical scores. These smaller numerical sets are used to describe the original observations. A descriptive analysis is the first action a researcher takes to understand the data that have been collected. There are several techniques or descriptive statistics for reducing data. Included in this category of statistics are frequency distribution, measures of central tendency (mode, median,

and mean), variances, contingency tables, and correlational analyses. These descriptive statistics are concerned with direct measures of population characteristics. Let us examine each type of descriptive statistic.

### Frequency distribution

The first and most basic descriptive statistic is the *frequency distribution*. This term refers to both the distribution of values for a given variable and the number of times each value occurs. The distribution reflects a simple tally or count of how frequently each value of the variable occurs in the set of measured objects. As discussed in Chapter 18, frequencies are used to clean raw data files and to ensure accuracy in data entry. Frequencies are also used to describe the sample or population.

Frequency distributions are usually arranged in table format in which the values of a variable may be arranged from lowest to highest or highest to lowest. Frequencies provide information about two basic aspects of the data that have been collected. They allow the researcher to identify the most frequently occurring class of scores and any pattern in the distribution of scores. In addition to a count, frequencies can

| Table 19-2 | Relationship of level of knowledge to type of question and level of statistical analysis | | |
|---|---|---|---|
| *Level of knowledge* | | *Type of question* | *Level of statistical analysis* |
| Little to nothing is known. | | Descriptive Exploratory | Descriptive |
| Descriptive information is known, but little to nothing is known about relationships. | | Explanatory | Descriptive Inferential |
| Relationships are known, and well-defined theory needs to be tested. | | Predictive Hypothesis testing | Descriptive Inferential Associational |

produce what are referred to as relative frequencies, which are the observed frequencies converted into percentages based on the total number of observations. For example, relative frequencies tell us at a glance what percentage of subjects has a score on any given value.

Consider the following example. Let us assume you want to develop a drug prevention program in a high school. To adequately plan, you will need to know the ages of the students who will participate. You will obtain a list of ages of 20 participants (Table 19-3); the ages are measured at the interval level and are listed in the order in which the students register. However, the list is difficult to interpret or derive meaning from. For example, the average age of the group, the age distribution among the categories, or the youngest and oldest ages represented of those who signed up for the program are not immediately apparent on the list. To understand the data, you can develop a simple frequency table (Table 19-4). This table orders the ages of the sample in ascending order and indicates the number and percentage of students at each age. There is only one variable presented and its level of measure is interval. This simple rearrangement of the data provides important information that you can immediately understand. From this table, it is immediately apparent that ages range from 14 to 18 years and the most frequently occurring ages are 15 and 17 years.

You can reduce the data further by grouping the ages to reflect an ordinal level of measurement. For example, you may want to know how many students fall within the age range of 14 to 16 and 17 to 18 years (Table 19-5). It is often more efficient to group data based on a theoretical basis for variables in which there is a

large number of response categories. Frequencies are commonly used with categorical data rather than with continuous data in which the possible number of scores is high, such as test grades or income. It will be difficult to derive any immediate understanding from a table of a large distribution of numbers.

In addition to a table format, frequencies can be visually represented by graphs, such as a pie chart, histogram or bar graph, and polygon (dots connected by lines). Let us use another hypothetical data set to illustrate the value of representing frequencies using some of these formats. Assume you conducted a study with

**Table 19-3 Ages of high school students**

| | | | | |
|----|----|----|----|----|
| 18 | 15 | 14 | 16 | 17 |
| 17 | 17 | 15 | 17 | 18 |
| 16 | 15 | 14 | 15 | 16 |
| 15 | 17 | 16 | 14 | 18 |

**Table 19-4 Frequency distribution of ages of students (N = 20)**

| Age | Frequency | Percent |
|-----|-----------|---------|
| 14 | 3 | 15 |
| 15 | 5 | 25 |
| 16 | 4 | 20 |
| 17 | 5 | 25 |
| 18 | 3 | 15 |

**Table 19-5 Frequency distribution by age interval (in years)**

| Age interval | Frequency | Percent |
|--------------|-----------|---------|
| 14 to 16 | 12 | 60 |
| 17 to 18 | 8 | 40 |

1000 persons 65 years of age or older in which you obtained scores on a measure of life satisfaction. If you examine the raw scores, you will be at a loss to understand patterns or how the group behaves on this measure. One way to begin will be to examine the frequency of scores for each response category of the life satisfaction scale using a histogram. There are five response categories: 5 = very satisfied, 4 = satisfied, 3 = neutral, 2 = unsatisfied, and 1 = very unsatisfied. Figure 19-1 depicts the distribution of the scores by percentage of responses in each category (relative frequency).

You can also visually represent the same data using a polygon. A dot is plotted for the percentage value, and lines are drawn among the dots to yield a picture of the shape of the distribution, as well as the frequency of responses in each category (Figure 19-2).

Frequencies can be described by the nature of their distribution. There are several dif- ferent shapes of distributions. Distributions can be symmetrical (Figures 19-3, *A* and *B*) in which both halves of the distribution are identical. This distribution is referred to as a normal distribution. Distributions can be nonsymmetrical (Figures 19-3, *C* and *D*) and are characterized as positively or negatively skewed. A distribution that has a positive skew has a curve that is high on the left and a tail to the right (Figure 19-3, *E*). A distribution that has a negative skew has a curve that is high on the right and a tail to the left (Figure 19-3, *F*). A distribution can be characterized by its shape, or kurtosis, and is either characterized by its flatness (platykurtic; Figure 19-3, *G*) or peakedness (leptokurtic; Figure 19-3, *H*). Not shown is a bimodal distribution, which is characterized by two high points. If you plot the age of the 20 students who registered for the drug prevention course (data shown in Table 19-4), you will have a bimodal distribution.

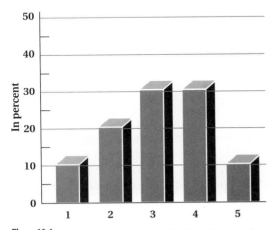

**Figure 19-1** Histogram depicts distribution of scores by percentage of responses in each category.

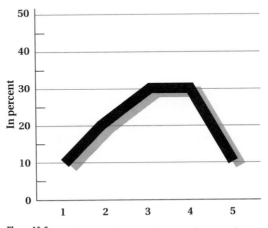

**Figure 19-2** Polygon depicts distribution of scores by percentage of responses in each category.

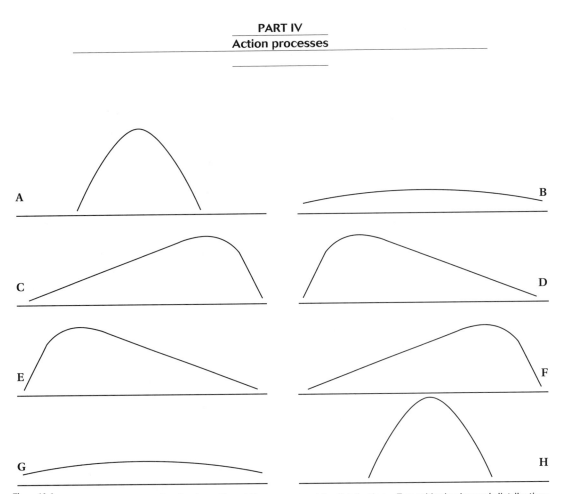

Figure 19-1  **A** and **B**, Symmetric distribution;  **C** and **D**, nonsymmetric distribution;  **E**, positively skewed distribution;  **F**, negatively skewed distribution;  **G**, platykurtosis (flatness);  **H**, leptokurtosis (peakedness).

It is good practice to examine the shape of a distribution before proceeding with other statistical approaches. The shape of the distribution will have important implications for determining central tendency and the types of other analyses that can be performed.

## Measures of central tendency

A frequency distribution reduces a large collection of data into a relatively compact form. Al-though we can use terms to describe a frequency distribution (e.g., bell-shaped, kurtosis, or skewed to the right), we can also summarize the frequency distribution by using specific numerical values. These values are called *measures of central tendency* and provide important information regarding the most typical or representative scores in a group. The three basic measures of central tendency are the mode, median, and mean.

**Mode.** In most data distributions, observations tend to cluster heavily around certain values. One logical measure of central tendency is the value that occurs most frequently. This value is referred to as the modal value or the *mode*. For example, consider the data collection of nine observations, such as the following values:

| | | | | | | | | |
|---|---|---|---|---|---|---|---|---|
| 9 | 12 | 15 | 15 | 15 | 16 | 16 | 20 | 26 |

In the above distribution of scores, the modal value is 15 because it occurs more than any other score. The mode therefore represents the actual value of the variable that occurs most often. It does not refer to the frequency associated with that value.

Some distributions can be characterized as bimodal in that two values occur with the same frequency. Let us use the age distribution of the 20 students who plan to attend the drug abuse prevention class (see Table 19-4). In this distribution, two categories have the same high frequency. This is a bimodal distribution; 14 is the value of one mode, and 17 is the value of the second mode.

In a distribution based on data that have been grouped into intervals, the mode is often taken as the midpoint of the interval that contains the highest frequency of observations. For example, let us reexamine the frequency distribution of the students' ages (see Table 19-5). The first category of ages, 14 to 16 years, represents the highest frequency. However, because the exact ages of the individuals in that category are not known, we select 15 as our mode because it is the midway point in this category.

The advantage of the mode is that it can be easily obtained as a single indicator of a large distribution. Also, the mode can be used for statistical procedures with categorical variables (numbers assigned to a category; e.g., 1 = male and 2 = female).

**Median.** The second measure of central tendency is the *median*. The median is the point on a scale above or below which 50% of the cases fall. It lies at the midpoint of the distribution. To determine the median, arrange a set of observations from lowest to highest in value. The middle value is singled out so that 50% of the observations fall above and below that value. Consider the following values:

| | | | | | | | | |
|---|---|---|---|---|---|---|---|---|
| 22 | 24 | 24 | 25 | 27 | 30 | 31 | 35 | 40 |

The median is 27, because half the scores fall below the number 27 and half are above. In an odd number of values, as in the above case of nine, the median is one of the values in the distribution. When an even number of values occurs in a distribution, the median may or may not be one of the actual values, since there is no middle number; in other words, an even number of values exist on both sides of the median. Consider the following values:

| | | | | | | | | | |
|---|---|---|---|---|---|---|---|---|---|
| 22 | 24 | 24 | 25 | 27 | 30 | 31 | 35 | 40 | 47 |

The median lies between the fifth and sixth values. The median is therefore calculated as an average of the scores surrounding it. In this case the median is 28.5 because it lies halfway between the values of 27 and 30. If the sixth value had been 27, the median would have been 27. Look at Table 19-4 again. Can you determine the median value? Write out the complete array of ages based on the frequency of their occurrence. For example, the age of 14 occurs 3 times, so you will list 14 three times; the age of 15 occurs five times, so list 15 five times, and so forth. Count until the 10th and 11th value. What age did you obtain? If you identified 16, you are correct. The age of 16 years occurs in the 10th and 11th value and is therefore the median value of this group of students.

In the case of a frequency distribution based on grouped data, the median can be reported as the interval in which the cumulative frequency equals 50 percent (or midpoint of that interval).

The major advantage of the median is that it is insensitive to extreme scores in a distribution; that is, if the highest score in the set of numbers shown had been 85 instead of 47, the median would not be affected. Income is a good example of how the median is a good indicator of central tendency because it is not affected by extreme values.

*Mean.* The *mean,* as a measure of central tendency, is the most fundamental concept in statistical analysis. The mean serves two purposes. First, it serves as a data reduction technique in that it provides a summary value for an entire distribution. Second and most importantly, it serves as a building block for many other statistical techniques. As such, the mean is the most important measure of central tendency. There are many common symbols for the mean (Box 19-1).

### Box 19-1 Common symbols for the mean

- $Mx$ = mean of variable x
- $My$ = mean of variable y
- $\overline{X}$ = x bar or mean value of a variable
- $M$ = mu, mean of a sample

The formula for calculating the mean is simple:

$$M = \frac{\Sigma X_i}{N}$$

where $\Sigma X_i$ = sum of all values, $M$ = mean, and $N$ = total number of observations.

The major advantage of the mean over the mode and median is that in calculating this statistic, the numerical value of every single observation in the data distribution is considered and used. When the mean is calculated, all values are summed and then divided by the number of values. However, this strength can be a drawback with highly skewed data in which there are outliers or extreme scores.

Consider an example to illustrate this point. Suppose you have just completed teaching a continuing education course in cardiopulmonary resuscitation (CPR). You test your students to determine their competence in CPR knowledge and skill. Of a possible 100, the following scores were obtained:

*100  100  100  95  95*

To calculate the mean, you will add each value and divide the sum by the total number of values $(100 + 100 + 100 + 95 + 95 = 490/5 = 98)$. The mean score of your group is 98. You are satisfied with the scores and with the high level of knowledge and skill. Now let us see what happens in the following distribution of test scores:

*100  100  100  90  35*

The mean is calculated as $100 + 100 + 100 + 90 + 35 = 425/5 = 85$. The mean (85) presents quite a different picture even though only one member of the group scored poorly. If only the mean were reported, you will have no way of knowing that the majority of your class did well and that one individual or outlier score was responsible for the lower mean.

Now that you are aware of the three measures of central tendency, how do you determine which measure or measures you should calculate? Although investigators often calculate all three measures, all may not be useful. Their usefulness depends on the purpose of the analysis and the nature of the distribution of scores. In a normal curve, the mean, median, and mode are in the same location (Figure 19-4). In this case it is most efficient to use the mean, because it is the most widely used measure of central tendency and forms the foundation for subsequent statistical calculations.

However, in a skewed distribution the three measures of central tendency fall in different places (Figure 19-5). In this case you will need to examine all three measures and select the one that most reasonably answers your question without providing a misleading picture of the findings.

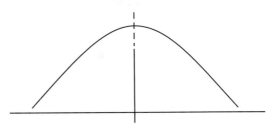

**Figure 19-4** Normal curve, where mean, median, and mode are in same location.

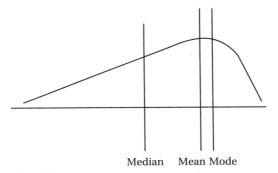

Median     Mean Mode

**Figure 19-5** Skewed distribution, where the three measures of central tendency fall in different places.

## Measures of variability

We have learned that a single numerical index, such as the mean, median, or mode, can be used to describe a large frequency of scores. However, each has certain limitations, especially in the case of a distribution with extreme scores. Most groups of scores on a scale or index differ from one another or have what is termed variability. (Other terms for variability are spread or dispersion.) Variability is another way of summarizing and characterizing large data sets. The measure of variability simply indicates the degree of *dispersion* or the differences among scores. If scores are similar, there is little dispersion, spread, or variability across response categories. On the other hand, if scores are dissimilar, there is a high degree of dispersion. Even though a measure of central tendency provides a numerical index of the average score in a group, it is also important to know how the scores vary or how they are dispersed around the measure of central tendency. Measures of variability provide additional information about the scoring patterns of the entire group.

Consider for example the two groups of life satisfaction scores (Table 19-6).

In both groups the mean satisfaction score is equal to 100. However, the variability or dispersion of scores around the mean is quite different. The scores in group 1 are more homogeneous. In the second group, the scores are more variable, dispersed, or heterogeneous. The dispersion of scores for the two groups are shown in Figure 19-6. Therefore knowing the mean will not help ascertain differences in the two groups, even though they exist. Let us assume you had to develop a support-group educational program for both groups. You will approach the focus of each group differently, based on your knowledge of the variability in scores.

To more fully describe a data distribution, a summary measure of the variation or dispersion of the observed values is important. We discuss five basic measures of variability—range, interquartile range, sum of squares, variance, and standard deviation.

***Range.*** The *range* represents the simplest measure of variation. It refers to the difference between the highest and lowest observed value in a collection of data. The range is a crude measure, since it does not take into account all values of a distribution, only the lowest and highest. It does not indicate anything about the values that lie between these two extremes. In group 1 data listed in Table 19-6, the range is 96 to 103, or a range of 7 points. In group 2 data, the range is 78 to 128, or a range of 50 points.

***Interquartile range.*** A more meaningful measure of variability is called the *interquartile range* (IQR). The IQR refers to the range of the middle 50% of subjects. This range describes the middle of the sample or range of a majority of subjects. By using the range of 50% of subjects, the investigator ignores the extreme scores or outliers. Assume your study sample ranges in age from 20 to 90 years as shown:

| *20* | *20* | *21* | *34* | *35* | *35* | *35* | *38* | *39* | *45* | *85* | *90* |

If you only use the range, you will report a range of 20 to 90 with a 70-point spread. However, most individuals are approximately 35 years of age. By using the IQR, you will separate the lowest 25% (ages 20, 20, 22 years) and the highest 25% (70, 85, 90 years) from the middle or 50% (30, 35, 35, 35, 38, 39 years). You will report the range of scores that fall within 50th percentile. In this way you ignore the outliers of 85 and 90. Usually, when reporting the median

| Table 19-6 | Life satisfaction scores for two groups | |
|---|---|---|
| | *Group 1* | *Group 2* |
| | 102 | 128 |
| | 99 | 78 |
| | 103 | 93 |
| | 96 | 101 |

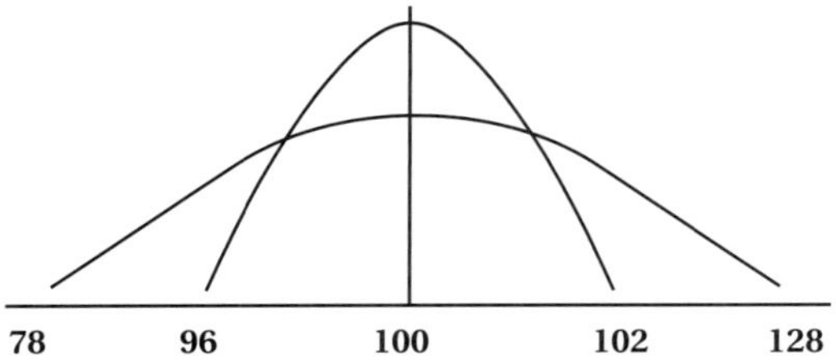

Figure 19-6 Homogeneous and heterogeneous IQ scores.

score for a distribution, the IQR is also used. To calculate the median, you will count to the middle of the distribution. Similarly, with IQR, you will count off the top and bottom quarters.

***Sum of squares.*** Another way of interpreting variability is by squaring the difference between each score from the mean. These squared scores are then summed and referred to statistically as the *sum of squares* (SS). The larger the value of SS, the greater the variance. The SS is used in many other statistical manipulations. The equation for SS is as follows:

$$SS = \Sigma\,(X - X)^2$$

***Variance.*** The *variance* (V) is another measure of variability and is calculated using the following equation:

$$V = \frac{\Sigma\,(X - X)^2}{N}$$

As the equation shows, variance is the mean or average of the sum of squares. The larger the variance, the larger the spread of scores.

***Standard deviation.*** The *standard deviation* (SD) is the most widely used measure of dispersion. It is an indicator of the average deviation of scores around the mean or, simply, the square root of the variance. In reporting the SD, researchers often use sigma (S) or $\sigma$. Similar to the mean, SD is calculated by taking into consideration every score in a distribution. The standard deviation is based on distances of sample scores away from the mean score and equals the square root of the mean of the squared deviations. It is derived by computing the variation of each value from the mean, squaring the variation, and

taking the square root of that calculation. The standard deviation represents the sample estimate of the population standard deviation and is calculated by the following formula:

$$S = \sqrt{\frac{\Sigma\,(y - y)^2}{n - 1}}$$

Examine the following calculation of the standard deviation for these observations and a mean of 15.5 (or 16):

| *14  21  15  12* |
| --- |

$$S = \sqrt{\frac{(16-14)^2 + (21-16)^2 + (16-15)^2 + (16-12)^2}{4 - 1}}$$

$$S = \sqrt{\frac{4 + 25 + 1 + 16}{4 - 1}}$$

$$S = \sqrt{\frac{46}{3}}$$

$$S = 3.9$$

The first step is to compute deviation scores for each subject. Deviation scores refer to the difference between an individual score and the mean. Second, each deviation score is squared. If the deviation scores were added without being squared, the sum would equal zero, because the deviations above the mean always exactly balance the deviations below the mean. The standard deviation overcomes this problem by squaring each deviation score before adding. Third, the squared deviations are added; the result is divided by one less than the number of cases, and then the square root is obtained. The square root takes the index back to the original units; in other words, the standard deviation is expressed in the units that are being measured.

The standard deviation is an index of variability of scores in a data set. It tells the investigator how scores deviate on the average from the mean. For example, if two distributions have a mean of 25 but one sample has an SD of 70 and the other sample an SD of 30, we know the second sample is more homogeneous. We know that the scores more closely cluster around the mean or that there is less dispersion (Figure 19-7).

Based on a normal curve, approximately 68% of the means from samples in a population will fall within one standard deviation from the mean of means, 95 percent will fall within two standard deviations, and 99 percent will fall within three standard deviations.

The mean and standard deviation are often reported together in a data table. It is important to know the measure of central tendency for a particular variable, as well as its measure of dispersion, to fully understand the distribution that is presented.

## Bivariate descriptive statistics

Thus far we have discussed descriptive data reduction approaches for one variable. The pro-

cedures we have described are for a univariate distribution; another aspect of describing data involves looking for relationships among two or more variables. We describe two methods: contingency tables and correlational analysis.

***Contingency tables.*** One method for describing a relationship between two variables (bivariate relationship) is a contingency table, which is also referred to as a cross tabulation. A contingency table is a two-dimensional frequency distribution that is primarily used with categorical data. In a contingency table, the attributes of one variable are related to the attributes of another. Let us return to our earlier example of the 20 high school students who register for a drug abuse prevention program. Since you know the ages, you will want to know the number of male and female students for each age category. You can easily develop a contingency table that displays the number of male and female students for each age category (Table 19-7).

This table shows that there is an unequal distribution, with more male than female students registering for the course. You can also add a column on the table that indicates the percentage of male and female students for each

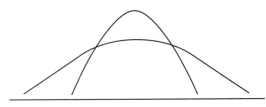

Figure 19-7 Standard deviation, an index of variability of scores in a data set, reveals how much scores deviated, on average, from the mean.

| Table 19-7 | Contingency table of age by gender (N = 20) | | |
|---|---|---|---|
| | **Gender** | | |
| *Age* | *Male* | *Female* | *Total* |
| 14 | 2 | 1 | 3 |
| 15 | 3 | 2 | 5 |
| 16 | 2 | 2 | 4 |
| 17 | 4 | 1 | 5 |
| 18 | 1 | 2 | 3 |
| **Total** | **12** | **8** | **20** |

age. Also, there are a number of statistical procedures that you can use to determine the nature of the relationships displayed in a contingency table and whether the number of male students is significantly greater than the number of female students and not a chance occurrence.

***Correlational analysis.*** A second method of determining relationships among variables is correlational analysis. This approach examines the extent to which two variables are related to each other across a group of subjects. There are numerous correlational statistics. Selection is primarily dependent on the level of measurement and sample size. In a correlational statistic an index is calculated that describes the direction and magnitude of a relationship. Three types of directional relationships can exist among variables: positive correlation, negative correlation, and zero correlation (no correlation). A positive correlation indicates that as the value of one variable increases or decreases, the other variable also changes in the same direction. Conversely, a negative correlation indicates that each variable is related in an opposing direction; as one variable increases, the other variable decreases. For example, the relationship between age and height in children younger than 12 years demonstrates a positive correlation, whereas the relationship between illiteracy and years of education represents a negative correlation.

To indicate the magnitude or strength of a relationship, the value that is calculated in correlational statistics ranges from −1 to +1. The value of −1 indicates a perfect negative correlation, and +1 signifies a perfect positive correlation. By perfect, we mean that each variable changes at the same rate as another. For ex-

ample, assume you find a perfect positive correlation (+1) between years of education and reading level. This statistic will tell you that for each year (unit) of education, reading level will improve 1 unit. A zero correlation is demonstrated in the previous table, which displays the relationship between life satisfaction and age. As you can surmise, the closer a correlational statistical value falls to |1| (absolute value of 1), the stronger the relationship (Figure 19-8). As the value approaches zero, the relationship weakens.

Two correlation statistics are frequently used in social science literature: the Pearson product–moment correlation, known as the Pearson *r*, and the Spearman rho. Both statistics yield a value between −1 and +1. The Pearson *r* is calculated on interval level data, whereas the Spearman *rho* is used with ordinal data.

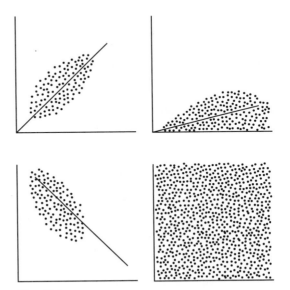

**Figure 19-8** Correlational analyses.

To illustrate the use of the Pearson *r*, let us examine a study by Rozier et al. that investigates job satisfaction in occupational therapy faculty.[5] The researchers examined numerous variables measured with interval level data to determine which were related to job satisfaction in a sample of 538 faculty members. To ascertain the extent of the relationships among selected demographic variables and attitudes, the researchers conducted a series of Pearson *r* calculations. They found that the strongest correlation (r=0.38) existed between the highest degree earned and the attitude, "Research is exciting." The weakest correlation (r = −.014) existed between previous opportunity to teach in the clinical setting and the attitude, "Seeing students grow is exciting." Note that the first correlation is positive and the second is negative. If the investigators had used ordinal data in their measurements, they would have used the Spearman *rho* to examine these relationships.

You may ask several questions. Are these findings valuable? Could the relationships reported by Rozier et al. be a function of chance? Are these important in light of such seemingly low correlations? To answer these questions, investigators must first submit the data to a test of significance, which determines the extent to which a finding occurs by chance. The investigator selects a *level of significance,* which is a statement of the expected degree of accuracy of the findings based on the sample size and on the convention in the relevant literature. The investigator locates the correlation coefficient in a table in the back of a statistics book or examines a computer printout. If the correlation value exceeds the number listed in the table or if the computer presents an acceptable level of significance, the investigator can assume with a degree of certainty that the relationship was not caused by chance.

Consider how this is done. Let us suppose that Rozier et al. selected 0.05 as their confidence level. This number means the results will be caused by chance 5 times out of 100. The investigators locate a table of critical values and find that their number of 0.38 exceeds the value they need to determine that the finding is significant or not caused by chance. Therefore they conclude that 0.38 is significant at the 0.05 level and report it to the reader as such. The investigators may have also searched a computer file to determine the corresponding level of significance, calculated for the value of r = 0.38. If it were .05 or smaller, the investigators would have concluded that this finding was significant.

There are other statistical tests of association that are used with different levels of measurement. For example, investigators often calculate the point biserial statistic to examine a relationship between a nominal variable and an interval level measure. When two nominal variables are calculated, the phi correlation statistic is often selected by researchers as an appropriate technique.[6]

## Level 2: Drawing inferences

Descriptive statistics are useful for summarizing univariate and bivariate sets of data obtained from either a population or a sample. However, researchers also want to determine the extent to which observations of the sample are representative of the population from which the sample was selected. Inferential statistics provide the action processes for drawing conclusions about a population, based on the data that are obtained from a sample. Remember, the purpose of testing or measuring a sample is to gather data that allow statements to be made about the characteristics of the population from which the sample has been obtained (Figure 19-9). Statistical inference, which is based on probability theory, is the process of generalizing from samples to populations from which the samples are derived. The tools of statistics help identify valid generalizations and those that are likely to stand up under further study. Thus the second major role of statistical analysis is to make inferences. Inferential statistics include statistical techniques for evaluating differences among sets of data. These techniques are used to evaluate the degree of precision and confidence of measurements.

Consider an example that illustrates how inferential statistics are used to determine the extent to which findings about a sample apply to the population from which it is selected. Assume you are a mental health provider and are interested in testing the effect of a new rehabilitation technique on the functional level of persons with schizophrenia who are hospitalized in long-term care institutions. In this study you will evaluate the rehabilitation technique for its effectiveness on one unique group. You will also evaluate its value for the population of persons with schizophrenia residing in institutional settings, which the sample represents. First, you will need to define your population carefully in terms of specific inclusion and exclusion criteria. You will randomly select a sample from your defined or targeted population using an appropriate random sampling technique. Next, you will randomly assign the obtained sample to either an experimental or a control-group condition. You will pretest all subjects, expose the experimental group to the intervention, and posttest all subjects. Hypothetically, the scores on your measure of functional status range from 1 to 10, with 1 the least functional and 10 the

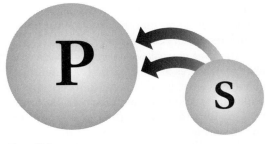

**Figure 19-9** Relationship between sample (S) and population (P).

most functional. Now you have a series of scores—pretest scores from both groups and posttest scores from both groups.

Let us assign hypothetical means to each group to illustrate. The experimental group has a pretest mean of 2 and a posttest mean of 6, whereas the control group has a pretest mean of 3 and a posttest mean of 5. (In a real study you will calculate measures of dispersion as well; however, for instructive purposes, we will omit this measure.)

To answer your research question, you must examine these scores at several levels. First, you will want to know if the groups are equivalent before the intervention. You hypothesize that there will be no difference between the two groups before participation in the intervention. Also, you will hypothesize that the groups adequately represent the population. Visual inspection of your pretest mean scores shows different scores. Is this difference occurring by chance or as a result of actual group differences? To determine whether the difference in mean scores is caused by chance, you will select a statistical analysis (e.g., an independent t-test) to compare the two sets of pretest data (e.g., experimental and control group mean scores).

At this point you will hope to find that the scores are equivalent and that therefore both sample groups represent the population.

Second, you will want to know whether the change in scores at the posttest is a function of chance or what is anticipated to occur in the population. You will therefore choose a statistical analysis to evaluate these changes. (The analysis of covariance [ANCOVA] is the statistic of choice for the true-experimental design). In actuality, you will hope that the experimental group demonstrates change on the dependent or outcome variable at posttest time. You will hypothesize that the change will be greater than that which may occur in the control group and greater than the scores observed at pretest time. Thus as a consequence of participating in the experimental group condition, you will want to show that the sample is significantly different than the control group and thus the population from which the sample was drawn. In actuality you will be testing two phenomena: inference—the extent to which the samples reflect the population both at pretest and posttest time, and significance—the extent to which group differences are a function of chance.

As you may recall, the population refers to all possible members of a group as defined by the researcher (see Chapter 13). A sample refers to a subset of a population from which the researcher wants to generalize. The accuracy of inferences from sample to population depends on how representative the sample is of the population. The best way to ensure representativeness is to use probability sampling techniques. To use an inferential statistic, you will follow the five action processes that were introduced in Chapter 13 and summarized in Box 19-2.

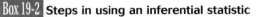

**Box 19-2** | **Steps in using an inferential statistic**

- Action 1: State the hypothesis.
- Action 2: Select a significance level.
- Action 3: Compute a calculated value.
- Action 4: Obtain a critical value.
- Action 5: Reject or fail to reject the null hypothesis.

## Action 1: State the hypothesis

Stating a hypothesis is both simple and complex. In experimental-type designs that test the differences between population and sample, most researchers state a "hunch" of what they expect to occur. This statement is called a working hypothesis. However, for statistical analysis, a working hypothesis is transformed into the null hypothesis. The null hypothesis is a statement of no difference between or among groups. In some studies, the investigator hopes to accept the null hypothesis, whereas in other studies, the hope is to fail to accept it. Initially, as in the example of the experimental design given earlier, we hope to accept the null hypothesis between the pretest mean scores of the experimental and control groups to ensure that our experimental and control groups are equivalent. We do not want our sample scores to differ from the population scores nor do we want the experimental and control groups to differ from one another at baseline before the introduction of the treatment intervention. We pose and test the null hypothesis and hope that in testing it our statistical value will fall below the critical value in the statistical tables. However, for our posttest and change scores, we hope to reject the null hypothesis. We want to find differences between the posttest scores and a change in the experimental group scores that are not representative of the population that has not received the intervention.

Why is the null hypothesis used? Theoretically, it is impossible to prove a relationship among two or more variables.[6] It is only possible to negate the null hypothesis of no difference.[7,8] Nonsupport for the null hypothesis is similar to stating a double negative. If it is not "not raining," it logically follows that it is raining. Applied to research, if there is no "no difference among groups," differences among groups can be assumed, although not proven.

## Action 2: Select a significance level

A level of significance defines how rare or unlikely the sample data must be before the researcher can reject the null hypothesis. The level of significance is a cut-off point that indicates whether the samples being tested are from the same or a different population. It indicates how confident the researcher is that the findings regarding the sample are not attributed to chance. For example, if you select a significance level of 0.05, you are 95% confident that your statistical findings did not occur by chance. If you repeatedly draw different samples from the same population, you will find similar scores 95 out of 100 times. Similarly, a confidence level of 0.1 indicates that the findings may be caused by chance, 1 out of every 10 times.

As you can see, the smaller the number, the more confidence the researcher has in his or her findings and the more credible the results. Because of the nature of probability theory, the researcher can never be certain that his or her findings are 100% accurate. Significance levels are selected by the researcher on the basis of sample size, level of measurement, and conventional norms in the literature. As a rule of thumb, the larger the sample size, a smaller numerical value in the level of significance. This principle makes a lot of sense when you consider it. If you have a small sample size, you risk obtaining a group that is not highly representative of the population; thus your confidence level drops. A large sample size includes more elements from the population, and thus the chances of representation and confidence of findings increase. You therefore can use a stringent level of significance (0.01 or smaller).

***One- and two-tailed levels of significance.*** Consider the normal curve (see Figure 19-4). Extreme scores can occur either to the left or right of the bell shape. The extremes of the curve are called tails. If a hypothesis is nondirectional, it usually assumes that extreme scores can occur at either end of the curve or in either tail. If this is the case, the researcher will then use a two-tailed test of significance. He or she uses a test to determine whether the 5% of statistical values that are considered statistically significant are distributed between the two tails of the curve. If, on the other hand, the hypothesis is directional, the researcher will use a one-tailed test of significance. The portion of the curve in which statistical values are considered significant are in one side of the curve, either the right or left tail. It is easier to obtain statistical significance with a one-tailed statistical test, but the researcher will run the risk of a Type I error (see discussion that follows). A two-tailed test is a more stringent statistical approach.

Because in statistical inference researchers deal with probabilities, two types of statistical inaccuracy or error can contribute to the inability to claim full confidence in findings. These are called Type I and Type II errors.

***Type I error.*** In a *Type I error* (also called an alpha error),[4] the researcher fails to accept the null hypothesis when it is true. In other words, the researcher claims a difference between groups when, if the entire population were measured, there would be no difference. This error can occur when the most extreme members of a population are selected by chance in a sample. Assume, for example, that you set the level of significance at 0.05, indicating that 5 times out of 100 the null hypothesis can be rejected when it is accurate. Because the probability of making a Type I error is equal to the level of significance chosen by the investigator, reducing the level of significance will reduce the chances of making this type of error. Unfortunately, as the probability of making a Type I error is reduced, the potential to make another type of error increases.

***Type II error.*** A Type II error (also called a beta error)[4] occurs if the null hypothesis is accepted when it should be rejected. In other words, the researcher fails to ascertain group differences when, in fact, they occur. If you make a Type II error, you will conclude, for example, that the intervention did not have a positive outcome on the dependent variable when it actually did. The probability of making a Type II error is not as apparent as making a Type I error.[2] A Type II error is based in large part on the power of the statistic to detect group differences.[4]

Type I and II errors are mutually exclusive. However, as you decrease the risk of a Type I error, you increase the chances of a Type II error. Furthermore, it is difficult to determine whether either error has been made, because actual population parameters are not known by the researcher. It is often considered more serious to make a Type I error, because the researcher is claiming a significant relationship or outcome when there is none. Because other researchers or practitioners may act on that finding, the researcher wants to ensure against Type I errors. On the other hand, failure to recognize a positive effect from a treatment program, a Type II error, can also have serious consequences for practice.

## Action 3: Compute a calculated value

To test a hypothesis, the researcher must choose and calculate a statistical formula. The selection of a statistic is based on his or her research question, level of measurement, number of groups that the researcher is comparing, and sample size. There are two classifications of inferential statistics from which an investigator chooses a statistic: parametric and nonparametric procedures. Both are similar in that they (1) test hypotheses, (2) involve a level of significance, (3) require a calculated value, (4) compare against a critical value, and (5) conclude with decisions about the hypotheses.

***Parametric statistics.*** *Parametric statistics* are mathematical formulas that test hypotheses based on three assumptions (Box 19-3).

The data must be derived from a population in which the characteristic is distributed normally. Second, the variances within groups must be homogeneous. Homogeneity is displayed by the scores in one group having approximately the same degree of variability as the scores in another group. Third, the data must be measured at the interval level. Parametric statistics can test the extent to which numerous sample structures are reflected in the population. For example, some statistics test differences between only two groups, whereas others test differences among many groups. Some statistics test main effects (i.e., the direct effect of one variable on another), whereas other statistics have the capacity to test both main and interactive effects (i.e., the combined effects that several variables have on another variable). Furthermore, some statistical action processes test group differences only one time, whereas others test differences over time. We cannot present the full spectrum of parametric statistics in this text. Most researchers attempt to use parametric tests when possible because they are the most robust of the inferential statistics. By robust we mean statistics that most likely detect a significant effect or increase power and decrease Type II errors.

Let us examine a few of the most frequently used statistical tests to illustrate the power of parametric testing. Three techniques are used to compare two or more groups to determine whether the differences between group means are large enough to assume that the corresponding population means are different. These tests include the t-tests, analysis of variance, and multiple comparisons.

**t-Test.** The t-test is the most basic statistical procedure in this grouping. It is used to compare two sample means on one variable. For example, suppose you want to compare the life satisfaction level of physical therapy (PT) students with occupational therapy (OT) students. You administer a general life satisfaction scale to a randomly selected sample of students and obtain a mean score for each group. Let us assume the OT students have an average score of 125.6 and PT students have an average of 120.3. At first glance it appears as if the OT group has the larger mean. However, it is not much larger than the mean derived from the PT group. The statistical question is: Are the two sample means sufficiently different to allow the researcher to conclude, with a high degree of confidence, that the population means are different from one another (even though we will never see the actual population means)?

The t-test provides an answer to this question. If the researcher finds a significant difference between the two sample means, the null hypothesis will be rejected. As a test of the null hypothesis, the $t$ value indicates the probability that the null hypothesis is correct. There are several principles that influence the t-test. First, the larger the sample size, the less likely that a difference between two means is a consequence of an error in sampling. Second, the larger the observed difference between two means, the less likely the difference is a consequence of a sampling error. Third, the smaller the variance, the less likely the difference between the means is also a consequence of a sampling error.

The t-test can be used only when the means of two groups are compared. For studies with more than two groups, the investigator must select other statistical procedures. Similar to all parametric statistics, t-tests must be calculated with interval level data and should be selected only if the researcher believes that the assumptions for the use of parametric statistics have not been violated. The t-test yields a $t$ value that is reported as $t = x$, $p = 0.05$; $x$ is the calculated $t$ value and $p$ is the level of significance set by the researcher. There are two types of t-tests. One type is for independent or uncorrelated data and the other type is for dependent or correlated data. To understand the difference between these two types of t-tests, return to the example of the two-group randomized design to test an experimental intervention for patients with schizophrenia. We stated that one of the first statistical tests that is performed determines whether the experimental and control group subjects differ at the first testing occasion, or pretest. The pretest data of experimental and control group subjects reflect two independent samples. A t-test for independent samples will be used to compare the difference between these two groups. However, let us assume we want to compare the pretest scores to posttest scores for only the experimental subjects. In this case you will compare scores from the same subjects at two points in time. The scores will be more similar because they are drawn from the same sample, and pretest scores serve as a good predictor of posttest scores. In this case the scores are drawn from the same

group and are highly correlated. Therefore the t-test for dependent data will be used, which considers the correlated nature of the data. To learn the computational procedures for the test, we refer you to statistical texts.

**One-way analysis of variance.** The one-way analysis of variance (ANOVA), also referred to as the F-test, serves the same purpose as the t-test. It is designed to compare sample group means to determine whether a significant difference can be inferred in the population. However, ANOVA can manage two or more groups. It is an extension of the t-test for a two or more group situation. The null hypothesis for an ANOVA, as in the t-test, states that there is no difference between the two or more population means. The procedure is also similar to the t-test. The original raw data are put into a formula to obtain a calculated value. The resulting calculated value is compared against the critical value, and the null hypothesis is rejected if the calculated value is larger than the tabled critical value or accepted if the calculated value is less than the critical value. Computing the one-way ANOVA yields an $F$ value that may be reported as $F(a,b) = x$, $p = 0.05$; $x$ equals computed $F$ value, $a$ equals group degrees of freedom, $b$ equals sample degrees of freedom, and $p$ equals level of significance. Degrees of freedom refer to the "number of values, which are free to vary"[6] in a data set.

There are many variations of ANOVA. Some test relationships when variables have multiple levels and some examine complex relationships among multiple levels of variables. For example, assume you are interested in determining the effects of rehabilitation intervention, family support, and functional level on the recovery time for persons with closed head injuries. Measuring the relationship between each independent variable and the outcome will be valuable. However, it will seem prudent to consider the interactive effects of the variables on the outcome. Several variations of the ANOVA (i.e., analysis of covariance [ANCOVA]) exist that should be considered.

When a one-way ANOVA, also known as a single-factor ANOVA, is used to compare three or more groups, a significant $F$ value means that the sample data indicate that the researcher should reject the null hypothesis. However, the $F$ value, in itself, does not tell the investigator which of the group means are significantly different; it only indicates that one or more are different. There are several procedures referred to as multiple comparisons (i.e., *post hoc* comparisons) to determine which group is greater than the others. These procedures are computed after the occurrence of a significant $F$ value and are capable of identifying which group or groups differ among those being compared.

***Nonparametric statistics.*** *Nonparametric statistics* are statistical formulas used to test hypotheses when the data violate one or more of the assumptions for parametric procedures (see Box 19-3). If variance in the population is skewed or asymmetrical, if the data generated from measures are ordinal or nominal, or if the size of the sample is small, the researcher needs to use a nonparametric statistic.

Each of the parametric tests mentioned thus far has a nonparametric analog. For example, the nonparametric analog of the t-test for categorical data is the chi-square. The chi-square test ($X^2$) is used when the data are nominal and when computation of a mean is not possible. The chi-square test is a statistical procedure that uses proportions and percentages to evaluate group differences. The test examines differences between observed frequencies and the frequencies that can be expected to occur if the categories were independent of one another. However, if differences are found, the analysis does not indicate where the significant differences are. For example, let us assume you want to know whether 100 men and 100 women differ with regard to their political party affiliation (Republican or Democrat). Your first step will be to develop a contingency table (a 2 x 2 table) and carry out a chi-square analysis. If there are no differences, you will expect each cell to have the same number of observations. The same number of men and women will have indicated the same party preference (e.g., 50 men indicate Republican, 50 men indicate Democrat, and likewise 50 women indicate Republican and 50 women indicate Democrat). However, the actual data look somewhat different with unequal cells. The chi-square evaluates whether differences in cells are statistically significant or whether the differences are not attributable to chance, but it will not tell you where the significance lies in the table.

The Mann-Whitney U test is another powerful nonparametric test. It is similar to the t-test in that it is designed to test differences between groups, but it is used with data that are ordinal. There are, of course, many other nonparametric tests that are useful, and we suggest you consult other texts to learn about these.

For some of the nonparametric tests, the critical value may have to be larger than the computed statistical value for findings to be significant. Nonparametric statistics, as well as parametric statistics, can be used to test hypotheses from a wide variety of designs. Because nonparametric statistics are less robust than parametric tests, researchers tend not to use them unless they believe that the assumptions necessary for the use of parametric statistics have been violated.

***Choose a statistical test.*** Choosing a statistical test is based on several considerations (Box 19-4).

The answers to these questions guide the researcher to the selection of specific statistical procedures. A discussion of the tests frequently used by researchers follows. This section should be used only as a guide. We refer you to other texts and, in particular, the statistical decision trees constructed by Andrews et al., which should help lead you to the selection of appropriate statistical techniques.[9]

### Action 4: Obtain a critical value

The researcher must locate a critical value in an appropriate table in the back of a statistical book. The critical value is a criterion related to the level of significance and tells the researcher what number he or she must derive from the statistical formula to have a significant finding.

### Action 5: Reject or fail to reject the null hypothesis

The final action process is the decision about whether to reject or fail to reject the null hypothesis. So far we have indicated that a statistical formula is selected, along with a level of significance. The formula is calculated, yielding a nu-

| Box 19-4 | Deciding on a statistical test |
| --- | --- |

- What is the research question?
  - Is it about differences?
  - Is it about degrees of a relationship between variables?
  - Is it an attempt to predict group membership?
- How many variables are being tested, and what types of variables are they?
  - How many variables do you have?
  - How many independent and dependent variables are you testing?
  - Are variables continuous or discrete?
- What is the level of measurement? (Interval level can be used with parametric procedures.)
- What is the nature of the relationship between two or more variables being investigated?
- How many groups are being compared?
- What are the underlying assumptions about the distribution of a measurement in the population from which the sample was selected?
- What is the sample size?

merical value. How do researchers know whether to reject or fail to reject the null hypothesis based on the obtained value? Before the use of computers, the researcher would set a significance level and calculate degrees of freedom for his or her sample or number of sample groups (or both). Degrees of freedom are closely related to sample size and number of groups. Calculating degrees of freedom is dependent on the statistical formula used. Suffice it to say, by examining the degrees of freedom in a study, the researcher can closely ascertain sample size and number of comparison groups without reading anything else. As an example, in the t-test, degrees of freedom are calculated only on the sample size. Group degrees of freedom are not calculated because only two groups are analyzed, and therefore only one group mean is free to vary. When degrees of freedom for sample size are calculated, the number 1 is subtracted from the total sample ($DF = n - 1$), indicating that all measurement values with the exception of one are free to vary. For the $F$ ratio, degrees of freedom are also calculated on groups means because more than two groups may be compared. Once the researcher has calculated the degrees of freedom and the statistical value, he or she locates the table that illustrates the distribution for the statistical values that were conducted. The critical values are located by observing the value that is listed at the intersection of the calculated degrees of freedom and the level of significance. If the critical value is larger than the calculated statistic, in most cases the researcher accepts the null hypothesis (i.e., no significance differences between groups). If the calculated value is larger than the critical value, the researcher rejects the null hypothesis and within the confidence level selected accepts that the groups differ. With the increasing use of computers, researchers rarely make use of tables. The computer is capable of calculating all values and further identifying the $p$ value at which the calculated statistical value will be significant.

## Level 3: Associations and relationships

The third major role of statistics is the identification of relationships between variables and whether knowledge about one set of data allows the researcher to infer or predict characteristics about another set of data. Included among these statistical tests are factor analyses, discriminant function analysis, multiple regression, and modeling techniques. The commonality among these tests is that they all seek to predict one or more outcomes from multiple variables. Some of the techniques can further identify time factors, interactive effects, and complex relationships among multiple independent and dependent variables.

To illustrate this level of statistical analysis, let us consider the study by Palmore in which he investigated predictors of outcome in nursing homes. Palmore obtained data on 22 variables that had the potential of predicting outcomes on two variables: length of stay and whether the conditions of nursing home residents would deteriorate. Included among the independent or predictor variables was the extent of participation in rehabilitation, diagnosis, current health status, impairment status, and prognosis. Palmore used an analysis technique called automatic interaction detector, a statistical procedure that can reveal predictive relationships and the strength of those relationships to examine the effect of the 22 variables on both outcomes.[10] As you can see, predictive statistics are extremely valuable in that they suggest what may happen in one arena (outcome in nursing home placement), based on knowledge of certain indicators (22 predictive variables).

Consider an example of the use of one of these statistics that is frequently seen in the literature, multiple regression. Multiple regression is used to predict the effect of multiple independent (predictor) variables on one dependent (outcome or criterion) variable. Multiple regression can be used only when all variables are measured at the interval level. Discriminant function analysis is a similar test used with categorical or nominal dependent variables. In the article by Rozier et al. that examined the job satisfaction of occupational therapy faculty, the investigators were interested in predicting the extent to which four variables could predict teaching satisfaction. The four variables were "pleasant environment, much satisfaction with teaching, designing learning experiences, and the lack of constraints posed by higher education on the teaching process."[5] As illustrated, multiple regression is an equation based on correlational statistics in which each predictor variable is entered into an equation to determine how strongly it is related to the outcome variable and how much variation in the outcome variable can be predicted by each independent variable. In some cases a stepwise multiple regression is performed, in which the predictors are listed from least related to most related and the cumulative effect of variables is reported. In the Rozier study, it was found that all four predictor variables were important influences on the variance of the outcome variable.[5]

Other techniques, such as modeling strategies, are frequently used to understand complex system relationships. Assume you are interested in determining why some persons with chronic disability live independently and others do not. With so many variables, you may choose a modeling technique that will help identify mathematical properties of relationships, allowing you to determine which factor or combination of factors will best predict success in independent living. We cannot cover these complex, advanced statistical procedures in this introductory text and refer you to the list of references to begin reading about these techniques.

## Summary

Statistical analysis is an important action process in experimental-type research that occurs at the conclusion of data collection and data preparation efforts. There are hundreds of statistical tests that can be categorized as representing one of three levels of analysis: descriptive, inferential, or associational. The level of statistical analysis that is used depends on a number of factors. Chief among these factors are the research question, level of measurement of study variables, sample size, and distribution of scores. Each level of analysis builds on the other. Descriptive analyses are always conducted first, followed by inferential and associational, if the question and data warrant each subsequent form of analysis.

As you can see, the decisions made in each previous step of the research process determine the specific statistical actions that will be taken. Thus embedded in the investigator's research question, in the operational definitions of key concepts, and in th sampling procedures are the statistical manipulations that the investigator will be able to use.

The statistical stage of the research process represents for many researchers the most exciting action process. It is at this juncture that data become meaningful and lead to knowledge building that is descriptive, inferential, or associational. The researcher does not have to be a mathematician to appreciate and understand the logic of statistical manipulations. If the investigator does not have a strong background in mathematics, it is wise for him or her to consult an expert or a statistician at the start of the study to ensure that the question and data collection methods are compatible with the statistical approaches that best answer the research question.

The purpose of this chapter is to "jump start" your understanding of this action research process. There are many different guides and statistical books that describe in detail the hundreds of tests from which to choose.

## Exercises

1. Select a research article that uses statistical procedures. (a) Determine the level of statistical techniques used. (b) Ascertain the rationale behind the selection of the specific statistics used. (c) Critically analyze the statistical tests and determine whether they were appropriate to answer the question the investigator initially posed, level of measurement, and sample size.

2. Given the following scores, develop a frequency table and find the mode, median, mean, range, and standard deviation:

```
12 35 34 26 26 13 21 22 22 22 24 35
36 37 39 51 23 42 41 21 21 22 25 26
27 44 42 13 35 43 12
```

## Exercises

3. Identify a research article that reported in a table format the mean and standard deviation scores to describe the basic characteristics of the study sample. Examine the table; in your own words, write a description of the study based on the numbers presented. Compare your description with that of the study authors.

### References

1. Kachigan SK: *Statistical analysis: an interdisciplinary introduction to univariate and multivariate methods,* New York, 1986, Radius Press.
2. Huck SW, Cormier WH, Bounds WG: *Reading statistics and research,* New York, 1974, Harper & Row.
3. Royeen C, editor: *Clinical research handbook,* Thorofare, NJ, 1989, Slack.
4. Knoke D, Bohrnstedt GW: *Basic social statistics,* Itasca, Ill, 1991, Peacock.
5. Rozier CK, Gilkeson GE, Hamilton BL: Job satisfaction of occupational therapy faculty, *Am J Occup Ther* 45:160-165, 1991.
6. Pilcher D: *Data analysis for the helping professions: a practical guide,* Newbury Park, Calif, 1990, Sage.
7. Mohr L: *Understanding significance testing,* Newbury Park, Calif, 1990, Sage.
8. Henkel RE: *Tests of significance,* Newbury Park, Calif, 1976, Sage.
9. Andrews FM, Klem L, Davidson TN, et al: *A guide for selecting statistical techniques for analyzing social science data,* ed 2, Ann Arbor, Mich, 1981, University of Michigan.
10. Palmore E: Predictors of outcome in nursing homes, *J Appl Gerontol* 9:172-184, 1990.

# Chapter 20

# Analysis in naturalistic inquiry

| | |
|---|---|
| **Key terms** | Categories |
| | Constant comparative method |
| | Credibility |
| | Interpretation |
| | Taxonomy |
| | Theme |
| | Truth value |

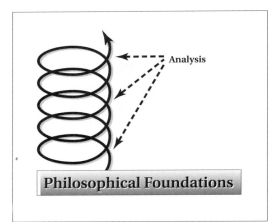

Analysis

**Philosophical Foundations**

We are now ready to turn our attention to the way in which researchers who use the naturalistic inquiry approach the analysis of data. As you may have guessed, the action process of analysis in naturalistic inquiry is quite different from the statistical decision making used in experimental-type research. Analysis in naturalistic research represents a dynamic process. Although analytical strategies reflect a logical approach, there is not a step-by-step, recipe-like set of rules that can be followed by an investigator. Many different analytical strategies can be used. In this chapter we cannot adequately discuss the many approaches to analysis that are used in naturalistic inquiry. We would need to write one or more books to provide an in-depth examination of the many approaches to description and interpretation. After you read this chapter, you may want to refer to other sources listed in the bibliography, which provide in-depth descriptions of specific analytical approaches in naturalistic inquiry.[1-4] The following discussion provides an overview of the basic principles that underlie the general thinking and action processes of researchers involved in different forms of analysis across the traditions of naturalistic inquiry.

Consider the different purposes of the analytical process, the selection of which depends on the primary purpose of the research study, the scope of the query, and the particular design. Table 20-1 summarizes the basic purpose and analytical approach used by seven different designs in naturalistic inquiry.

Some analytical strategies in naturalistic inquiry are extremely unstructured and interpretative, such as in phenomenology, heuristic, and some ethnographic studies. Other analytical strategies are highly structured, such as in grounded theory. Still other types of naturalistic inquiry may incorporate numerical descriptions and may vary in the type of analysis that is used, such as in certain forms of ethnography, endogenous, or participatory action research. Further, some forms of naturalistic inquiry are interpretative but use a specific strategy, such as in life history. In this type of study the investigator identi-

| Table 20-1 | Study design, purpose, and basic analytical strategy | | |
|---|---|---|
| | *Study design* | *Main purpose* | *Basic analytical strategy* |
| | Endogenous | Varies | Varies |
| | Participatory action research | Varies | Varies |
| | Phenomenology | Identifies essence of personal experiences | Groups statements based on meaning; develops textual description |
| | Heuristic | Discovers personal experiences | Describes meaning of experience for researcher and others |
| | Life history | Provides biographical account | Describes chronological events; identifies turning points |
| | Ethnography | Describes and explains cultural patterns | Identifies themes and develops interpretative schema |
| | Grounded theory | Constructs or modifies theory | Provides constant comparative method to name and frame theoretical constructs and relationships |

fies epiphanies, or key turning points, using a chronological or biographical account. Each analytical approach provides a different understanding and reveals a distinct aspect of field experience. Furthermore, in any given study a researcher may use a combination of analytical strategies at different points in the course of fieldwork. For example, let us assume you are conducting a microethnographic study of the meaning of daily life in an assisted living facility for older residents. You may use several different data collection strategies, such as interviewing residents and family members, observing daily activities, and videotaping staff interactions with residents. The initial purpose of your analysis will be to describe daily routines and behaviors of the residents. One analytical strategy may involve counting the number of activities in which residents are engaged and then grouping activities by the categories they represent, such as self-care, leisure, and social activities. Another purpose of the analysis will be to identify themes that explain the meanings attributed by residents to their daily life in the facility. Analysis will involve an interpretative process by which statements that reflect core meanings of the experience of assisted living are identified. Assume that, based on these two analytical steps, you discover that staff relationships are a salient factor in the experiences of residents. To better understand this particular finding, you may add another analytical strategy such as frame-by-frame video analysis of staff-resident verbal interactions. In this particular study you will use three different approaches to analysis. Each approach will reflect a specific purpose and yield a particular understanding of the phenomenon of interest. The findings from each approach will then be inte-

grated to contribute to an understanding of the initial research query (e.g., What is the experience and meaning of living in assisted living?).

Although each type of naturalistic design uses a different analytical strategy or combination of approaches, the researcher can conceptualize the analytical process across these designs as occurring in two overlapping stages. The first stage of analysis occurs at the exact moment the investigator enters the field. It involves trying to make sense of what is observed and heard, or what has been referred to as "learning the ropes."[2] At this stage the purpose of analysis is primarily descriptive and yields "hunches" or initial interpretative schemes. The second stage follows the conclusion of fieldwork and involves a more formal review and analysis of all the information that has been collected. The investigator refines or evolves an interpretation that is recorded in a written report for dissemination to the scientific community. In each stage the researcher may use a different analytical approach. The actions in each stage are best conceptualized as a spiral in which each loop of the spiral involves a set of analytical tasks that lead to the next loop in successive fashion until a complete understanding of the field or phenomenon under study is derived.

## Stage one: Analysis in the field

The process of naturalistic inquiry is iterative. Let us examine what this means in the initial analytical stage. First, data analysis occurs immediately as the researcher enters the field. Analysis continues throughout the investigator's engagement in the field. It is the basis from which all field decisions are made—who to interview, what to observe, and which piece of information to explore further. Data collection efforts are inextricably connected to the initial impressions and "hunches" that are formulated by the investigator; that is, an observation, or datum gives rise to an initial understanding of the phenomenon under study. This initial understanding informs or shapes the next data collection decision. Each collection-analytical action builds successively on the previous action. Thus during fieldwork the researcher begins the process of systematically examining data—field notes, recorded observations, and transcriptions of interviews—to obtain initial descriptions, impressions, "hunches." From this information, direction is derived for further data collection efforts. The investigator also notes his or her own perceptions, biases, or opinions, and begins to group information into meaningful categories that describe the phenomenon of interest. This descriptive analysis is especially critical in the early stages of fieldwork and is essential to the process of reframing the initial query and setting limits regarding who and what is investigated.

This initial set of analytical steps involve four interrelated thinking and action processes (Box 20-1).

Keep in mind that the analytical process is dynamic. In naturalistic research the four aspects of the process are not neat, separate entities that occur in sequence at a particular time in fieldwork. Rather, they are ongoing, overlapping processes that lead to refinement of interpretations throughout the data-gathering effort.

## Inductive and abductive thinking process

Naturalistic inquiry is based on either an inductive or abductive thinking process (see Chapter 1). This thinking process is key to all the analytical approaches of naturalistic inquiry. One of the first analytical efforts of the researcher is to engage in a thoughtful process. This may sound rather obvious and a basic element of any research endeavor. However, the active engagement of the investigator in thinking about each datum in naturalistic inquiry assumes a different quality and level of importance than in other research endeavors. David Fetterman describes this basic analytical effort in ethnographic research as follows:

> The best guide through the thickets of analysis is at once the most obvious and most complex of strategies: clear thinking. First and foremost, analysis is a test of the ethnographer's ability to process information in a meaningful and useful manner.[5]

More specifically, an inductive and abductive thinking process is characterized by the development of an initial organizational system and the review of each datum. The organizational system must emerge from the data itself. The investigator must avoid imposing constructs or theoretical propositions before becoming involved

## Box 20-1 Analytical thinking action processes

- Inductive and abductive thinking
- Developing categories
- Grouping categories into higher level of abstractions
- Discovering meanings and underlying themes

with the data. For example, in the case of data collected through an interview, the researcher will read and reread the transcriptions. From these initial readings, ideas and "hunches" will be formulated. In a phenomenological, heuristic, or life history approach, the investigator will continue working inductively until all meanings of an experience are explicated.

In an abductive approach the thinking process begins inductively with an idea. The investigator explores information or behavioral actions and formulates a working hypothesis, which is examined in the context of the field to see whether it fits. The investigator works somewhat deductively to draw implications from the working hypothesis as a way of verifying its accuracy. This process characterizes the actions of the investigator throughout the field experience, especially for grounded theory [6] and ethnography. [7]

In ethnography, Fetterman labels this process as "contextualization," or the placement of data into a larger perspective. [5] While in the field the investigator continually strives to place each piece of datum into a context to understand the bigger picture or how the parts fit together to make the whole. One way the investigator strives to understand how a datum fits into the larger context is by grouping information into categories.

## Developing categories

We have discussed in previous chapters the volume of information that is gathered in the course of fieldwork. The need to manage the immense amount of data collected occurs quickly. Consider when you had to review a large body of literature for a course in college. Perhaps you first went to the library to obtain information from the literature. You probably realized that your notes from the readings soon became overwhelming and that you needed to develop some organization to make sense of the information you gathered. The same principle applies in the initial stages of analysis in naturalistic inquiry. The researcher must find a way to organize analytically and make sense of the information as it is being collected. One of the first meaningful ways in which the investigator begins to organize information is to develop *categories*. This action process represents a major step in naturalistic analysis. How do categories emerge? As Wax describes:

> The student begins "outside" the interaction, confronting behaviors he finds bewildering and inexplicable: the actors are oriented to a world of meanings that the observer does not grasp...and then gradually he comes to be able to categorize peoples (or relationships) and events. [8]

The researcher enters the field to see and understand phenomena without imposing *a priori* concepts, labels, categories, or meanings. Thus categories emerge from researcher-field interactions and from the initial information that is obtained and synthesized. Preliminary categories are developed and become the tools used to sort and classify subsequent information as it is received.

Spradley and McCurdy describe the process of generating categories as the process of classifying objects according to their similarities and differences from other objects. [9] Categories such as "student," "provider," or "client" make it easier to anticipate the behavior of individuals in these groups and to identify the cultural rules that govern their behavior. As Spradley and McCurdy point out, categories are basic cultural elements, enabling people to organize experiences. Categories are social inventions, since there is no natural way in which objects are grouped. These groupings change from culture to culture. Consider, for example, the way in which colors are classified in different cultures. Although most people living in the United States have only one basic category for the color "white," Eskimo Indians refer to numerous categories. This difference is not surprising, considering the prevalence of "white" in the natural environment in Alaska. Categories are therefore embedded within a cultural context and reveal at the most basic level the way in which a culture classifies objects and establishes its system of meanings.

How do you find or identify categories? The researcher searches for commonalities among different objects, experiences, or events. Agar suggests that recurrent topics are prime candidates for categories.[7] Consider a study conducted by Gitlin et al. that examined the meanings attributed to mobility aids and other assistive devices by patients in rehabilitation who had experienced strokes and were first-time users of the equipment.[10] The initial analytical strategy involved using a pile-sorting technique in which two members of the research team independently read each statement about the devices, which had been generated by patients in the course of brief interviews. These comments were independently sorted by each researcher into basic categories, based on perceived similarities and differences. The cate-gories reflected the underlying topics expressed in patient statements. (A statement about a reacher device such as, "It's good for picking up things," was categorized as representing a comment that explicitly focused on the instrumental utility of the device.) The summary lists of the categories generated by each researcher were compared. Differences were discussed and the categories were refined. A final comprehensive list was prepared and reviewed by all investigators. This process yielded 11 basic topics or categories of meaning.

As data collection activity proceeds, the naturalistic investigator uses the original categories as the basis for analyzing new data. New data are either classified into existing categories or serve to modify or create new categories to accurately depict the phenomenon of interest. Lofland and Lofland suggest that the researcher "file" data by placing them into categories based on characteristics that the data share. The researcher decides on the filing scheme and considers both descriptive and analytical cataloging. Data placed in the descriptive categories answer who, what, where, and when queries and do not involve interpretation. Analytical or more interpretative categories answer how and why queries.[11]

The development of categories is based on repeated review and examination of narrative, videotape, or other types of information that have been collected. The investigator assigns codes to each category. A number of methods can be used, depending on the investigator's personal style and preferences of working. For example, some researchers generate multiple copies of a data set (e.g., a transcription from an interview) and literally cut sections from the transcript that reflect the identified categories. Each cut section is pasted in a notebook or on an index card and filed by the category it represents. (As discussed in Chapter 18, some researchers prefer to use word processors to organize data.) Computer software programs such as Nudist, Zyindex, or Ethnograph can facilitate the coding process for large data sets and make it easier to create separate files of information that reflect multiple categories. These programs automatically assign codes to similar passages or key words identified by the investigator. For example, the researcher may program the computer to automatically assign the code "self-care" to every datum that has the term "bathing" in it. As you see, key words can be selected based on categories that arise from the data set, and the computer can be programmed to automatically assign codes based on a key word list.

## Developing taxonomies

Developing a *taxonomy* represents the next level of organizing information. Taxonomic analysis involves two processes: (1) organizing or grouping similar or related categories into larger categories, and (2) identifying differences between sets of subcategories and larger or overarching categories. In this process, related subcategories are grouped. For example, basic categories such as whales and dogs belong to the larger category of animals; basic categories such as blocks and dolls belong to the larger category of toys. In a taxonomy, sets of categories are grouped on the basis of similarities. The investigator must uncover the thread or inclusionary criterion that link categories. Taxonomic analysis is therefore an analytical procedure that re-

sults in an organization of categories and describes their relationships. In a taxonomic analysis the focus is on identifying the relationship between wholes and parts.

In the Gitlin et al. study of stroke patients, the 11 initial categories identified were grouped into 6 larger categories or dimensions.[10] One dimension was labeled "issues posed by device use." This dimension included four subcategories that reflected concerns ranging from the physical interface between the equipment and the user to the social consequences of being a device user.

## Discovering underlying themes

One of the main purposes of naturalistic research is to understand how each observation or part fits into the whole to make sense of the layers of meaning and the multiple perspectives that make up field experience. The major inductive method to accomplish this task is to search for relationships among categories and to reveal the underlying *theme* or meaning in categories and their components beyond what is immediately visible. Agar suggests that it is from the "simple" process of first establishing topics, categories, and codes that "...you begin building a map of the territory that will help you give accounts, and subsequently begin to discuss what 'those people' are like."[7]

According to Glaser and Strauss, the researcher engages in the thinking process of "integrating" in which he or she finds relationships among categories and further searches for overlap, exclusivity, or hidden meanings among categories.[6] In their grounded theory method, Glaser[12] and Strauss[13] use the term "theoretical sensitivity" to refer to the researcher's sensitivity and ability to detect and give meanings to data, to go beyond the obvious, and to recognize what is important in the field.

In Spradley and McCurdy's terms, the ethnographer looks for patterns of thought and behavior by examining repeated actions.[9] Categories and taxonomies are compared, contrasted, and sorted until a discernible thought or behavioral pattern becomes identifiable and the meaning of the pattern is revealed. As exceptions to rules emerge, variations on themes are detectable. As themes are developed based on abstractions (categories and taxonomies), they are examined in depth in light of ongoing observations. Also, literature review or other theoretical concepts may be used at this point by the investigator to derive an understanding and explanation of the categories. These rigorous methods are part of an inductive approach to analysis, and they move the researcher up each loop of the spiral toward understanding and interpretation. Each analytical step from category and taxonomy to thematic identification allows the researcher to uncover the multiple meanings and perspectives of individuals and to develop complex understandings of their experience and interactions.

Savishinsky, in his study of the culture of a nursing home, notes the multiple levels of insights that occur in naturalistic inquiry and the way in which new data can influence previously held notions:

> The lives of the residents were absorbing because beneath the deceptively simple style in which they told their stories, there was often depth of passion, or the moral twists of fable, or one small detail which transformed the meaning of all the other details.[14]

## Stage two:  Formal report writing

Analysis, as an active component of the data collection process. Analysis also continues once the investigator formally leaves the field and has completed collecting information. However, this stage of the process is a more formal and analytical step in which the investigator enters into an intensive report writing effort that furthers the interpretative process. The main objective is to consolidate the investigator's understandings and impressions by writing one or more manuscripts or a final report. This writing effort involves a self-reflective and highly interpretive process, the ease of which often depends on how well the investigator initially organizes and cross-references the voluminous records and field notes gathered in fieldwork. In this more formal analytical stage the investigator reexamines materials and refines categories, taxonomies, themes, and derives an *interpretation*. The investigator must also purposely and carefully select quotes and examples to illustrate and highlight each aspect of the refined interpretation. Selections are carefully made to ensure adequate representation of the interpretation or theme the investigator wishes to convey and to remain true to the voice that is being quoted and to the context in which the narrative occurred.

In the final interpretation the investigator moves beyond the information to suggest a deeper understanding of the data through theory development or an explication of the themes and general principles that emerge from the study of the phenomenon of interest.

## Examples of the analytical processes

Researchers use the basic analytical processes somewhat differently and often label these activities distinctly. One of the most formal and systematic analytical approaches is found in grounded theory. Developed by Glaser and Strauss, the purpose of this approach is to develop theory.[6] We highlight aspects of the analytical process of grounded theory that demonstrate its highly structured approach in naturalistic inquiry.

### Grounded theory

Glaser and Strauss suggest specific procedures to examine data. Their approach to grounded theory systematizes the inductive incremental analytical process and the continuous interplay between previously collected and analyzed data and new information.[6] The authors label their analytical approach as the *constant comparative method.* As information is obtained, it is compared and contrasted with previous information to inductively fit all the pieces together into a bigger puzzle. Patterns emerge from the data set, which are then coded. Data filing occurs by categorizing and coding. In the constant comparative method the researchers not only search for themes to emerge but also code each piece of raw data according to the categories in which it belongs.

Initially, codes are "open," which refers to a "process of breaking down, examining, com-

paring, conceptualizing and categorizing data."[13] "Axial coding" then occurs, which refers to "a set of procedures whereby data are put back together in new ways after open coding by making connections between categories."[13] "Selective coding" occurs next, which is the "process of selecting the core category, systematically relating it to other categories."[13] Codes reflect the similarities and differences among themes and continue to test the category system through analysis of each datum and categoric assignment as it is collected. In this way the analysis is grounded in and emerges from each datum. Theory emerges from the data, is intimately linked to the field reality, and reflects a synthesis of the information gathered.

This method is perhaps one of the most systematic and procedure-oriented processes in naturalistic inquiry. In various books listed in the bibliography, Strauss and Glaser—together, individually, and with other authors—systematically walk the researcher through each analytical step of coding and categorizing and use a prescribed language to identify each procedure and task.

### Ethnography

Most field studies of the ethnographic-type use a range of analytical approaches, depending on the specific purpose and nature of the study. The researcher may borrow techniques from grounded theory or use a more general thematic analysis, depending on the particular philosophical stance and analytical orientation of the researcher. To illustrate one way in which a field study analysis may be conducted from beginning to end, we examine DePoy and Archer's study, which was designed to discover the meaning of the quality of life and independence to nursing home residents.[15]

Because of the limited theory that explained the quality of life and meaning of independence from the perspective of the elderly residents, DePoy and Archer initially chose a qualitative approach to address their research query.[15] As the primary data collector, Archer began by examining the "social situation" of a nursing home in rural New England, or what Spradley and McCurdy refer to as the place where the research takes place.[8] Archer recorded her data by separating her observational log into two categories: the physical environment and the human environment. This organizational framework is based on an environmental competence model that envisions a person's competence as influencing and, in turn, being influenced by aspects of the physical and social surroundings in which behaviors occur.

Archer answered three basic queries with this organizing scheme. (1) What bounds the environment in which the residents live? (2) What physical characteristics does the environment display? (3) What types of interaction occur within the physical environment? Data were collected and preliminary analyses evolved, determining the similarities between objects to derive descriptive categories. Once Archer was able to collect descriptive data about the environment and who was in it, she and DePoy sampled segments of the data set to examine relationships and types of interaction patterns that occurred within the environment. After reading and rereading observational notes, they identified a pattern of the daily schedule followed by both residents and formal providers in the insti-

tution. This schedule was conceived as a category of its own, and Archer returned to the field to observe specific times of the day to elaborate or broaden the meaning of this category. For example, she observed morning care, meal times, and visiting hours. This set of observations provided greater insight as to the reasons people acted in the way that they did during these times and the meaning of the activity for these individuals. Thus the initial query became reformulated as, "Why do they do what they do, and what is the meaning of the activity?"

In addition to developing descriptive categories, DePoy and Archer[15] used constant comparison[13] and taxonomic analysis.[4,9] When the constant comparison approach was used, two categories of resident activity emerged from the first set of field notes—self-care and rehabilitation. For example, Archer documented in her field notes an observation of a woman dressing herself with the assistance of an occupational therapist. This datum was initially coded as reflecting two categories of self-care and rehabilitation. The coding occurred as a result of constant comparison in which the observation was compared with previous data in each category and was determined to be sufficiently similar to be included in both.

However, as a consequence of comparing new and previous data, discrepancies emerged. This dissonance required reflection and action involving the revision of the category scheme initially developed to depict the nature of the datum. Further along in fieldwork, DePoy and Archer's constant comparisons revealed that the category of self-care was characterized by residents conducting their morning routine with assistance in dressing by the occupational therapist. However, other observations revealed that numerous residents were sitting in their beds during the morning self-care time schedule calling for nursing staff. Did these observations fit into the category of self-care? Because the residents were exercising their right to obtain help from staff, the data could have been coded as self-care. However, because residents appeared to need and be dependent on requested assistance, the data did not seem to fit the concept of independence inherent in the category of self-care. Self-care was thus reconceptualized to reflect a new meaning and was eliminated as a category by itself. The example of the woman dressing with the assistance of the occupational therapist was now coded as "functional relationships," whereas observations of those remaining in their beds were revised as subcategories of "in waiting," and "confinement" (Figure 20-1).

As categories emerged from the data set and became clarified by constant comparison, DePoy and Archer examined relationships among them. Figure 20-1 depicts the simple taxonomy of nursing home experience that inductively emerged from the full data set. As you can see, the lines demonstrate bidirectional connections among categories of findings. For example, the category of confinement was di-

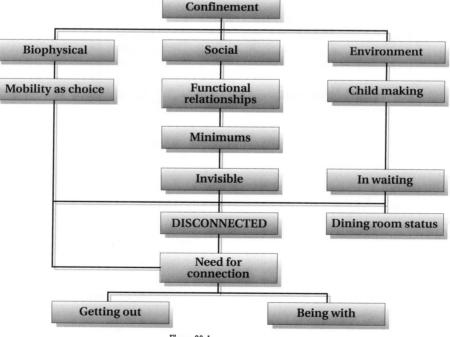

**Figure 20-1** Taxonomy.

vided into three subcategories, biophysical, social, and environmental confinement. Biophysical confinement was both caused by and resulted in mobility choices that were intimately related to the category of "functional relationships" (relationships between residents and staff based on resident need).

## Accuracy and rigor in analysis

In naturalistic research a major concern is obtaining an in-depth, rich description and explanation of phenomena. The investigator may not be concerned with the generalizability or external validity of study findings. Rather, the primary focus is obtaining a comprehensive and truthful representation of a particular context. At this point, however, you may be wondering how you, as a consumer of naturalistic research, can trust an investigator's final interpretations as representing scientific "truth." How can you determine the accuracy or the *truth value* of an investigator's interpretation of field data? How can you be assured that the experiences of research participants are "accurately" represented in a final report? The question is whether the findings reveal meanings that will be shared by other researchers if they had conducted the same set of interviews, observations, and analytical orientation. The issue of validity and truth is obviously important.

In naturalistic research the debate continues on how to construct standards for conducting and evaluating data-gathering and analytical efforts. Lincoln and Guba, in numerous books and articles, have labeled this as a concern with the trustworthiness or *credibility* of an account.[16,17] They and others identify a

number of strategies by which an investigator can enhance the confidence in the truth of the findings from naturalistic inquiry. The concern with credibility of an account or interpretative scheme is similar to the issue of internal validity in experimental-type research. In reading a report involving naturalistic inquiry the critical reader needs to ask two primary questions: (1) To what extent are the biases and personal perspectives of the investigator identified and considered in the data analysis and interpretation? (2) What actions has the investigator taken to enhance the credibility of the investigation? There are six basic actions that are often used by researchers to enhance the accuracy of representation of data and credibility of the interpretation (Box 20-2). When reading a published study using naturalistic inquiry, check whether the investigator has used any of these strategies. Let us review each approach to see how it applies to the analytical process. (See discussions on these techniques in Chapter 17, "Accuracy in data collection.")

### Triangulation

Triangulation is a basic aspect of data gathering that also shapes the action process of data analysis. It is an approach in which one source of in-

Box 20-2 **Techniques to enhance credibility of analysis**

- Triangulation
- Saturation
- Member checks
- Reflection
- Audit trail
- Peer debriefing

formation is checked against one or more other different types of sources to determine the accuracy of hypothetical understandings. For example, one approach to triangulation may involve the comparison of a narrative from an interview with published materials such as a journal. Triangulation enables the investigator to validate a particular finding by examining whether different sources provide convergent information. Also, the comparison of different sources enables the researcher to develop a more comprehensive analytical understanding of the phenomenon of interest.

## Saturation

Saturation refers to the point at which an investigator has obtained sufficient information from fieldwork. As you may recall, there are several indicators that data collection can be terminated (see Chapter 17). For example, the investigator obtains saturation when the information gathered does not provide additional insights or new understandings. Another indication that saturation has been achieved is when the investigator can guess what a respondent is going to say or do in a particular situation. If saturation is not achieved, the investigator reports only partial information that is preliminary, and a credible and comprehensive account or interpretative schema cannot be developed.

## Member checks

Member checking is a technique in which the investigator checks an assumption or a particular understanding with one or more informants. Affirmation of a particular revelation from a re-

search participant strengthens the credibility of the interpretation and decreases the potential of introducing investigator bias. This technique is often used throughout the data collection process. It is also introduced in the formal stage of analysis to confirm the truth value of specific accounts.

## Reflexivity

In the final report or manuscript it is important for the researcher to discuss his or her personal biases and assumptions in conducting the study. Personal biases are revealed in the course of collecting data and during the active process of reflection. The investigator purposely engages in a reflexive process in which his or her own perspectives and personal biases are examined to determine how they may have influenced not only what is learned but also how it is learned.

## Audit trail

Another way an investigator can increase truth value is using an audit trail. Lincoln and Guba suggest that an investigator should leave a path of his or her thinking and coding decisions so others can review the course of logic and decision making that was followed.[16]

## Peer debriefing

Peer debriefing is another strategy that can be used to affirm emerging interpretations. In this approach the investigator purposely involves peers in the analytical process. An investigator may convene a group of peers to review his or her audit trail and emerging findings, or he or she may ask a peer to independently code a randomly selected set of data. The investigator compares the outcomes with his or her own coding scheme. Areas of agreement and disagreement are identified and discussed. Either approach provides an opportunity for the investigator to reflect on other possible competing interpretations of the data. Peer debriefing may occur at different junctures in the analytical process.

### Summary

There are many different purposes and strategies for analysis in naturalistic inquiry. Some researchers seek to generate theory, whereas others aim to reveal and interpret human experiences. Regardless of purpose, the essential characteristic of the analytical process is that it involves an ongoing inductive and abductive thinking process that is interspersed with the activity of gathering information. Although we have described the essential components of the analytical process, each form of naturalistic inquiry approaches this effort differently.

One of the most difficult aspects of naturalistic inquiry is being prepared for the voluminous amount of data that is obtained. Even in a small-scale study, such as a life history of a single individual, the amount of information obtained and its analysis can be overwhelming. The analytical process begins with the simple act of reading or reviewing on multiple occasions the interviews, observational notes, or videotapes that were collected. This step begins the thinking process that is essential to the research. Through inductive and abductive reasoning the boundaries of the study become reformulated and defined, and initial descriptive queries are answered. Further data collection efforts

are determined by the need to more fully explore the depth and breadth of categories and to answer why and how queries. As data are obtained they are coded and organized into meaningful categories. The boundaries and meanings of categories are further refined through the process of establishing relationships among categories. Queries that ask "Why?" and "How?" lead to the development of taxonomies. This in turn leads to emergent patterns, meanings, and interpretations of how observations fit into a larger context. Existing theoretical frameworks or constructs in the literature may be brought into the analytical process to refine emerging interpretations or serve as points of contrast. A refined and final interpretation is usually derived after the investigator exits the field and begins the writing process. Gubrium eloquently summarizes the analytical process as follows:

> Analysis proceeds incrementally with the aim of making visible the native practice of clarification, from one domain of experience to another, structure upon structure.[3]

### Exercises

1. Return to exercise 1 in Chapter 17, which asks you to observe a public place to determine characteristic behavior patterns. Now examine your raw data and search for categories. Based on the categories, code each datum and develop a descriptive taxonomy of behavior.

2. Develop an audit trail for your data collection and analysis activities in the previous inquiry.

*Continued*

## Exercises

3. Give your raw data set from exercise 1 to a colleague for analysis and to establish an audit trail. When your colleague has completed the task, compare your conclusions. Reconcile any differences by reexamining your data and your audit trails.

### References

1. Wolcott HF: *Transforming qualitative data: description, analysis, and interpretation*, Thousand Oaks, Calif, 1994, Sage.
2. Gubrium JF, Holstein JA: *The new language of qualitative method*, New York, 1997, Oxford University Press.
3. Gubrium J: *Analyzing field reality*, Newbury Park, Calif, 1988, Sage.
4. Miles MB, Huberman AM: *Qualitative data analysis: a sourcebook of new methods*, Newbury Park, Calif, 1984, Sage.
5. Fetterman DL: *Ethnography step by step*, Newbury Park, Calif, 1989, Sage.
6. Glaser B, Strauss A: *The discovery of grounded theory*, Chicago, 1967, Aldine.
7. Agar MH: *The professional stranger: an informal introduction to ethnography*, ed 2, San Diego, 1996, Academic Press.
8. Wax M: On misunderstanding verstechen: a reply to Abel, *Sociol Soc Res* 51:323-333, 1967.
9. Spradley JP, McCurdy DW: *The cultural experience: ethnography in a complex society*, Prospect Heights, Ill, 1988, Waveland Press.
10. Gitlin LN, Luborsky M, Schemm R: Emerging concerns of older stroke patients about assistive devices in rehabilitation, *The Gerontologist* 38(2):169-180, 1998.
11. Lofland J, Lofland L: *Analyzing social settings: a guide to qualitative observation and analysis*, ed 2, Belmont, Calif, 1984, Wadsworth.
12. Glaser BG: *Theoretical sensitivity: advanced in the methodology of grounded theory*, Mill Valley, Calif, 1978, Sociology Press.
13. Strauss AL, Corbin JM: *Basics of qualitative research: grounded theory procedures and techniques*, Newbury Park, Calif, 1990, Sage.
14. Savishinsky JS: *The ends of time: life and work in a nursing home*, New York, 1991, Bergen & Garvey.
15. DePoy E, Archer L: Quality of life in a nursing home, *Topics Geriatr Rehabil* 7:64-74, 1992.
16. Lincoln YS, Guba EG: *Naturalistic inquiry*, Newbury Park, Calif, 1985, Sage.
17. Guba EG: Criteria for assessing the trustworthiness of naturalistic inquiries, *Educ Commun Technol J* 29:75-92, 1981.

# Chapter 21

# Reporting and disseminating conclusions

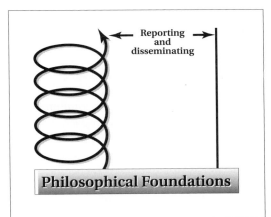

Reporting
and
disseminating

**Philosophical Foundations**

Reporting and disseminating the results of a study are two important action processes in research. These action processes usually occur at the conclusion of a research project. However, often there are opportunities to report the progress of a study or report some of the methodologic challenges of a study before completing the actions of data collection and analysis.

Research, in essence, is not complete unless it is shared with others who can benefit from it. Remember the definition of research presented in Chapter 1? Four criteria to which a study must conform were specified: logical, understandable, confirmable, and useful. Reporting and disseminating are two research action processes that also reflect these criteria. However, usefulness is the unique research criterion that cannot be accomplished without telling others about the findings of a completed study and their meanings.

Any research study may generate one or more reports. Reports are designed to fit the particular avenue or context chosen to disseminate research findings. The method chosen for reporting and disseminating research is purposeful. It is driven by several factors, the most important of which are the question or query and the particular audience or community in which the researcher wants to impact.

As suggested throughout this book, there are multiple research languages and structures. Likewise, there are multiple ways in which you may choose to present and structure the reporting and disseminating of your research. The reporting language and structure you use must be congruent with the epistemological framework of your study; it must fit the purpose for dissemination and the target audience.

Writing and disseminating a research project is analogous to telling a story. As indicated by Richardson:

> Whenever we write science, we are telling some kind of story, or some part of a larger narrative. Some of our stories are more complex, more densely described, and offer greater opportunities as emancipatory documents; others are more abstract, more distanced from lived experience and reinscribe existent hegemonies.[1]

## Principles for writing

Let us now consider the writing action process for both naturalistic and experimental-type inquiries. Each type of inquiry has a distinct language or set of languages and structures that organize the reporting action process. However, all reporting that involves written research has a common set of principles that can be used to guide this important action process.[2]

### Clarity

As stated clearly by Babbie, writing a report serves little purpose if it is not understood.[3] Therefore an investigator should be certain that his or her report is clear and well-written. There are many books on writing and many ways of approaching this task, which is often difficult, particularly for the new investigator. As in any professional activity, the more you do it, the more proficient and easier the task will become. It is important to recognize that writing is an important aspect of the research process; it takes time, thought, and creative energy.

### Purpose

There are multiple purposes that drive the selection of action processes in research. These purposes also structure the nature of the reporting action process.[4] Consider, for example, two different purposes for writing a report—a publication in a professional journal and an evaluation for a community organization. Researchers who write for the purpose of publishing their research in scholarly journals must conform to the style and expectations of the journal to which the manuscript is submitted. The researcher may also consider writing an article for practitioners and thus will present results and interpretations somewhat differently. The researcher who has just completed an evaluation of a community program may need to write a report to the funding agency to ensure continuation of financial support. In this case the researcher may emphasize positive programmatic outcomes and write the research report consistent with the expectations of the funding agency. There are many purposes for conducting and reporting research, and each purpose must be carefully considered.

## Audience specific

Along with purpose, the audience for which the report is written determines, in large part, how the report will be structured and the degree of specificity that will be included. The audience may vary in areas of expertise and knowledge of research methodology. The important point is to identify your reason for writing a report to a particular audience and to assess the way in which that purpose can be communicated to that audience. You need to write in a style that is consistent with the level of understanding and knowledge of the targeted reader.

## Citations

There are several other important points you need to be aware of as you develop written reports and methods for dissemination. The first is the issue of plagiarism. We realize that most researchers who plagiarize do not intend to do so. To avoid this potential and devastating mistake, you need to be aware of the norms for citation and credit. All work written by another person, even if not directly quoted in your work, must be cited. There are many different citation formats used in health and human service research. We refer you to your publication source for the correct format and urge you to become familiar with it. If necessary, have someone else check your work to ensure that you have properly credited other authors.

Another important point to remember in report writing is that it is not an acceptable practice to quote from other research studies in the literature review of an article for a journal. Many students of research like to review a body of literature by stringing a series of quotes together from different articles. However, the review of the literature section in a report must reflect a summation and critical analysis of the most salient aspects of existing studies.

Another common error among newcomers to formal writing is the use of citations that you have not directly read. For example, let us assume you read an article by an author, Dr. Smith, and in her review of the literature she cited a number of other authors and their studies. You are interested in these other studies and include them in your study based on your reading of Dr. Smith's article, and you cite them in your reference list. However, you have never obtained and read the original articles. In this case you are actually using Dr. Smith's interpretations of these studies. Remember, Dr. Smith selected the most salient points from these studies that supported her particular approach. Therefore her interpretation may be different from the intent of the original work. Perhaps if you had read the articles yourself, a different understanding would have been derived. In writing a research report, only primary citations are acceptable. Therefore you have two choices. You can report Dr. Smith's interpretation of the studies she reviewed and cite her article in your reference list. For example, you may say: "According to Dr. Smith, the literature on the adequacy of home care for elders is underdeveloped." A second strategy is to retrieve the articles cited in Dr. Smith's report, read them, and report your interpretation of this body of literature. In the latter case, you will then cite each study you read and include it in your reference list.

With these common-sense principles, let us now consider the specific writing considerations for each tradition.

## Writing an experimental-type report

Reports of experimental-type research use a common language and follow a standard format and structure for presenting a study and its findings. The language used by the experimental-type researcher is "scientific" in nature. It is logical and detached from personal opinion. Interpretations are supported by numerical data. There are usually seven major sections of an experimental-type report (Box 21-1). Although investigators sometimes deviate from this order of

presentation, these sections are usually considered the critical components of a scientific report.

Let us examine each section. The abstract appears before the full report and briefly summarizes or highlights the major points in each subsequent section of the report. It includes a statement of the research purpose, brief overview of method, and summary of the major findings and implications of the study. Usually the abstract does not exceed one or two paragraphs. Professional journals usually specify the length of the abstract; some journals require brief abstracts that are no longer than 100 words.

The introduction presents the problem statement, the purpose statement, and an overview of the questions that the study addresses. In this section the researcher embeds the study in a particular body of literature and highlights the specific contribution that the research is intended to make to professional knowledge and practice.

**Box 21-1** **Major sections of an experimental-type report**

- Abstract
- Introduction
- Background and significance
- Method
  - Design
  - Research question(s)
  - Population and sample
  - Measures
  - Data analysis strategies
  - Procedures
- Results
- Discussion
- Conclusion

The background and significance section reviews the literature that provides the conceptual foundation for your research study. In this section, key concepts, constructs, principles, and theory of the study are critically summarized. (Refer back to your literature chart or concept matrix to help organize the background and significance section.) The degree of detail in presenting the literature will depend on the researcher's purpose and intended audience. For example, in a journal article the researcher usually limits the literature review to the seminal works that precede the study, whereas in a doctoral dissertation all previous work that directly or indirectly informs the research question is included. Some researchers combine the introduction and literature review into one section. Grinnell has named the combined introduction and literature review "the problem statement."[4]

The method section consists of several subsections, including a clear description of the design, an explication of the research question or questions, the population and sample, the measures or instrumentation, the specific data analysis strategies, and the procedures used to conduct the research. The degree of detail and specificity is once again determined by the purpose and audience. However, sufficient information must be provided in each subsection of methods so that the reader has a clear understanding of how data were collected and the specific procedures that were implemented.

In the results section, the analyzed data are presented. Usually, researchers begin by presenting descriptive statistics of their sample and then proceed to a presentation of inferential and associational types of statistical analyses. A rationale for statistical analysis is presented, and the findings are usually explained. However, interpretation of the data is not usually presented in this section. Data may be presented in narrative, chart, graph, or table form. You should be aware that there are prescribed formats for presenting statistical analyses. We suggest that you consult Huck et. al.[5] and Pilcher[6] that appear in the bibliography or seek guidance from actual research reports.

The discussion section is perhaps the most creative part of the experimental-type research report. In this section the researcher discusses the implications and meanings of the findings, poses alternative explanations, relates the findings to previously published work, and suggests the potential application or use of the research results. Most researchers include a statement of the limitations of the study in this section as well, although it can also be found in the sections that discuss methods or findings.

The conclusion section is a short summary that draws conclusions about the findings of the study with regard to future directions for research or health care practices.

As you can see, writing an experimental-type report follows a logical, well-accepted sequence that includes seven essential sections. The degree of detail and precision in each section is dependent on the purpose and audience for the report.

## Writing a naturalistic report

Because there are many epistemologically and structurally different types of research designs that reflect naturalistic inquiry, there is not one single, accepted format for writing a final report. However, there are some basic commonalties among the varied designs that can guide report writing in this tradition. Unlike experimental-type reporting, naturalistic reporting does not follow a prescribed format with clear expectations for language and structure. Written reports are rich in detail and description and draw on case material in the form of narratives to illustrate major themes and interpretations. The structure of the presentation is not standardized, and there is great variation in the format, sequencing of information, and approach. The approach used by the researcher reflects his or her underlying interpretative scheme. Interpretative schemes are often presented in storylike fashion in which main themes and subtexts unfold as the story is told. For example, in her ethnography of children diagnosed with leukemia, Bluebond-Langner presented her analysis of the children's experiences in the form of a play with acts and scenes.[7] The characters in the play represented a composite of the children, families, and medical personnel she had interviewed and observed. In this way, Bluebond-Langner was able to creatively and immediately immerse the reader into the worlds of dying children, their parents, and medical staff. Her approach showed the sequence of events experienced by children as they moved through stages of diagnosis, remission, relapse, and finally death; and to highlight the interactions between children and parents, physicians, and nursing staff. The style of reporting reflected the way in which the children presented themselves to the investigator.

In contrast, in a study of 26 African-American women with breast disease, Mathews et al. began their report with an excerpt from an interview with one of their informants.[8] The au-thors provided a brief overview of the theoretical foundation for understanding narratives and the relationship between personal accounts and cultural systems. The rest of the report was structured more traditionally and included, "Background for the Study," "Profile of the Patient Population and Description of Methodology," "Results of the Narrative Analysis," and "Conclusions."

Another important aspect of reporting in naturalistic inquiry is the inclusion of a section that describes the researcher's personal biases and feelings in conducting the study. Bluebond-Langner, for example, included an appendix in her book entitled, "Doing the fieldwork: A Personal Account."[7] Other researchers discuss their personal perspective on conducting the study as part of the introduction to their report.

Although the report may be structured in many different ways, it contains some of the same basic elements used in report writing for experimental-type research. Using the language of naturalistic research, the basic sections for writing a report are shown in Box 21-2. Reporting in naturalistic research may not follow the sections in the sequence as shown, but each report usually contains these basic elements.

| Box 21-2 | Basic sections of a report of naturalistic inquiry |
| --- | --- |

- Introduction
- Query
- Epistemological foundation
- Theoretical framework(s)
- Research process
- Information
- Analysis
- Meaning and implications

Let us examine each section. The introduction in naturalistic design contains the purpose for conducting the research. An investigator may include personal purposes, as well as a purpose that is related to the development and advancement of professional knowledge.

The query, epistemological foundation, and theoretical framework may appear separately or combined in one section of the report. As previous chapters have described, these thought and action processes are integrated throughout the conduct of naturalistic research and therefore can be presented as such. However, consistent with the principle of clarity in presentation, investigators need to select a format that is clear and easily understood by the target audience and consistent with the purpose of the study and report.

By now you may have noticed that we have not listed literature review as part of the reporting process. Consistent with this research tradition, literature may be presented as a conceptual foundation for the query, or as evidence that supports the data or main interpretations presented by the investigator. In most reports the literature is used to ground the research in a body of knowledge, to support the main findings, or to examine competing interpretations of the findings.

Reporting naturalistic research departs from experimental-type reporting in the presentation of the research process and information. As indicated by Richardson, naturalistic investigators rely heavily on the narrative to report their data.[1] It is not uncommon to find quotations from informants woven throughout the narrative text. Visual and numerical display of information, such as taxonomic charts and content analyses, are also used in naturalistic reporting, depending on the query, epistemological foundation, purpose, and intended audience. Let us consider how the reports from different naturalistic designs may be structured.

## Ethnography

Although there are divergent approaches to ethnography, the primary function of this approach is to identify patterns and characterize a cultural group. The report therefore tells a story about the underlying values, roles, beliefs, and normative practices of the culture. It is not unusual for ethnographers to begin with method; that is, the investigator frequently begins by reporting how he or she gained access to the cultural setting. The report may be developed chronologically, and literature, other sources of information, and conclusions are interspersed throughout and summarized in the end. In his book, *Tally's Corner,* Liebow exemplifies this structure.[9] In the book, *Living and Dying at Murray Manor,* Gubrium's approach is another example of how interpretation is integrated throughout and is reflected in the way he describes what it is like to live in a nursing home.[10] Each chapter builds on the previous but focuses on a different aspect of life in the nursing home facility (e.g., "The Setting," "Top Staff and its World"). The entire book represents his findings. He introduces formal literature through the use of footnotes, which are designed to either support his points or lead the reader to other literature for more discussion of a particular concept that is introduced.

A written report in ethnography is usually lengthy because of the expansiveness of the domain and nature of narrative data.

## Phenomenology

Because the focus in phenomenological research is on the unique experience of one or more persons, the report is often written in the form of a story. If specific points about the lived experience of the informants are made, they are fully supported with information from the informants themselves, frequently in the form of direct quotes from the field notes. Because the length of phenomenological studies varies extensively, they may appear as full-length journal articles, books, or other literary styles in between. The reports highlight life experience and its interpretation by those who experience it, and they minimize interpretations imposed by the investigator.

As you can see, the nature and purpose of each of these designs differ, as does the reporting format. In both cases, form follows function. In ethnography the function of the investigator is to make sense of what he or she has observed, whereas in a phenomenological study the investigator reports how others make sense of their experience. These differences are clearly reflected in the written report.

In summary, naturalistic researchers use a variety of reporting action processes to share their findings. Although there is a heavy reliance on narrative data, the naturalistic investigator has the option of using numerical and visual representations, as well as other media. All reports contain the basic sections (see Box 21-2), but the order and emphasis differ among naturalistic designs and the preferences and personal styles of the investigator.[1,11,12]

### Writing an integrated report

Because integrated reports have made a relatively recent appearance in the research world, there are no guidelines for language and format. In addition, the nature and structure of the report depend on the level of integration, types of designs used, purpose of the work, and audience who will receive the report. We do, however, offer two principles that may help your writing action process. First, you should include the components of a complete research report (see Boxes 21-1 and 21-2). Regardless of its length, organization, or complexity, your report should contain a statement of purpose, review of the literature, methodology section, presentation of findings, and conclusions. Second, because integrated design is not as well-established as designs that are distinctly experimental-type or naturalistic, it is often useful to include an evaluation of the methodology in the report and the justification for the use of each design and the way in which each complements the other.

## Dissemination

There are many ways in which you may choose to disseminate your research. Let us examine three popular modes of disseminating.

## Sharing written reports

Sharing a written report is one of the most common ways of disseminating research findings. As we have already discussed, written reports may reflect different formats, depending on the purpose of the report and the audience. Although journal articles are perhaps the most popular outlet for disseminating a written report, there are many other valuable formats. These include research briefs in periodicals and newsletters, summary articles in professional newsletters, local newspapers, and university newsletters, as well as reports to funding agencies, masters and doctoral theses, chapters in edited books, and full-length books. Once you have written a report, the next action process is publication.

## Publishing your work

The process of publishing your work is exciting but sometimes frustrating, if you are new to the process. The first step in considering publication is to ensure that your work is high quality and meets the rigorous standards for research as discussed in previous chapters. However, writing a sound report does not ensure publication. If you are attempting to publish your first piece of written work, we suggest that you consult with someone who is knowledgeable about the process. It is critical to select a medium that is compatible with the design, purpose, focus, and level of development of your work. Each publication has a set of guidelines and requirements for authors that are usually available in one or more of the yearly issues of the publication. Scholarly and professional journals usually publish instructions for authors at least twice a year. These guidelines include a list of the required format for writing, typing and notation style, and submission processes. For refereed journals, once you submit your work, it is sent out to several (usually three) reviewers for comment and evaluation. This process takes between 3 and 6 months. Do not be surprised if your work is rejected. Most journals have many more submissions than they can publish, and rejection does not mean your work is poor. It is not unusual for journal editors to suggest alternative journals that may accept your work. If your written report is accepted, frequently it will be accompanied with requested revisions from the reviewers or the editor. After revisions, the work is placed in an issue, and galley proofs are sent to you for your review. These galleys are typeset models of your work. Be vigilant in reviewing them to ensure that no mistakes have occurred in the typesetting process. Celebrate your work as you read it in publication. You have met the research criterion of "usefulness!"

## Sharing your research through other methods

Written dissemination is not the only method for sharing your work. There are many other outlets, including presentations at professional and scholarly conferences, oral presentations in other forums, continuing and in-service education, collaborative work with colleagues, and many other formats. Sharing your work is not only useful to others but also helps you receive constructive criticism that will advance your own thinking and conceptual development.

## Summary

Disseminating your research is a major and essential part of the research process. Sharing your work provides knowledge to others to inform practice, tests existing knowledge and theory, develops new knowledge and theory, and ultimately promotes the collective advancement of knowledge in health and human services.

# Exercises

1. Find a research article reported in a professional research journal. Identify a research report published in a practice-oriented newsletter for a professional association. Compare the style of writing and the basic elements of the research process that in light of the intended audiences.

2. Identify a published research study that used an experimental-type design and a published research study that used a naturalistic-type design. Compare the style of writing, the basic elements of the report, and, particularly, the presentation of data.

## References

1. Richardson L: *Writing strategies: reaching diverse audiences,* Newbury Park, Calif, 1990, Sage.
2. Gitlin LN, Lyons KJ: *Successful grant writing: strategies for health and humans service professionals,* New York, 1996, Springer.
3. Babbie E: *The practice of social research,* ed 6, Belmont, Calif, 1992, Wadsworth.
4. Grinnell RM: *Social work research and evaluation,* Itasca, Ill, 1988, Peacock.
5. Huck SW, Cormier WH, Bounds WG: *Reading statistics and research,* New York, 1974, Harper & Row.
6. Pilcher DM: *Data analysis for the helping professions: a practical guide,* Newbury Park, Calif, 1990, Sage.
7. Bluebond-Langner M: *The private worlds of dying children,* Princeton, NJ, 1978, Princeton University Press.
8. Mathews HF, Lannin DR, Mitchell JP: Coming to terms with advanced breast cancer: black women's narratives from eastern North Carolina, *Soc Sci Med* 38(6):789-800, 1994.
9. Liebow E: *Tally's corner,* Boston, 1967, Little, Brown.
10. Gubrium JF: *Living and dying at Murray Manor,* New York, 1975, St Martin's Press.
11. Emerson RM, Fretz RI, Shaw LL: *Writing ethnographic fieldnotes,* Chicago, 1995, University of Chicago Press.
12. Wolcott HF: *Writing up qualitative research,* Newbury Park, Calif, 1990, Sage.

# Chapter 22
## Stories from the field

 Here we are at the end of our book but certainly not, we hope, at the end of your involvement in research. The beauty of research is that you learn from doing, and it is a never-ending process. At each step of the process, new, more refined, and complex queries and questions will emerge and whet your appetite.

We have introduced you to what some may believe are "heavy" philosophical thoughts, technical language, and logical ways of thinking and acting. These are your tools for you to soar and creatively explore that which troubles or challenges you in your practice, daily life, or professional experience, or in your reading of the literature. As you apply these thinking and action tools to health and human service–related issues, you will discover both the artistry and science involved in research.

Research, like any other human activity, has its low and high points, its tedium and thrill, its frustrations and challenges, its drastic mistakes, and clever applications of research principles. Research is, above all, a thinking process. If you think about what you are doing and reflect on what you have done, you can learn from mistakes and keep refining your skill as an investigator.

We would like to share with you some of our own stories from the research field to highlight the twists and turns of research and how human this activity really is.

## Just beginning

It was an urban anthropology class, and we were split into groups to conduct urban ethnographies on health practices by different ethnic groups in the city. The big assignment? The Chinese community. The research group? A hippie-type woman, a rock musician, and a topless go-go dancer who dressed the part day and night. The threesome entered the Chinese community, a relatively self-contained 5- by 10-block area of the inner city. As you can imagine, we were quite a sight. How would we ever be able to "enter" the world of this community and engage in passive observation and active participation in community activities? We started out by walking around and scoping out the area. We made observations of the physical environment and spent some great times eating lunch and dinner in various restaurants.

We became Chinese restaurant experts for friends and family, but we had no breakthrough. Not one Chinese family agreed to meet with us or to be interviewed. Young people were curious and asked lots of questions about us, but their parents remained removed, detached, and unavailable. We caused quite a stir in the community. We split up a couple of times to see if

one of us could gain access, but we had no luck. Then one day we happened to pass a small building with an announcement for a Chinese Political Youth Club. The sign was posted in Chinese and English (a sign of a new acculturated generation?), and we walked directly to the address of the club. We were welcomed and engaged in long discussions of the political climate in the university and the dilemmas confronting the community. Bingo! This was a beginning. Although our access to the community remained through the ears, eyes, and thoughts of this radical subgroup, we were able to delineate health practices and health issues as perceived by this group. This was a lesson in nonreactive research, gaining access, and the impact of key informants on the type of information and understandings that are obtained.

## "I'll do it for you, sweetie"

It was my first important research position. I was working with a gerontological research institute and learning the ropes of how to coordinate a large, federally funded research grant. I was responsible for putting together a rather lengthy face-to-face interview that included questions generated by me and the research team, as well as an arsenal of standardized instruments used in gerontology. Finally, we were ready for pretesting. We pretested the battery with five older adults who immediately became bored and uninterested and found the interview questions tedious and irrelevant. "I'll do it for you, sweetie," became the constant song. I was devastated but assured by my mentors that this is a common response and that the interview schedule was indeed comprehensive and asked what was intended. This was my first big disillusionment with standardized questionnaires.

### In search of significance!

Five years of intensive interviewing, data entry, data cleaning, and sophisticated statistical analyses, but where is the significance? Accepting no significance when you want to find statistically significant differences between an experimental and control group can be difficult. Nonsignificance can be as an important finding as obtaining significant differences, but it can also present a challenge to get the findings published.[1]

### Is health care effective?

In our research class, students are required to develop a research question or query and a proposal that describes how they intend to answer the problem. Our most frustrating but popular "research question" is the one posed by many beginning students in research, "Is nursing effective?," or "Is occupational therapy effective?"

Is this a researchable question? Can you explain what is wrong with the way this question is posed?

### Elevator insight

The values of occupational therapy students in a particular program were studied by administering a values test to incoming students, first-year students, and second-year students. It was hypothesized that a change in values would occur, which would indicate that students had acquired the professional values that were intricate components of the curriculum. After the test was administered, some of the students were talking about it on the elevator without realizing that the investigator was present. The students discussed the content of the questions; they were comparing responses and hoped that they had answered them correctly! The investigator realized at that incredible, serendipitous moment that the students had answered the questions as they thought they should. They thought it was a test with only one set of correct answers. Their responses did not reflect how they actually felt or believed but what was socially and professionally desirable.[2]

### A "good" research subject

We established what we believed were clear, objective criteria by which to identify eligible subjects from a pool of older adults who were in rehabilitation for a stroke, a lower limb amputation, or an orthopedic deficit. The purpose of the study was to identify the initial perceptions and attitudes of older patients toward the assistive devices they received in the hospital and whether these issued devices were used at home after hospitalization. As the recruitment process began, periodic meetings were held with therapists who were responsible for identifying potential study subjects. At one of these initial meetings, we asked how recruitment was proceeding and if everyone understood the study criteria. Therapists relayed that all was going well, and that they were very pleased that they had been able to identify the first few subjects who would "do very well" in this study. The therapists were asked what they meant by "doing well." We learned that therapists had referred patients to the study who they believed greatly valued their assistive devices and would use them at home. Therapists were systematically referring only the "good" patients and were ignoring the potential study eligibility of those patients who they did not like or who they suspected would be noncompliant to device use. This represented a fatal flaw in the recruitment process that would have contaminated the entire data collection effort and study results. We immediately changed the recruitment process and examined the hospital census records to determine who may have been available for study participation but systematically excluded by the therapists at this initial study phase.[3,4]

## A "bad" research subject

In a study of family caregiving, an eligible subject enrolled in the study and was randomly assigned to receive an experimental intervention. The experimental intervention involved in-home occupational therapy visits that were designed to help the caregiver modify the home environment to support his or her caregiving efforts. This particular subject had very unusual religious beliefs and social practices that personally upset and differed from the member of the research team who was providing the experimental intervention. Initially, the interventionist was unable to handle these value differences and suggested to the investigators that the subject was inappropriate for the study and should be considered ineligible. In actuality, there were no objective criteria for excluding this caregiver from the study. The caregiver fit all eligibility criteria. Additionally, the individual had agreed to participate in the study and had signed an informed consent form. It is for this very reason that criteria for subject selection are developed. Furthermore, oversight of their implementation and protection of the protocol must be maintained by the investigator. Subjective reasons for excluding individuals from study participation are a serious source of bias. In this case the investigators worked with the interventionist to alleviate her anxiety and to proceed with the implementation of the intervention according to protocol.[5,6]

## Wow, you got it!

Your heart starts to beat, you feel a rush; it all clicks, falls into place; you uncovered a pattern, a finding, something really striking, and it is significant. The data are right before your eyes. The result has the potential of having an impact on how professionals practice, on how clients feel, and on their health and well-being![3, 6-9] Wow, you got it! You feel great.

This is so important—you have to do it again.

*References*

1. Gitlin LN, Lawton MP, Landsberg LW, et al: In search of psychological benefits: exercise in healthy older adults, *J Aging Health* 4:174-192, 1992.
2. DePoy E, Merrill SC: Value acquisition in an occupational therapy curriculum, *Occup Ther J Res* 8:259-274, 1988.
3. Gitlin LN, Schemm RL, Landsberg LW, Burgh DY: Factors predicting assistive device use in the home by older persons following rehabilitation, *J Aging Health* 8(4):554-575, 1996.

4. Gitlin LN, Burgh DY, Dodson C, Freda M: Strategies to recruit older adults for participation in rehabilitation research, *Top Geriatr Rehabil* 11(1): 10-19, 1995.

5. Gitlin LN, Corcoran M: Expanding caregiver ability to use-environmental solutions for problems of bathing and incontinence in the elderly with dementia, *Technol Disabil* 2:12-21, 1993.

6. Gitlin LN, Corcoran M: Managing dementia at home: the role of home environmental modifications, *Top Geriatr Rehabil* 12(2):28-39, 1996.

7. Posner J, Gorman KM, Gitlin LN: Effects of exercise training in the elderly on the occurrence and time to onset of cardiovascular disease, *J Am Geriatr Soc* 38:205-210, 1990.

8. Burke JP, DePoy E: Emerging view of mastery, excellence and leadership in occupational therapy practice, *Am J Occup Ther* 45:1027-1032, 1991.

9. Gitlin LN, Luborsky M, Schemm R: Emerging concerns of older stroke patients about assistive devices in rehabilitation, *The Gerontologist* 38(2):169-180, 1998.

# Glossary

**Abductive reasoning** Patterns and concepts that emerge from an examination of information or data, which in some cases may relate to available theories and in other cases may not

**Abstract** Research report that appears before the full report and briefly summarizes or highlights the major points made in each subsequent section

**Abstraction** Symbolic representation of an observable or experienced referent

**Accidental sampling** *(see convenience sampling)*

**Action processes** Set of actions that researchers follow to implement a design; include setting boundaries of the study, collecting and analyzing information, and reporting and disseminating study findings

**Action research** Inquiry undertaken to generate knowledge to inform action

**Analysis of covariance** Statistical technique that removes the effect of the influence of another variable on the dependent or outcome variable

**Analysis of variance** Parametric statistic used to ascertain the extent to which significant group differences can be inferred to the population

**Artifact review** Data collection technique in which the meaning of objects in their natural contexts is examined

**Associational statistics** Set of procedures designed to identify relationships between multiple variables; determines whether knowledge of one set of data allows inference or prediction of the characteristics of another set of data

**Attention factor** *(also known as "Hawthorne" or halo effect)* Phenomenon in which research subjects may experience change simply from the act of participating in a research project

**Audit trail** Path of a person's thinking and action processes that enables others to follow the logic and manner in which knowledge was developed

**Axial coding** Set of procedures whereby data are put back together in new ways after open coding by making connections between categories *(see citation in Chapter 18)*

**Bias** Potential unintended or unavoidable effect on study outcomes

**Bimodal distribution** Distribution in which two values occur with the same frequency

**Boundary setting** One of the first action processes of research in which the investigator establishes the conceptual limits of the study, as well as the types of information and study participants that will be included

**Breakdowns** Point in data collection in naturalistic inquiry in which the expectation of the researcher does not match the observation or information gathered

**Case study** Detailed, in-depth description of a single unit, subject, or event

**Categories** Basic analytical step used in naturalistic inquiry in which the investigator groups phenomena according to similarities and labels the groups

**Celeration line** Approach to the visual analysis of data points obtained in single subject designs; drawn across pretest and posttest data points, it reflects the central tendency of the data

**Chi-square** Nonparametric statistic used with nominal data to test group differences

**Cleaning data** Action process whereby the investigator checks the inputted data set to ensure all data have been accurately represented

**Closed-ended question** Data gathering strategy in which a question is formed and the study participant is asked to choose a response among prescribed sets of answers

**Cluster sampling** Random sampling technique whereby the investigator begins with large units, or clusters, in which smaller sampling units are contained; the investigator then randomly selects elements from these clusters

**Codebook** Record of variable names for each variable in experimental-type research; record of categories, codes, and line placement in naturalistic inquiry

**Coding of categories** Repeated review and examination of the narrative in naturalistic data analysis

**Cohort study** Research that examines specific subpopulations as they change over time

**Concept** Symbolic representations of an observable or experienced referent

**Concept matrix** Two-dimensional organizational system that presents all information that the investigator reviews and evaluates

**Conceptual definition** (also known as lexical definition) Stipulates the meaning of concepts or constructs with other concepts or constructs

**Concurrent validity** Extent to which an instrument can discriminate the absence or presence of a known standard

**Confidentiality** Assurance, on the part of the investigator, that no one other than the research team can have access to a respondent's information unless those who see the data are identified to the person before participation; the information cannot be linked to a person's identity

**Confirmable** One of the four basic characteristics of research (defined in Chapter 1); the researcher must clearly and logically identify the strategies used in a study, enabling others to follow the sequence of thoughts and actions and to derive similar outcomes and conclusions

**Confirming cases** Naturalistic boundary-setting strategy in which the investigator purposely selects participants to support an emerging interpretation or theory

**Confounding variables** (see intervening variables)

**Constant comparison** Naturalistic data analysis technique in which each datum is compared and contrasted with previous information to fit inductively all the pieces together into a bigger puzzle

**Construct** Symbolic representation of shared experience that does not have an observable or directly experienced referent

**Construct validity** Fit between the constructs that are the focus of the study and the way in which these constructs are operationalized

**Content validity** Degree to which an indicator seems to agree with a validated instrument measuring the same construct

**Context specific** One of the central features of naturalistic inquiry, which refers to the specific environment or field in which the study is conducted and information is derived

**Contextualization** Placement of data into a larger perspective (see citation in Chapter 18)

**Contingency table** Two-dimensional frequency distribution primarily used with categorical data

**Continuous variables** Variables that take on an infinite number of values

**Control** Set of action processes that directs or manipulates factors to minimize extraneous variance in order to achieve an outcome

**Control group** Group in experimental-type design in which the independent variable is withheld; thus the control group represents the characteristics of the experimental group before being changed by participation in the experimental condition

***Convenience sampling*** *(also known as accidental, opportunistic, or volunteer sampling)* Boundary-setting action process that involves the enrollment of available subjects as they enter the study until the desired sample size is reached

***Correlational analysis*** Method of determining relationships among variables

***Counterbalance design*** Variation on experimental design in which more than one intervention is tested and in which the order of participation in each intervention is manipulated

***Credibility*** *(also referred to as truth value)* Truth value and accuracy of findings in naturalistic inquiry

***Criterion validity*** Correlation or relationship between a measurement of interest and another instrument or standard that has been shown to be accurate

***Critical theory*** World view that suggests both an epistemology and a social change purpose for conducting research; complex set of strategies that is united by the commonality of sociopolitical purpose designed to know about social justice and human experience as a means to promote social change

***Critical value*** Numerical value that indicates how high the sample statistic must be at a given level of significance to reject the null hypothesis

***Cronbach's alpha*** Statistical procedure used to examine the extent to which all items in the instrument measure the same construct

***Crossover design*** Variation on true experimental design in which one group is assigned to the experimental group first and to the control condition later, and then the order for the other group is reversed

***Cross-sectional studies*** Studies that examine a phenomenon at one point in time

***Culture*** Explicit and tacit rules, symbols, and rituals that guide patterns of human behavior within a group

***Data*** *(singular, datum)* Set of information obtained through systematic investigation; data can refer to information that is numerical or narrative

***Data reduction*** Procedures used to summarize raw data into more compact and interpretable forms

***Data set*** Set of raw numbers generated by experimental-type data collection

***Database management*** Set of actions necessary to develop and maintain the raw data and statistical control files that are developed in experimental-type studies

***Deductive reasoning*** Moving from a general principle to understanding a specific case

***Degrees of freedom*** Values that are free to vary in a statistical test

***Dependent variable*** Presumed effect of an independent variable

***Descriptive questions*** *(see Level 1 questions)*

***Descriptive research*** Research that yields descriptive knowledge of population parameters and relationships among those parameters

***Descriptive statistics*** Procedures used to reduce large sets of observations into more compact and interpretable forms

***Design*** Plan, or blueprint, that specifies and structures the action processes of collecting, analyzing, and reporting data to answer a research question or query

***Deviant case*** Naturalistic boundary-setting strategy in which the investigator selects participants that have experiences that deviate or are vastly different from the mainstream

***Directional hypothesis*** Type of hypothesis in which the direction of the effect of the independent variable on the dependent variable is clearly articulated

**Disconfirming cases** Naturalistic boundary-setting strategy in which the investigator selects participants who challenge an emerging interpretation or theory

**Discrete variables** Variables with a finite number of distinct values

**Dispersion** *(also referred to as variability)* Summary measure, such as range or standard deviation, which describes the distribution of observed values

**Effect size** Strength of differences in the sample values that the investigator expects to find

**Embedded case study** Design in which the cases are conglomerates of multiple subparts, or are subparts themselves, placed within larger contexts

**Emic perspective** "Insider's" or informant's way of understanding and interpreting experience

**Endogenous research** Inquiry that is conceptualized, designed, and conducted by researchers who are "insiders" of the culture, using their own epistemology and structure of relevance

**Epistemology** Branch of philosophy that addresses the nature of knowledge and how one comes to know

**Ethics** Integrity of the scientific process with specific concerns for the behavioral conduct of the investigator throughout the research process and for the ethical involvement of human subjects in research

**Ethnography** Primary research approach in anthropology that is concerned with description and interpretation of cultural patterns of groups, as well as the understanding of the cultural meanings people use to organize and interpret their experiences

**Etic perspective** Systematic understanding of phenomena developed by those who are external to a group

**Exempt status** Institutional review status in which a study protocol is exempt from formal review from either the full board or its subcommittee

**Ex post facto design** One type of non-experimental, passive observation design in which the phenomena of interest have already occurred and cannot be manipulated in any way

**Experimental group** Group in experimental design that receives the experimental condition

**Experimental-type research** Designs that are based in a positivist philosophical foundation and that yield numerical data for analysis

**Explanatory research** Research designed to predict outcomes

**Exploratory research** Studies conducted in natural settings with the explicit purpose of discovering phenomena, variables, theory, or combinations thereof

**External validity** Capacity to generalize findings and develop inferences from the sample to the study population

**Extraneous variables** *(see intervening variables)*

**Extreme or deviant case** Naturalistic boundary-setting technique in which the investigator selects a case that represents an extreme example of the phenomenon of interest

**Factorial design** Variation on true experimental design in which the investigator evaluates the effects of two or more independent variables ($X_1$ and $X_2$) or the effects of an intervention on different factors or levels of a sample or study variables

**Field notes** Naturalistic recordings written by the investigator that are composed of two basic components: (1) recordings of events, observations, and occurrences; and (2) recordings of the investigator's own impressions of events, personal feelings, hunches, and expectations

**Field study** Research conducted in natural settings

**Flexible design** One of the central characteristics of designs in naturalistic inquiry; refers to the unfolding nature of designs in which data-collection decisions are based on an interactive process of simultaneously collecting and analyzing information

*Focus group design* Naturalistic design that uses a small group process to facilitate data collection and analysis

*Frequency distribution* Distribution of values for a given variable and the number of times each value occurs

*Full integration* Method that integrates multiple purposes and thus combines design strategies from different paradigms, enabling each to contribute knowledge to the study of a single problem to derive a more complete understanding of the phenomenon under study

*Gaining access* Naturalistic action process of entering the context of a field study

*Grounded theory* Method in naturalistic research that is used to generate theory using primarily the inductive process of constant comparison

*Guttman scale* Unidimensional or cumulative scale in which the researcher develops a small number of items (four to seven) that relate to one concept and then arranges them so that endorsement of one item means an endorsement of items below it

*Halo effect* (also known as "Hawthorne" or attention factor; see attention factor)

*Hawthorne effect* (also known as attention factor or halo effect; see attention factor)

*Heuristic design* Research approach that encourages an individual to discover and methods that enable him or her to investigate further; design strategy that involves complete immersion of the investigator into the phenomenon of interest and self-reflection of the investigator's personal experiences

*History* Effect of external events on study outcomes

*Holistic* Philosophical approaches that view individuals as creating their own subjective realities that cannot be understood by atomizing, or separating, experience into discrete parts

*Holistic case study* Design in which the unit of analysis is seen as only one global phenomenon

*Homogenous selection* Naturalistic action process of boundary setting in which the investigator attempts to reduce variation in study participants, thereby simplifying the number of experiences, characteristics, and conceptual domains that are represented among study participants

*Hypothesis* Testable statements that indicate what the researcher expects to find, based on theory and level of knowledge in the literature

*Inclusion and exclusion criteria* Sets of criteria that determine who can and cannot participate in a study

*Independent variable* Presumed cause of the dependent variable (sometimes referred to as the predictor variable)

*Inductive reasoning* Human reasoning that involves a process in which general rules evolve or develop from individual cases or from observation of phenomenon

*Inference* Extent to which the samples reflect the population at both pretest and posttest times

*Inferential statistics* Used to draw conclusions about population parameters, based on findings from a sample

*Informants* Participants in a research study who play an active role of informing the investigator as to the context and its cultural rules

*Informed consent* Official statement developed by the researcher that informs study participants of the purpose and scope of the study

*Institutional Review Board (IRB)* Board of experts that must be established at each institution involved in a research process to oversee the ethical conduct of research

*Integrated design* Used to strengthen a study by selecting and combining designs and methods from both paradigms so that one complements the other to benefit the whole or contribute to an understanding of the whole

**Interactive effect** Changes that occur in the dependent variable as a consequence of the combined influence or interaction of taking the pretest and participating in the experimental condition

**Interactionists** Specific philosophical approach in naturalistic inquiry, which assumes that human meaning evolves from the context of social interaction; human phenomena are therefore understood through interpreting the meanings in social discourse and exchange

**Internal validity** Ability of the research design to answer accurately the research question

**Interpretation** Analytical step in naturalistic inquiry in which the investigator examines the derived categories and themes and develops a conceptual understanding of the phenomenon

**Interquartile range** Measure of variability in experimental-type research that refers to the range of scores that compose the middle 50% of subjects, or the majority responses

**Interrater reliability** Test involving the comparison of two observers measuring the same event

**Interrupted time series design** Quasi-experimental design in which there is repeated measurement of the dependent variable, both before and after the introduction of the independent variable, and in which there is no control or comparison group

**Interval numbers** Numbers that share the characteristics of ordinal and nominal measures but also have the characteristic of equal spacing between categories

**Intervening variables** (also known as confounding or extraneous variables) Phenomena that have an effect on the study variables but are not necessarily the object of the study

**Interview** Information-gathering action process conducted through verbal communication and occurring face-to-face or by telephone; process may be either structured or unstructured and are usually conducted with one individual

**Investigator involvement** One of the principal characteristics of most forms of naturalistic inquiry in which the investigator becomes fully immersed in the data collection and analytical process

**Judgmental sampling** (see purposive sampling)

**Kuder-Richardson formula** (K-R 20) Statistical procedure used to examine the extent to which all the items in the instrument measure the same construct

**Laboratory study** Research implemented in controlled environments

**Learning the ropes** Ongoing naturalistic action process that involves continued negotiation and renegotiation with members of a field site or with the individual or groups of individuals that are the focus of the study

**Level 1 questions** (also known as descriptive questions) Experimental-type research questions that aim to describe phenomena

**Level 2 questions** (also known as relational questions) Experimental-type research questions that explore relationships among phenomena that have already been studied at the descriptive level

**Level 3 questions** (also known as predictive questions) Experimental-type research questions that test concepts by manipulating one to affect the other

**Levels of abstraction** Four levels that guide theory development and testing: concept, construct, relationships, and propositions or principles

**Levels of significance** Probability that defines how rare or unlikely the sample data must be before the researcher can reject the null hypothesis

**Lexical definition** (see conceptual definition)

**Life history** Type of naturalistic inquiry concerned with eliciting life experiences and with how individuals interpret and attribute meanings to these experiences; a research approach designed to reveal the nature of the "life process traversed over time"

**Likert scale** Type of scale most frequently scored on a 5- to 7-point range, indicating the subject's level of positive or negative response to an item

**Literature review chart** Approach to organizing a literature review in which research studies are summarized in a table format along key categories, such as type of design, measures, and outcomes

**Logical deduction** Human process of reasoning that begins with an abstraction and then focuses on discrete parts of phenomena or observations

**Logical positivism** Philosophical school of thought characterized by a belief in a singular, knowable reality that exists separate from individual ideas and reductionism

**Logical process** One of the four criteria of research *(defined in Chapter 1)*; suggests that research must be clear and conform to accepted norms of deductive, inductive, or abductive reasoning, and proceed systematically and logically through the thinking and action processes

**Longitudinal study** Research design in which data collection occurs at discrete points over long periods of time

**Main effects** Direct effect of one variable on another

**Manipulation** Action process of maneuvering the independent variable so that the effect of its presence, absence, or degree can be observed on the dependent variable

**Maximum variation** Boundary-setting strategy that involves seeking individuals for study participation who are extremely different along dimensions that are the focus of the study

**Mean** Average score calculated by adding the objects or items and then dividing the sum by the number of objects or items

**Measure of variability** Degree of dispersion among scores

**Measures of central tendency** Numerical information regarding the most typical or representative scores in a group

**Measurement** Translation of observations into numbers

**Median** Point in a distribution at which 50% of the cases fall above and below

**Member check** Technique whereby the investigator "checks out" his or her assumptions with informants

**Memoing** Particular approach to coding segments of narrative that is used in naturalistic forms of analysis; investigator indicates personal notations as to emerging hypotheses and subsequent directions for analysis

**Mixed method design** Combination of multiple strategies and/or designs that answers a series of research questions

**Mode** Value that occurs most frequently in a data set

**Mortality** Subject attrition or dropping out of a study before its completion

**Multiple comparisons** Statistical tests used to determine which group is greater than the others

**Multiple regression** Equation based on correlational statistics in which each predictor variable is entered into the equation to determine how strongly it relates to the outcome variable and how much variation in the outcome variable can be predicted by each independent variable

**Multiple-case study** Design in which more than one study on single units of analysis are conducted

**Narrative** Set of words, derived from stories, interviews, written journals, and other written documents, which forms the data set in naturalistic inquiry

**Naturalistic inquiry** Set of research approaches that are based in holistic-type philosophical frameworks and that use inductive and abductive forms of reasoning to derive qualitative information

*Networking* *(see snowball sampling)*

*Nominal numbers* Numbers used to name attributes of a variable

*Nondirectional hypothesis* Type of hypothesis in which the research indicates an expected effect but not the direction of that effect

*Nonequivalent control group designs* Quasi-experimental designs in which there are at least two comparison groups, but subjects are not randomly assigned to these groups

*Nonexperimental designs* Experimental-type designs in which the three criteria for true experimentation do not exist

*Nonparametric statistics* Formulas used to test hypotheses when (1) normality of variance in the population is not assumed, (2) homogeneity of variance is not assumed, (3) data generated from measures are ordinal or nominal, and (4) sample sizes may be small

*Nonprobability sampling* Sampling in which nonrandom methods are used to obtain a sample

*Nonrandom error* *(see systematic error)*

*Nonreactive methodology* *(see unobtrusive methodology)*

*Null hypothesis* Hypothesis of no difference

*One-shot case study* Pre-experimental design in which the independent variable is introduced and in which the dependent variable is then measured in only one group

*Ontology* Term of philosophy that refers to a person's view or definition of reality

*Open-ended questions* Form of asking questions in which the response is open and in which participants are free to formulate specific verbal responses, rather than choose among fixed response options

*Operational definition* Reduces the abstraction of a concept to a concrete observable form by specifying the exact procedures for measuring or observing the phenomenon

*Opportunistic sampling* *(see convenience sampling)*

*Ordinal numbers* Numerical values that assign an order to a set of observations

*Panel study* Similar to cohort design, except that the same set of people are studied over time

*Parametric statistics* Mathematical formulas that test hypotheses based on three assumptions: (1) samples come from populations that are normally distributed, (2) there is homogeneity of variance, and (3) data that are generated from the measures are interval level

*Participant observation* Naturalistic data-collection strategy in which the researcher takes part in the context under scrutiny

*Participatory action research* Approach that directly involves study participants in each of the 10 research essentials; that is, it involves study participants that contribute to formulating the research question or query, study design, and approach to analysis

*Passive observation designs* Nonexperimental designs used to investigate phenomena as they naturally occur and to ascertain the relationship between two or more variables

*Pearson product–moment correlation* Statistic of association using interval level data and yielding a score between −1 and +1

*Peer debriefing* Use of more than one investigator as a participant in the analytical process, followed by reflection on other possible competing interpretations of the data

*Phenomenology* One form of naturalistic inquiry, the purpose of which is to uncover the meaning of how humans experience phenomena through the description of those experiences as they are lived by individuals

*Pluralism* Central characteristic of naturalistic inquiry that suggests there are multiple realities that can be identified and understood only within the natural context in which human experience and behavior occur

**Population** Group of persons, elements, or both that share common characteristics that are defined by the investigator

**Post hoc comparisons** Statistical tests used to determine which group is greater than the others

**Posttest** Observation or measurement subsequent to the completion of the experimental condition

**Practice research** Investigation of human experience in the context of health care and human service institutions, agencies, or settings

**Predictive questions** *(see Level 3 questions)*

**Predictive validity** Extent to which an instrument can predict or estimate the occurrence of a behavior or event

**Pre-experimental designs–experimental-type designs** Designs in which two of the three criteria necessary for true experimentation are absent

**Pretest** Observation or measurement before the introduction of experimental condition

**Principles** *(see propositions)*

**Probability sampling** Sampling plans that are based on probability theory

**Probe** Statement that is neutral, which is designed to encourage the study participant to provide additional information or elaboration

**Problem statement** Identifies the phenomenon to be explored and the reason(s) it needs to be examined or why it is a problem or issue

**Propositions** *(also called principles)* Statements that govern a set of relationships and give them a structure

**Prospective studies** Studies that describe phenomena, search for cause-and-effect relationships, or examine change in the present or as the event unfolds over time

**Purpose statement** Articulates the specific purpose of or reason for conducting the research study; identifies the particular goals of the study

**Purposive sampling** *(also known as judgmental sampling)* Deliberate selection of individuals by the researcher based on certain predefined criteria

**Quasi-experimental design** Experiments that have treatments, outcome measures, and experimental units, but do not use random assignment to create comparison from which treatment caused change is inferred; instead, the comparisons depend on nonequivalent groups that differ from each other in many ways other than the presence of the treatment whose effects are being tested *(see citation in Chapter 8)*

**Query** Broad statement that identifies the phenomenon or natural field of interest in naturalistic forms of inquiry

**Questionnaires** Written instruments that may be administered either face-to-face, by proxy, or through the mail; may vary as to the structure of questions (closed or open) that are included

**Quota sampling** Nonrandom technique in which the investigator purposively obtains a sample by selecting sample elements in the same proportion that they are represented in the population

**Random error** Error that occurs by chance

**Randomization** Selection or assignment of subjects based on chance

**Range** Difference between the highest and lowest observed value in a collection of data

**Ratio numbers** Numbers that have all the characteristics of interval numbers but also have an absolute 0 point

**Raw data file** Set of numbers in a computer file that is entered from a questionnaire or other data collection instrument used in experimental-type research; its creation is the first action step in the process of preparing data for statistical analysis

**Reflexivity** Process of self-examination

**Regression** Statistical phenomenon in which extreme scores tend to regress or cluster around the mean (average) on repeated testing occasion

*Relational questions* *(see Level 2 questions)*

*Reliability* Stability of a research design

*Research* Multiple, systematic strategies to generate knowledge about human behavior, human experience, and human environments in which the thought and action processes of the researcher are clearly specified so that they are (1) logical, (2) understandable, (3) confirmable, and (4) useful

*Research design* Plan that specifies and structures the action processes of collecting, analyzing, and reporting data to answer a research question

*Research question* Guides an experimental-type investigation; must be concise and framed in such a way that systematic inquiry can be carried out; establishes the boundaries or limits as to what concepts, individuals, or phenomena will be examined

*Research topic* Broad area of inquiry from which the investigator develops a more specific question or query

*Retrospective studies* Describe and examine phenomena after the fact or after the phenomena have occurred

*Sample* Subset of the population that participates in or is included in the study

*Sampling error* Difference between the values obtained from the sample and those that actually exist in the population

*Sampling frame* Listing of every element in the target population

*Saturation* Point at which an investigator has obtained sufficient information from which to obtain an understanding of the phenomena

*Scales* Tools for the quantitative measurement of the degree to which individuals possess a specific attribute or trait

*Secondary data analysis* Analysis of a data set that has been developed in a previous study or by another investigator; is conducted usually for the purpose of exploring specific research questions that were secondary to the primary study purpose

*Semantic differential* Scaling technique in which the researcher develops a series of opposites or mutually exclusive constructs that ask the respondent to give a judgment about something along an ordered dimension, usually of 7 points

*Significance level* Extent to which group differences are a function of chance

*Simple random sampling* (SRS) Probability sampling technique in which a sample is randomly selected from a population

*Single-case study* Design in which only one study on a single unit of analysis is conducted

*Snowball sampling* (also known as networking) Obtaining a sample through asking subjects to provide the names of others who may meet study criteria

*Solomon four-group design* True experimental design that combines true experiment and posttest-only designs into one design structure

*Spearman rho* Statistic of association using ordinal level data and yielding a score between $-1$ and $+1$

*Split-half technique* Reliability technique in which instrument items are split in half and a correlational procedure is performed between the two halves

*Standard deviation* Indicator of the average deviation of scores around the mean

*Static group comparison* Pre-experimental design in which a comparison group is added to the one-shot case study design

*Statistic* Number derived from a mathematical procedure as part of the analytical process in experimental-type research

*Statistical conclusion validity* Power of an investigator's study to draw statistical conclusions

*Statistical power* Probability of identifying a relationship that exists, or the probability of rejecting the null hypothesis when it is false or should be rejected

**Stratified random sampling** Technique in which the population is divided into smaller subgroups, or strata, from which sample elements are then chosen

**Sum of squares** Descriptive statistic for interpreting variability; derived by squaring the difference between each score from the mean, which are then summed

**Survey designs** Nonexperimental designs used to measure primarily characteristics of a population, typically conducted with large samples through mail questionnaires, telephone, or face-to-face interview

**Systematic error (also known as non-random error)** Refers to systematic bias or an error that occurs consistently with an instrument; impacts the extent to which an instrument is valid or represents the underlying construct or concept

**Systematic random sampling** Technique in which a sampling interval width $(K)$ is determined based on the needed sample size, and then every Kth element is selected from a sampling frame

**Target population** Group of individuals or elements from which the investigator is able to select a sample

**Taxonomic analysis** Naturalistic data analysis technique in which the researcher organizes similar or related categories into larger categories and identifies differences between sets of subcategories and larger or overarching categories

**Ten essentials** Ten thinking and action processes that compose any type of research that is experimental, naturalistic, or integrated (described in Chapter 2)

**Test-retest reliability** Reliability test in which the same test is given twice to the same subject under the same circumstances

**Theme** Analytical process used in naturalistic inquiry in which the investigator identifies patterns and topics from which a theme is derived

**Theoretical sensitivity** Researcher's ability to detect and give meaning to data

**Theory** Set of interrelated constructs, definitions, and propositions that presents a systematic view of phenomena by specifying relations among variables, with the purpose of explaining or predicting phenomena (see citation in Chapter 1)

**Theory-based selection** Approach in naturalistic inquiry wherein key informants or study participants are selected, based on their ability to illuminate the particular theoretical construct that is being explored

**Theory generating** One of the primary purposes of many forms of naturalistic inquiry; use of naturalistic approaches to inquiry to link each piece of datum from which concepts, constructs, relationships, and propositions are generated or derived

**Theory testing** One of the primary purposes of many forms of experimental-type research; use of experimental methodologies to formally test a set of propositions of a theory

**Thinking processes** Logical thought processes of research that involve deductive, inductive, or abductive thinking; include identifying a philosophical foundation and theoretical framework, framing a question or query, substantiating the research approach, and developing a design structure

**Time-series design** Quasi-experimental type design that involves multiple data collection over time for a single group

**Transcription** Typed narrative derived from an audiotape or a videotape of an interview with an individual or group; represents an action process primarily used in naturalistic forms of inquiry as the first step in the analysis and interpretation of narrative

**Trend study** Research examining a general population over time to see changes or trends that emerge as a consequence of time

**Triangulation** Use of multiple strategies or methods as a means to strengthen the credibility of an investigator's findings related to the phenomenon under study

***True-experimental design*** Classic two-group design in which subjects are randomly selected and randomly assigned *(R)* to either an experimental or a control group condition; before the experimental condition, all subjects are pretested or observed on a dependent measure *(O)*; in the experimental group, the independent variable or experimental condition is imposed *(X)*, and it is withheld in the control group; subjects are then posttested or observed on the dependent variable *(O)* after the experimental condition

***Truth value*** *(also referred to as credibility)* Used in naturalistic inquiry to refer to the accuracy of interpretation or how closely the analytical scheme reflects the natural context or focus of the investigation

***T-test*** Parametric test to ascertain the extent to which any significant differences existing between two sample group means can be inferred to the population

***Type I error*** Rejecting the null hypothesis when it is true

***Type II error*** Failing to reject the null hypothesis when it is false

***Typical case*** Naturalistic boundary setting strategy in which the investigator selects participants who are typical or representative of the particular event or experience that is the focus of the inquiry

***Understandable criteria*** One of the four criteria of research *(defined in Chapter 1)*; refers to the requirement that a study makes sense and that all study procedures are precisely articulated

***Univariate statistics*** Descriptive data reduction approaches for one variable

***Unobtrusive methodology*** *(also known as nonreactive methodology)* Observation and examination of documents and objects that bear on the phenomenon of interest

***Useful criteria*** One of the four criteria of research *(defined in Chapter 1)*; refers to the requirement that a research study contributes to knowledge building

***Validity*** Extent to which an investigator's findings are accurate or reflect the underlying purpose of the study

***Variability*** *(see dispersion)*

***Variable*** Concept or construct to which a numerical value is assigned; by definition, it must have more than one value, even if the investigator is interested in only one condition

***Variable label*** Applied to each variable in a computer file; follows certain conventions that are based on the particular statistical software that is used by the investigator

***Variance*** Descriptive statistic that reflects a measure of variability; reflects the mean or average of the sum of squares; the larger the variance, the larger the spread of scores

***Volunteer sampling*** *(see convenience sampling)*

***Vulnerable populations*** Considered to be vulnerable or at risk in participating in studies; require special set of ethical procedures to ensure their protection; examples include pregnant women, fetuses, children, individuals with cognitive impairments or mental illness, and prisoners

# Index

# Index

## V

Validity
    construct, 98-99
    definition of, 95, 316
    external, 97-99
    importance in measurements, 204-207
    internal, 95-97
    in naturalistic analysis, 283
    statistical conclusion, 98
    three degrees of, 204, 205
    types of, 206-207
Variability; *see also* dispersion
    measures of, 255-258, 310
    range, 256
Variable labels, 236-237
Variables
    analyzing two (bivariate), 258-260
    definition and description of, 75, 91t, 91, 316
    independent *versus* dependent, 89
    labeling, 236-237, 316
    manipulating and controlling, 93-94
    measurement levels of, 196-197

Variances (V)
    assumptions about in parametric statistics, 265
    definition of, 316
    formula for, 257
    one-way analysis of, 266-268
    as statistical indicator, 239
Verification, component in "asking," 224
Videotapes
    for collecting data, 227-228
    using in research, 5
Vocabulary, in research field, 5
Voluntarism, in research studies, 154-155
Volunteer sampling, 171, 316
Vulnerable populations, 156, 316

## W

Watching, 188
    in naturalistic research, 219-221
Wechler Adult Intelligence Scale, 205
Women, research vulnerability of pregnant, 156
Wood, M.J., on research question rules, 77, *78*

World Wide Web, 41
Writing
    clarity of, 288, 293
    experimental-type reports, 290-291
    formal reports, 279-280
    formal rules, 288-290
    literature reviews, 58, *59*
    naturalistic reports, 291-294
    principles for, 288-290
Written reports
    in experimental-type research, 290-291
    in naturalistic inquiry, 279-280
    publishing, 295
    sharing, 294-295

## Y

Yin, R.K., on case studies, 142-143, 146

## Z

Zero correlations, 259